FSH H

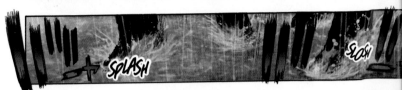

SPLASH SLOSH

FSH TH TH FTH

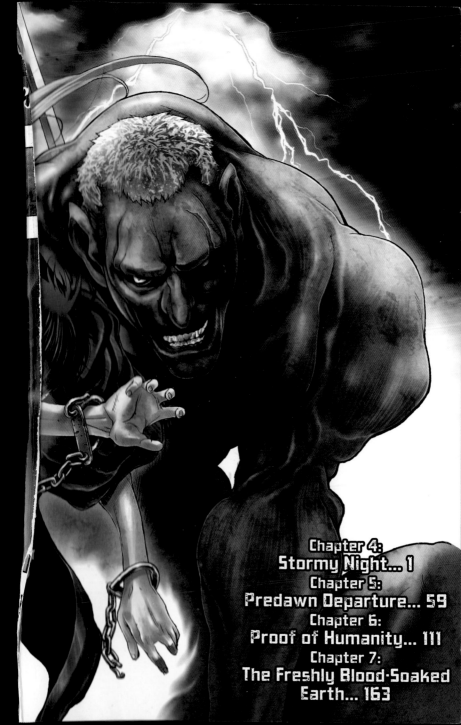

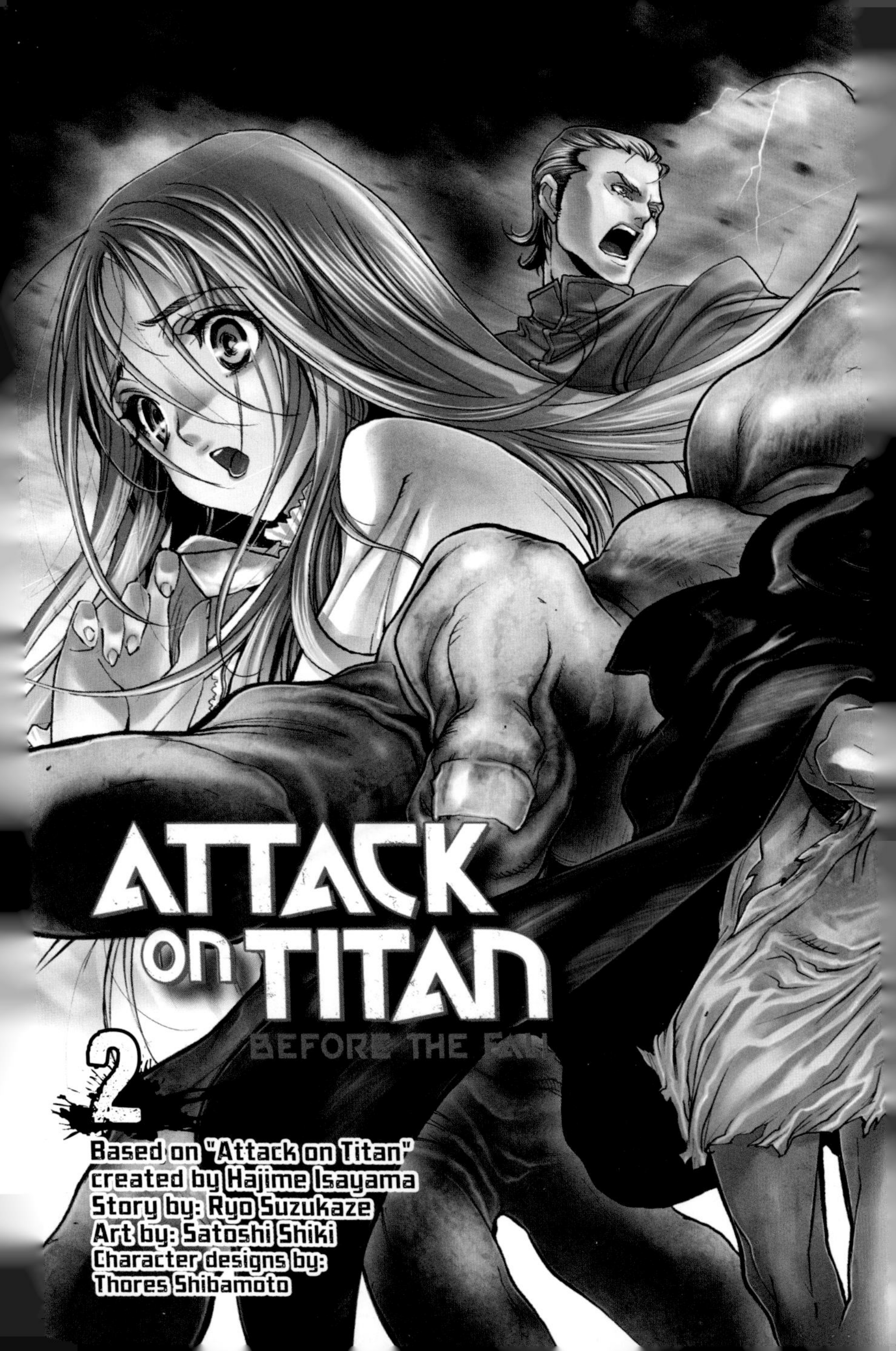

ATTACK on TITAN

BEFORE THE FALL

2

Based on "Attack on Titan"
created by Hajime Isayama
Story by: Ryo Suzukaze
Art by: Satoshi Shiki
Character designs by:
Thores Shibamoto

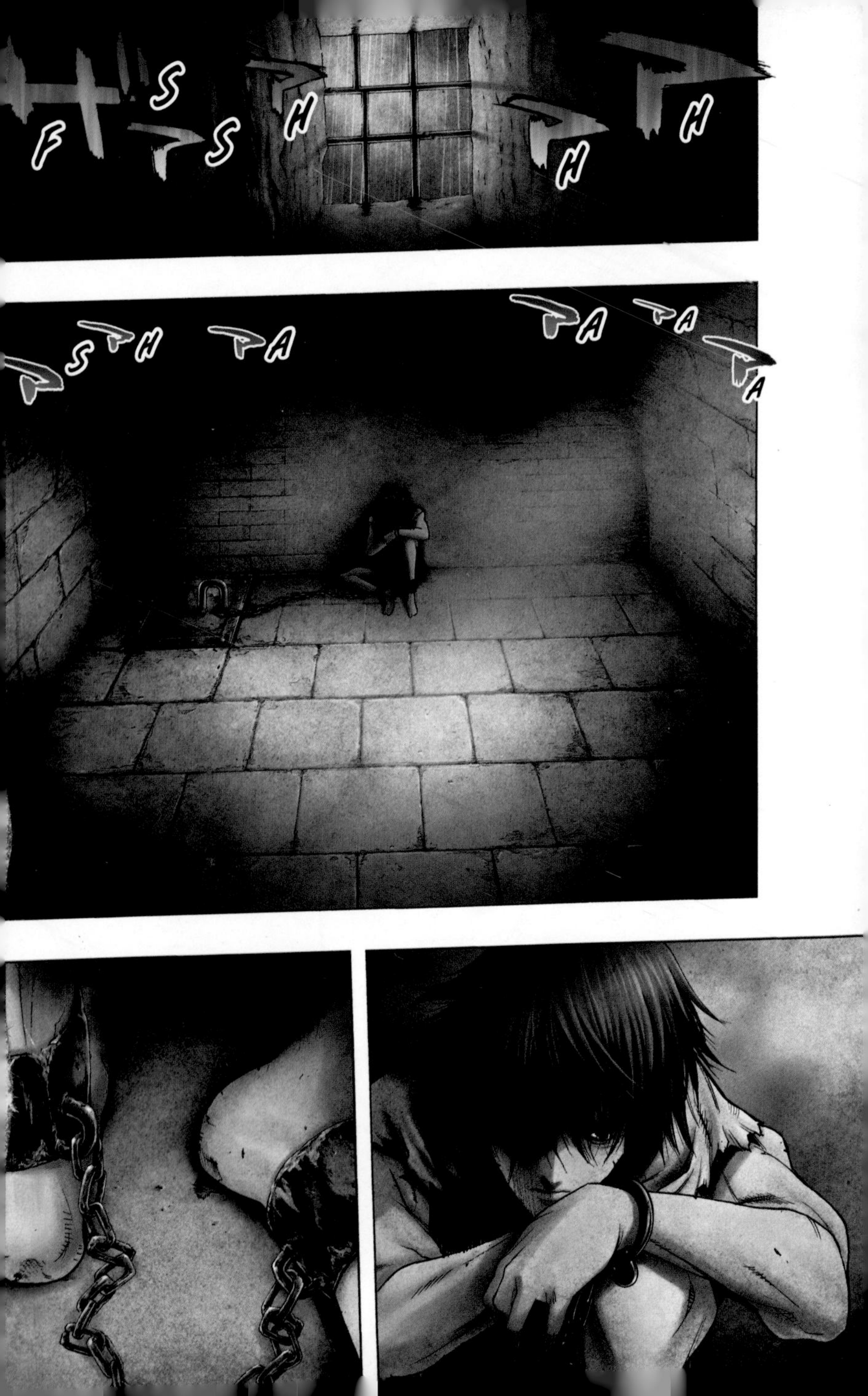
FSSH
HH
PSH PA
PA PA PA

ATTACK ON TITAN BEFORE THE FALL Character Profiles

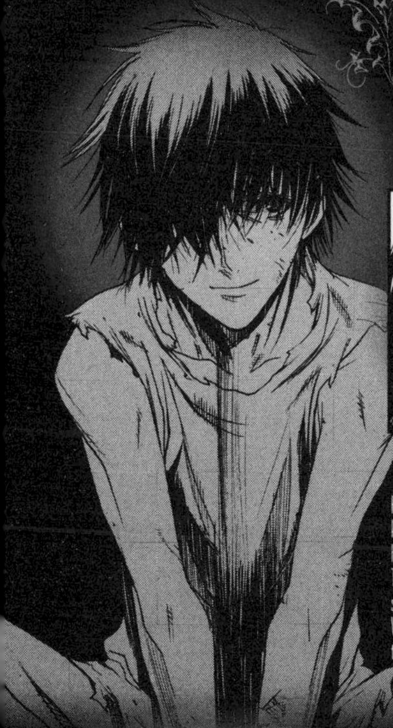

Kuklo

A boy born from a dead body packed into the vomit of a Titan, which earned him the moniker, "Titan's son." The wealthy Inocencio family bought him from a sideshow hut. His father was Heath Mansel, squad leader in the Survey Corps, and his mother was Elena, who helped bring a Titan inside the Wall. At the start of Volume 2, he is 15 years old.

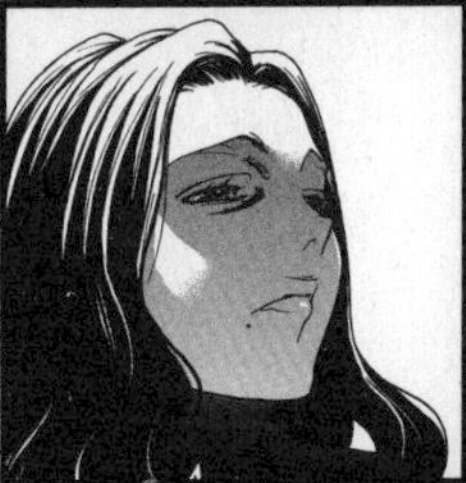

Elena

Kuklo's mother. Her husband Heath was killed by a Titan. When she saw his severed head, she went mad, and was drawn into a Titan-worshiping cult. Heavy with child, she led the cultists who opened the gate. When a Titan made its way inside, she was the first to be eaten.

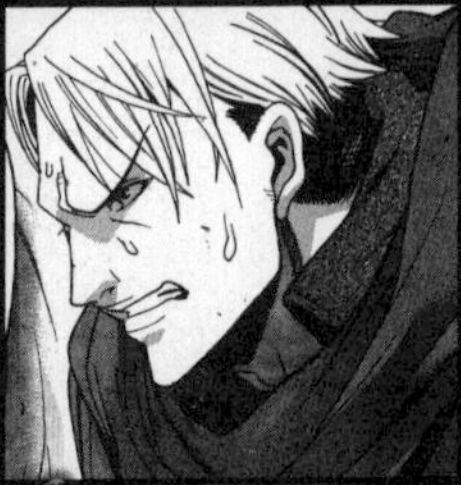

Carlo Pikale

Soldier in the Survey Corps. He was age 18 in the first chapter, having joined the same time as Heath, Kuklo's father. He discovered Elena's remains in the Titan's vomit, and witnessed Kuklo's birth. At the start of Volume 2, he is 33 years old.

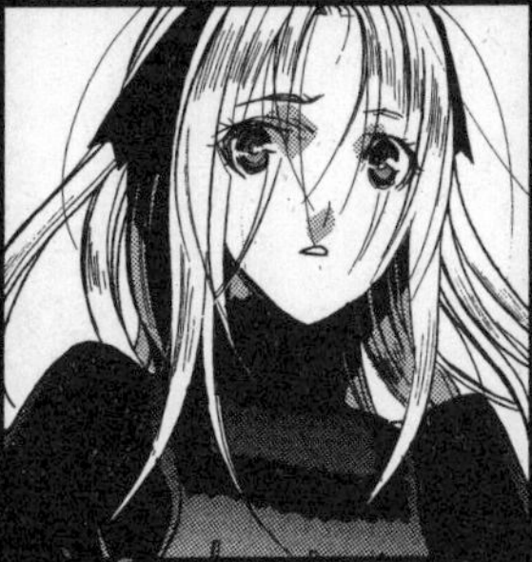

Sharle Inocencio

First daughter of the Inocencio family. She attempted to kill Kuklo after he was brought to the mansion, but became his only friend when she realized that he was human, not a monster. She decided to run away with Kuklo to avoid being forced into a strategic marriage. Like Kuklo, she is 15 at the start of Volume 2.

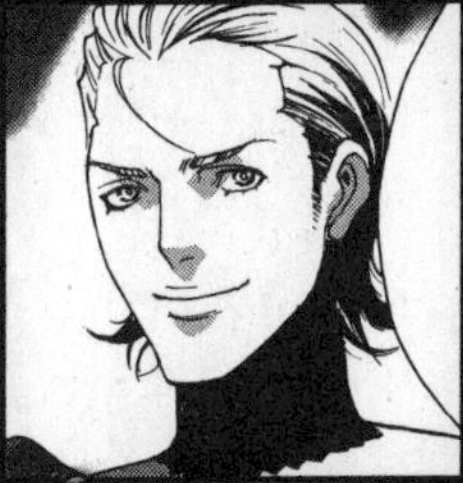

Xavi Inocencio

Sharle's brother, firstborn of the Inocencio children. His father Dario raised him to lead the military, and he will begin his training soon. He beat Kuklo nearly every day for two years, claiming to have "conquered the son of a Titan." This gave him an arrogant leader's air.

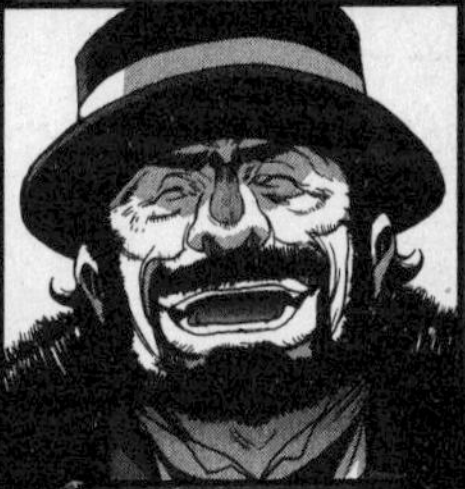

Dario Inocencio

One of the top merchants behind Wall Sheena, innermost of the walls. He has close ties to politicians, and hopes to arrange a marriage between Sharle and the son of Bruno Baumeister, a prominent conservative leader.

The Story So Far

Seventy years before the story of Eren, a Titan made it through Wall Maria for the first time. Amidst ingrained fear of the Titans, a small group of Titan worshipers took over the gate in Shiganshina District. Their leader was Elena, wife of a Survey Corps squad leader whose death at the hands of Titans drove her to madness. A single Titan made its way inside the gate, and its terrible onslaught left 5,000 people dead or missing.

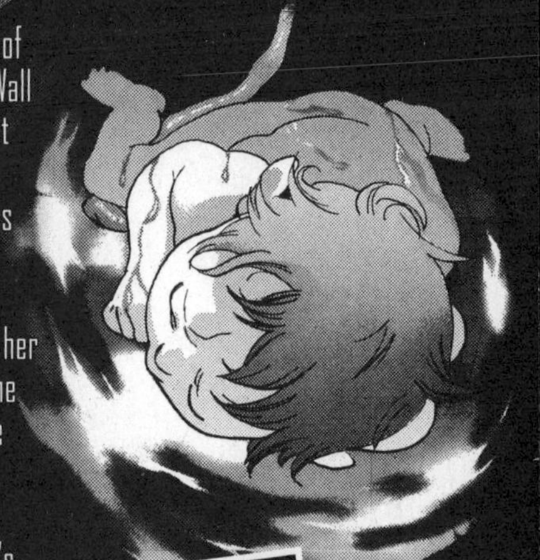

Elena was the first victim of the Titan's rampage through Shiganshina. But when her body was discovered in the Titan's vomit, her child was miraculously still alive. This boy was named Kuklo, the "Titan's son," and treated as a sideshow freak. Thirteen years later, the wealthy merchant Dario Inocencio bought Kuklo to serve as a punching bag for his son, Xavi. Meanwhile, Xavi's sister Sharle, who was terrified of the Titans, felt a secret duty to purge their house of the so-called monster. But when she saw Kuklo, she realized that he was a human being like any other, and Sharle decided to teach him about the world and human language instead.

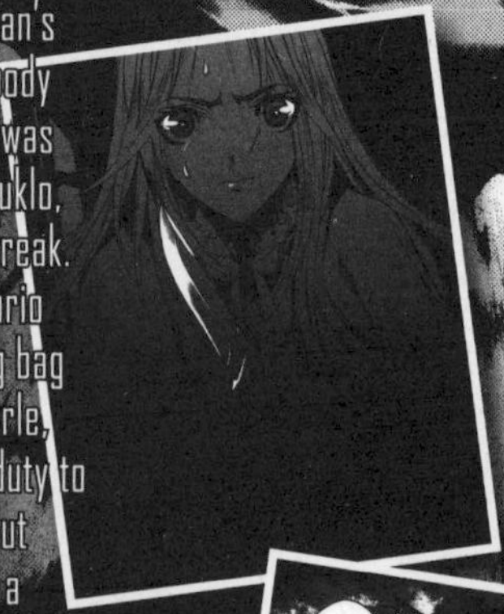

As he learned more and more from books and Sharle, Kuklo wanted to see a real Titan, to know whether he had truly been born of a Titan. To do that, he needed to escape the mansion and gain his freedom. So Kuklo put together a two-year escape plan. Meanwhile, when Sharle turned 15, the topic of her arranged marriage arose, a painful reminder that she was [redacted] but a tool to further her father's ambi[redacted]he two decided to escape the Inocencio mansion together.

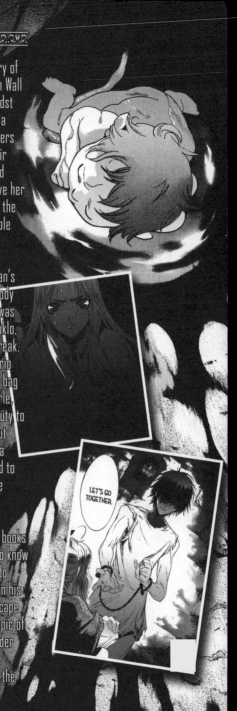

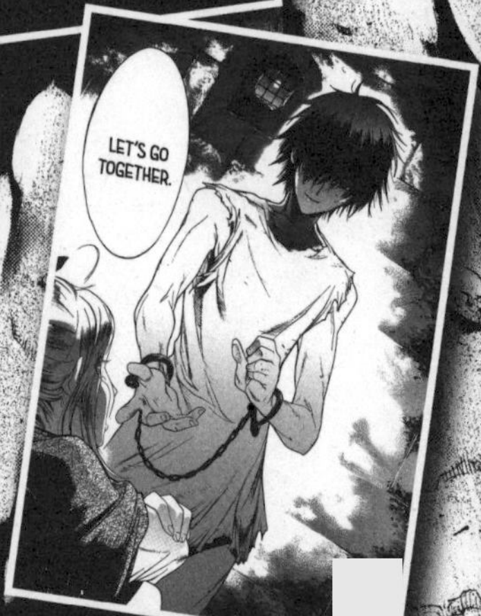
LET'S GO TOGETHER.

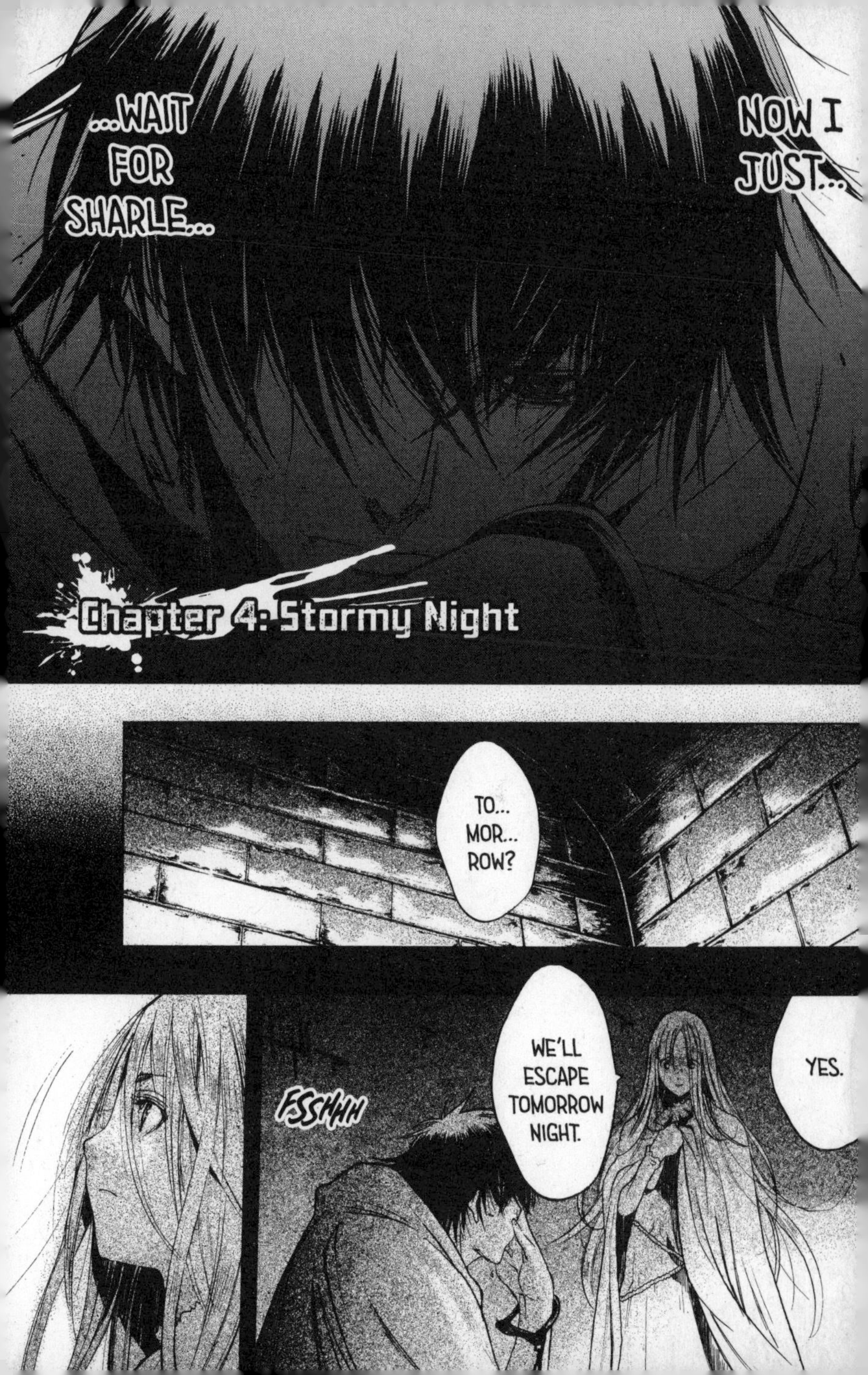

NOW I JUST...
...WAIT FOR SHARLE...
Chapter 4: Stormy Night
TO... MOR... ROW?
YES.
WE'LL ESCAPE TOMORROW NIGHT.
FSSHHH

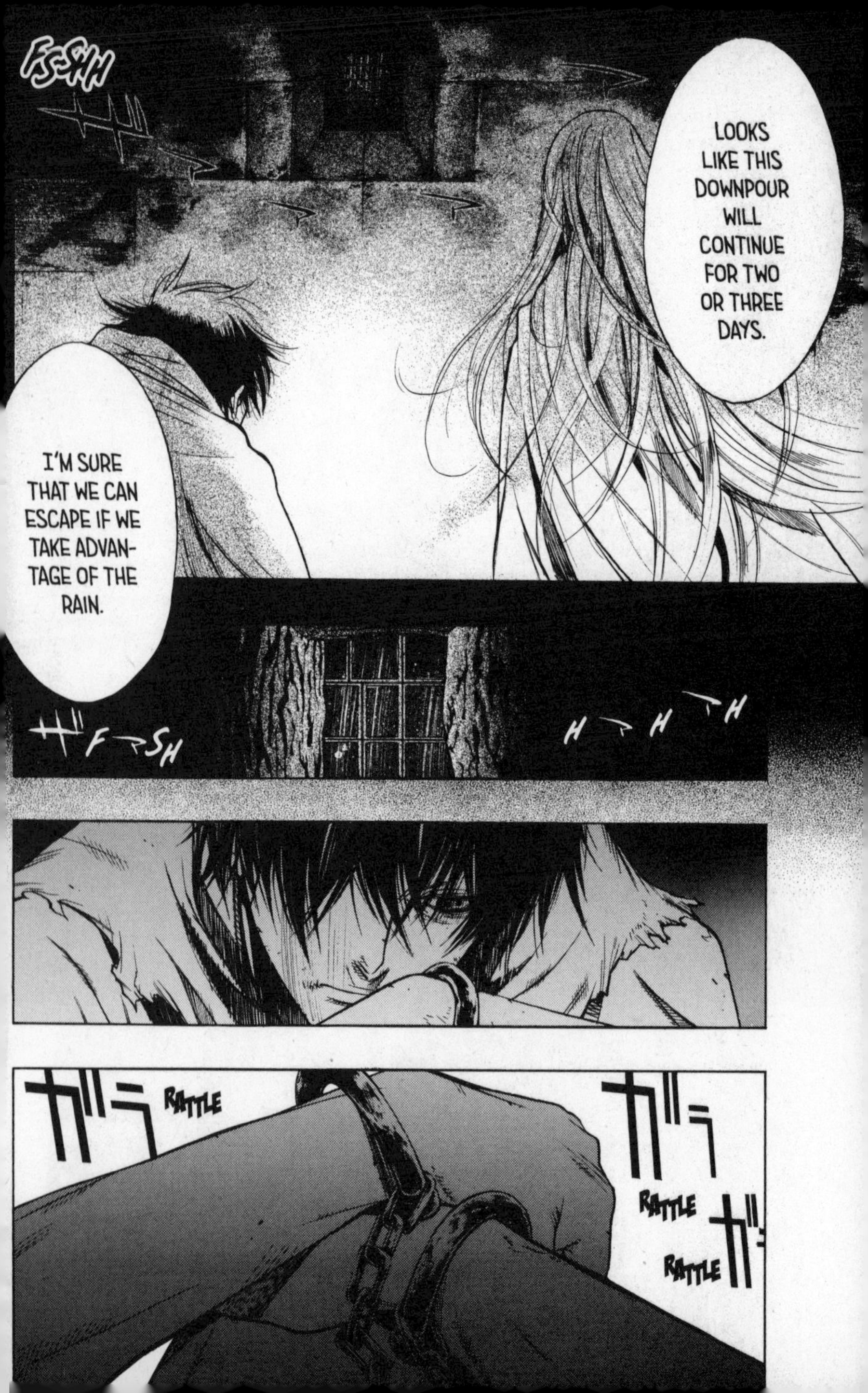
FSSHH
LOOKS LIKE THIS DOWNPOUR WILL CONTINUE FOR TWO OR THREE DAYS.
I'M SURE THAT WE CAN ESCAPE IF WE TAKE ADVAN-TAGE OF THE RAIN.
FSSH
HHHH
RATTLE
RATTLE
RATTLE

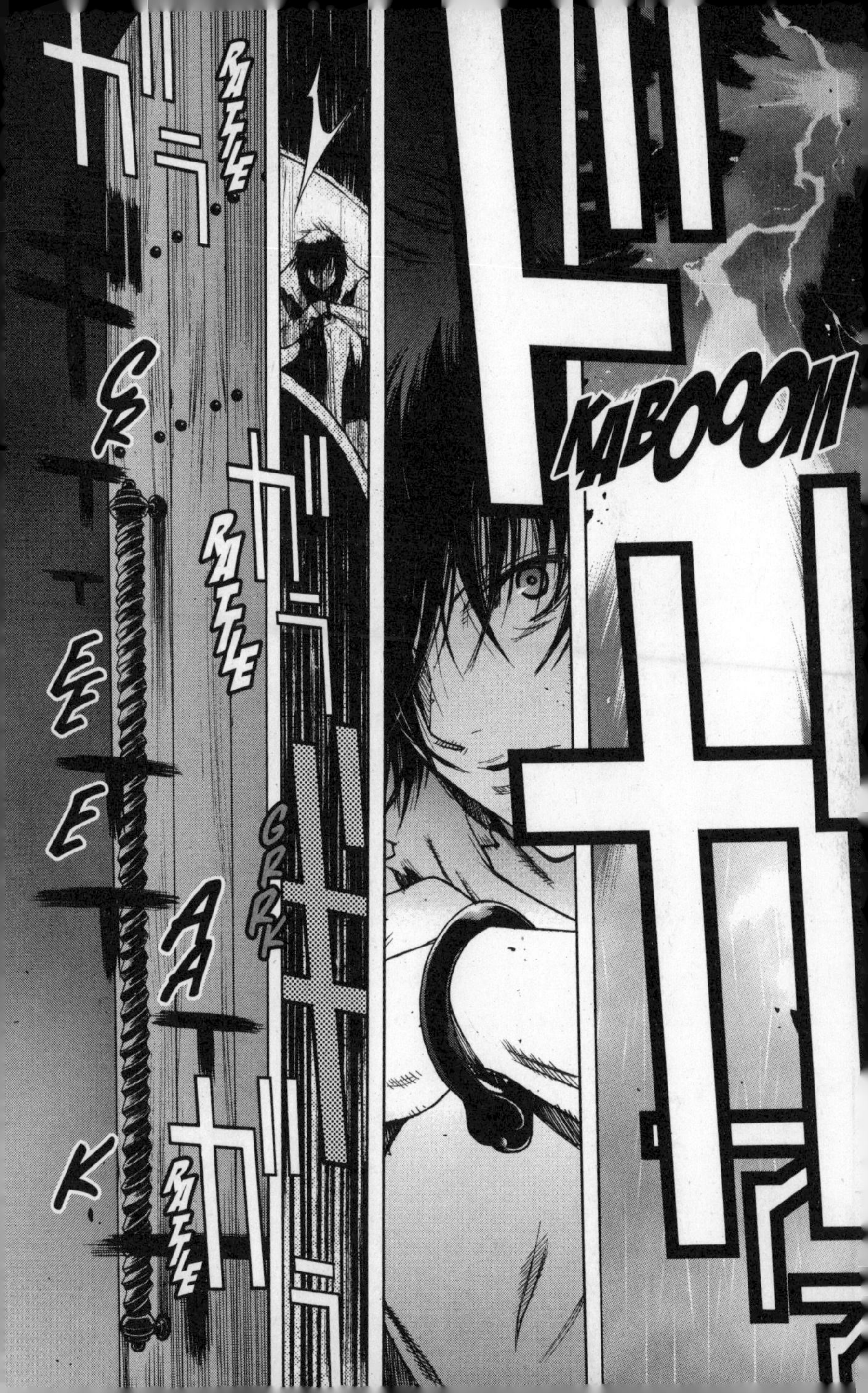
KABOOOM
RATTLE
GRRK
RATTLE
CREEEAK
RATTLE

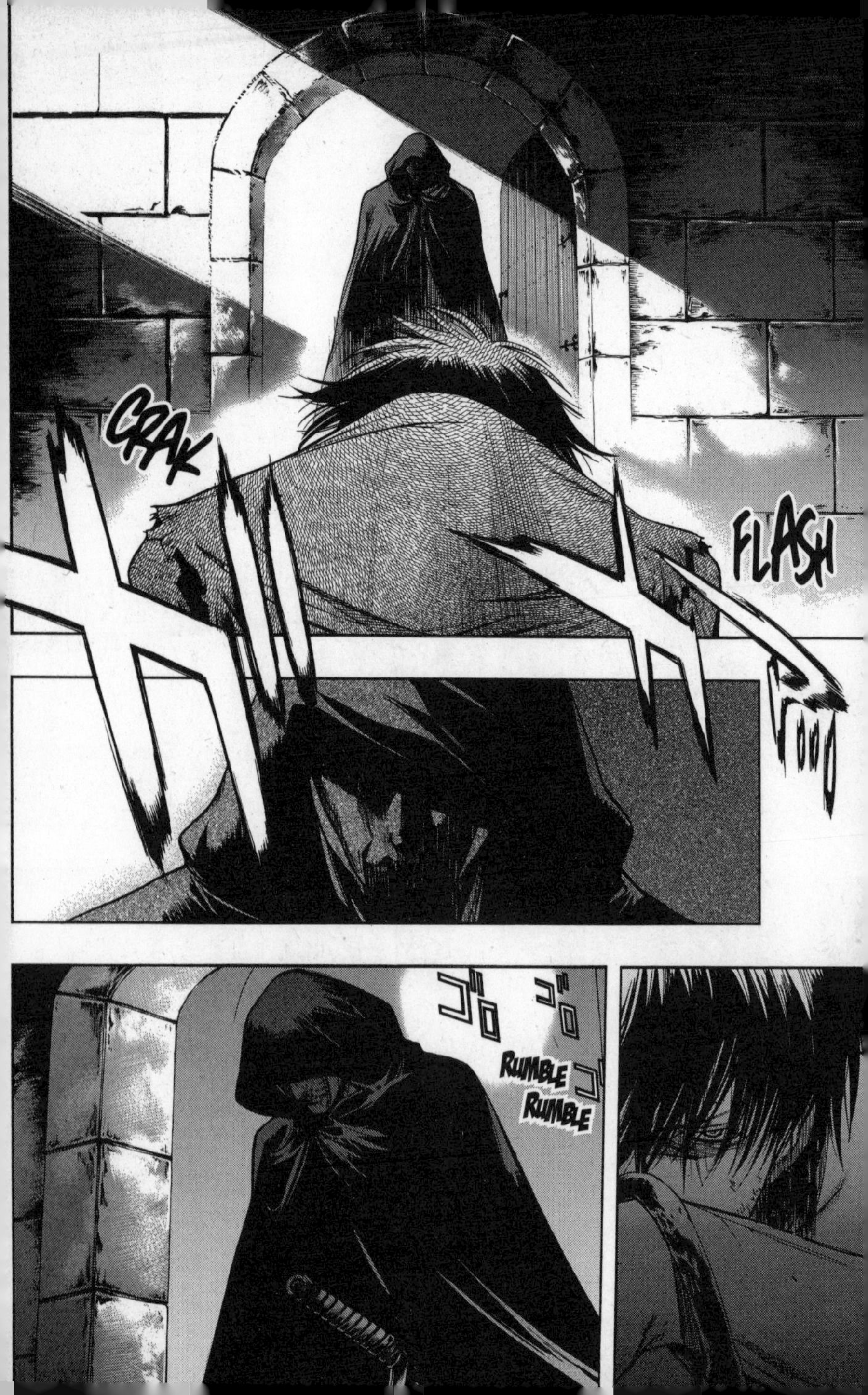
FLASH
CRAK
ゴロ ゴロ
RUMBLE
RUMBLE

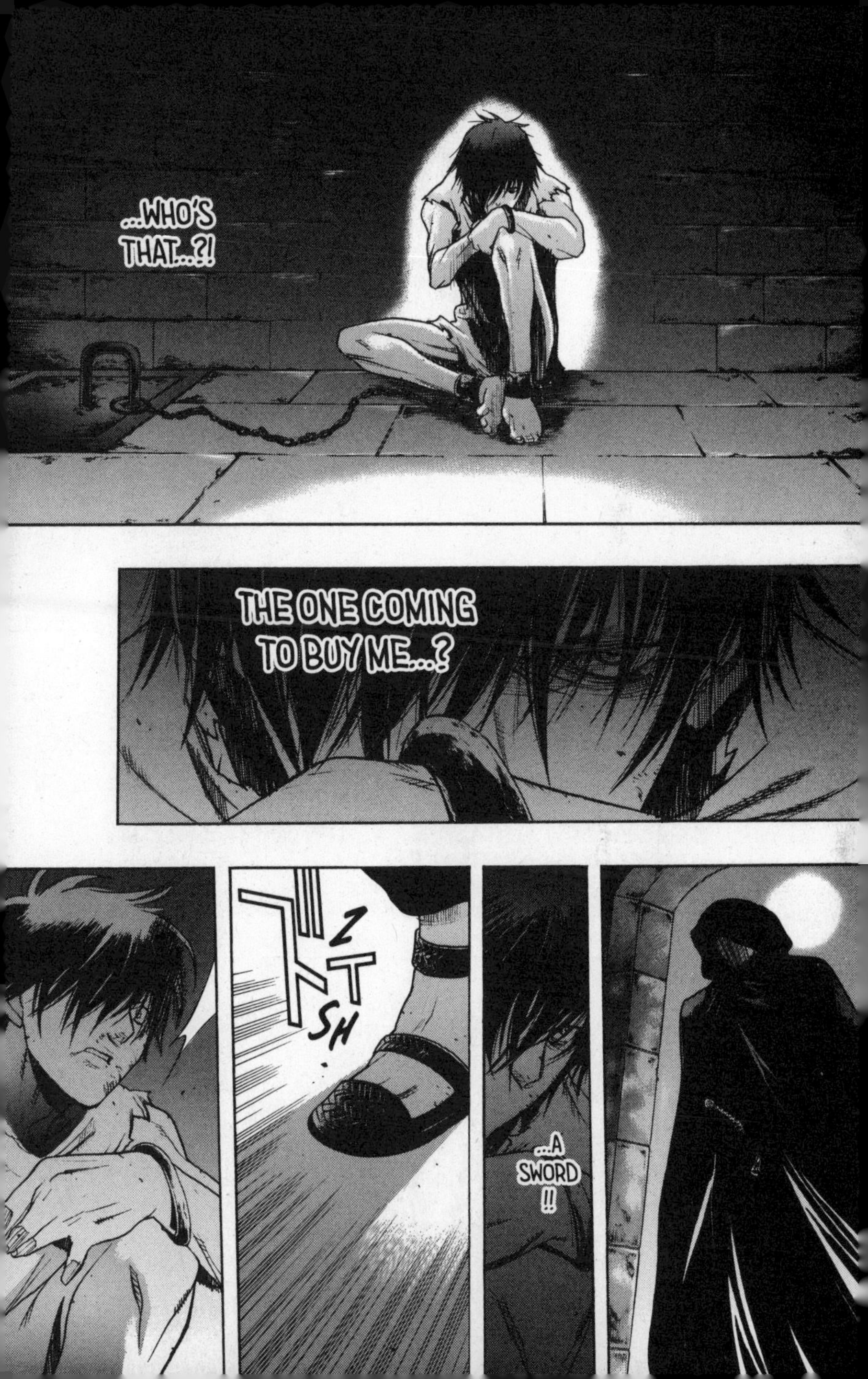

...WHO'S THAT...?!
THE ONE COMING TO BUY ME...?
...A SWORD !!
ZTSH

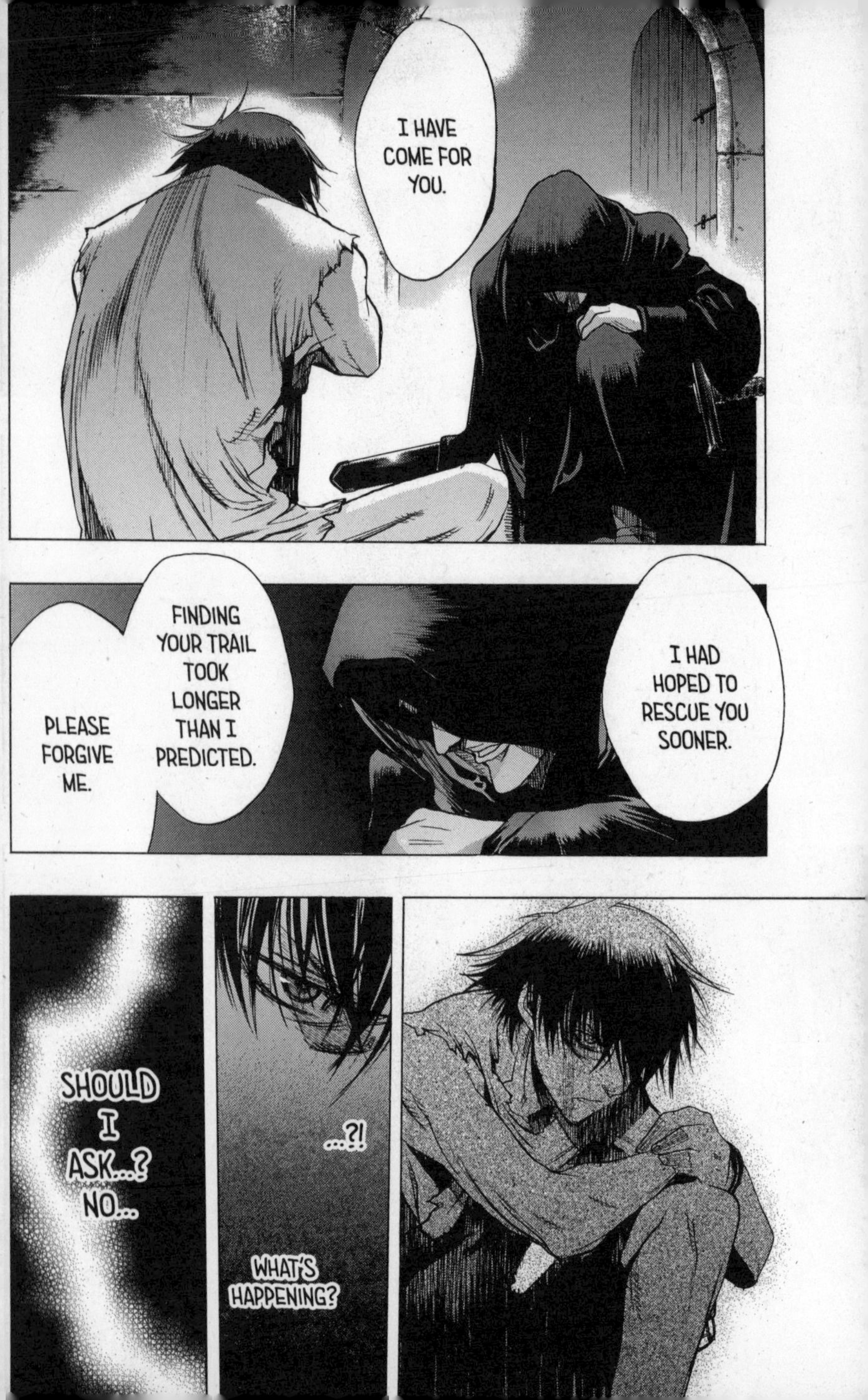
I HAVE COME FOR YOU.
I HAD HOPED TO RESCUE YOU SOONER.
FINDING YOUR TRAIL TOOK LONGER THAN I PREDICTED.
PLEASE FORGIVE ME.
...?!
WHAT'S HAPPENING?
SHOULD I ASK...? NO...

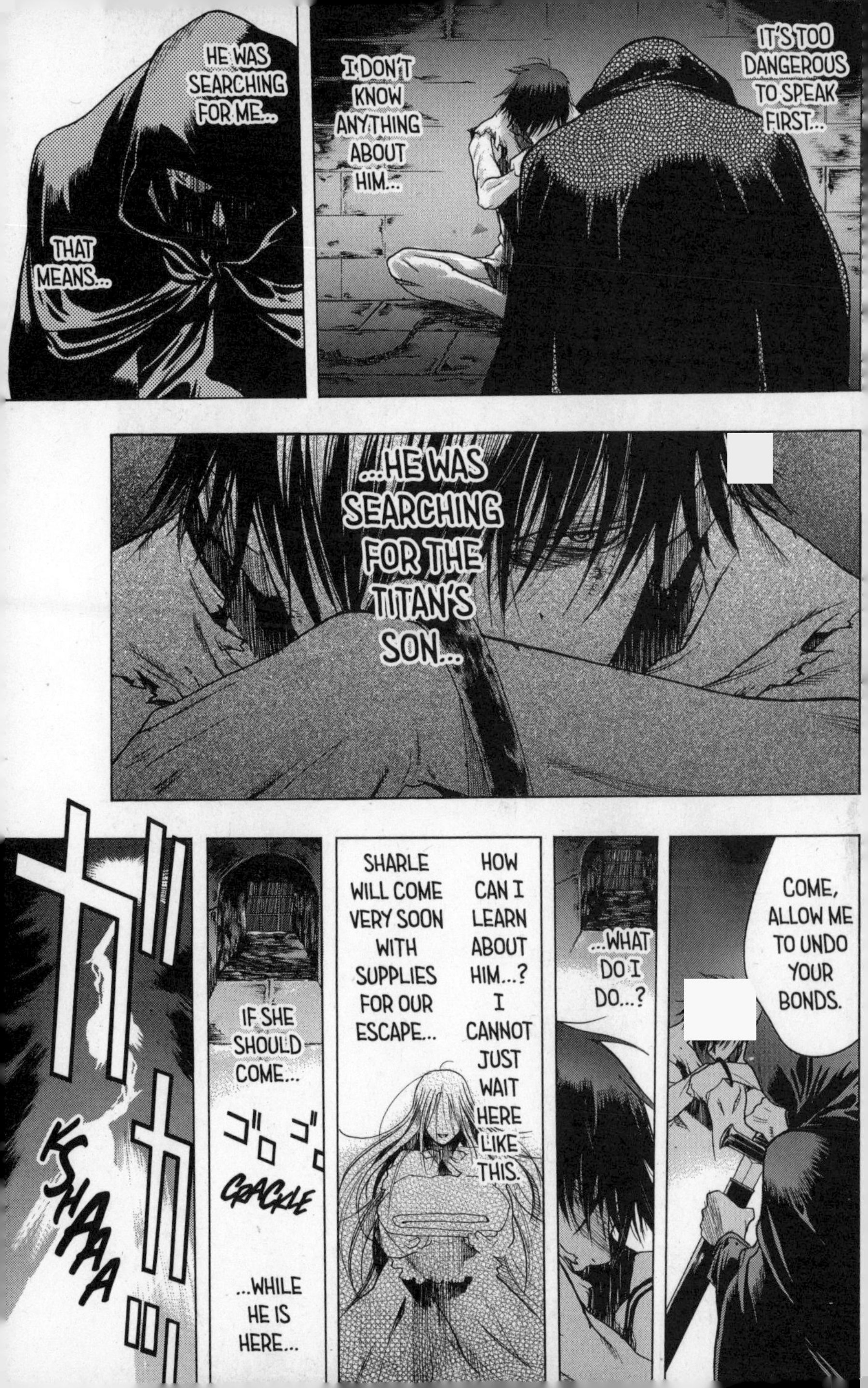
IT'S TOO DANGEROUS TO SPEAK FIRST...
I DON'T KNOW ANYTHING ABOUT HIM...
HE WAS SEARCHING FOR ME...
THAT MEANS...
...HE WAS SEARCHING FOR THE TITAN'S SON...
COME, ALLOW ME TO UNDO YOUR BONDS.
...WHAT DO I DO...?
HOW CAN I LEARN ABOUT HIM...? I CANNOT JUST WAIT HERE LIKE THIS.
SHARLE WILL COME VERY SOON WITH SUPPLIES FOR OUR ESCAPE...
IF SHE SHOULD COME...
CRACKLE
...WHILE HE IS HERE...
KSHAAA

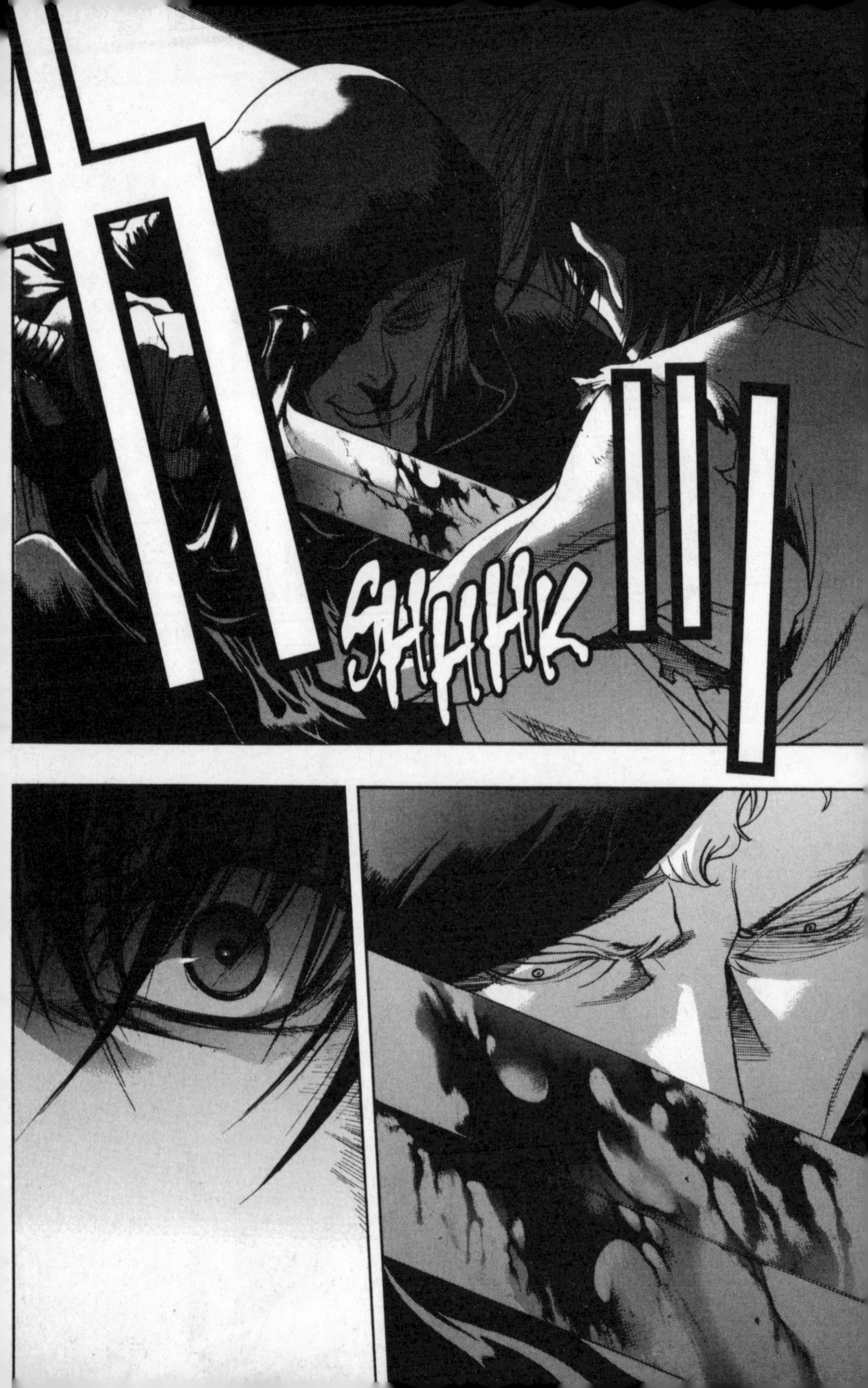
SHUHK

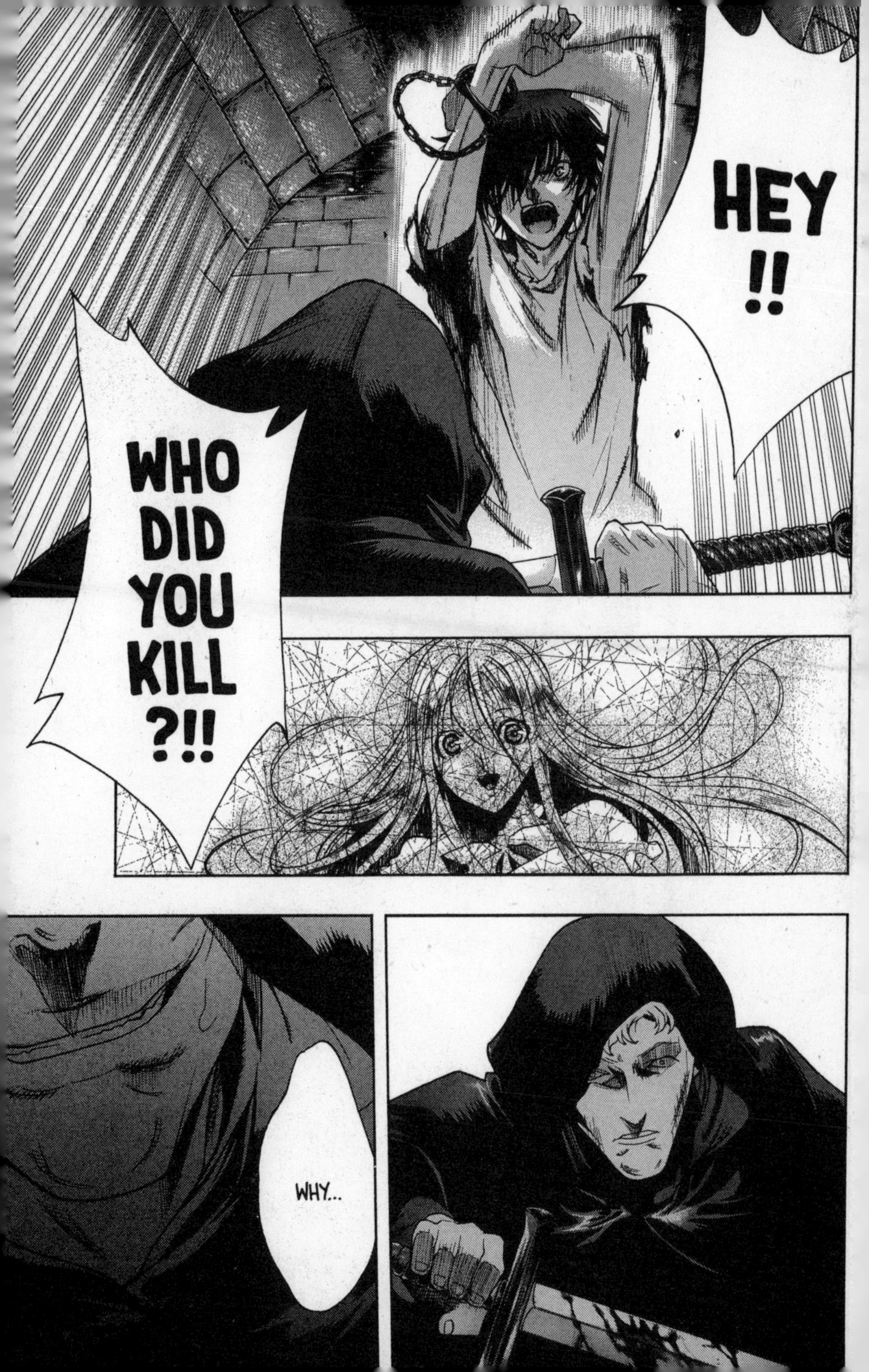
HEY!!
WHO DID YOU KILL?!!
WHY...

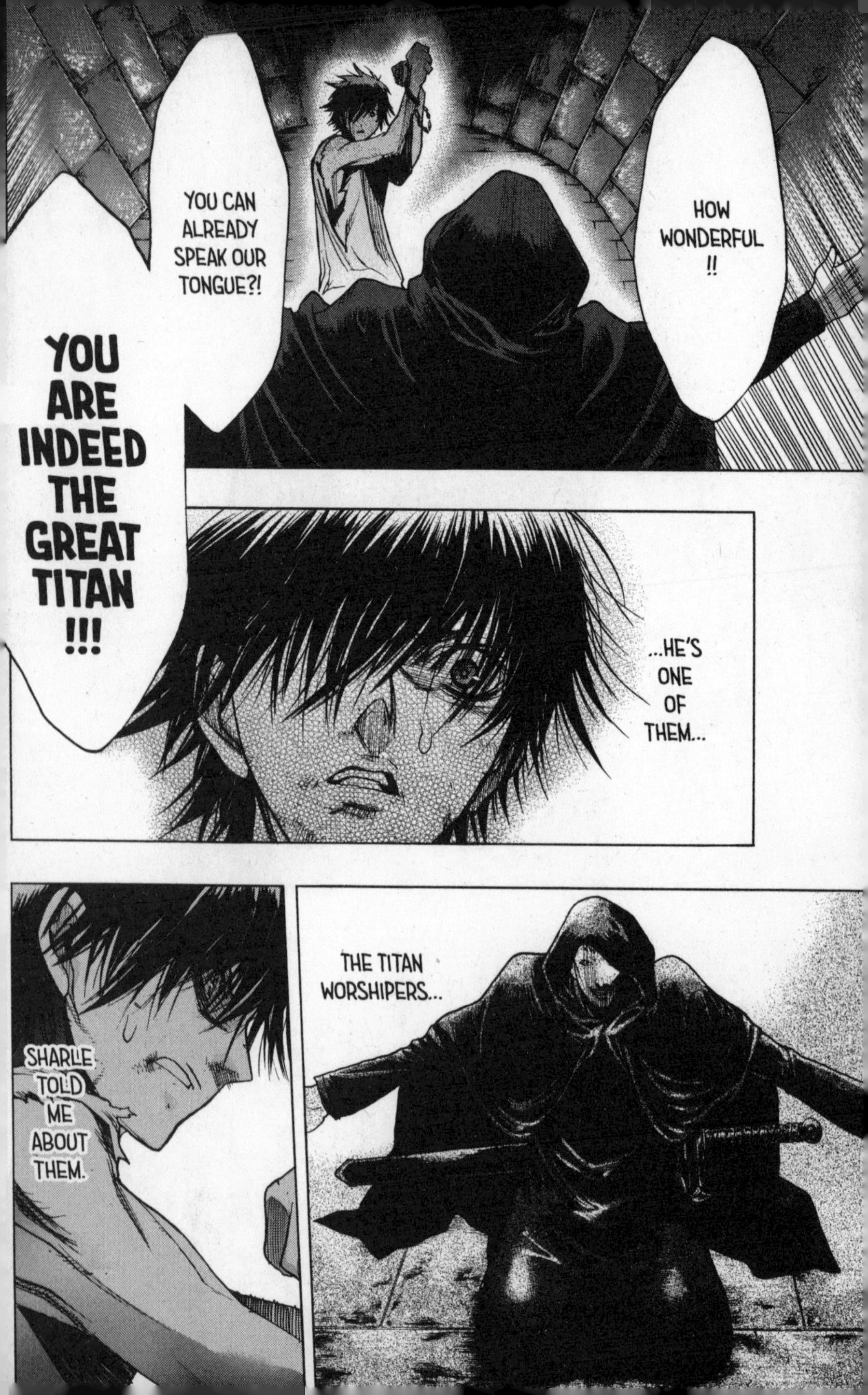
HOW WONDERFUL !!
YOU CAN ALREADY SPEAK OUR TONGUE?!
YOU ARE INDEED THE GREAT TITAN !!!
...HE'S ONE OF THEM...
THE TITAN WORSHIPERS...
SHARLE TOLD ME ABOUT THEM.

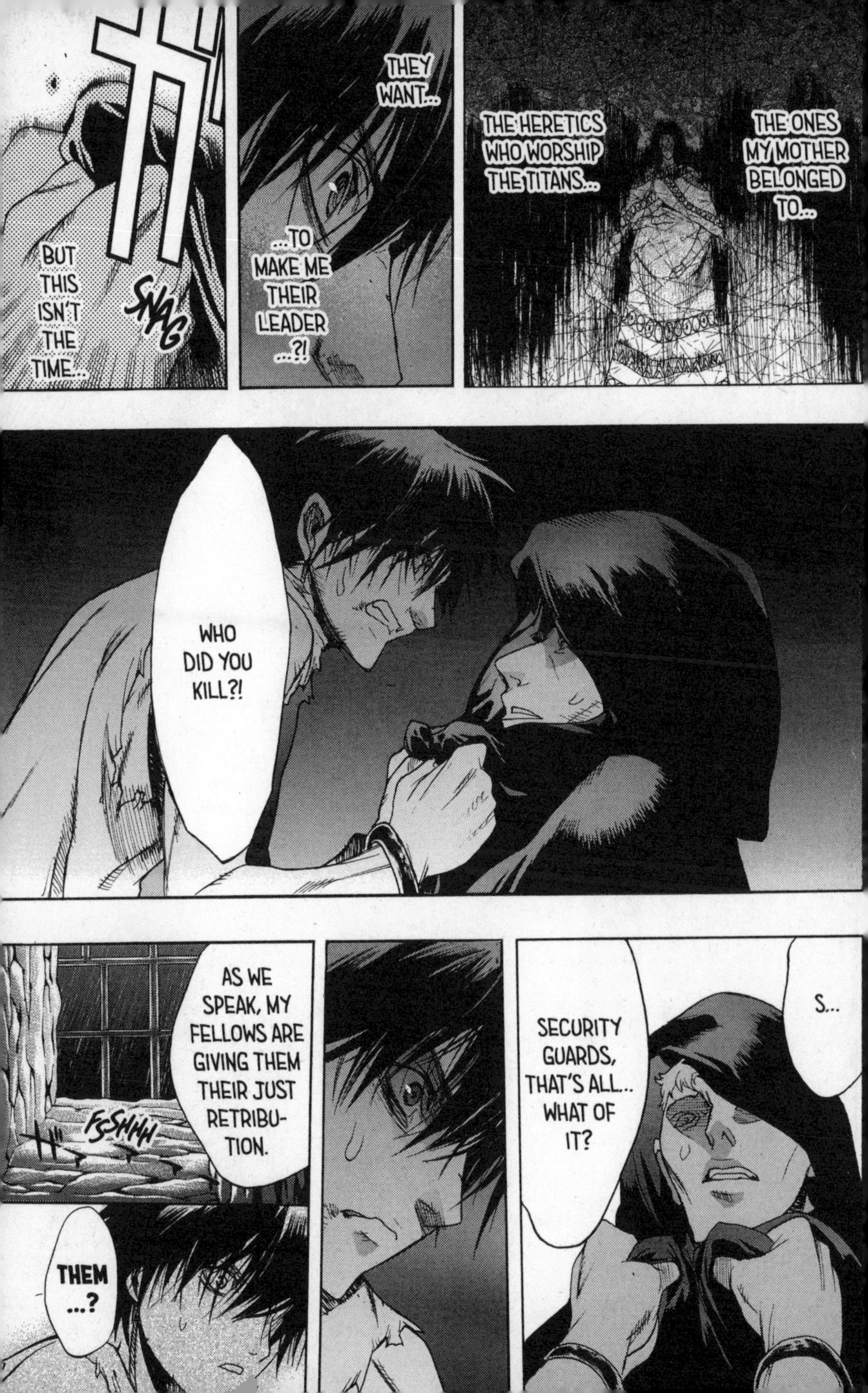
THE ONES MY MOTHER BELONGED TO...
THE HERETICS WHO WORSHIP THE TITANS...
THEY WANT...
...TO MAKE ME THEIR LEADER...?!
BUT THIS ISN'T THE TIME...
SNAG
WHO DID YOU KILL?!
S...
SECURITY GUARDS, THAT'S ALL.. WHAT OF IT?
AS WE SPEAK, MY FELLOWS ARE GIVING THEM THEIR JUST RETRIBU-TION.
FSSHHH
THEM...?

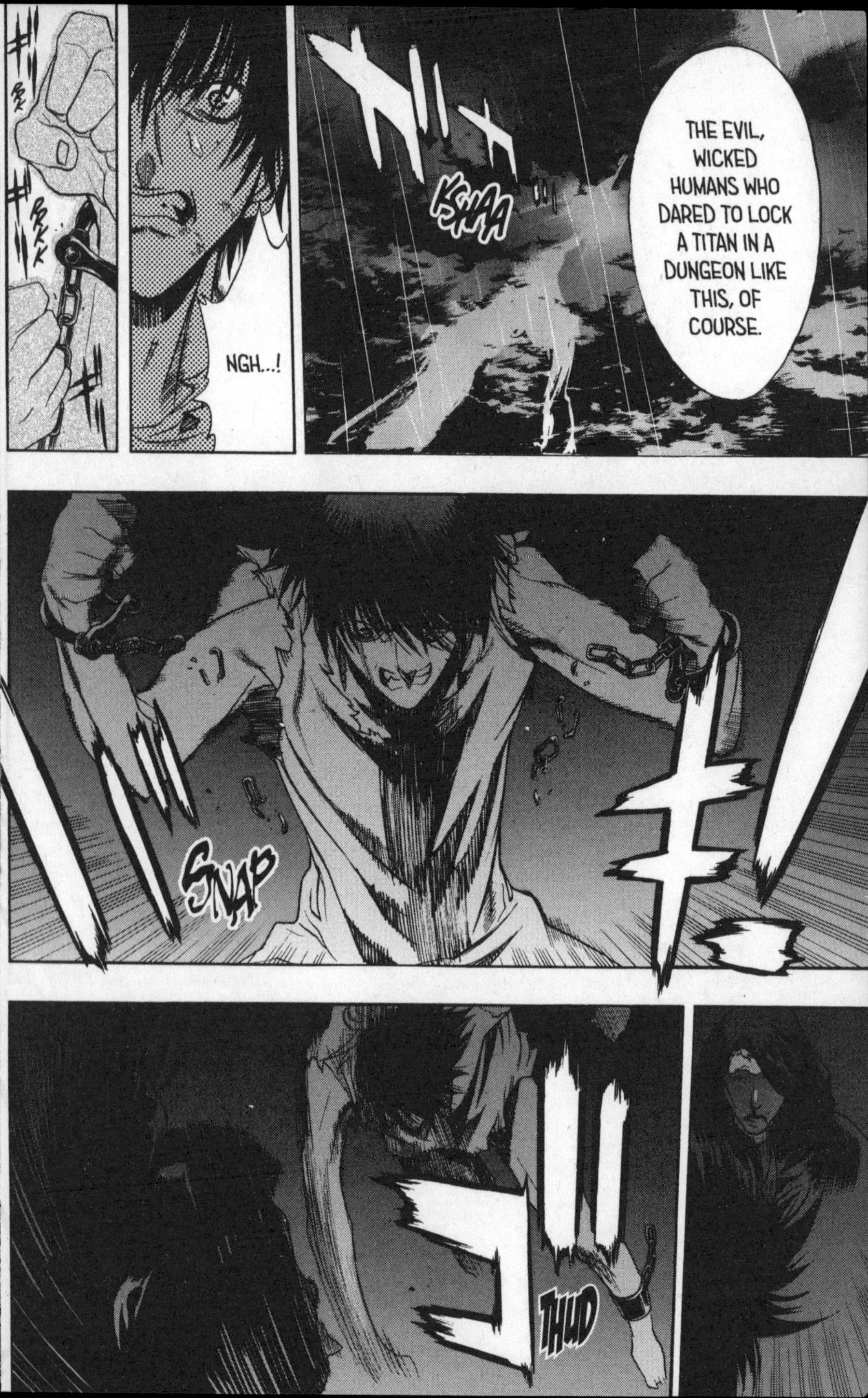
THE EVIL, WICKED HUMANS WHO DARED TO LOCK A TITAN IN A DUNGEON LIKE THIS, OF COURSE.
KSHAA
NGH...!
SNAP
THUD

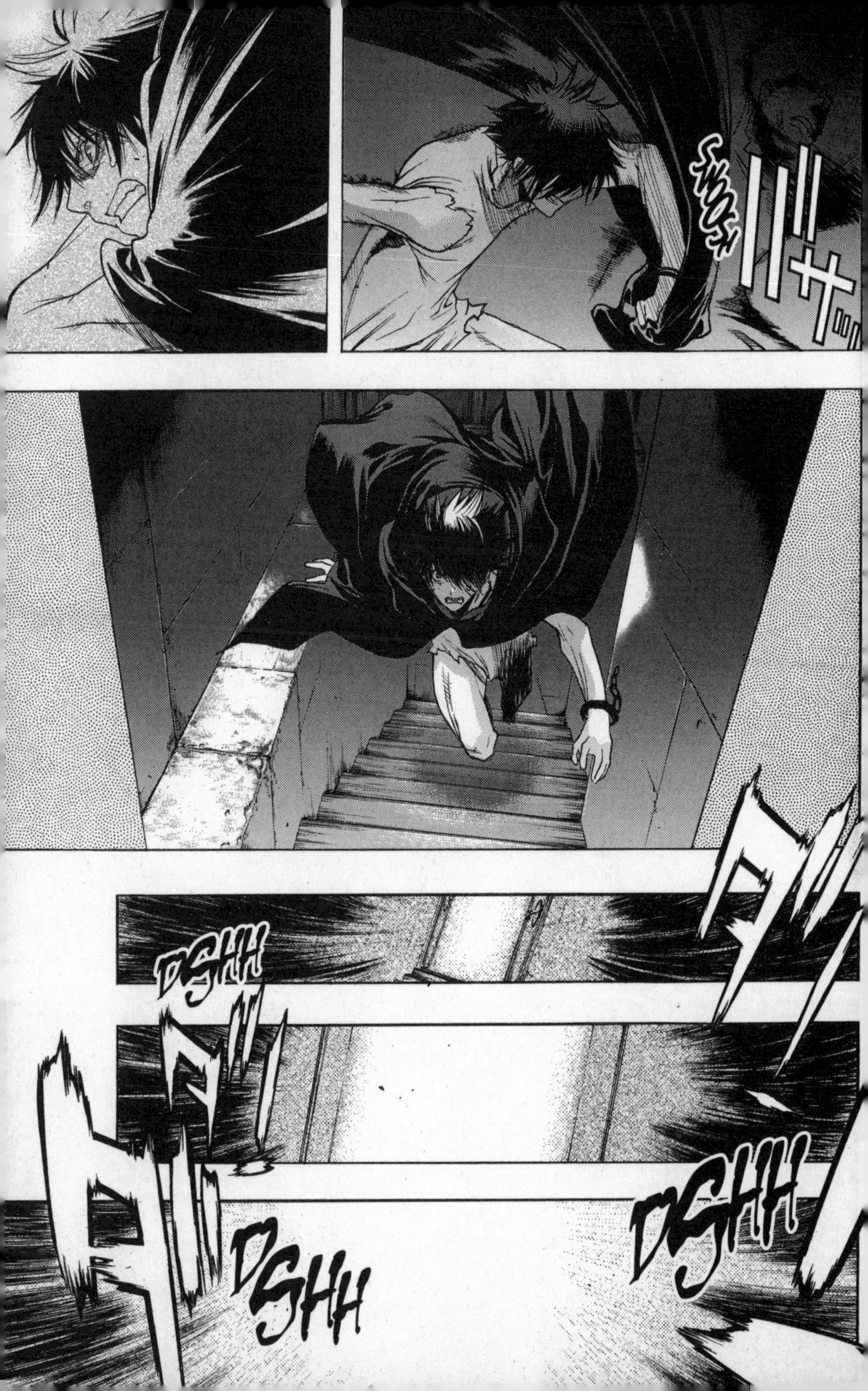
SWOOSH
DSHH
DSHH
DSHH

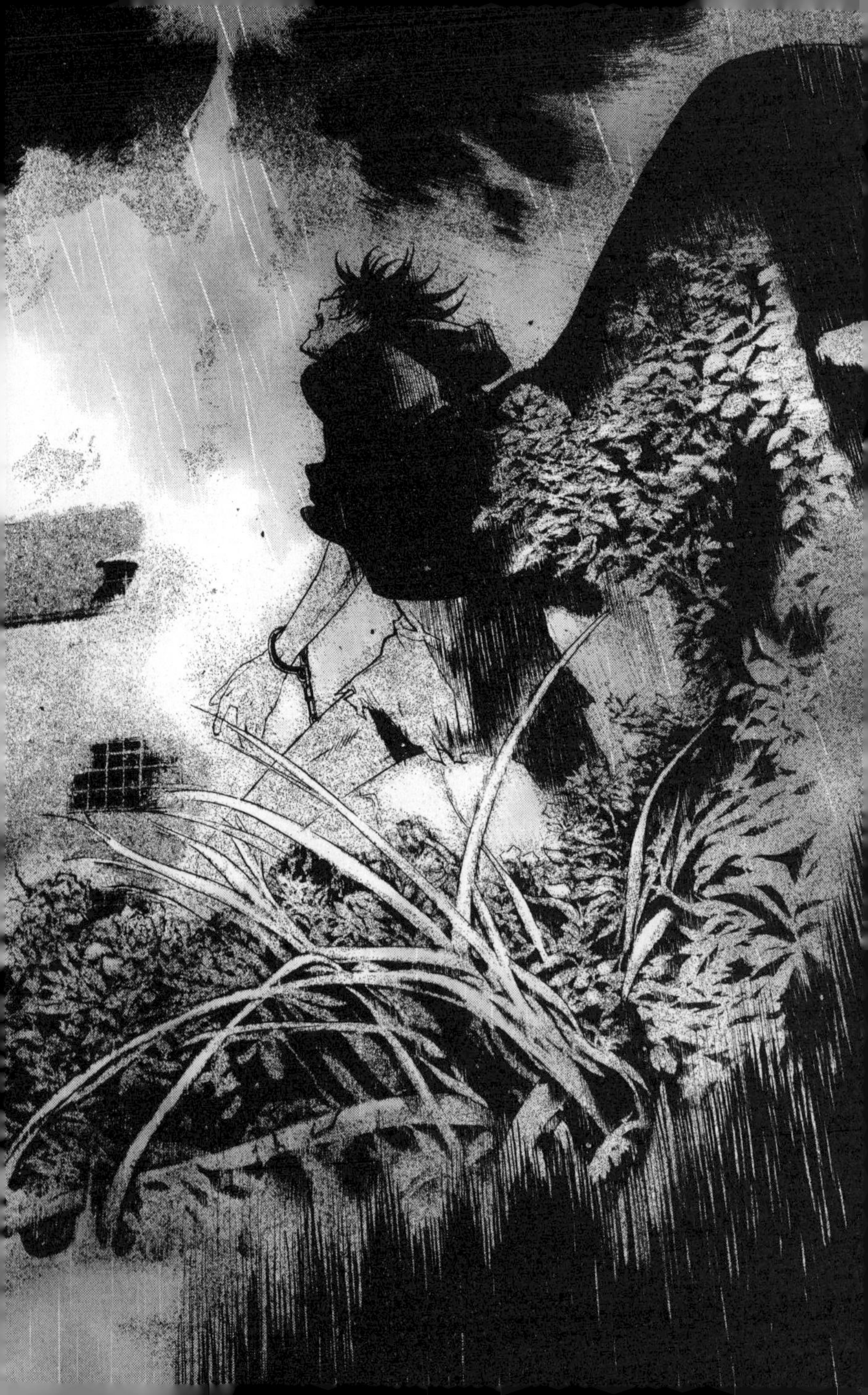

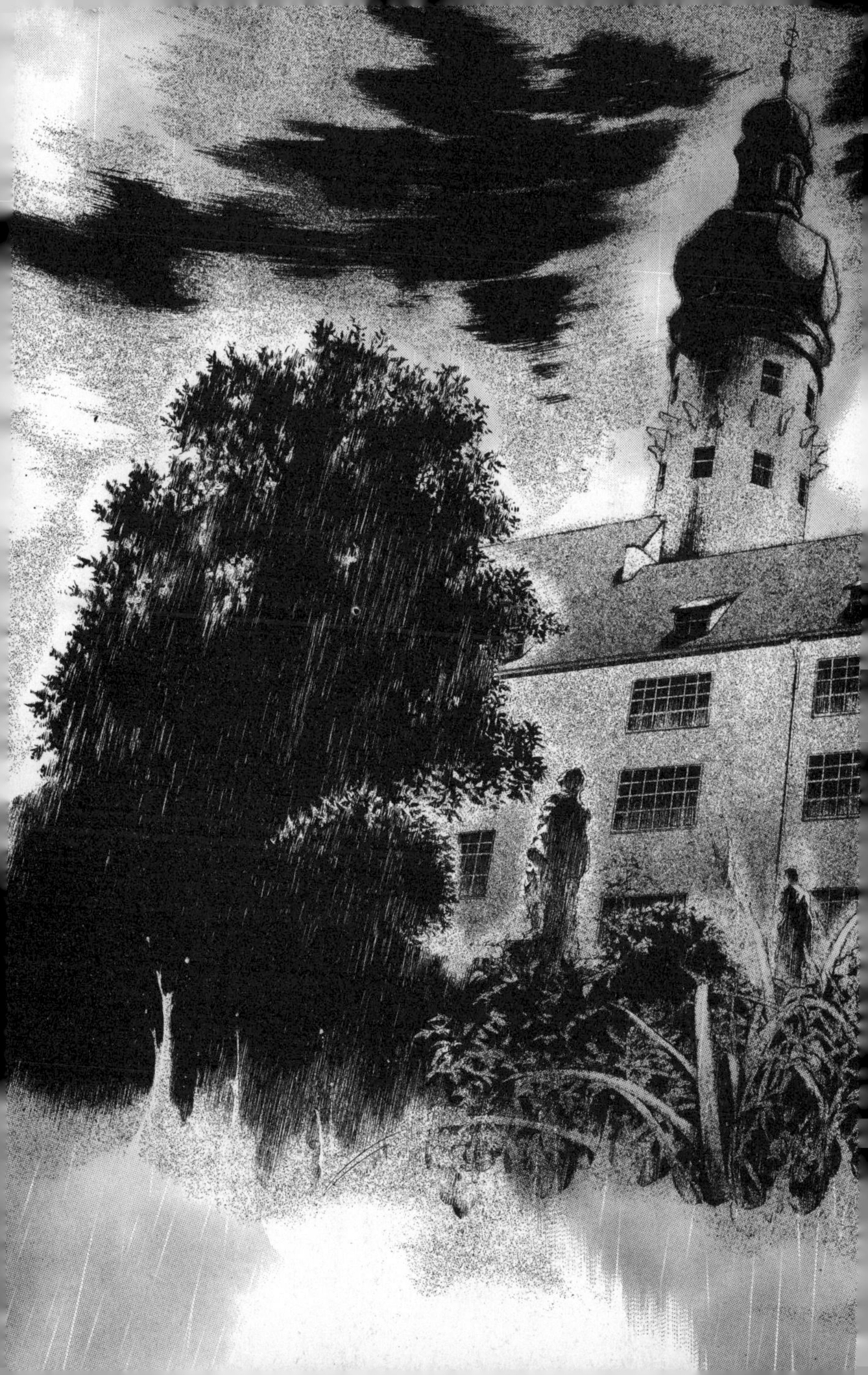

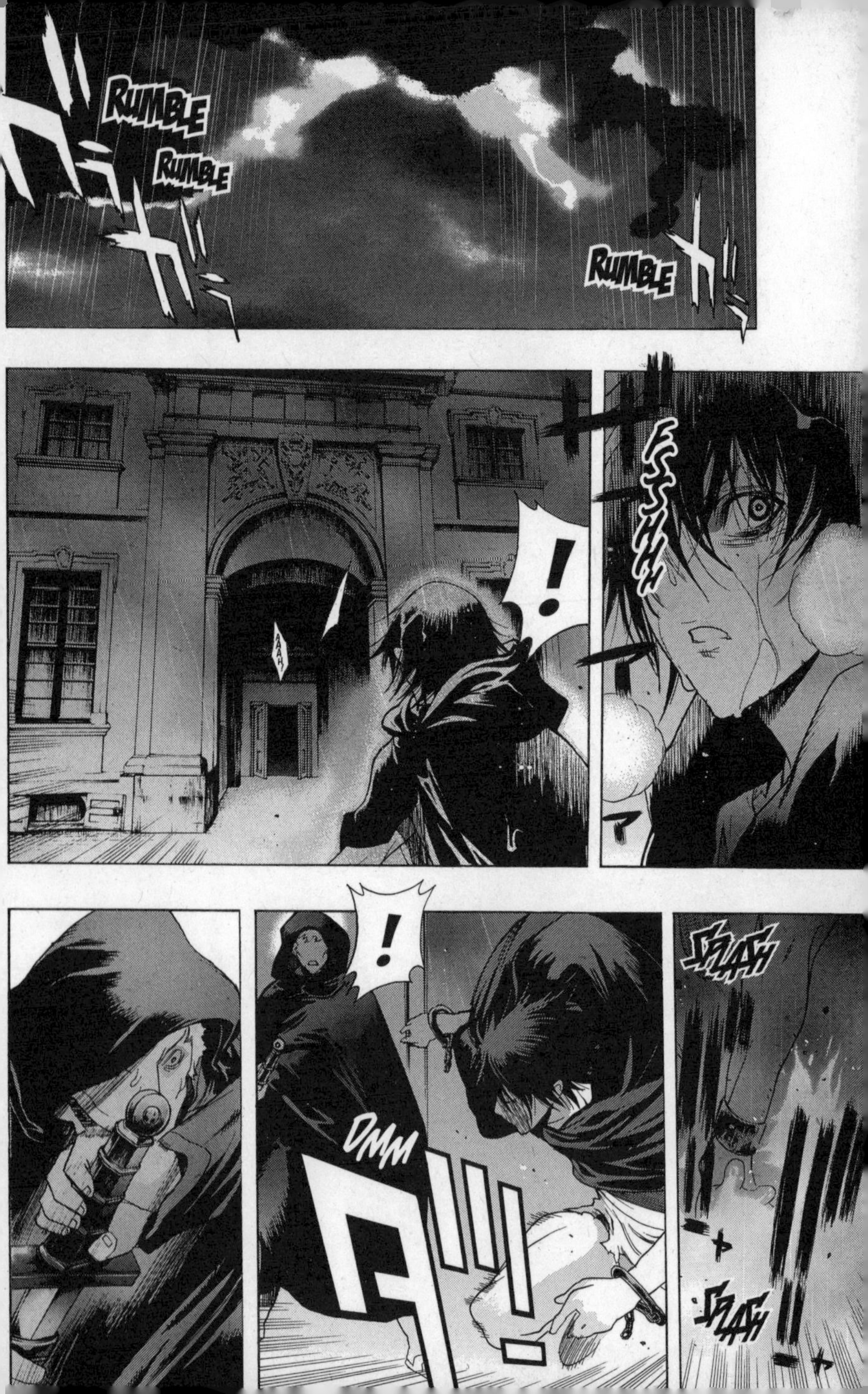
RUMBLE
RUMBLE
RUMBLE
FSSHHH
!
AAAH!
!
OMM
SPLASH
SPLASH

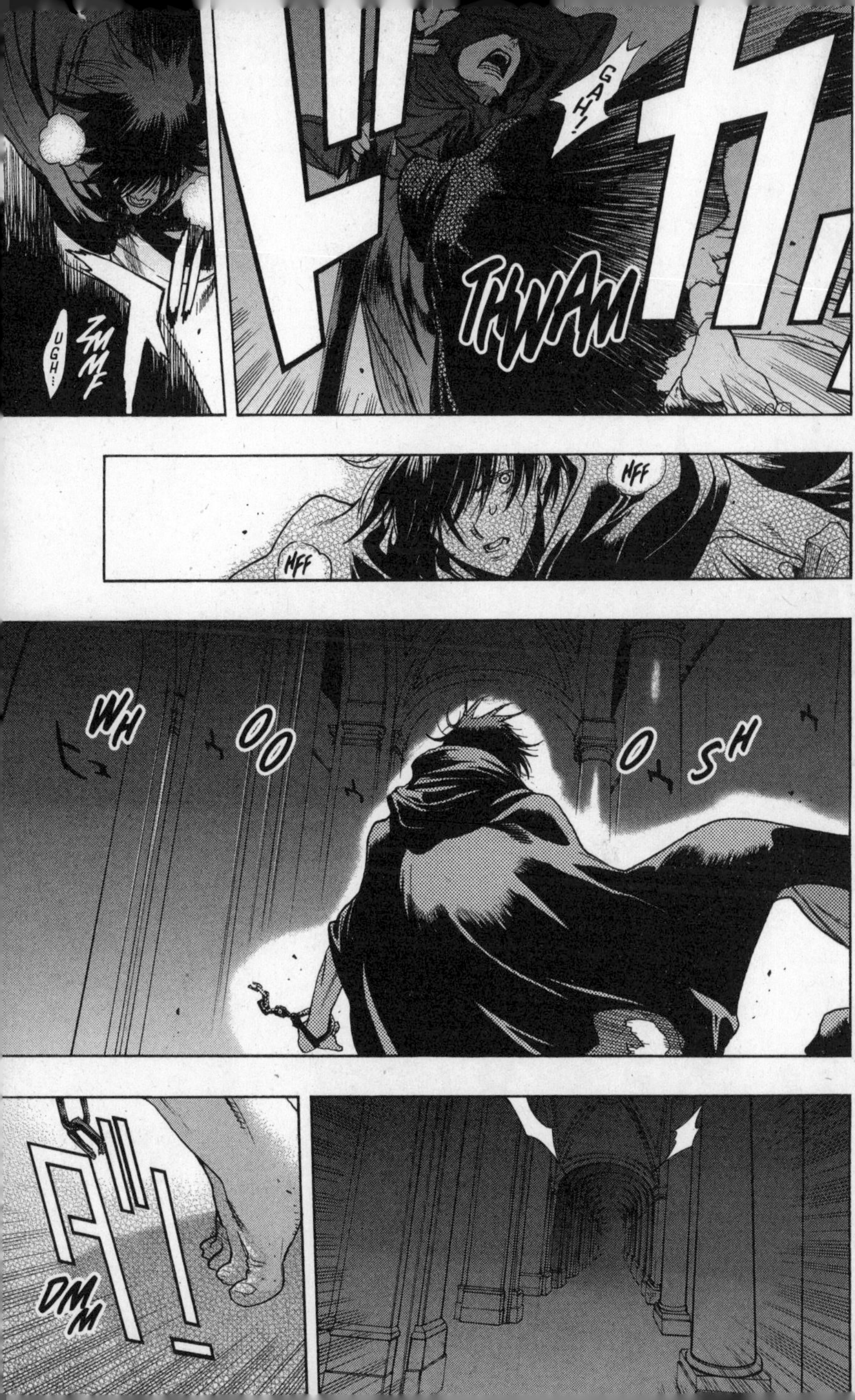

GAH!
THWAM
ZMMF
UGH...
MFF
MFF
WH OO O SH
DMM

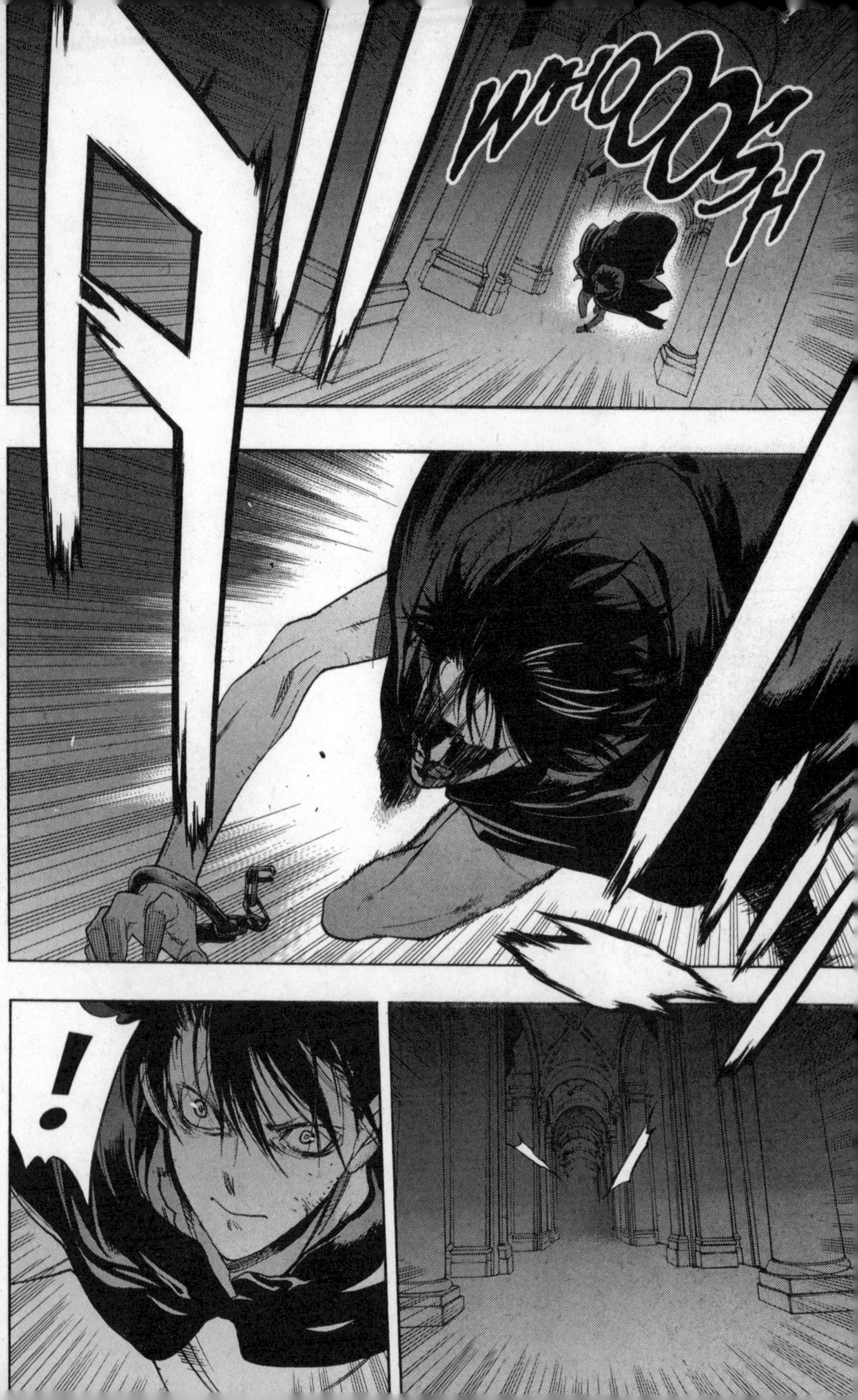

WHOOOSH
!

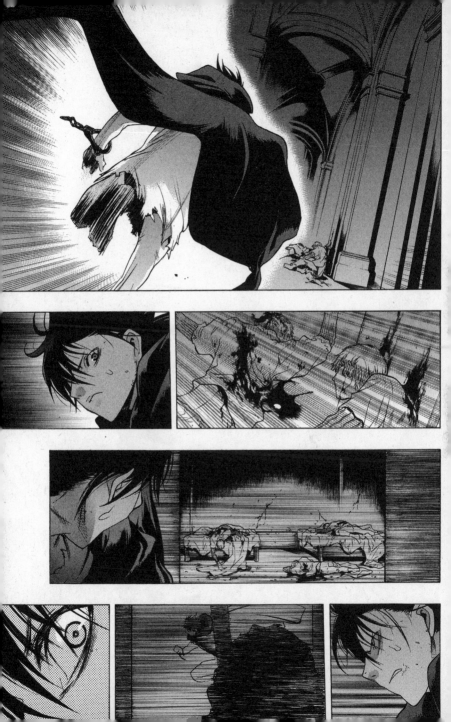

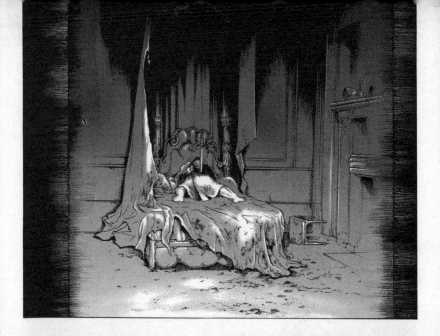

SHARLE!!!

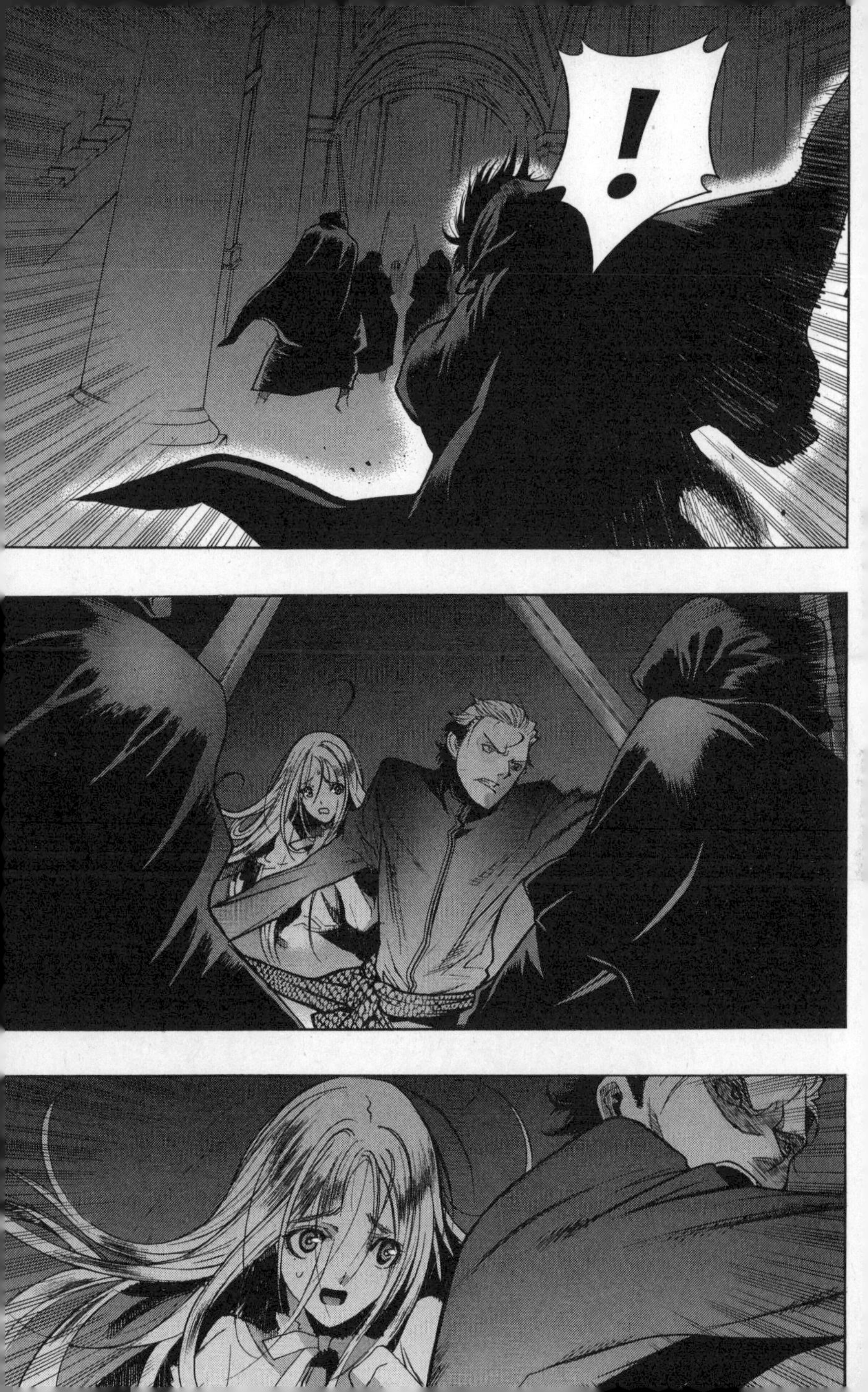
!

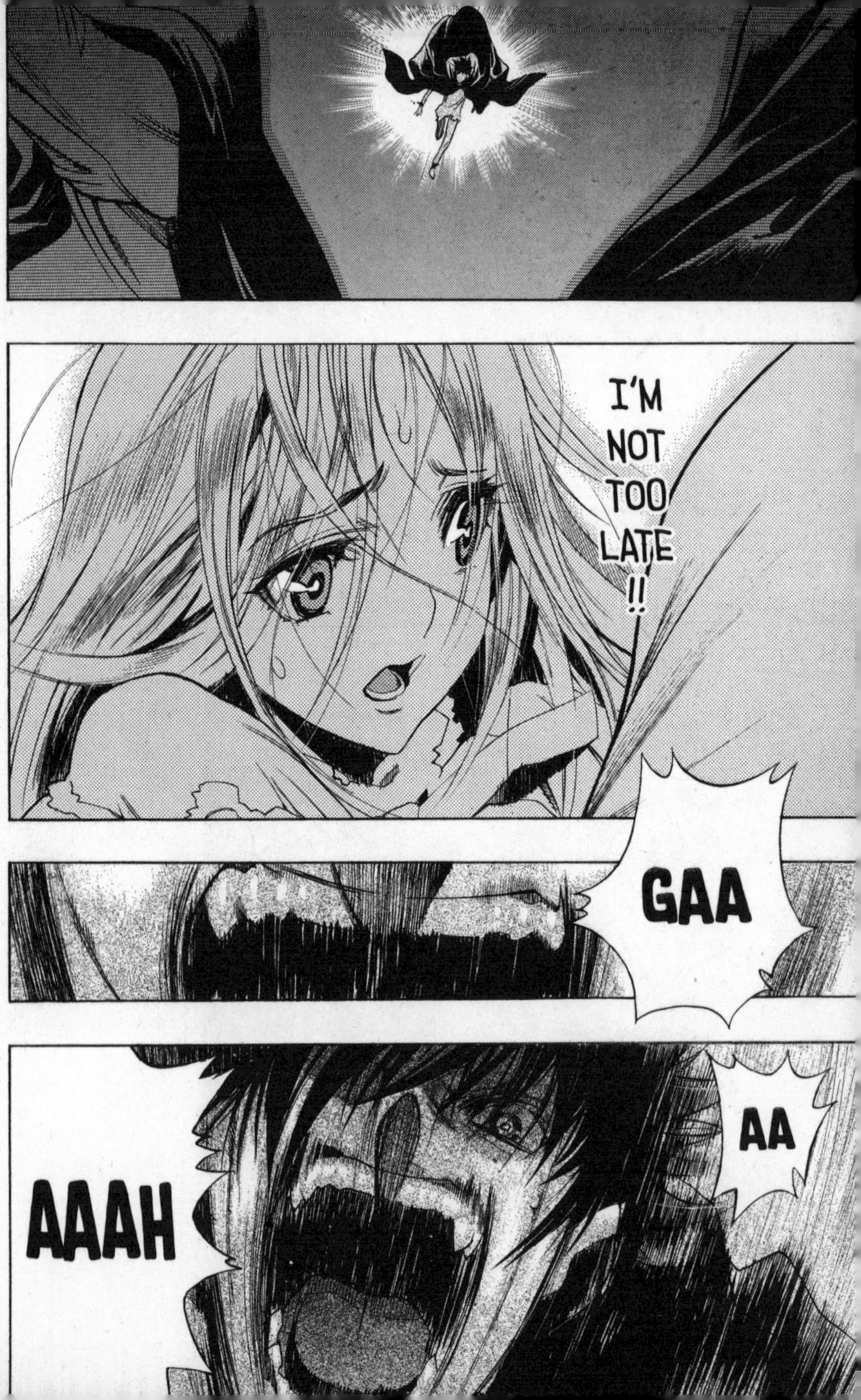
I'M NOT TOO LATE !!
GAA
AA
AAAH

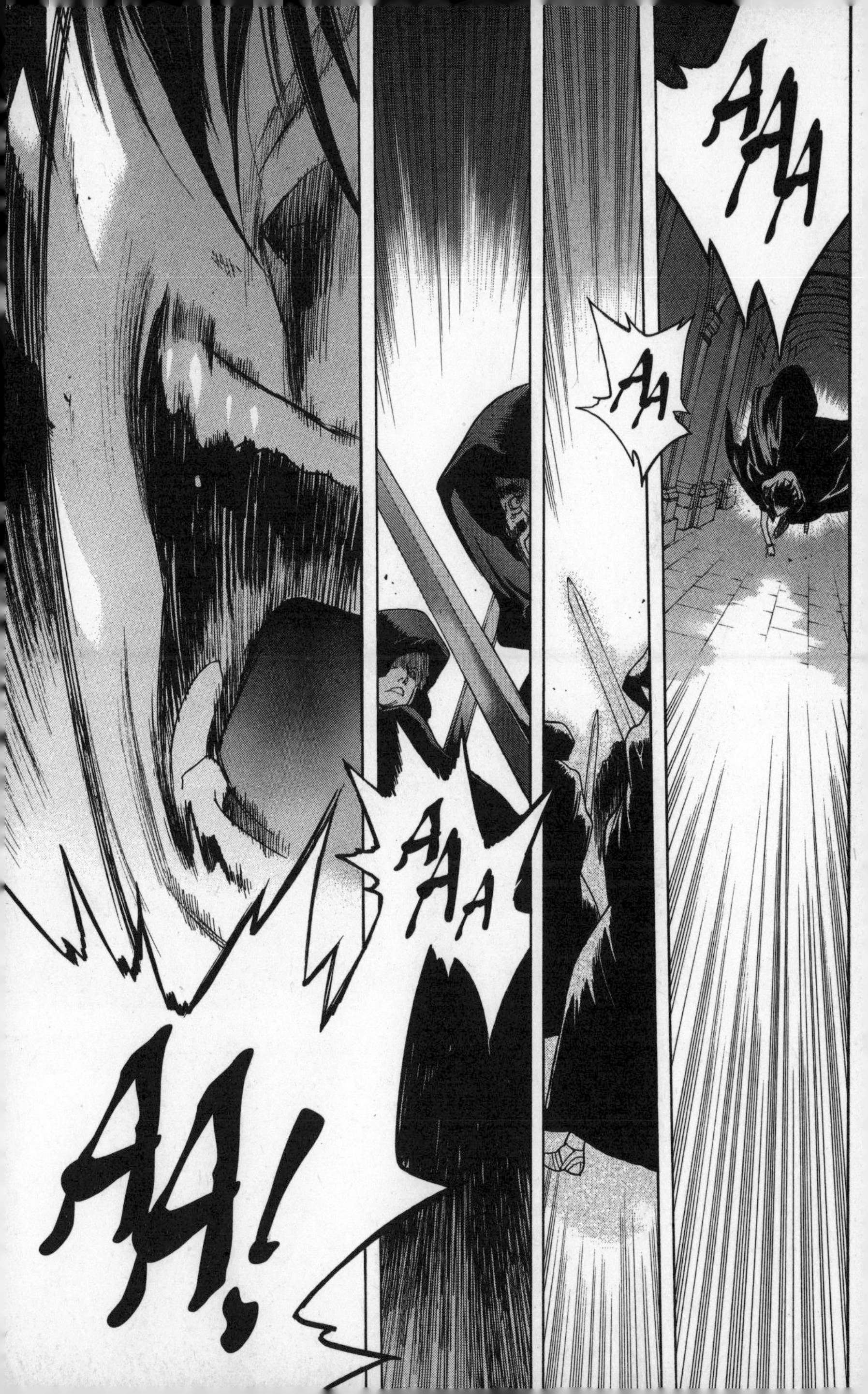
AAAA
AA
AAAA
AA!

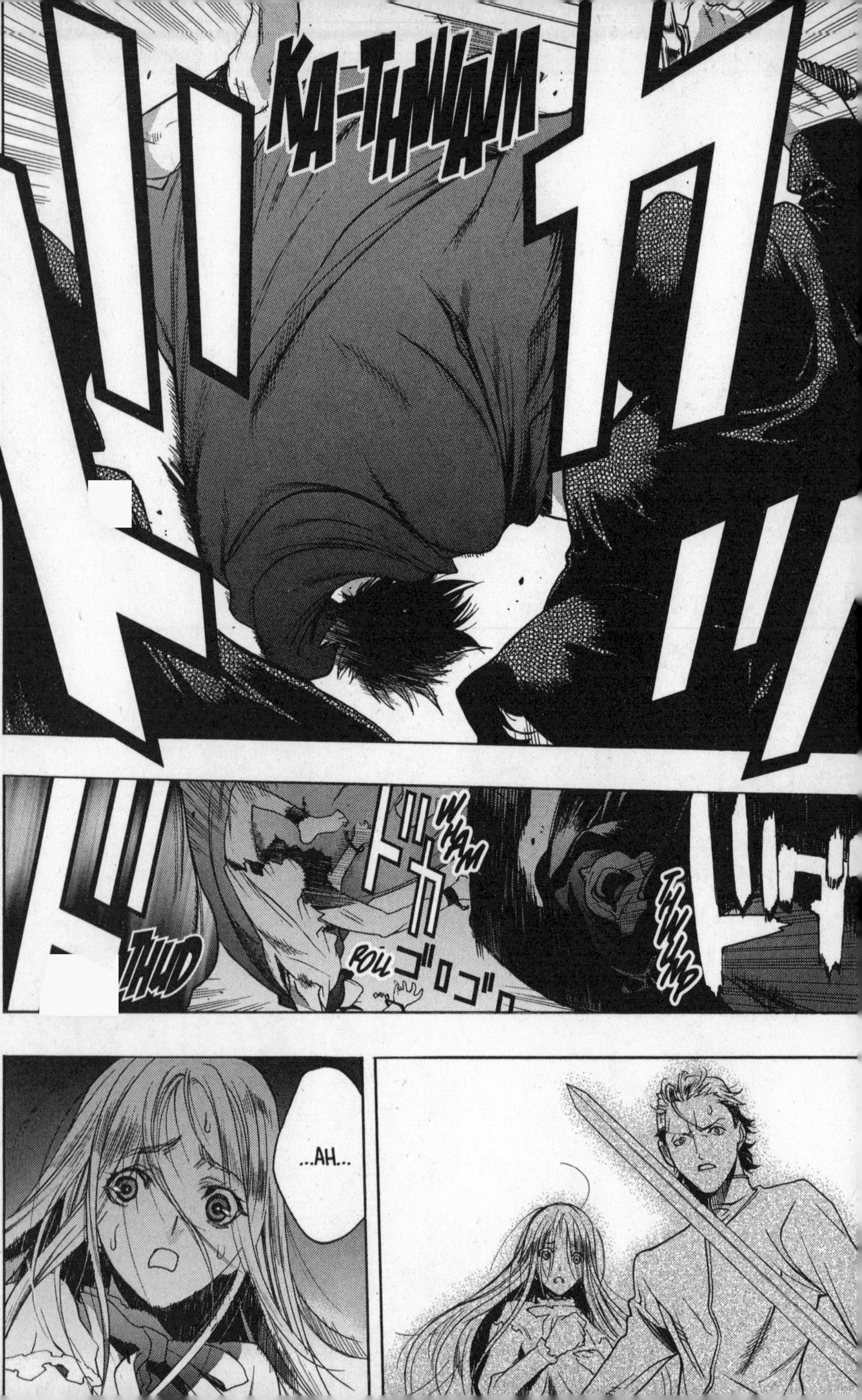

KA-THWAM
WHAM
THWUMP
THUD
ROLL
ゴロゴロ
...AH...

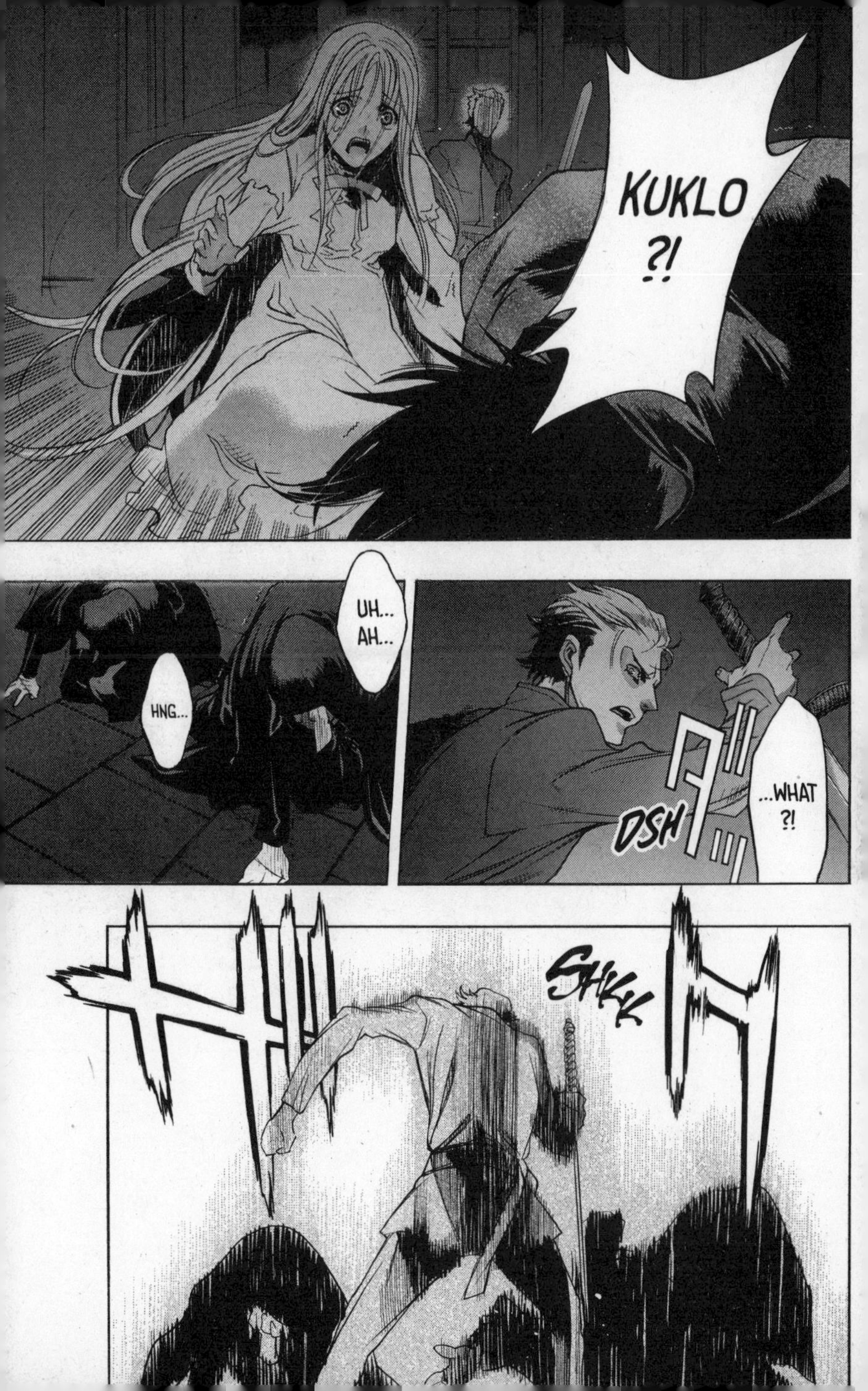
KUKLO ?!
UH... AH...
HNG...
...WHAT ?!
DSH
SHKK

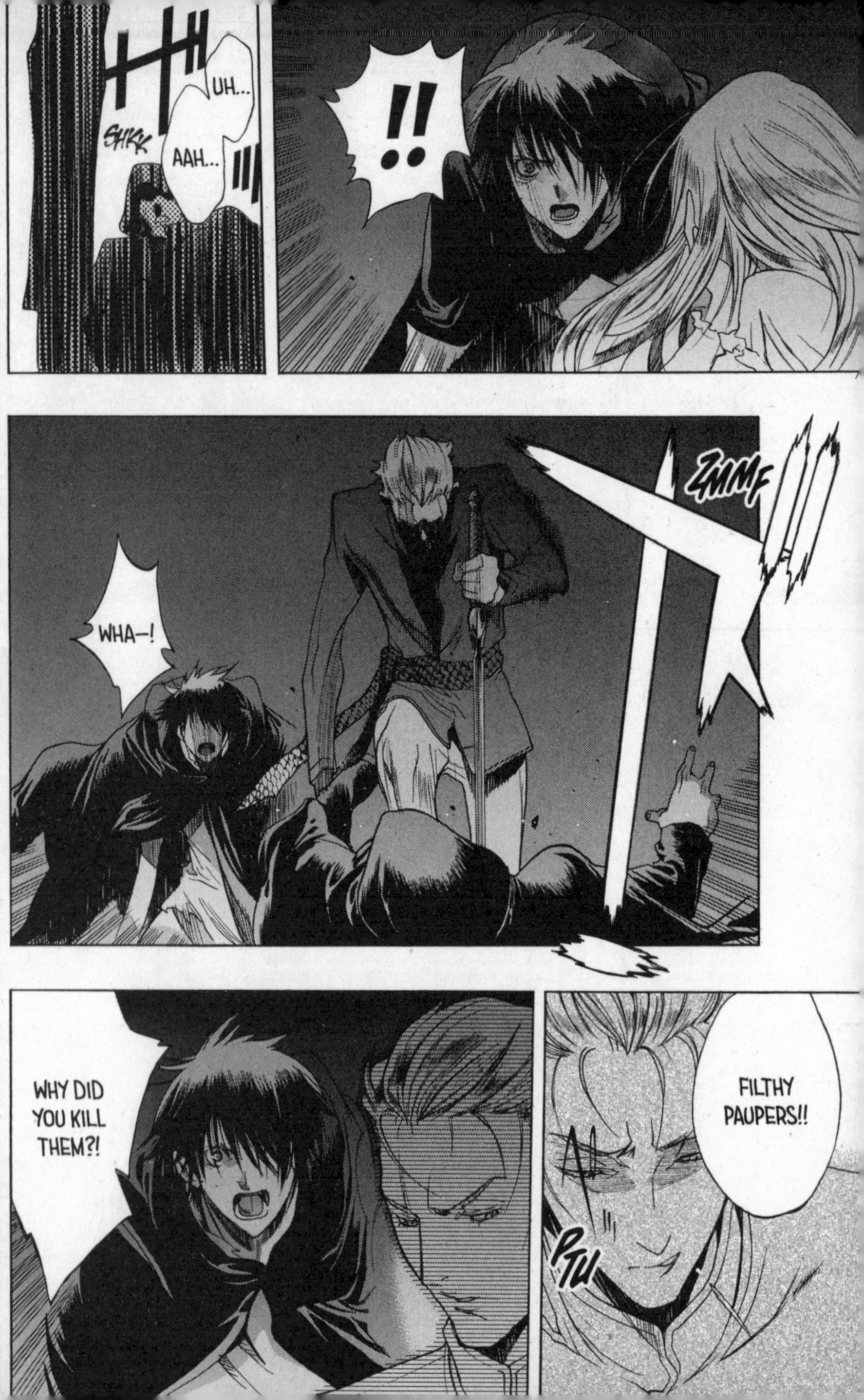
!!
UH...
AAH...
SHKK
ZMMF
WHA-!
FILTHY PAUPERS!!
PTU
WHY DID YOU KILL THEM?!

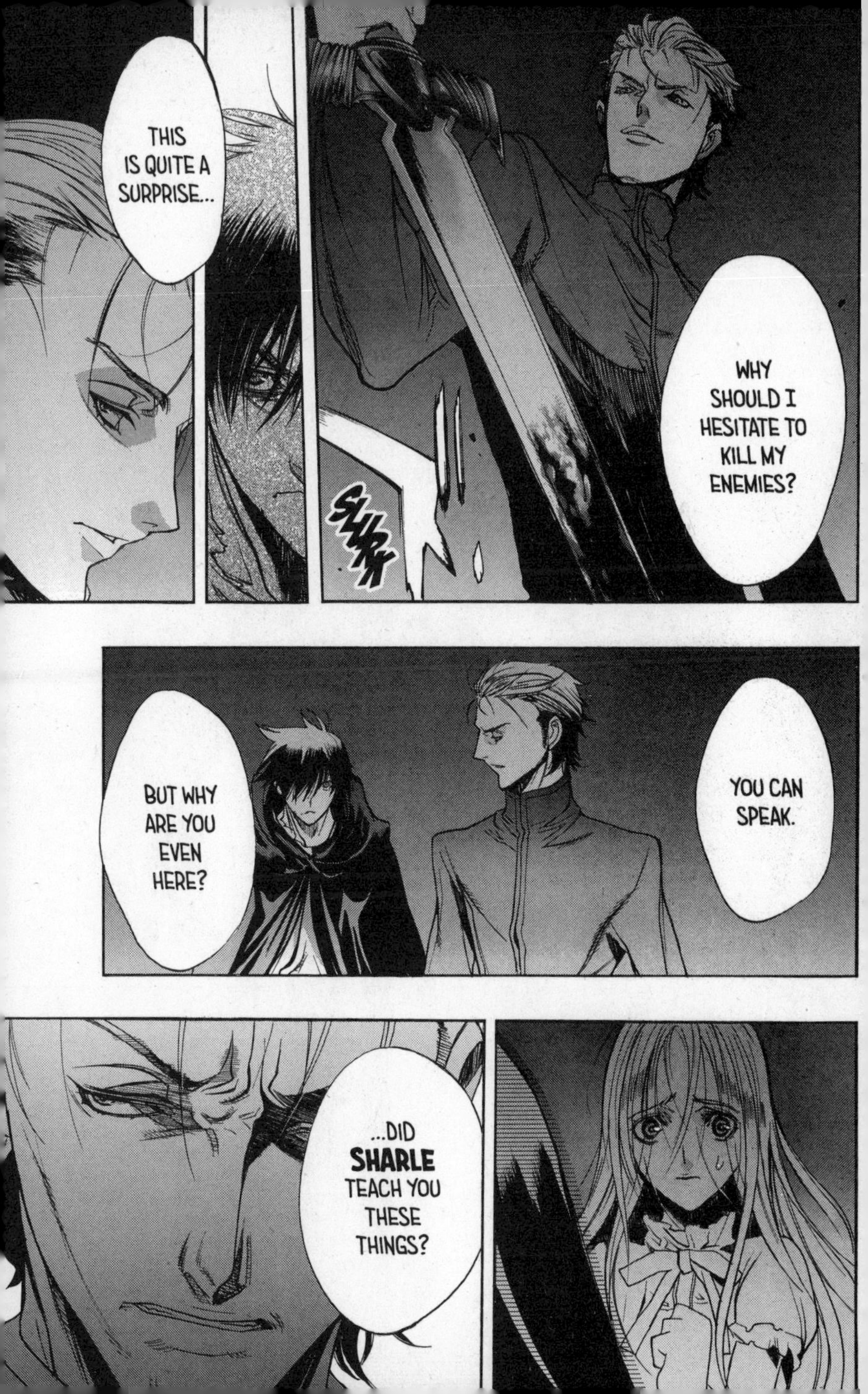
WHY SHOULD I HESITATE TO KILL MY ENEMIES?
SLURK
THIS IS QUITE A SURPRISE...
YOU CAN SPEAK.
BUT WHY ARE YOU EVEN HERE?
...DID **SHARLE** TEACH YOU THESE THINGS?

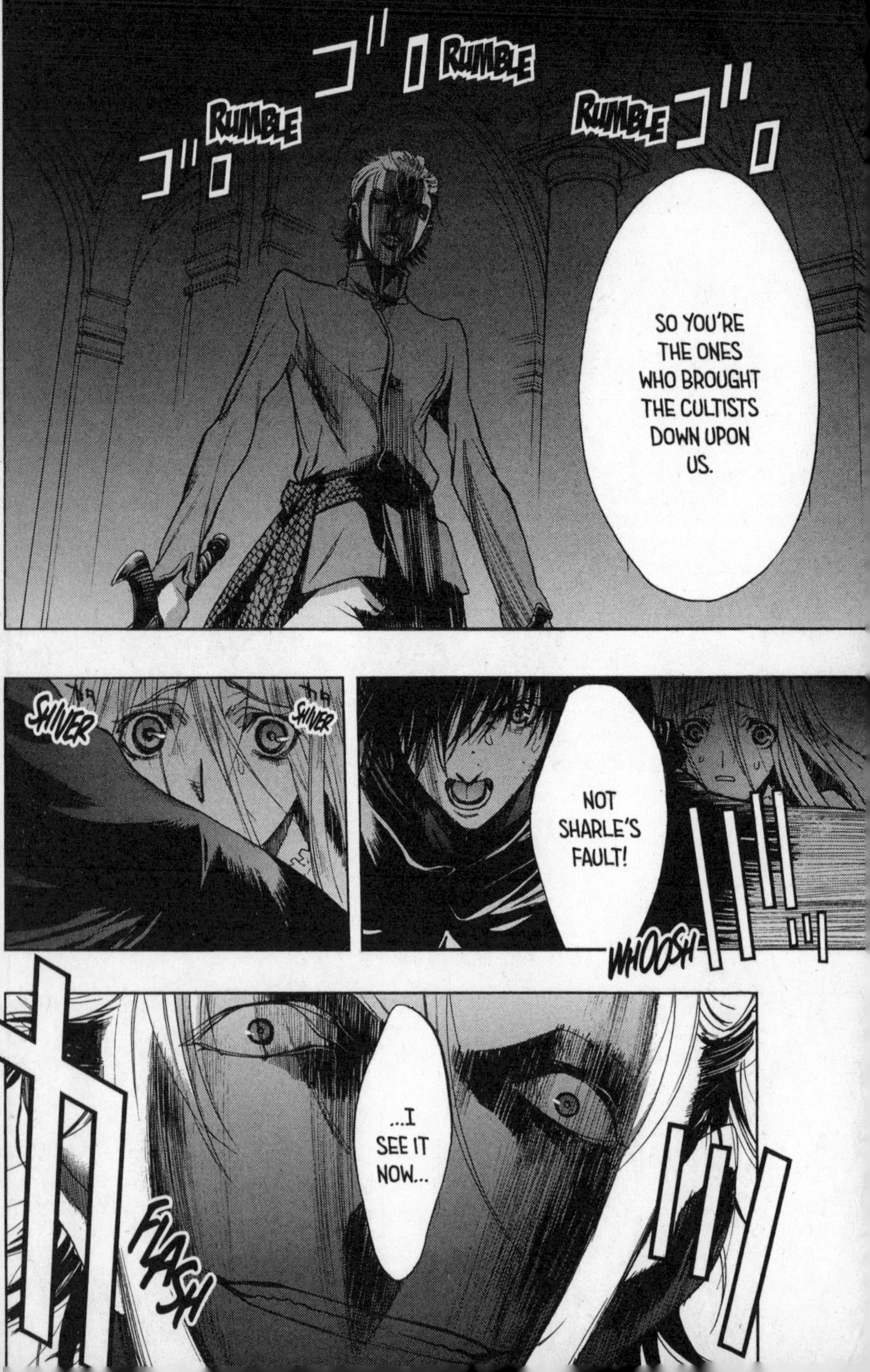
RUMBLE
RUMBLE
RUMBLE
SO YOU'RE THE ONES WHO BROUGHT THE CULTISTS DOWN UPON US.
NOT SHARLE'S FAULT!
WHOOSH
SHIVER
SHIVER
...I SEE IT NOW...
FLASH

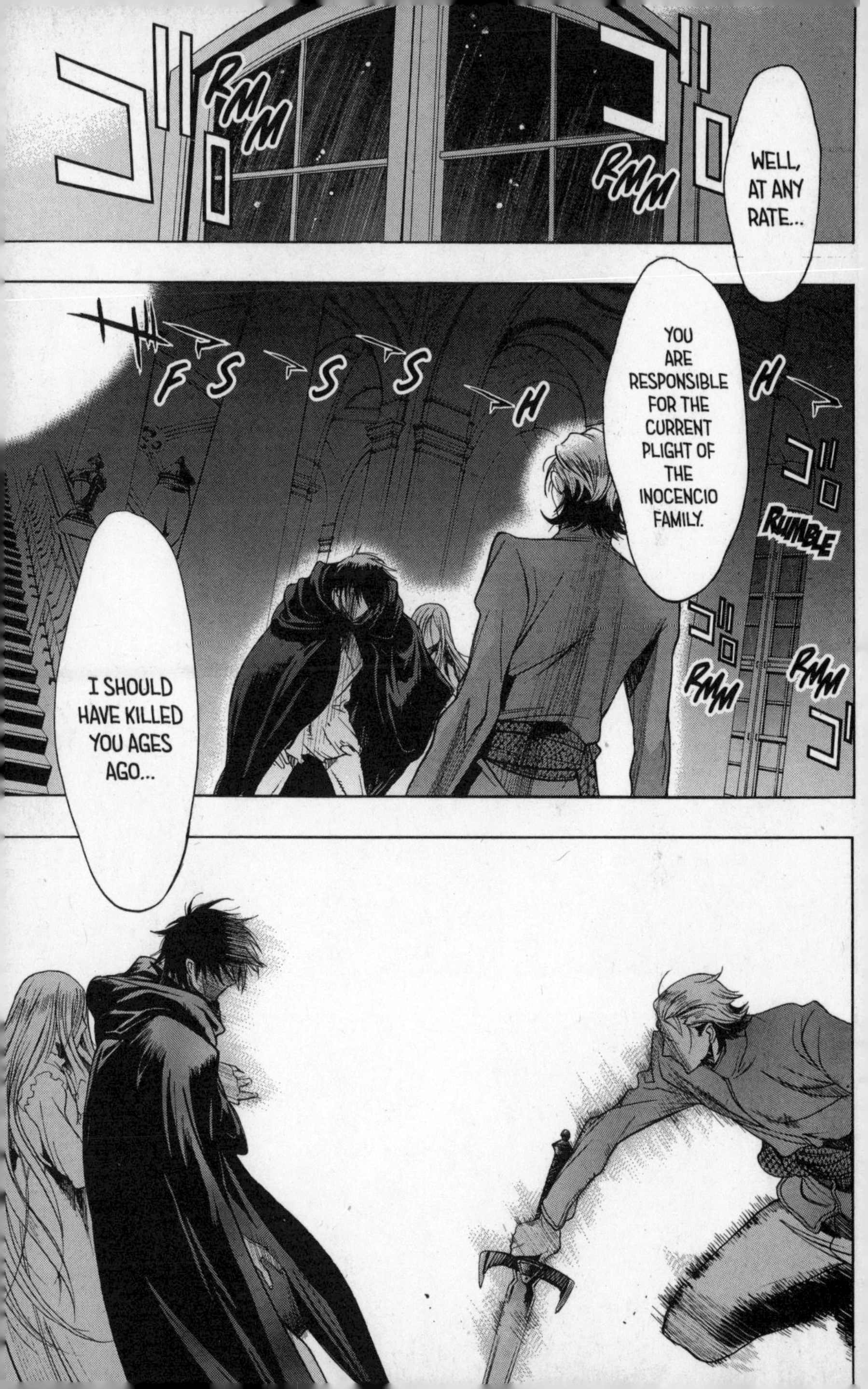
WELL, AT ANY RATE...
RMM
RMM
YOU ARE RESPONSIBLE FOR THE CURRENT PLIGHT OF THE INOCENCIO FAMILY.
H
RUMBLE
RMM
RMM
FSSSH
I SHOULD HAVE KILLED YOU AGES AGO...

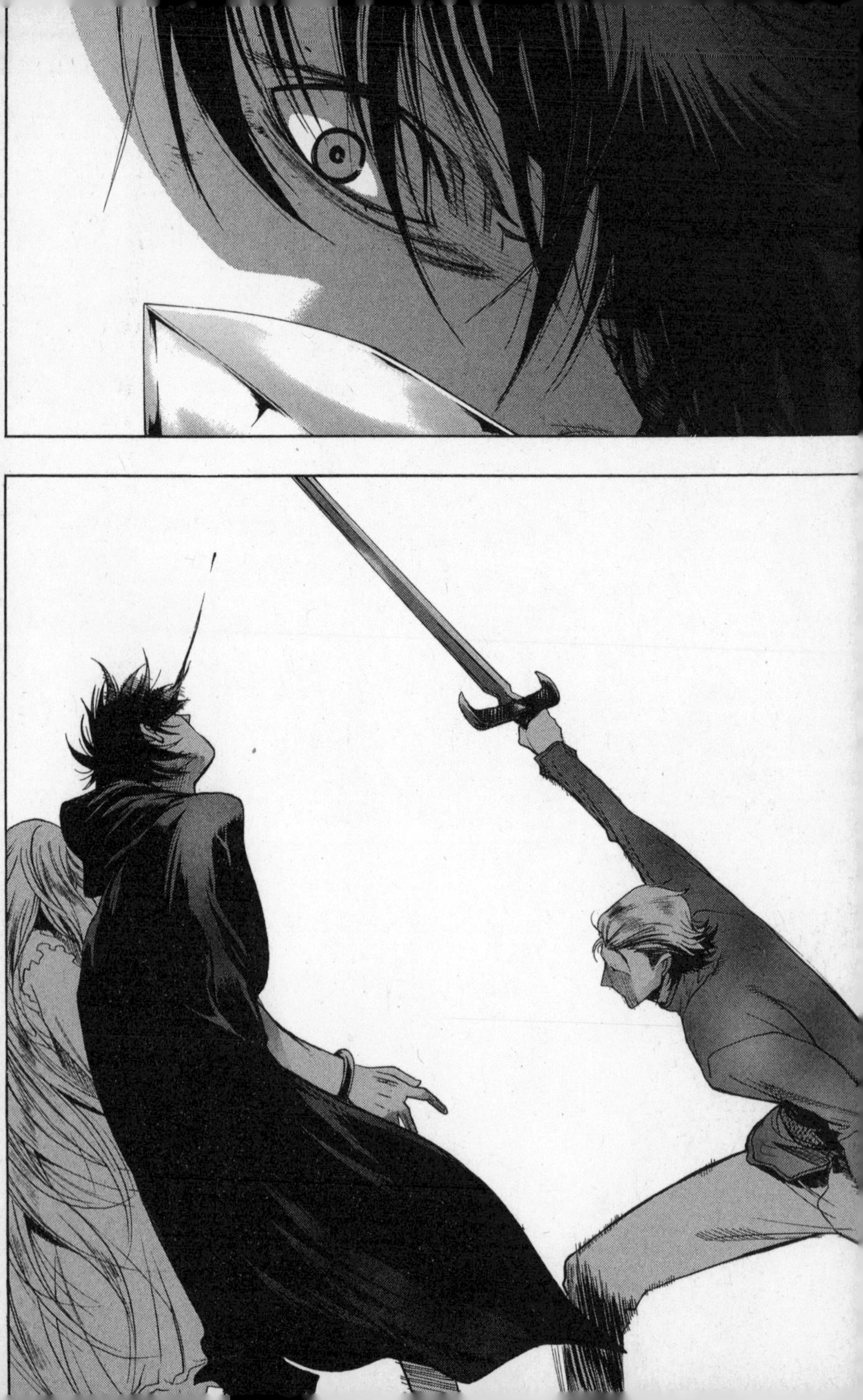

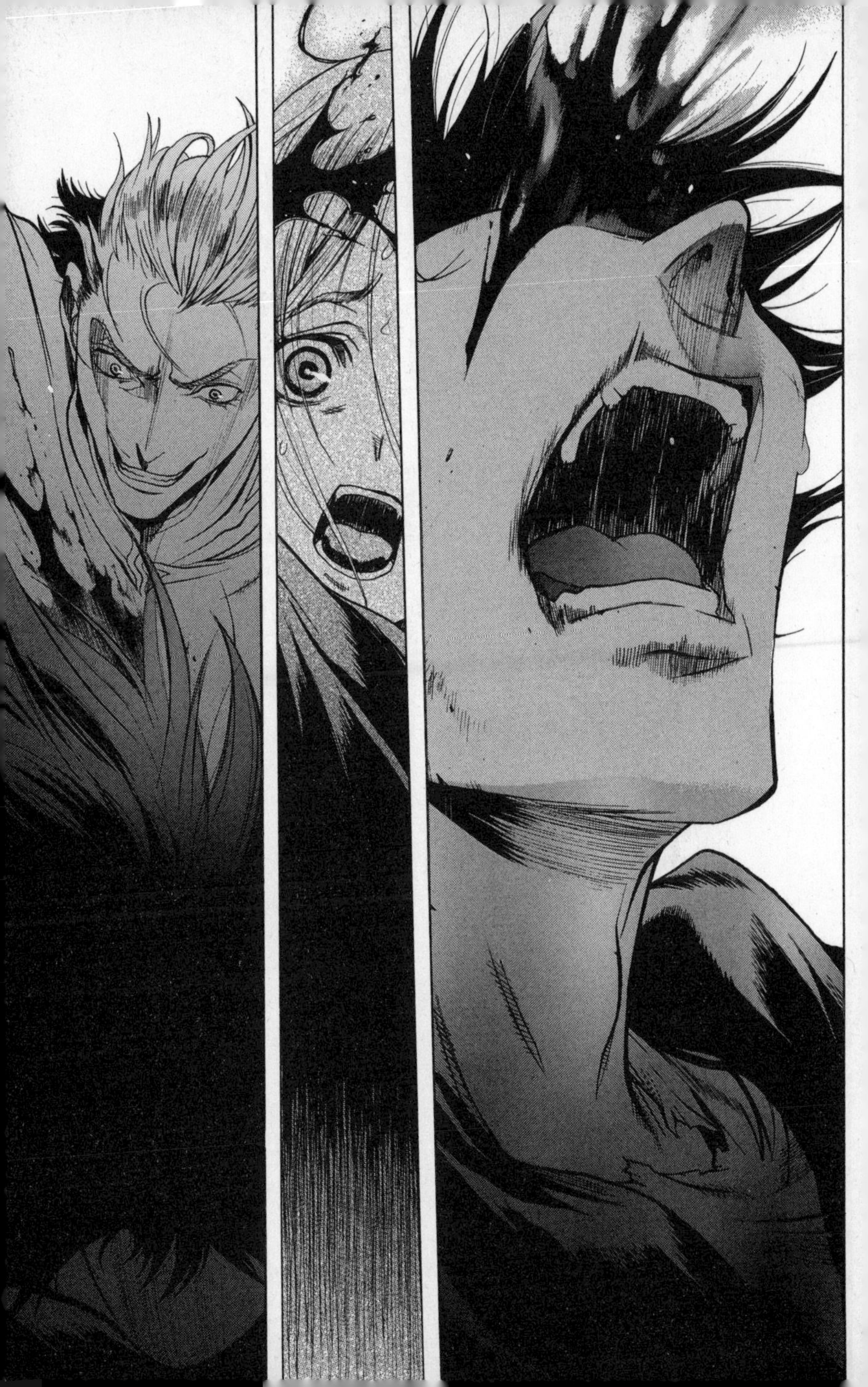

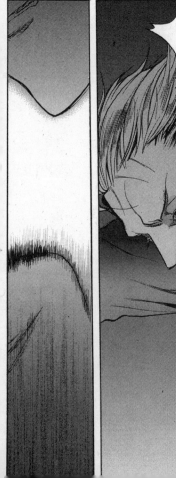

HRRG...
UH...

THUD

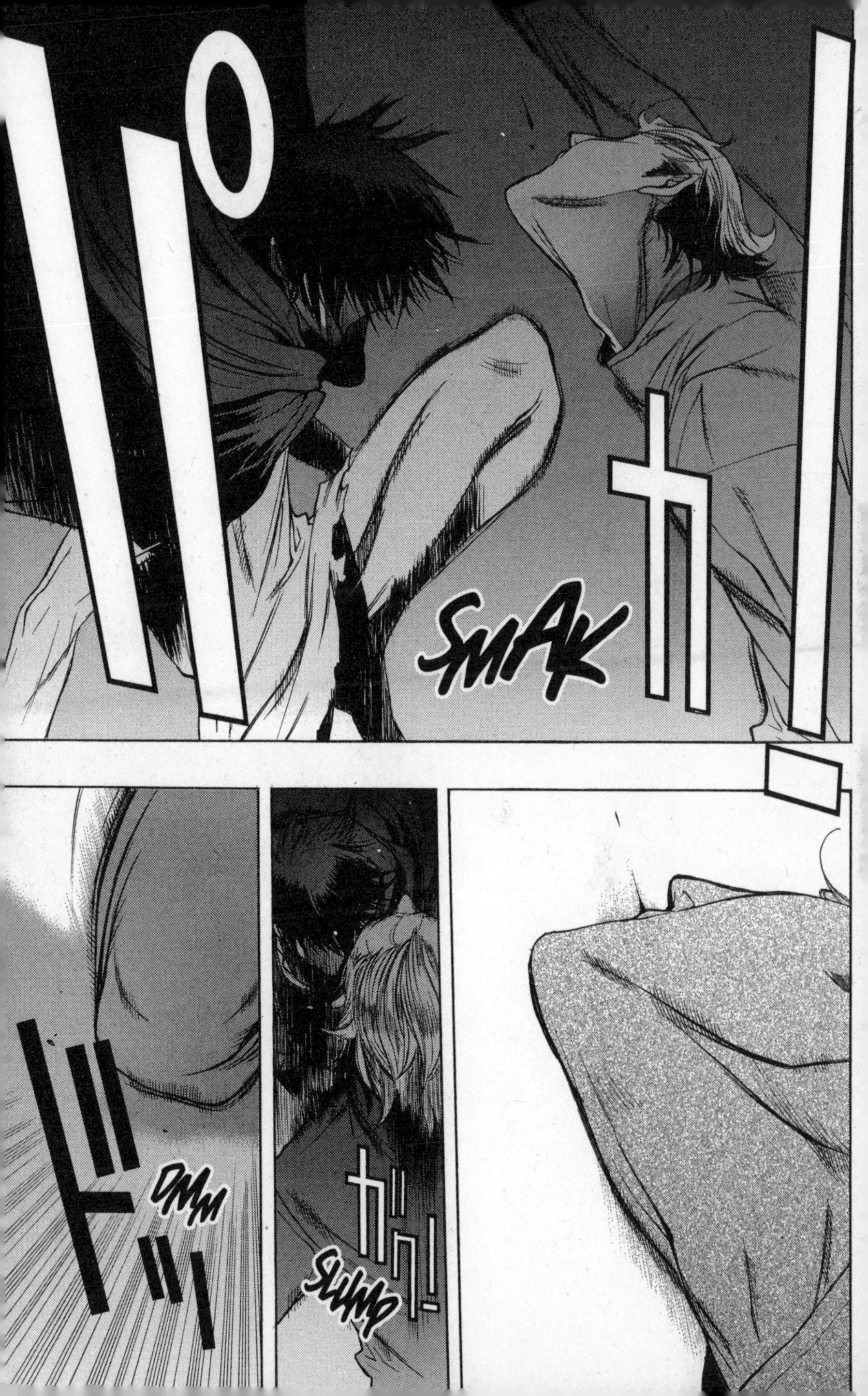
バッ
ガッ
SMAK
ドッ
DMM
ガクッ
SLUMP

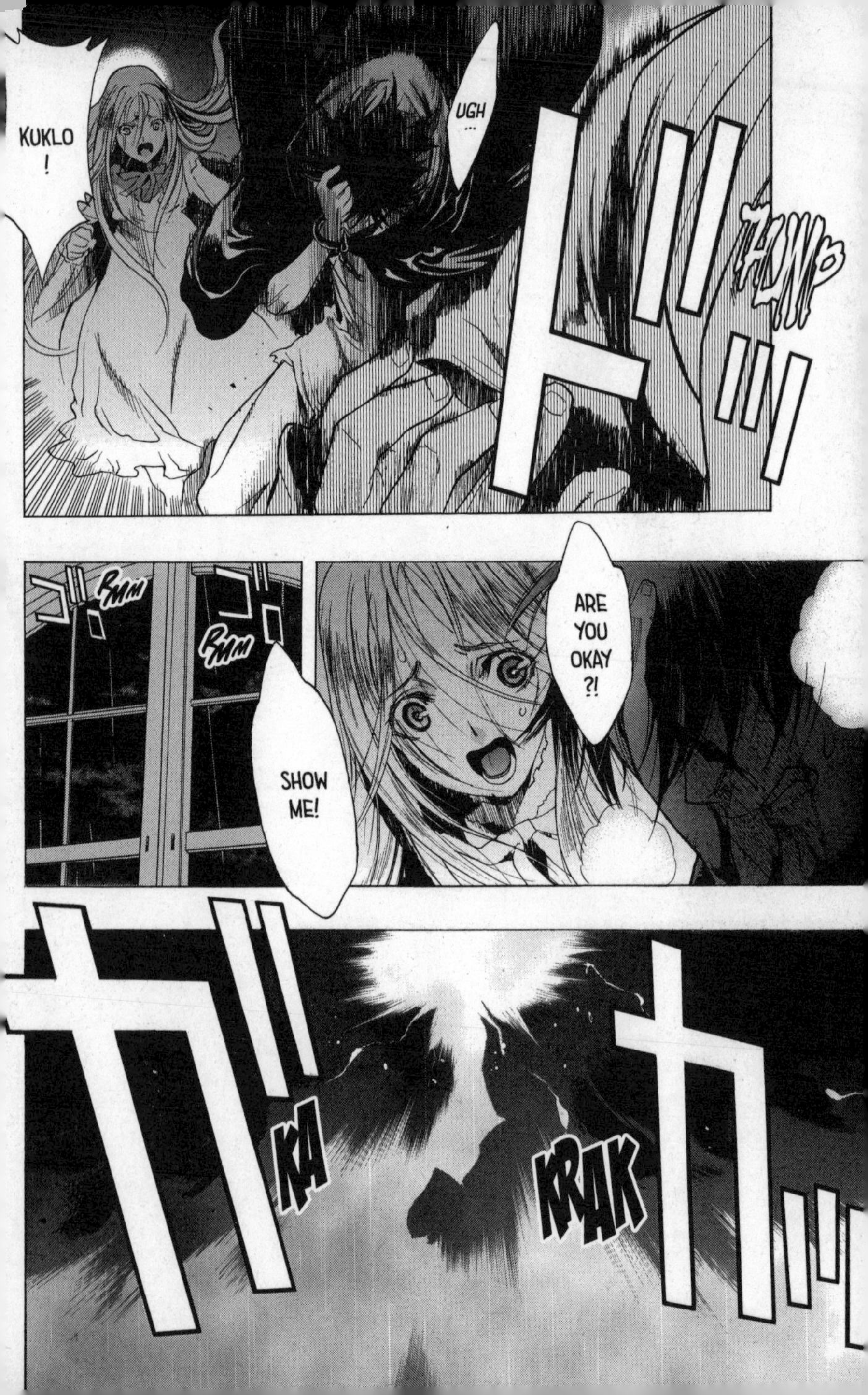
THOMP
UGH...
KUKLO!
ARE YOU OKAY?!
SHOW ME!
RMM
RMM
KRAK
KA

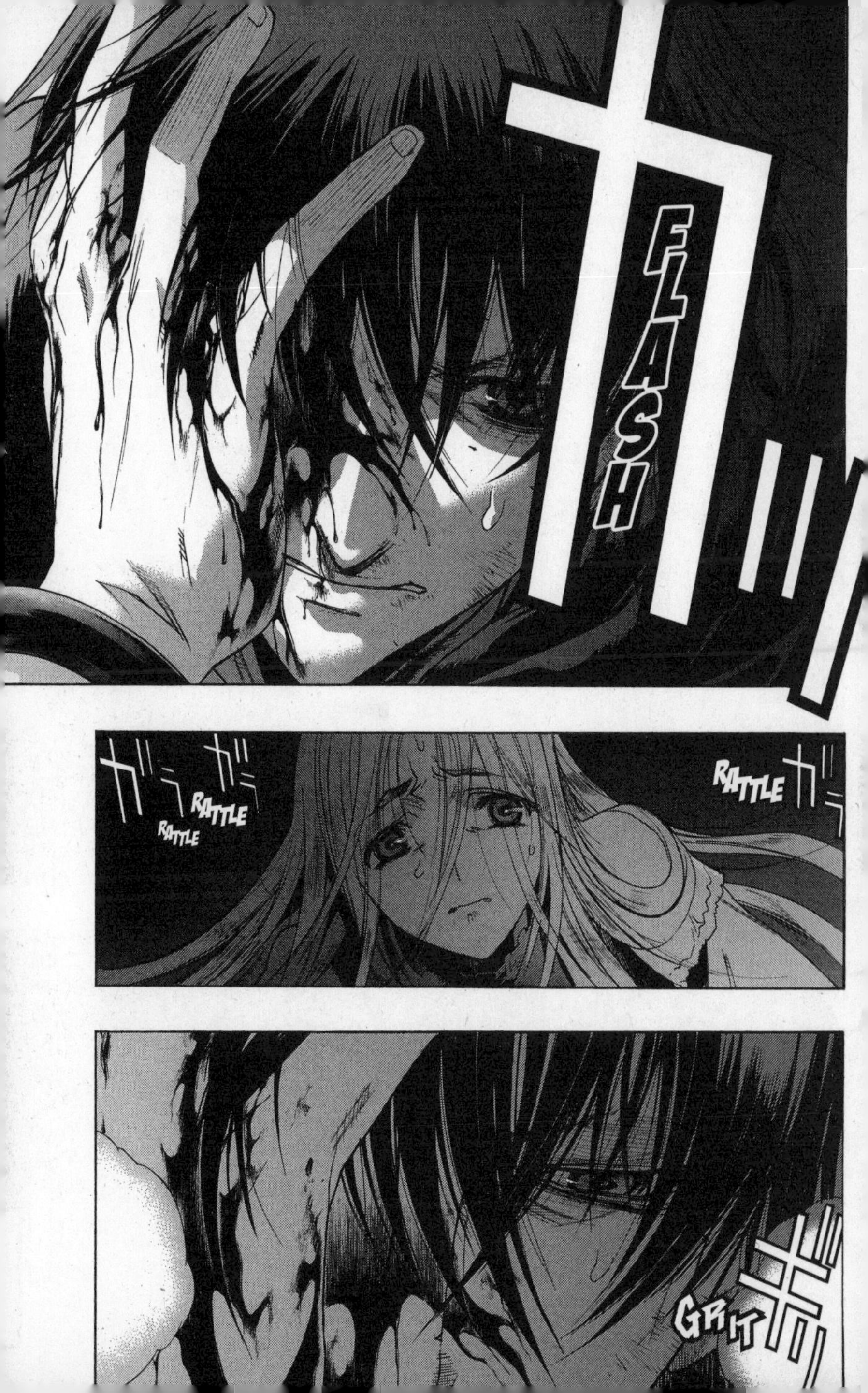
FLASH
RATTLE
RATTLE
RATTLE
GRIT

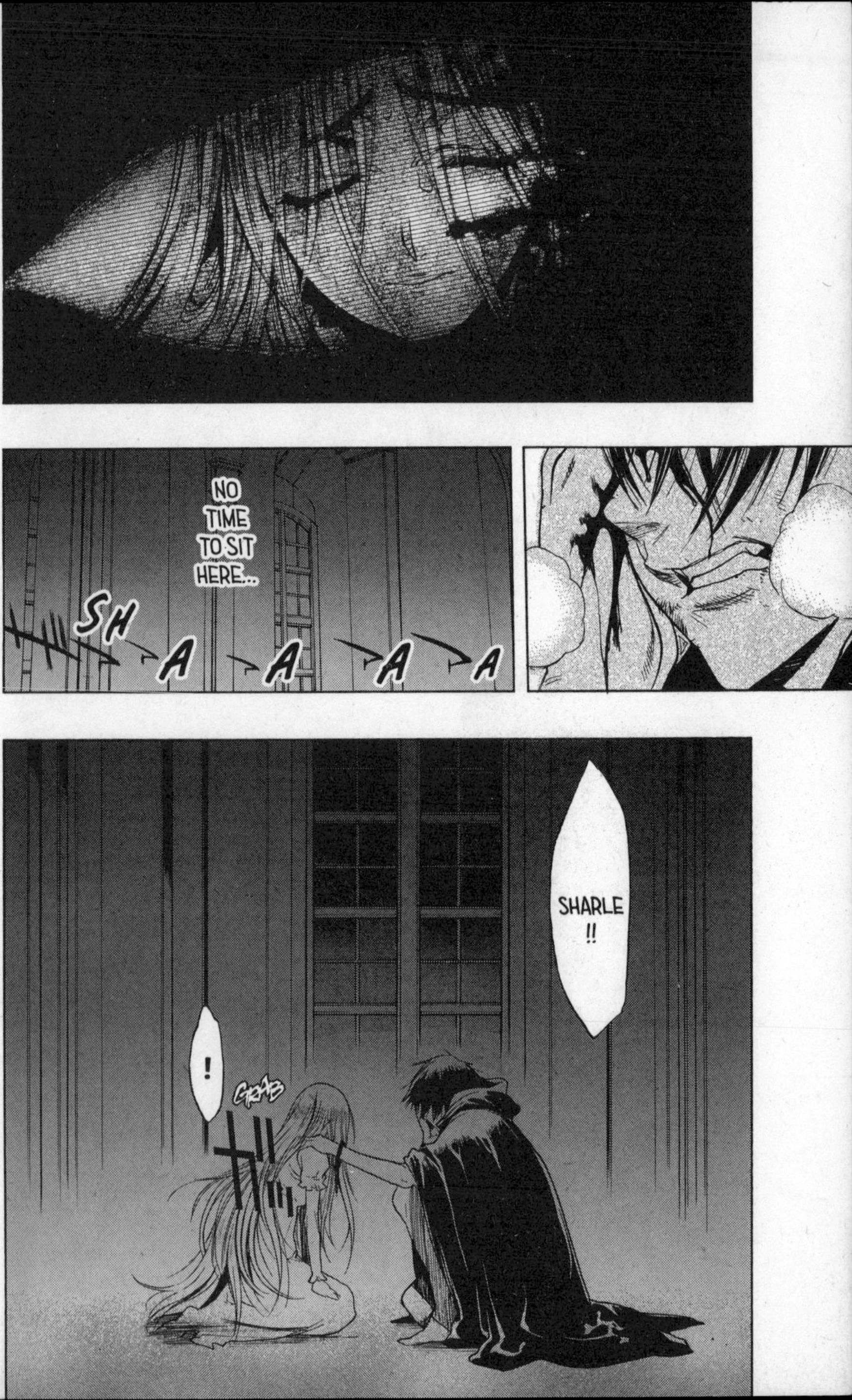
NO TIME TO SIT HERE...
SH-A-A-A-A
SHARLE !!
!
GRAB

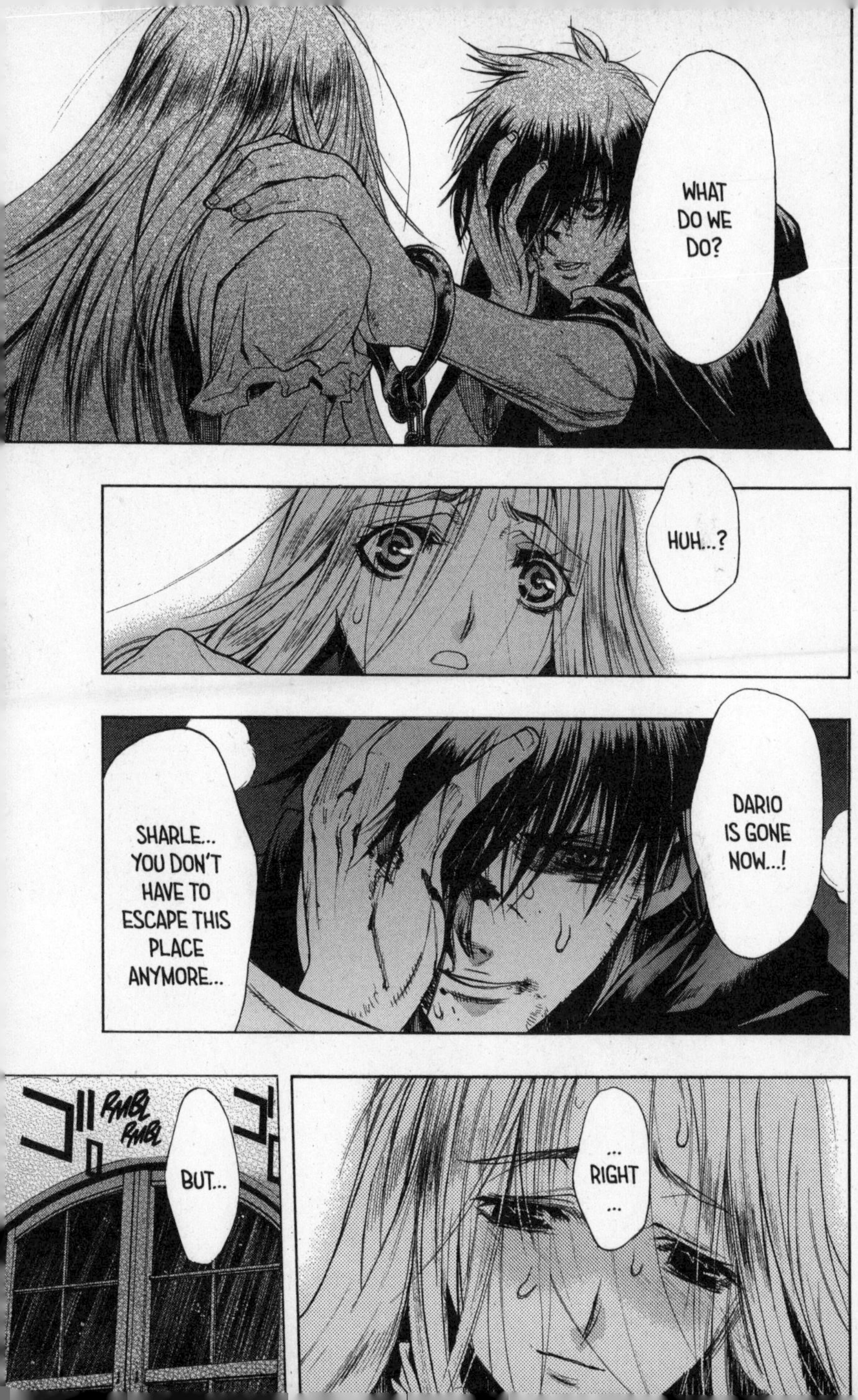
WHAT DO WE DO?
HUH...?
DARIO IS GONE NOW...!
SHARLE... YOU DON'T HAVE TO ESCAPE THIS PLACE ANYMORE...
... RIGHT ...
RMBL RMBL
BUT...

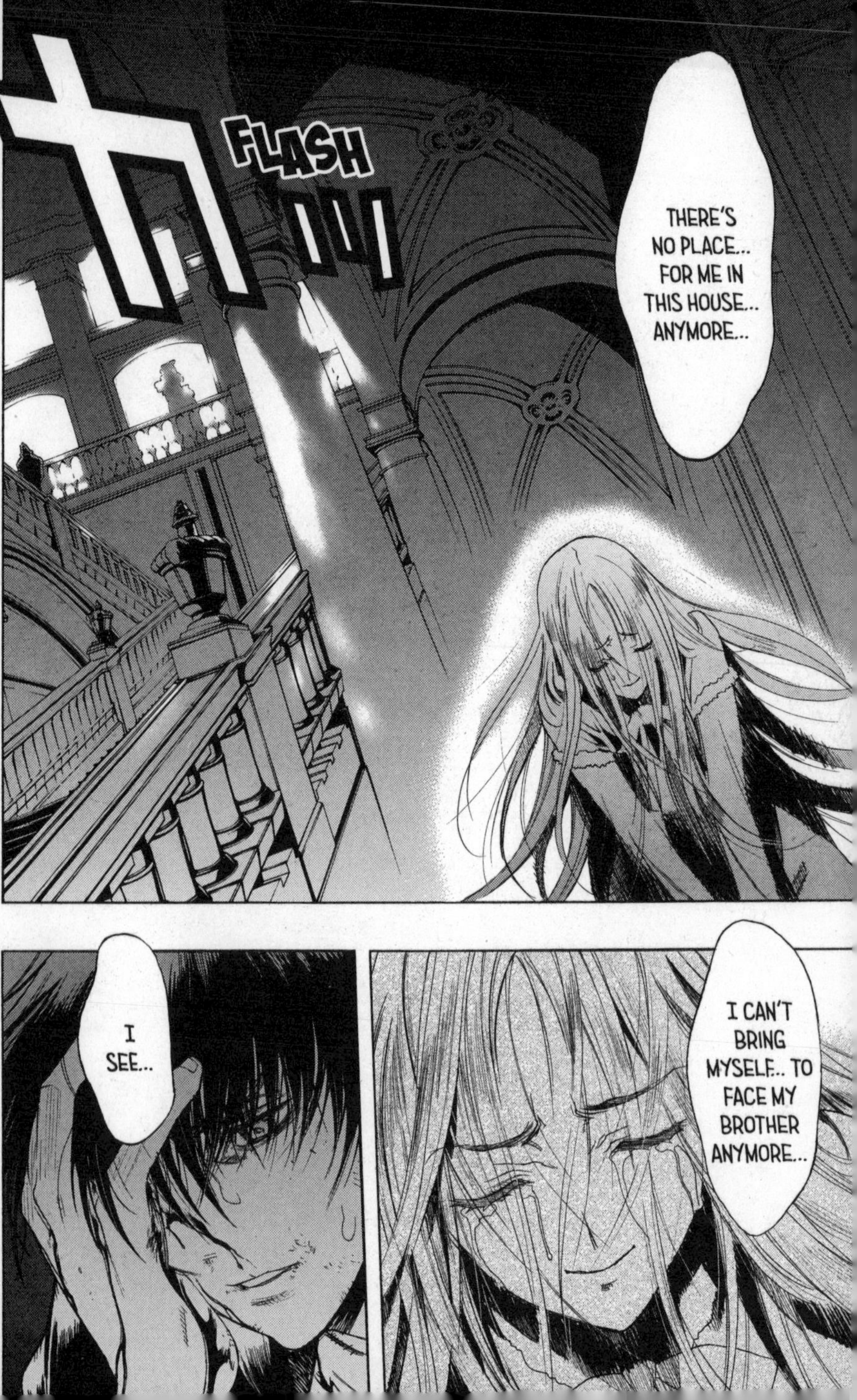
FLASH
THERE'S NO PLACE... FOR ME IN THIS HOUSE... ANYMORE...
I CAN'T BRING MYSELF... TO FACE MY BROTHER ANYMORE...
I SEE...

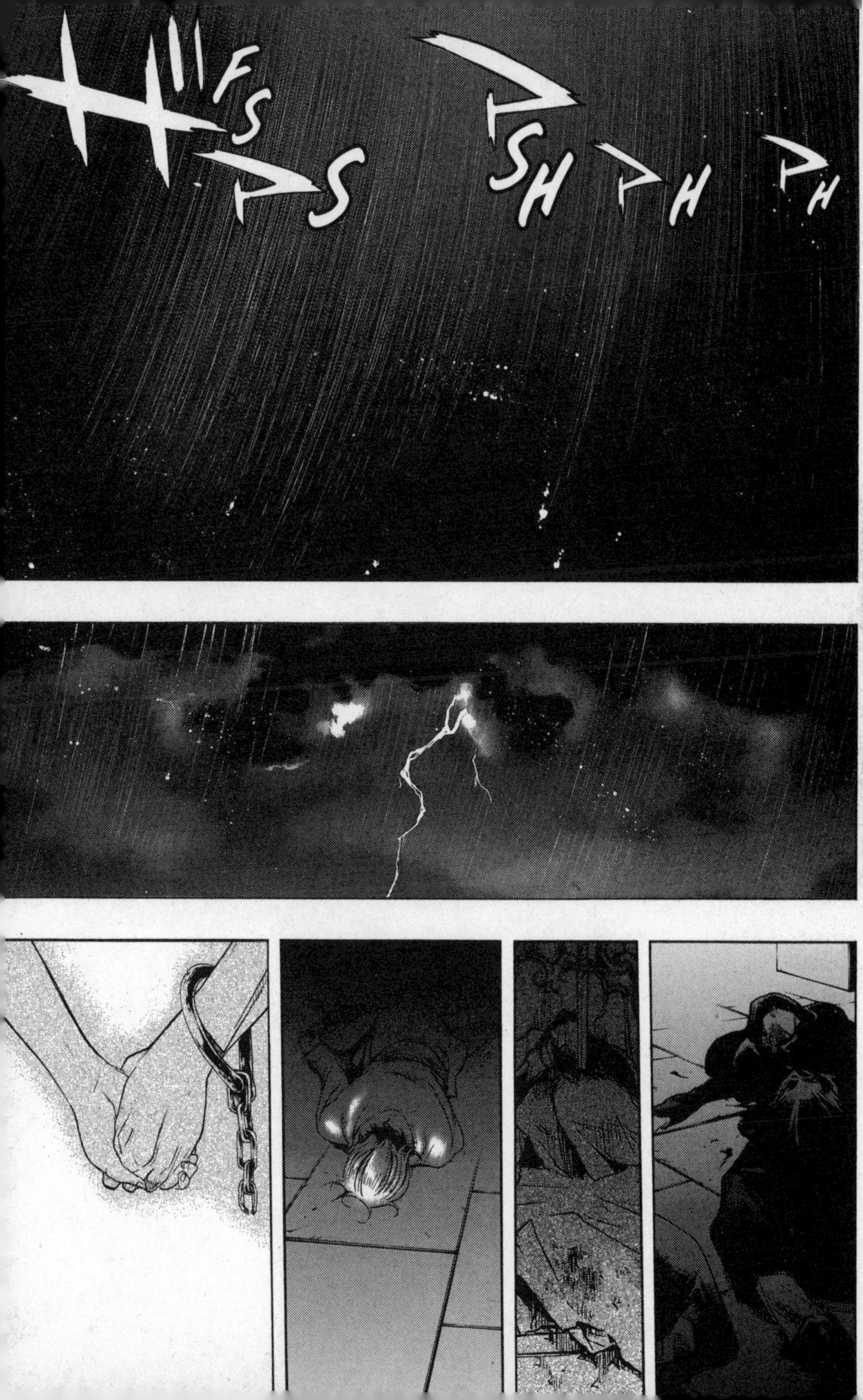
FS
PS
PSH PH PH

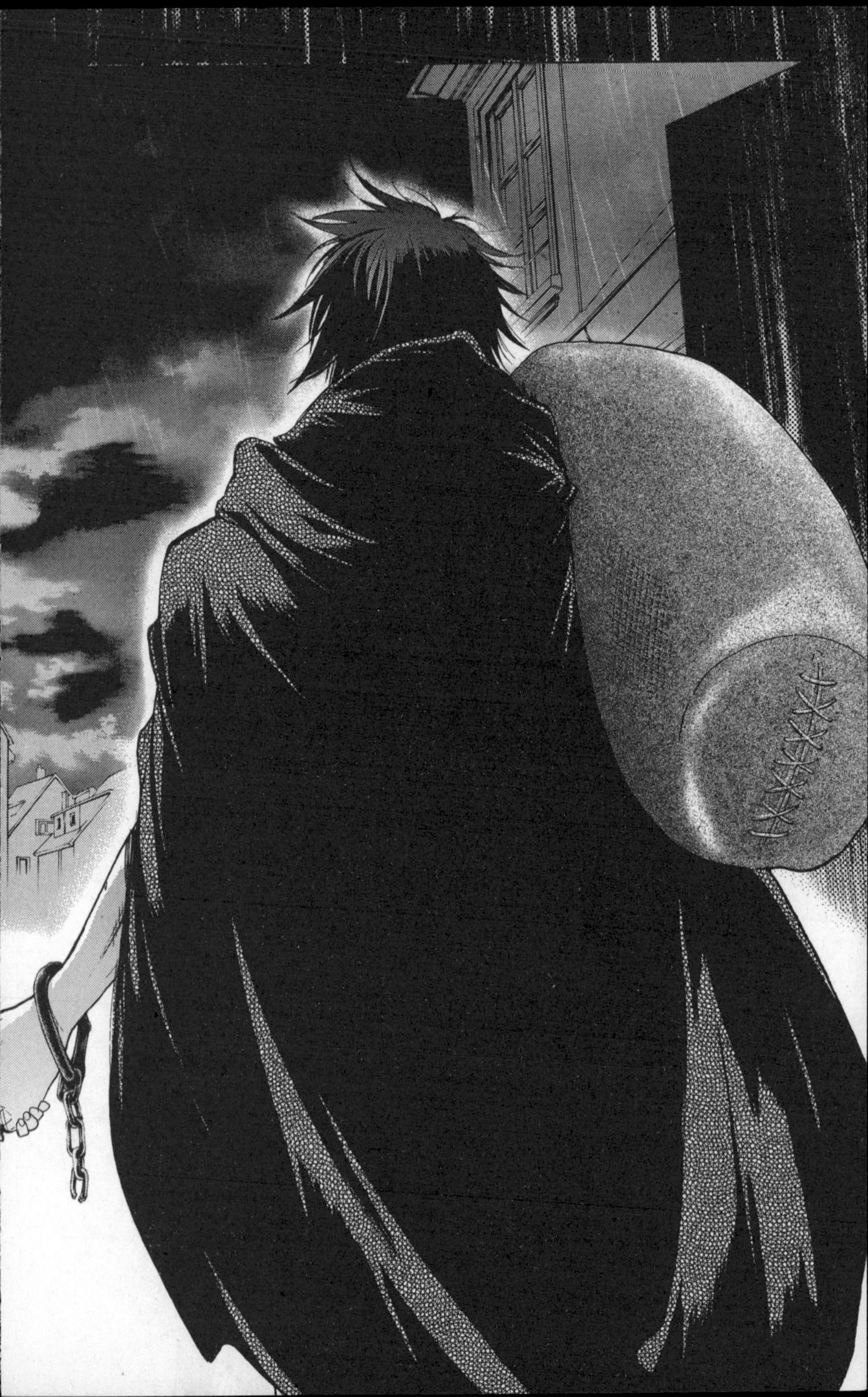

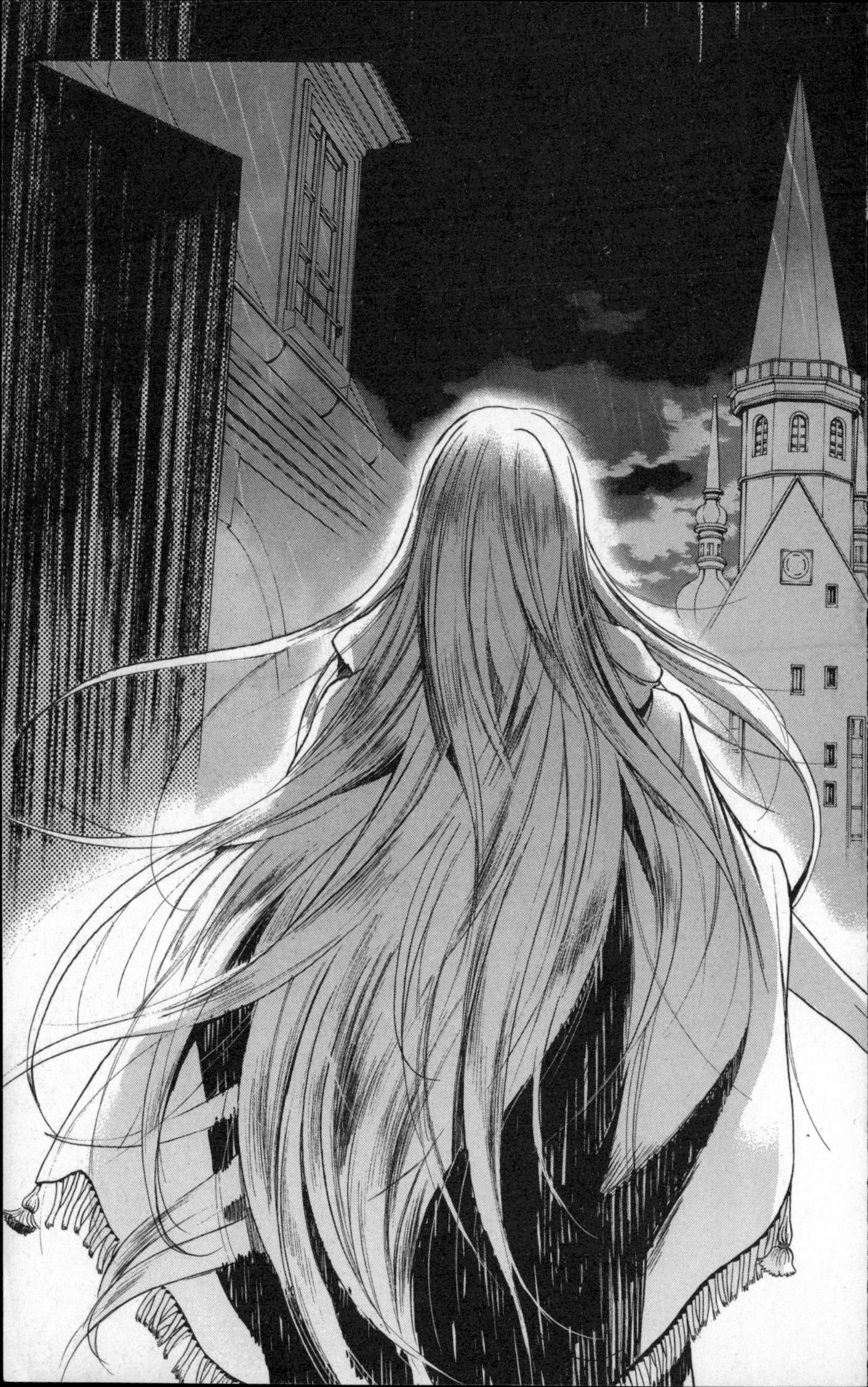

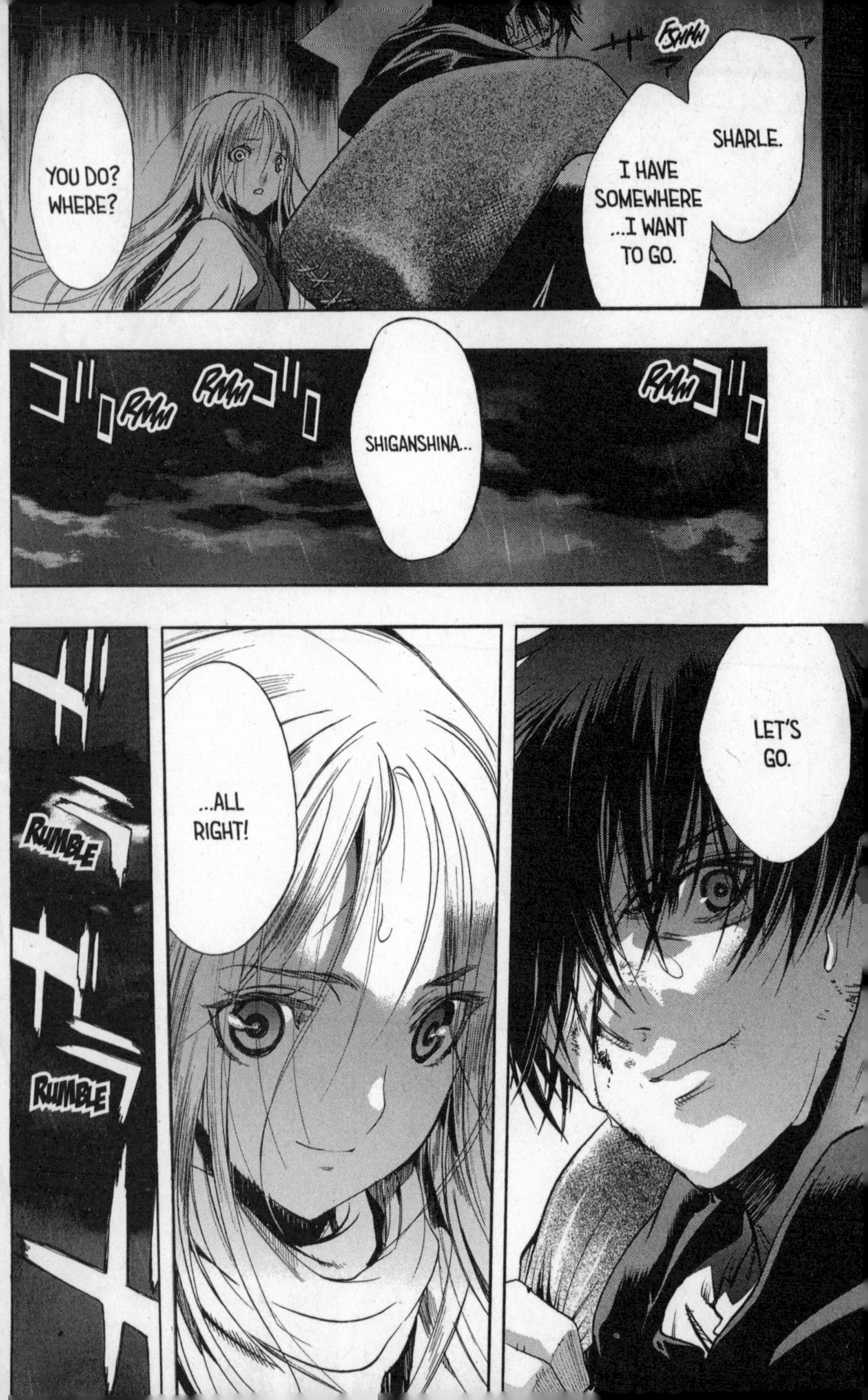
FSHHH
SHARLE.
I HAVE SOMEWHERE ...I WANT TO GO.
YOU DO? WHERE?
RMM
RMM
RMM
SHIGANSHINA...
LET'S GO.
...ALL RIGHT!
RUMBLE
RUMBLE

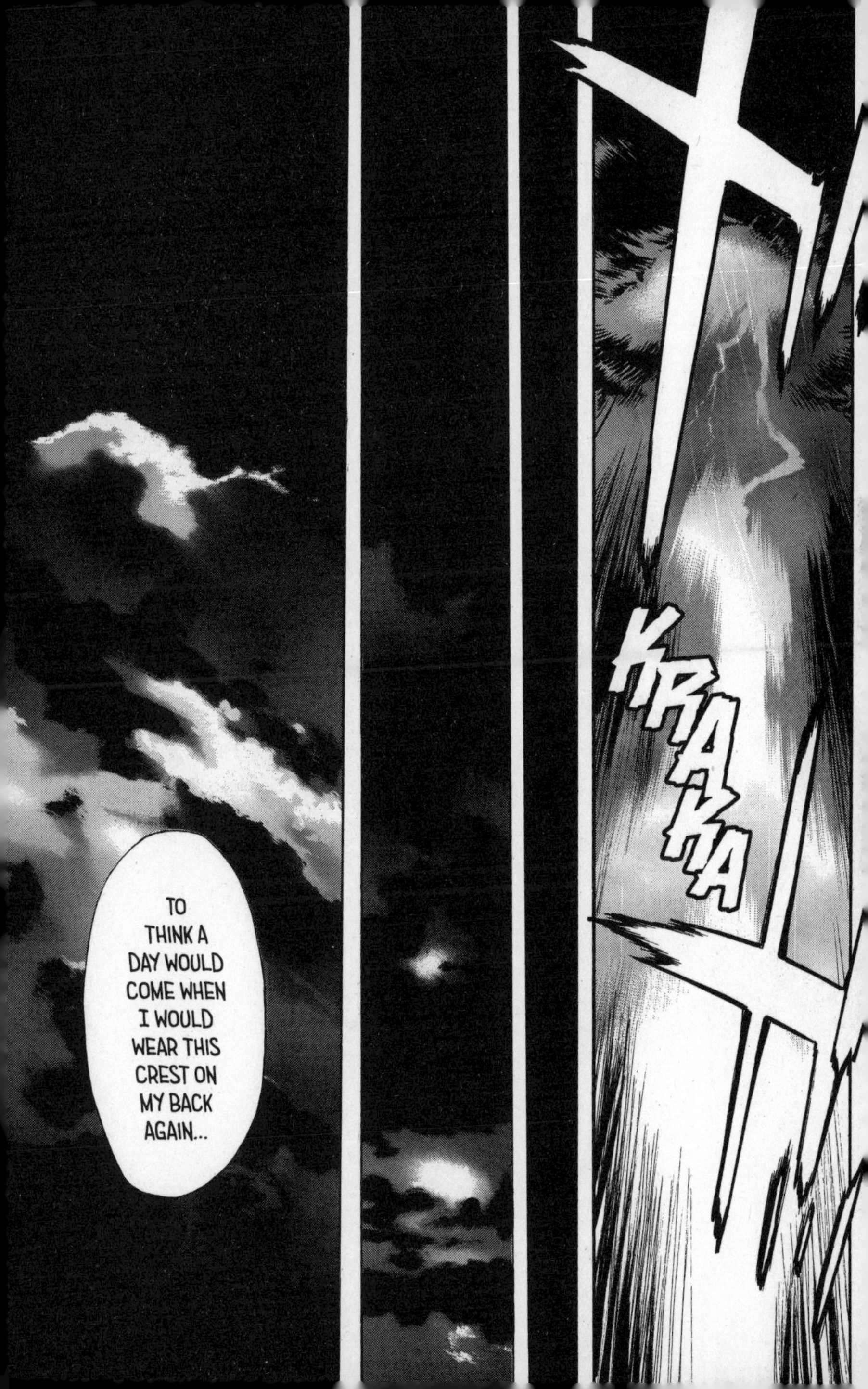
KRAKA
TO THINK A DAY WOULD COME WHEN I WOULD WEAR THIS CREST ON MY BACK AGAIN...

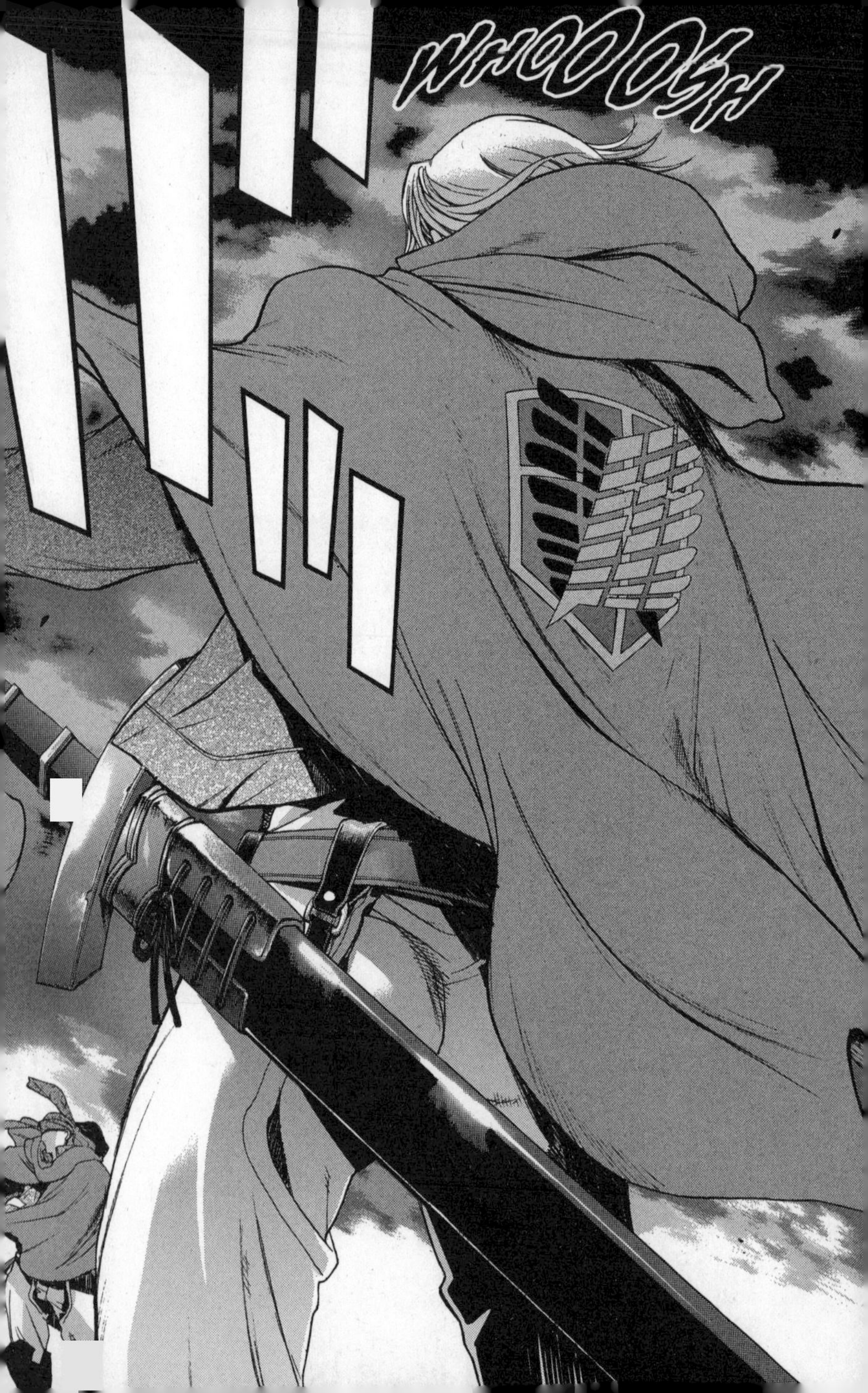
WHOOOSH

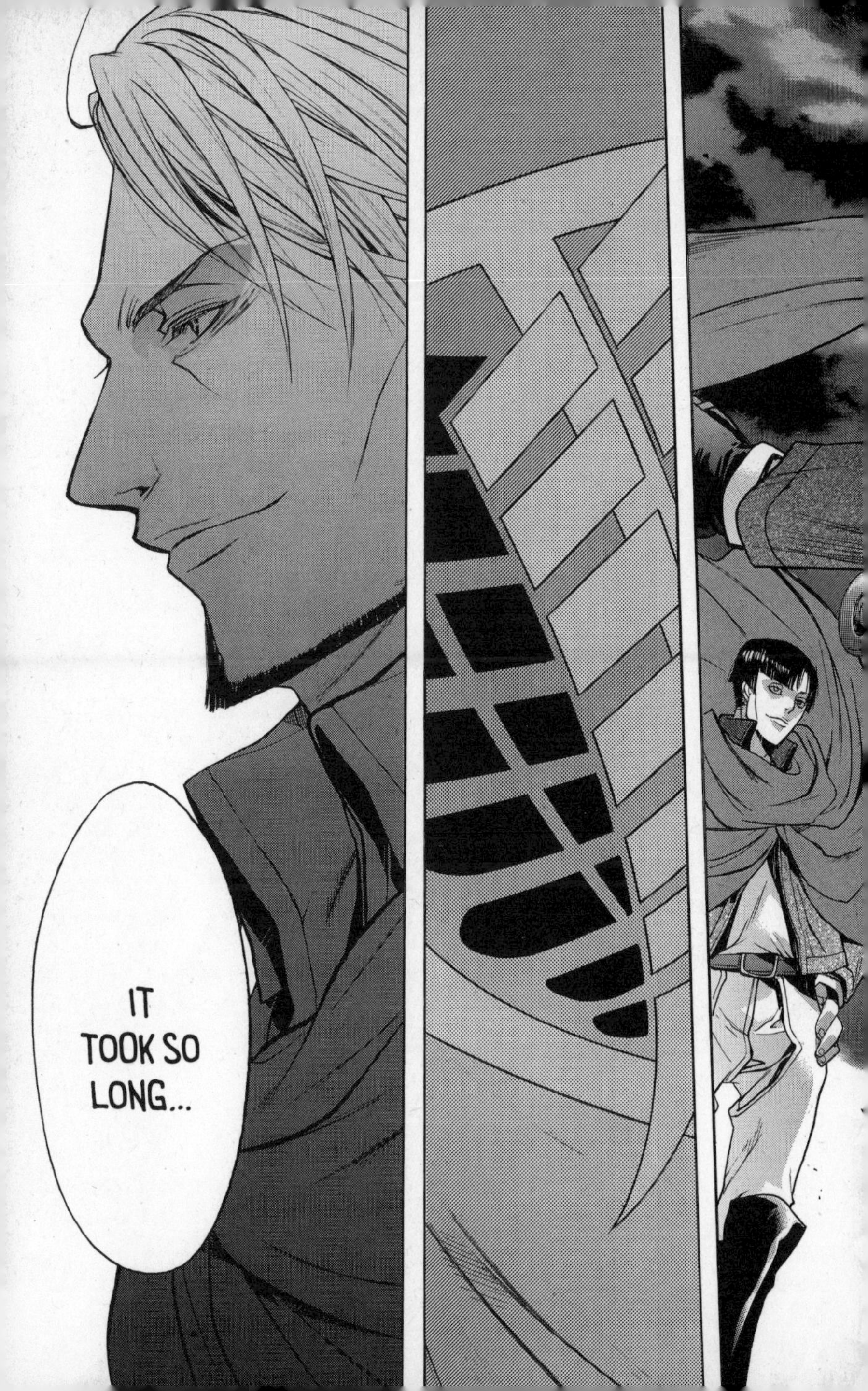
IT TOOK SO LONG...

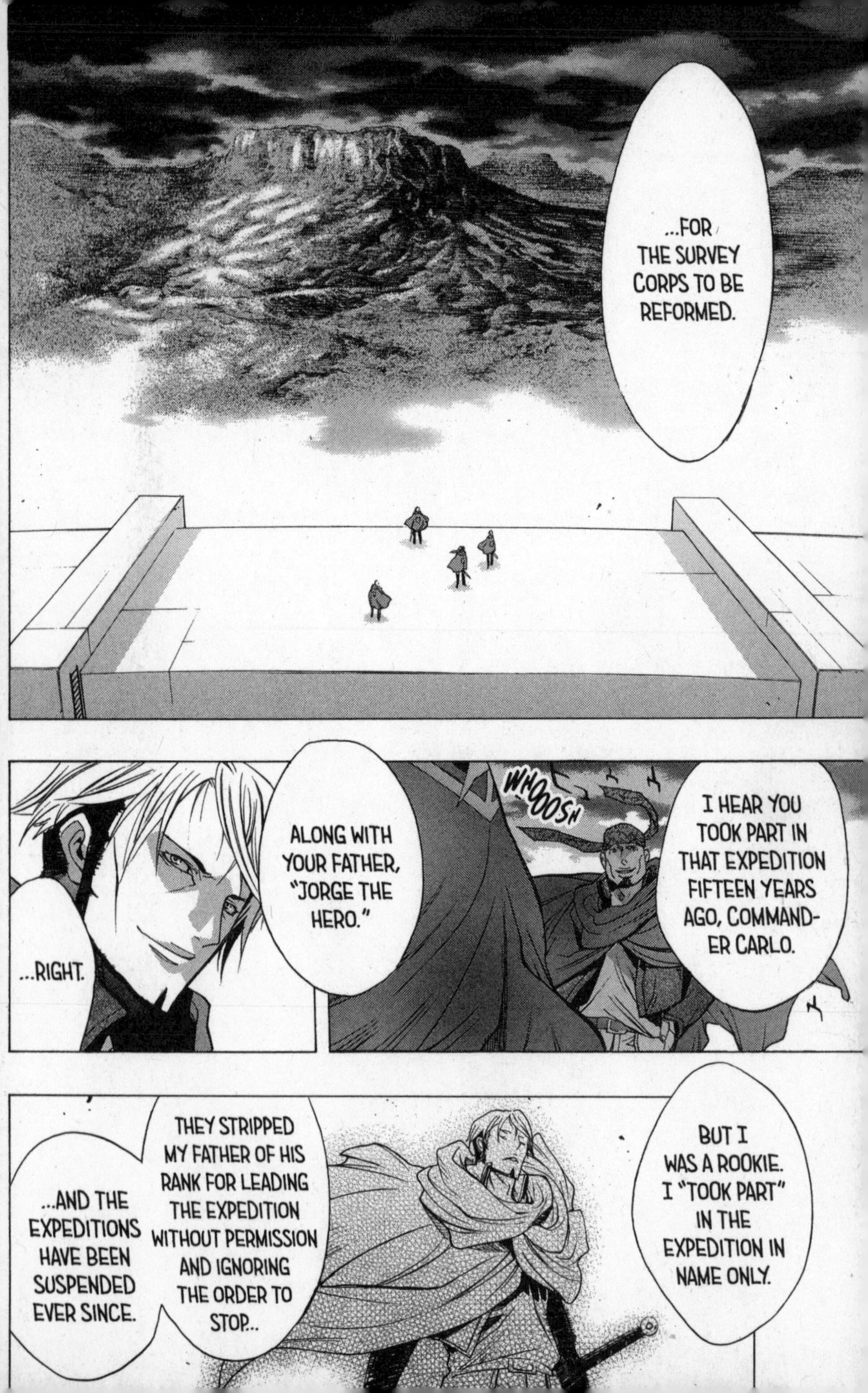
...FOR THE SURVEY CORPS TO BE REFORMED.
I HEAR YOU TOOK PART IN THAT EXPEDITION FIFTEEN YEARS AGO, COMMANDER CARLO.
WHOOOSH
ALONG WITH YOUR FATHER, "JORGE THE HERO."
...RIGHT.
BUT I WAS A ROOKIE. I "TOOK PART" IN THE EXPEDITION IN NAME ONLY.
THEY STRIPPED MY FATHER OF HIS RANK FOR LEADING THE EXPEDITION WITHOUT PERMISSION AND IGNORING THE ORDER TO STOP...
...AND THE EXPEDITIONS HAVE BEEN SUSPENDED EVER SINCE.

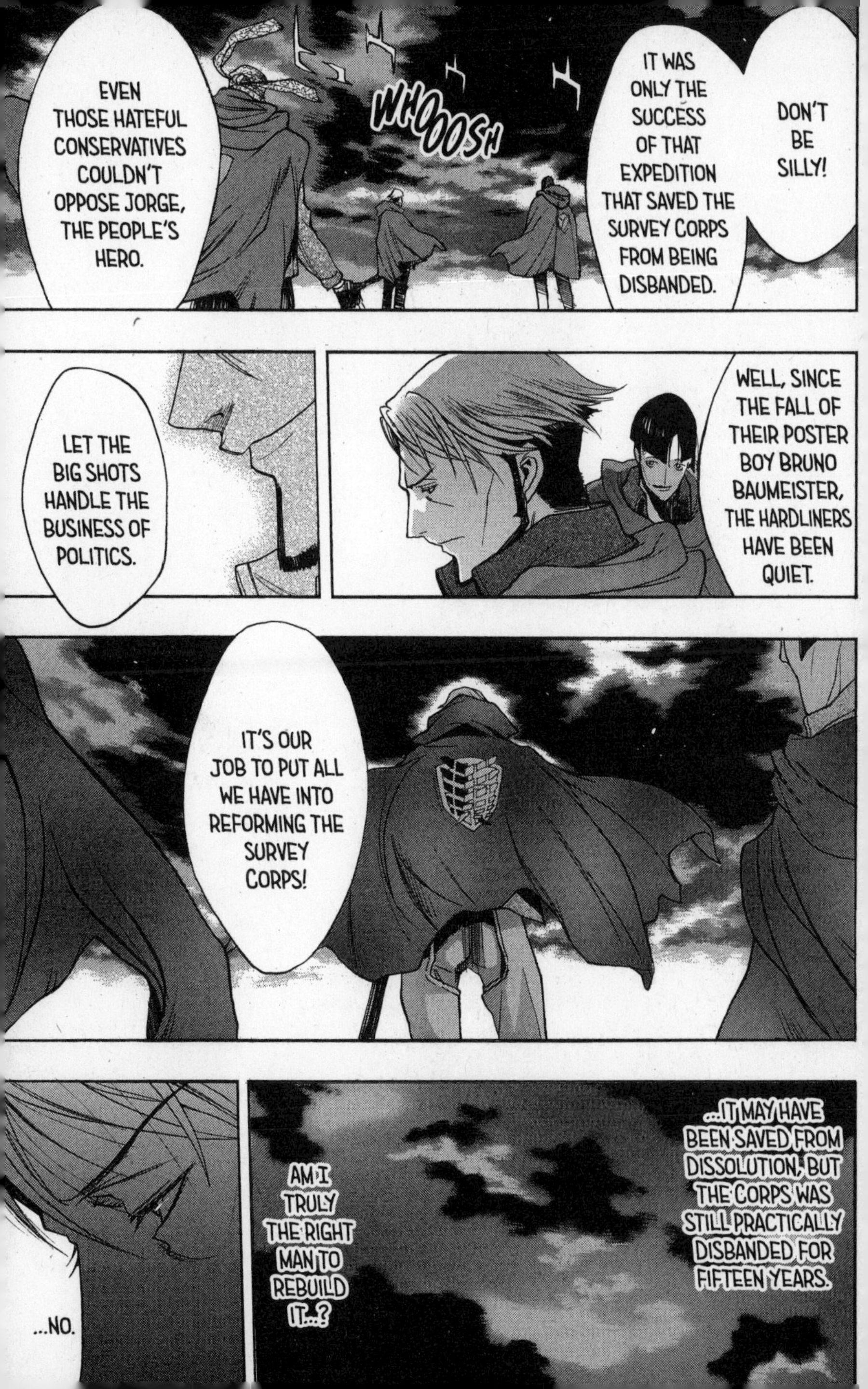
EVEN THOSE HATEFUL CONSERVATIVES COULDN'T OPPOSE JORGE, THE PEOPLE'S HERO.
WHOOOOSH
IT WAS ONLY THE SUCCESS OF THAT EXPEDITION THAT SAVED THE SURVEY CORPS FROM BEING DISBANDED.
DON'T BE SILLY!
LET THE BIG SHOTS HANDLE THE BUSINESS OF POLITICS.
WELL, SINCE THE FALL OF THEIR POSTER BOY BRUNO BAUMEISTER, THE HARDLINERS HAVE BEEN QUIET.
IT'S OUR JOB TO PUT ALL WE HAVE INTO REFORMING THE SURVEY CORPS!
...NO.
AM I TRULY THE RIGHT MAN TO REBUILD IT...?
...IT MAY HAVE BEEN SAVED FROM DISSOLUTION, BUT THE CORPS WAS STILL PRACTICALLY DISBANDED FOR FIFTEEN YEARS.

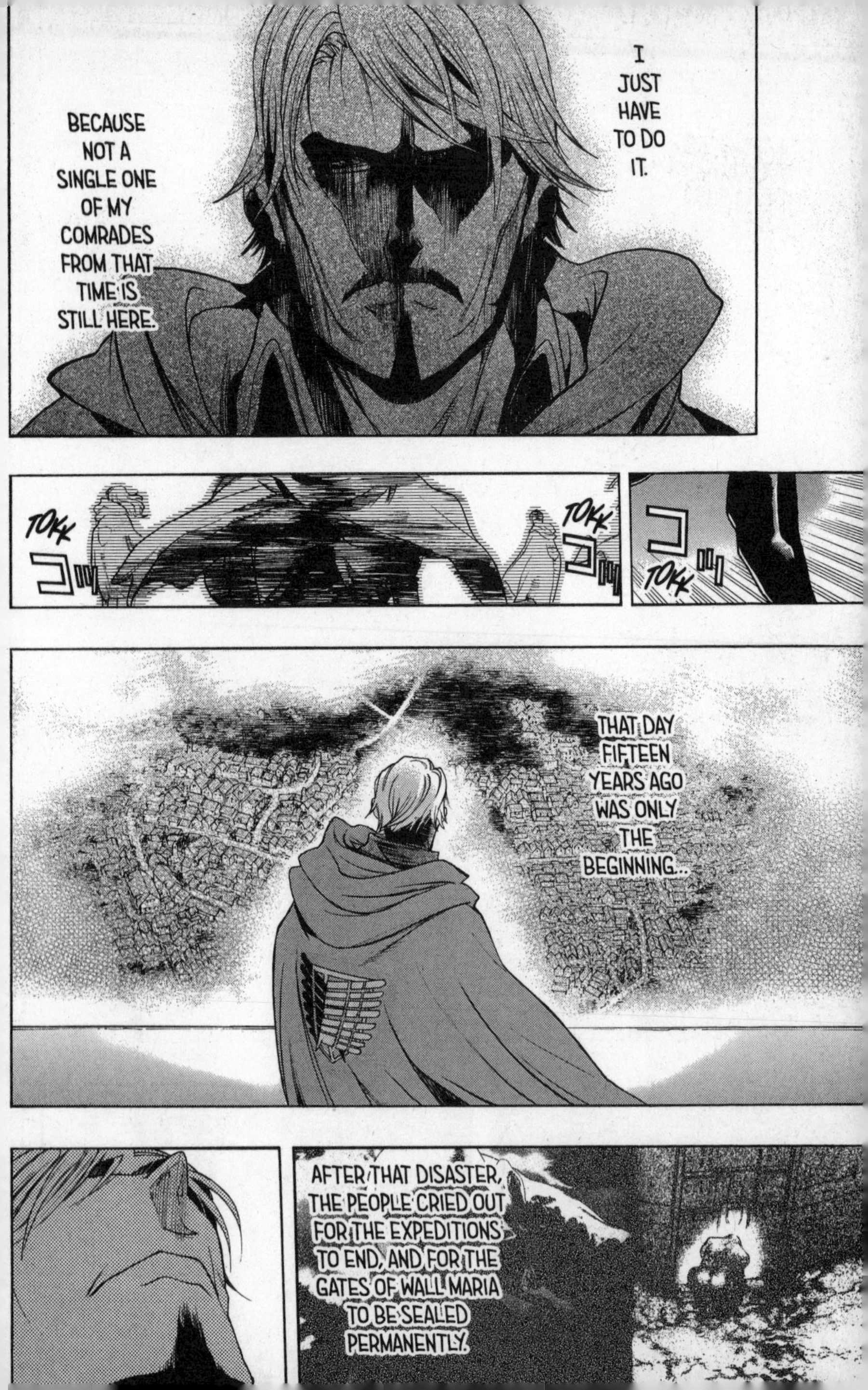
I JUST HAVE TO DO IT.
BECAUSE NOT A SINGLE ONE OF MY COMRADES FROM THAT TIME IS STILL HERE.
TOKK
TOKK
TOKK
THAT DAY FIFTEEN YEARS AGO WAS ONLY THE BEGINNING...
AFTER THAT DISASTER, THE PEOPLE CRIED OUT FOR THE EXPEDITIONS TO END, AND FOR THE GATES OF WALL MARIA TO BE SEALED PERMANENTLY.

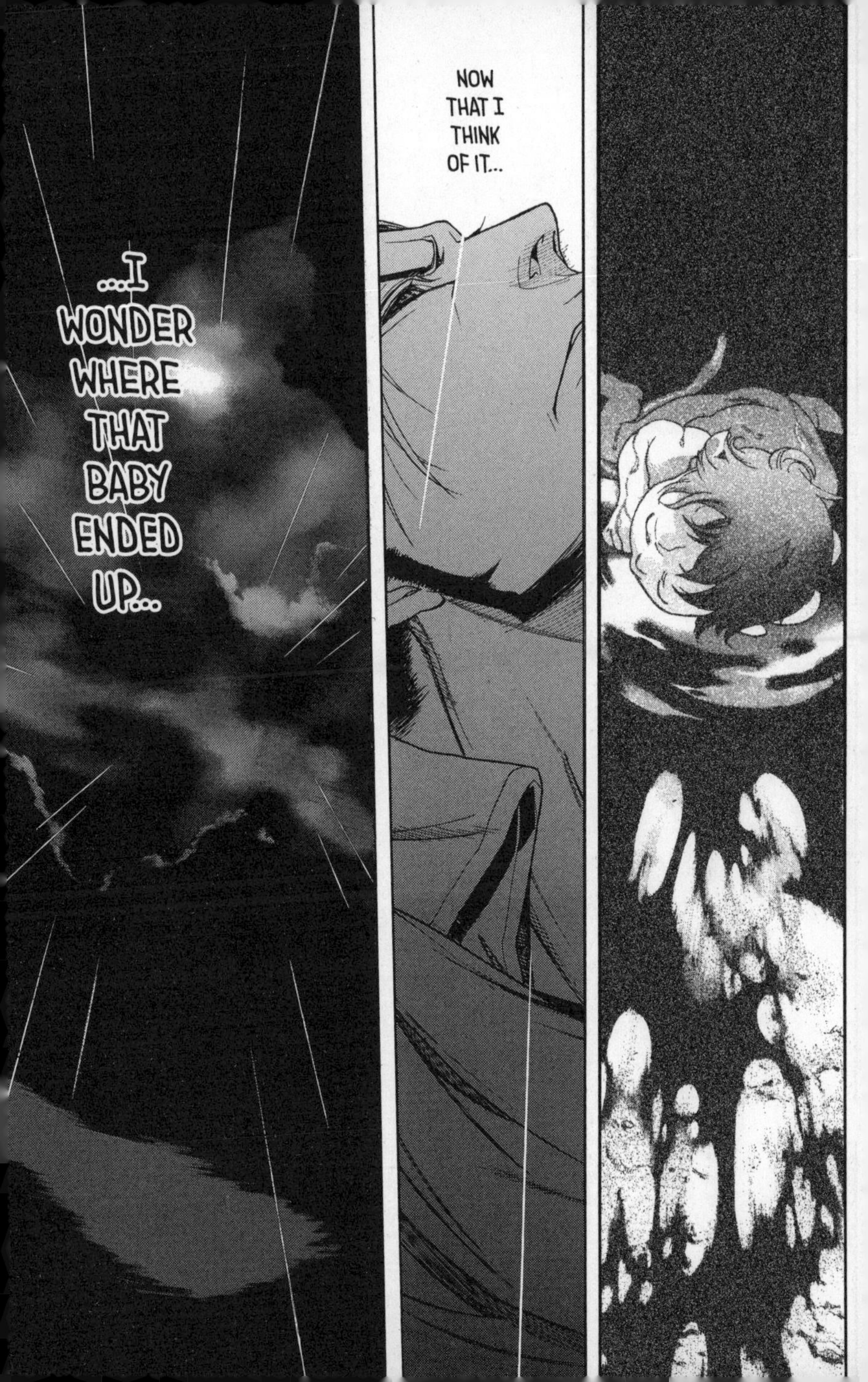
NOW THAT I THINK OF IT...
...I WONDER WHERE THAT BABY ENDED UP...

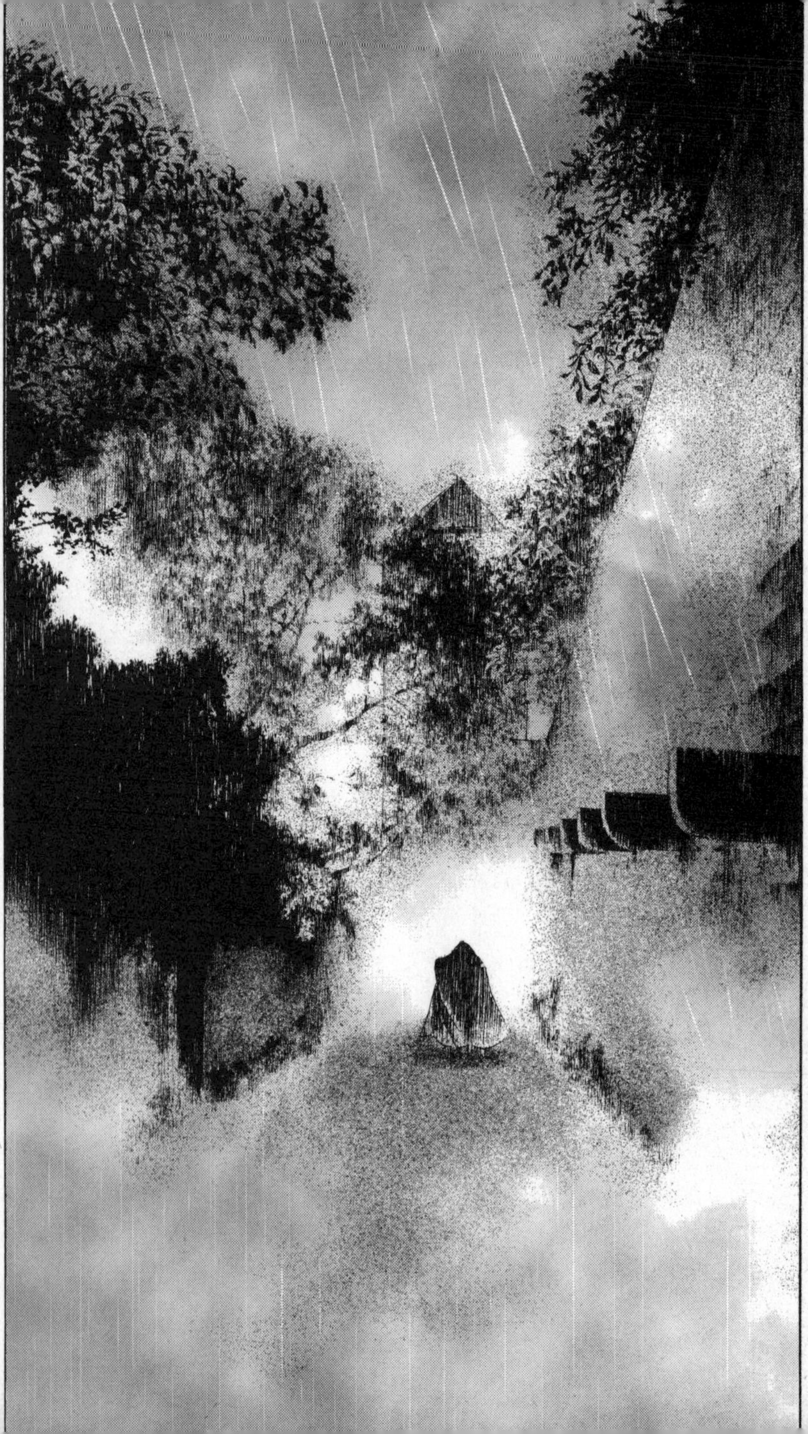

Chapter 4: Stormy Night - End

ATTACK on TITAN

BEFORE THE FALL

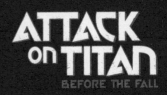

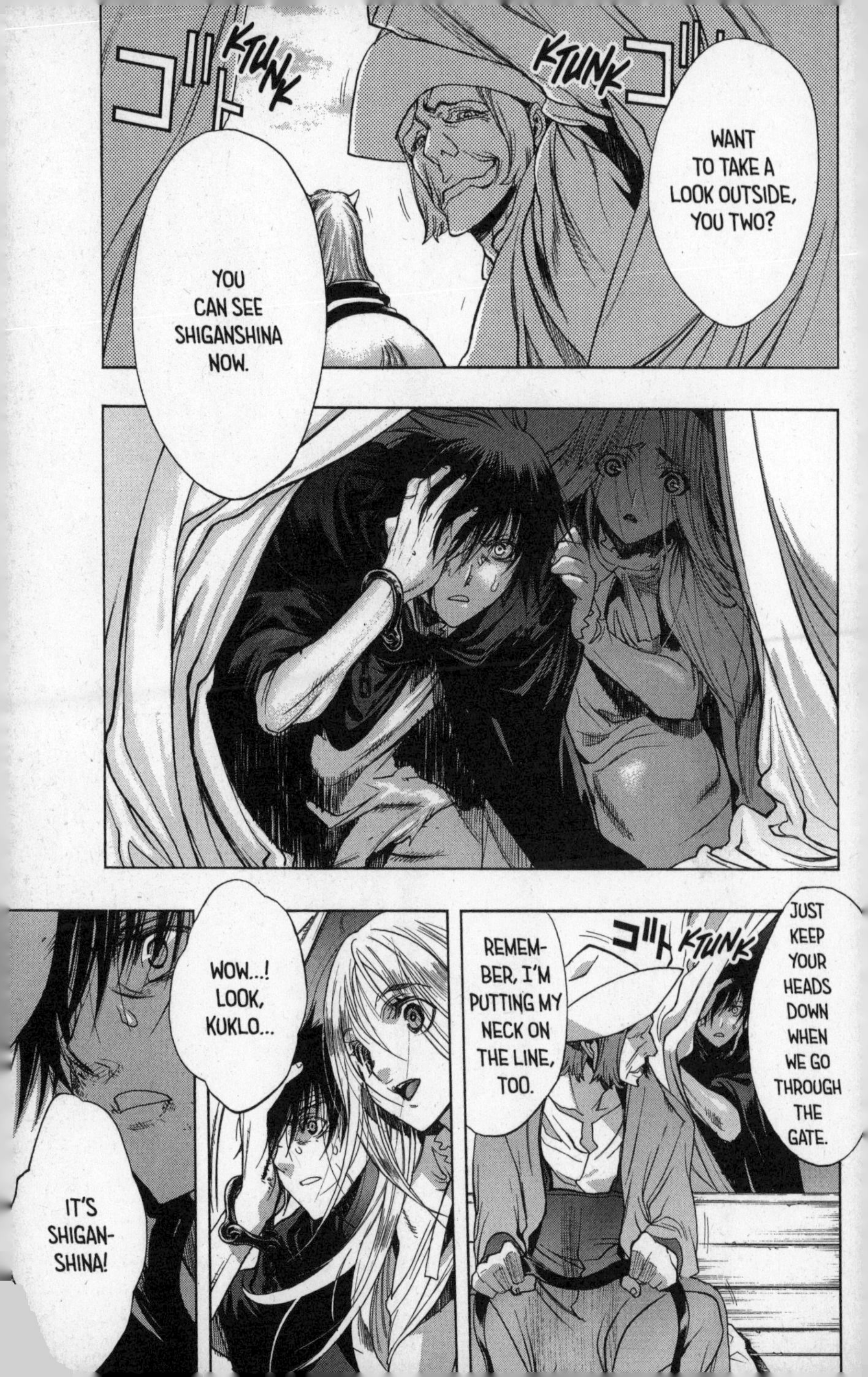
KTUNK
KTUNK
WANT TO TAKE A LOOK OUTSIDE, YOU TWO?
YOU CAN SEE SHIGANSHINA NOW.
KTUNK
JUST KEEP YOUR HEADS DOWN WHEN WE GO THROUGH THE GATE.
REMEMBER, I'M PUTTING MY NECK ON THE LINE, TOO.
WOW...! LOOK, KUKLO...
IT'S SHIGANSHINA!

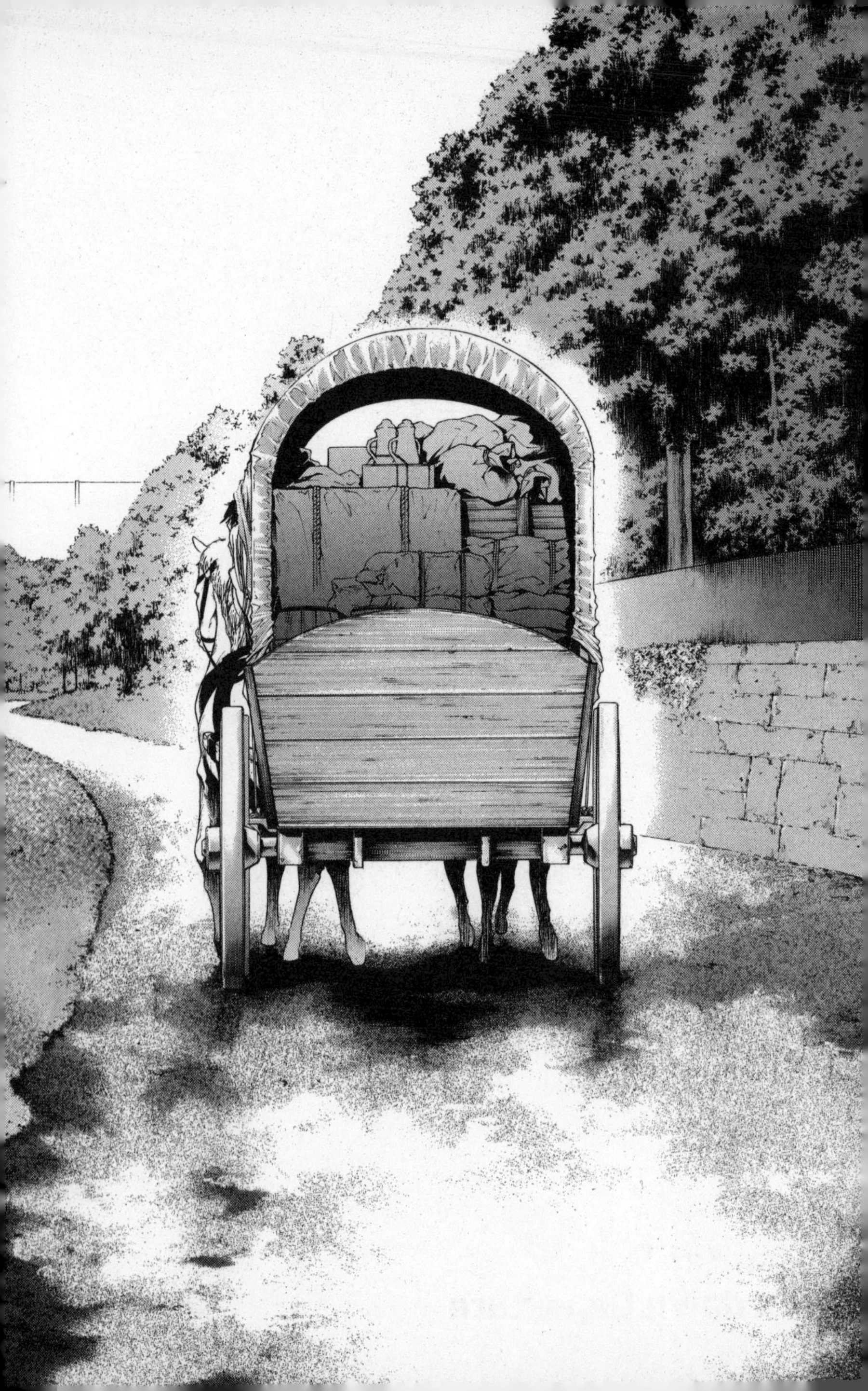

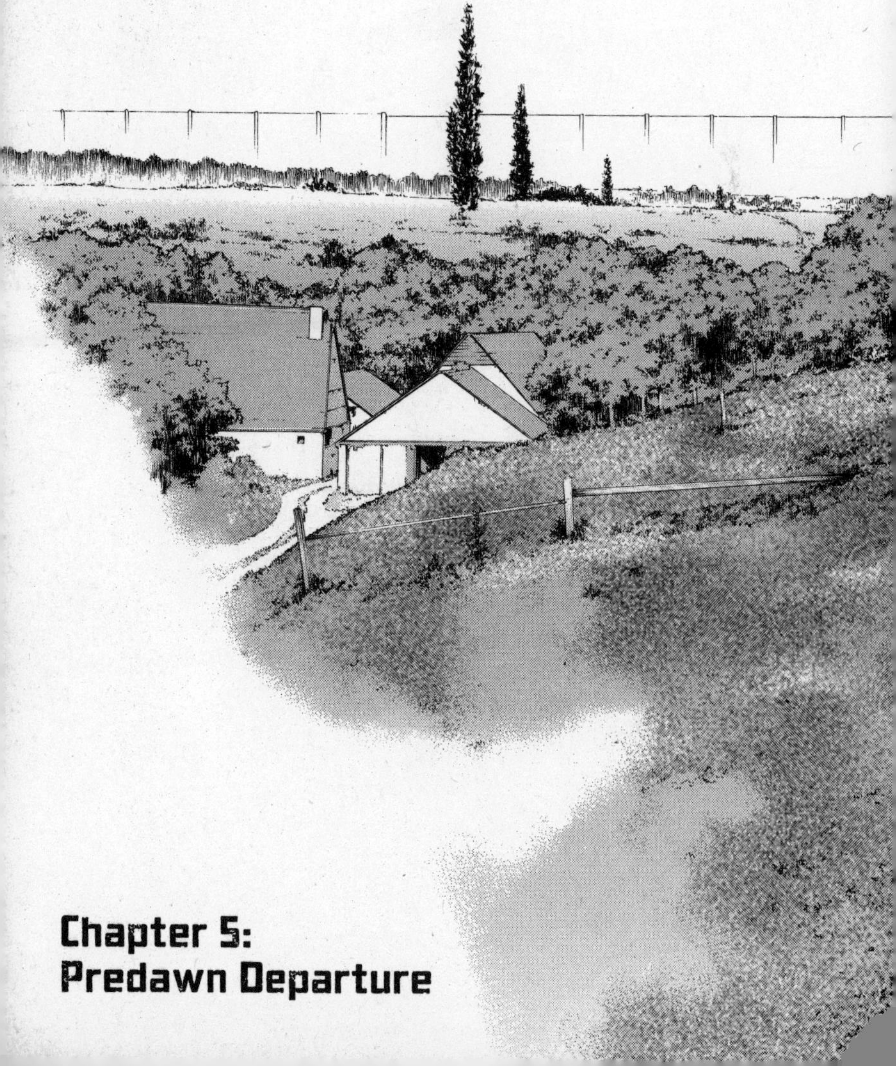

Chapter 5: Predawn Departure

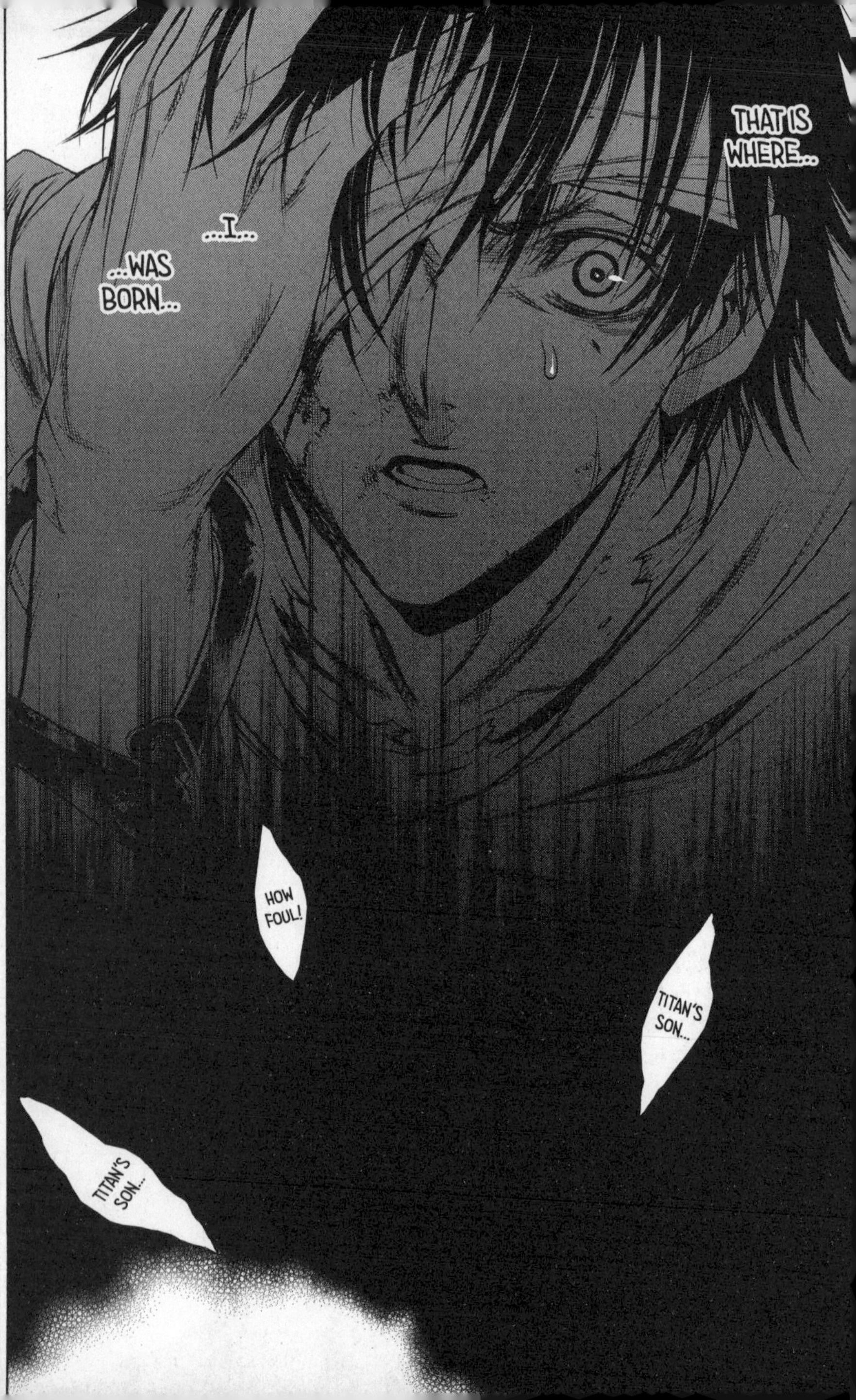
THAT IS WHERE...
...I...
...WAS BORN...
HOW FOUL!
TITAN'S SON...
TITAN'S SON...

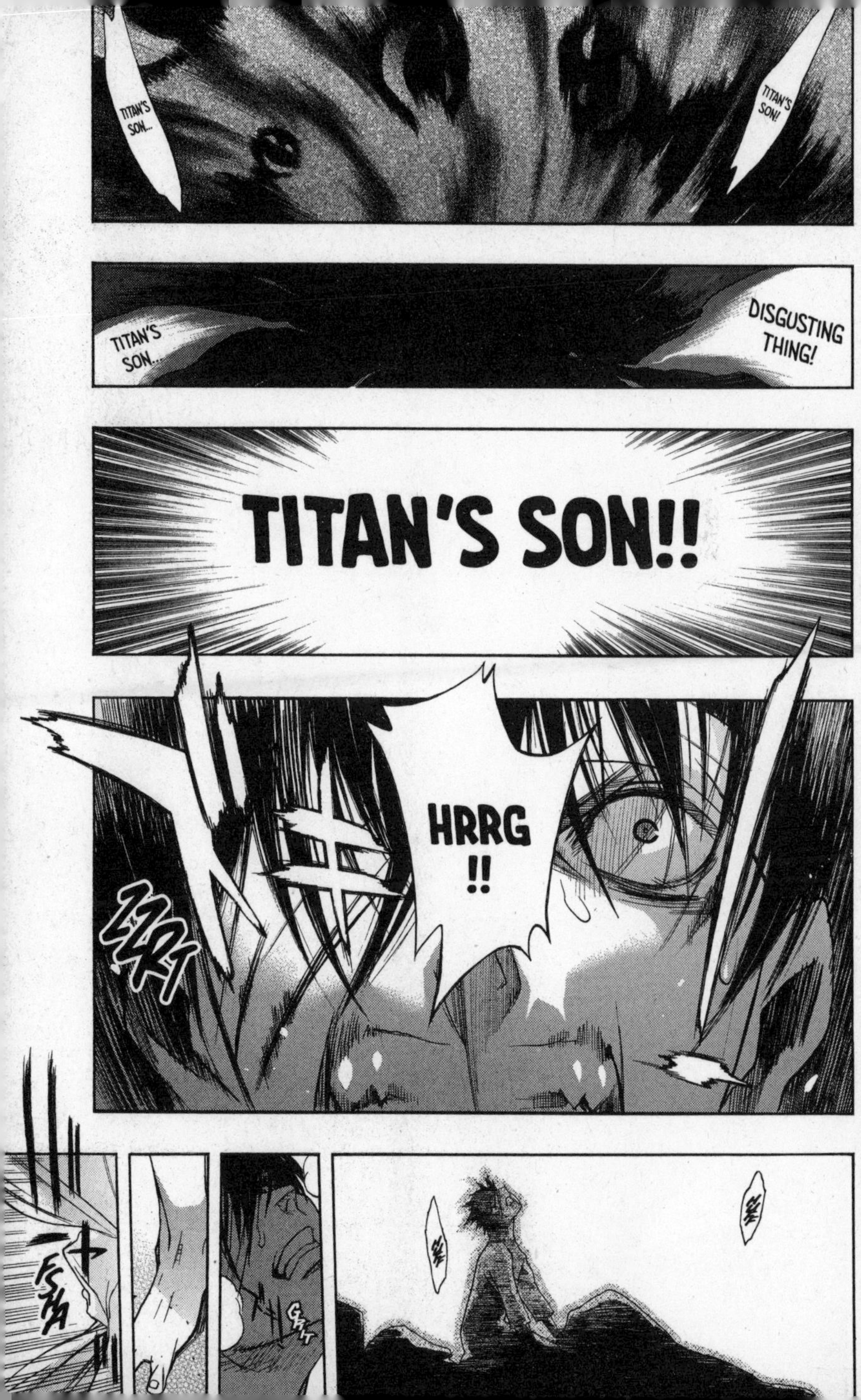
TITAN'S SON!
TITAN'S SON...
DISGUSTING THING!
TITAN'S SON...
TITAN'S SON!!
HRRG !!
GRIT
FSHA

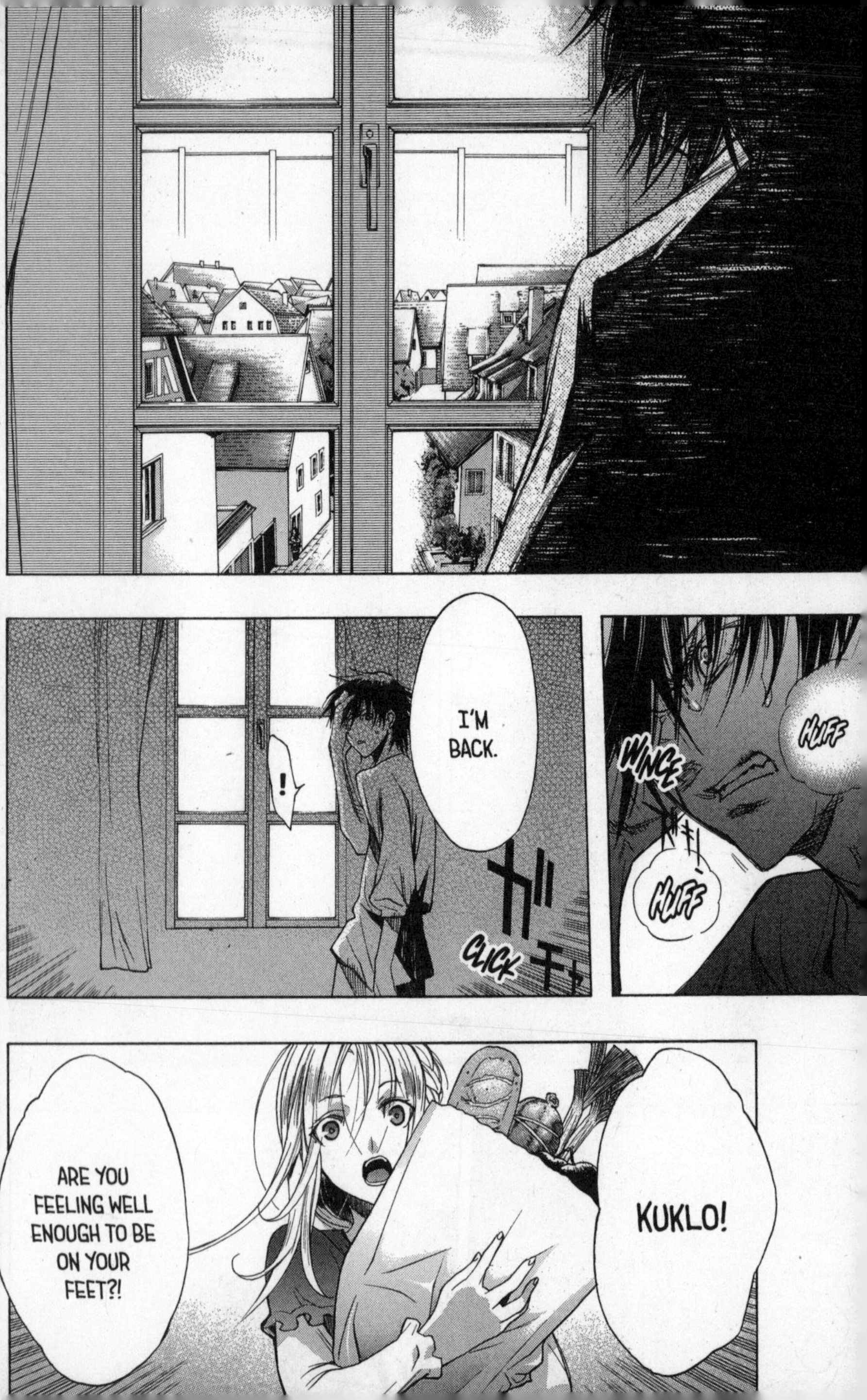
WINCE
HUFF
HUFF
I'M BACK.
!
CLICK
ガチャ
KUKLO!
ARE YOU FEELING WELL ENOUGH TO BE ON YOUR FEET?!

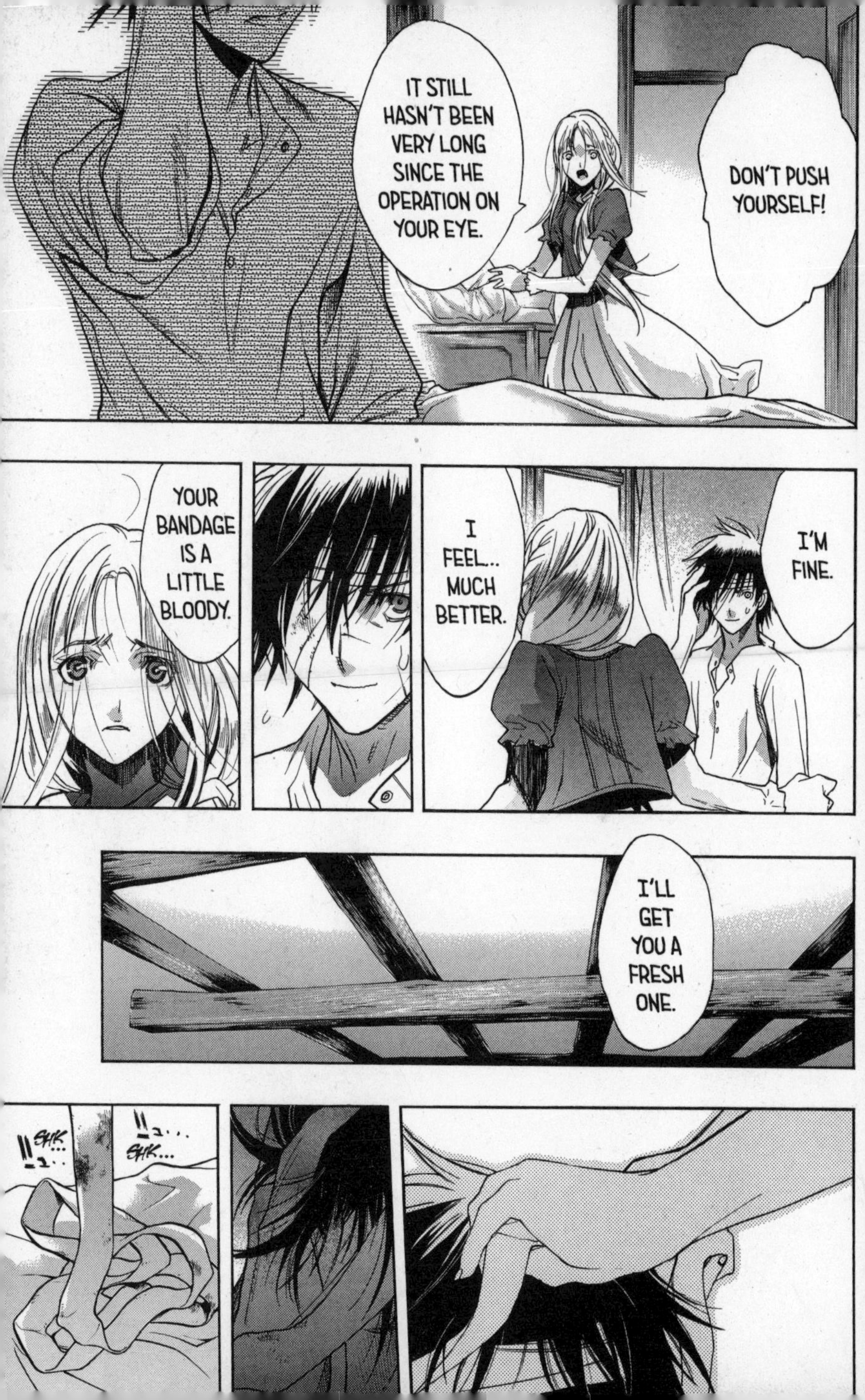
DON'T PUSH YOURSELF!
IT STILL HASN'T BEEN VERY LONG SINCE THE OPERATION ON YOUR EYE.
I'M FINE.
I FEEL... MUCH BETTER.
YOUR BANDAGE IS A LITTLE BLOODY.
I'LL GET YOU A FRESH ONE.
SHK...
SHK...

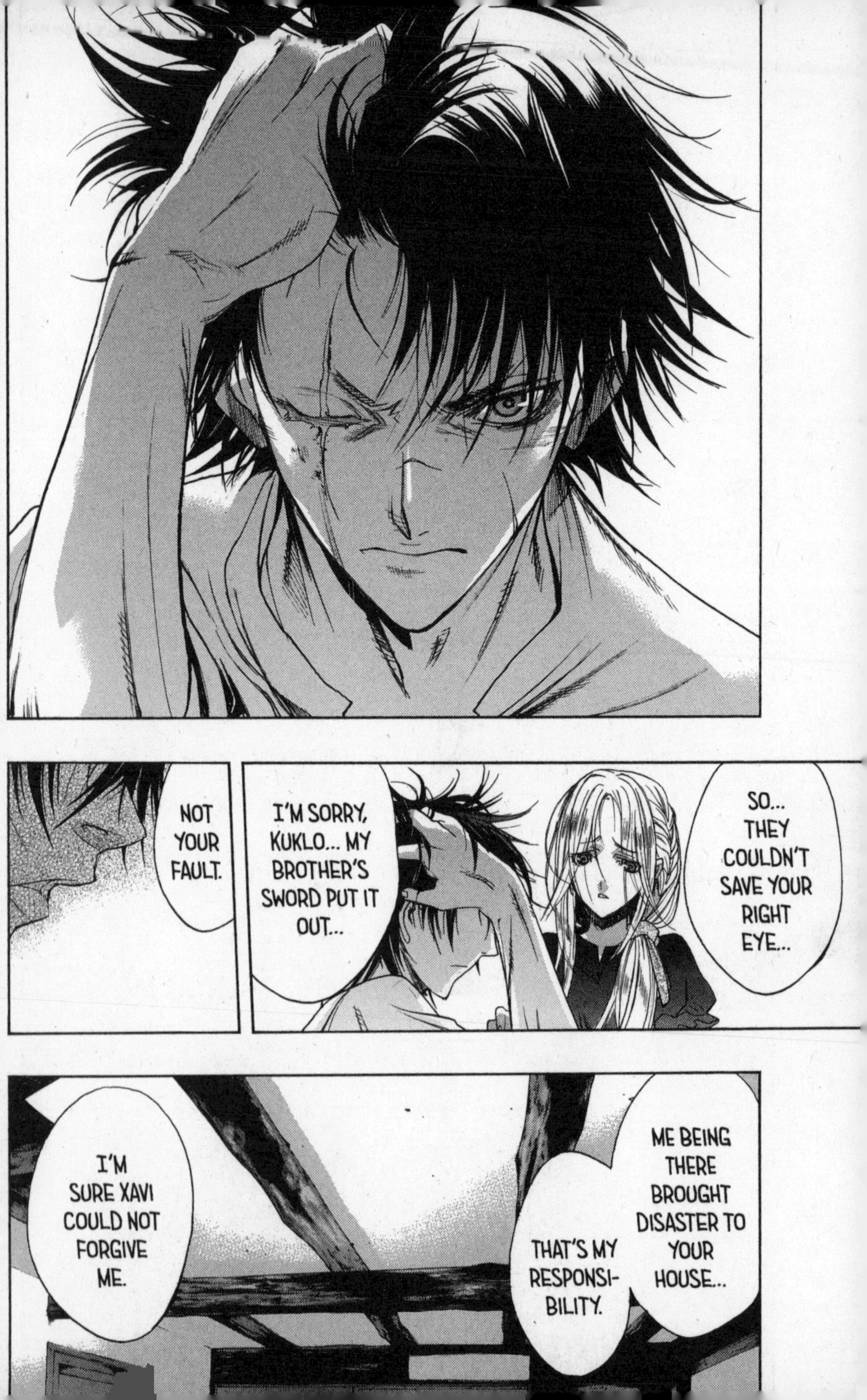
SO... THEY COULDN'T SAVE YOUR RIGHT EYE...
I'M SORRY, KUKLO... MY BROTHER'S SWORD PUT IT OUT...
NOT YOUR FAULT.
ME BEING THERE BROUGHT DISASTER TO YOUR HOUSE...
THAT'S MY RESPONSI-BILITY.
I'M SURE XAVI COULD NOT FORGIVE ME.

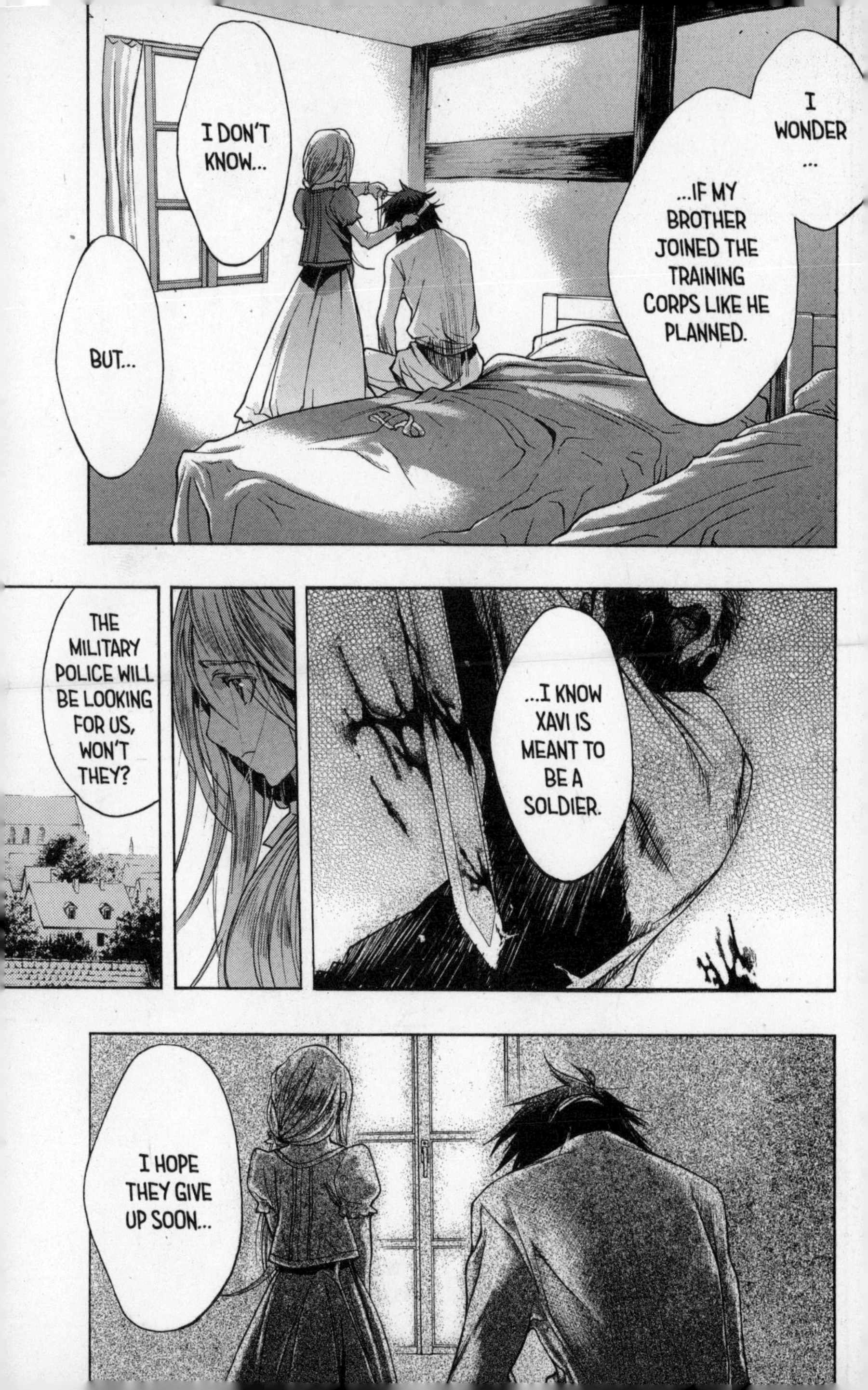
I WONDER ...
...IF MY BROTHER JOINED THE TRAINING CORPS LIKE HE PLANNED.
I DON'T KNOW...
BUT...
...I KNOW XAVI IS MEANT TO BE A SOLDIER.
THE MILITARY POLICE WILL BE LOOKING FOR US, WON'T THEY?
I HOPE THEY GIVE UP SOON...

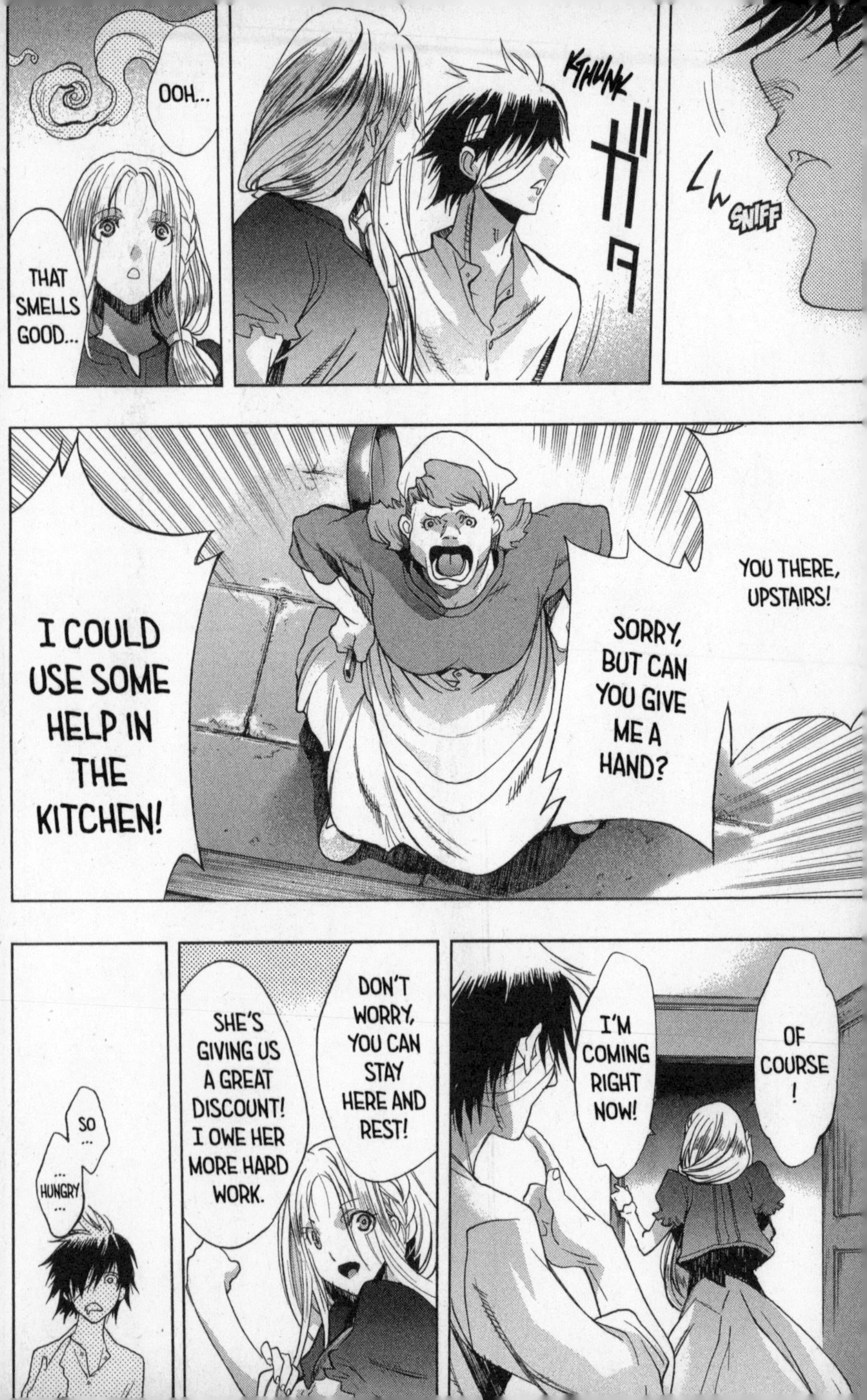
くん
SNIFF
KTHUNK
ガタ
OOH...
THAT SMELLS GOOD...
YOU THERE, UPSTAIRS!
SORRY, BUT CAN YOU GIVE ME A HAND?
I COULD USE SOME HELP IN THE KITCHEN!
OF COURSE!
I'M COMING RIGHT NOW!
DON'T WORRY, YOU CAN STAY HERE AND REST!
SHE'S GIVING US A GREAT DISCOUNT! I OWE HER MORE HARD WORK.
SO...
...HUNGRY...

キュル

GRRGG

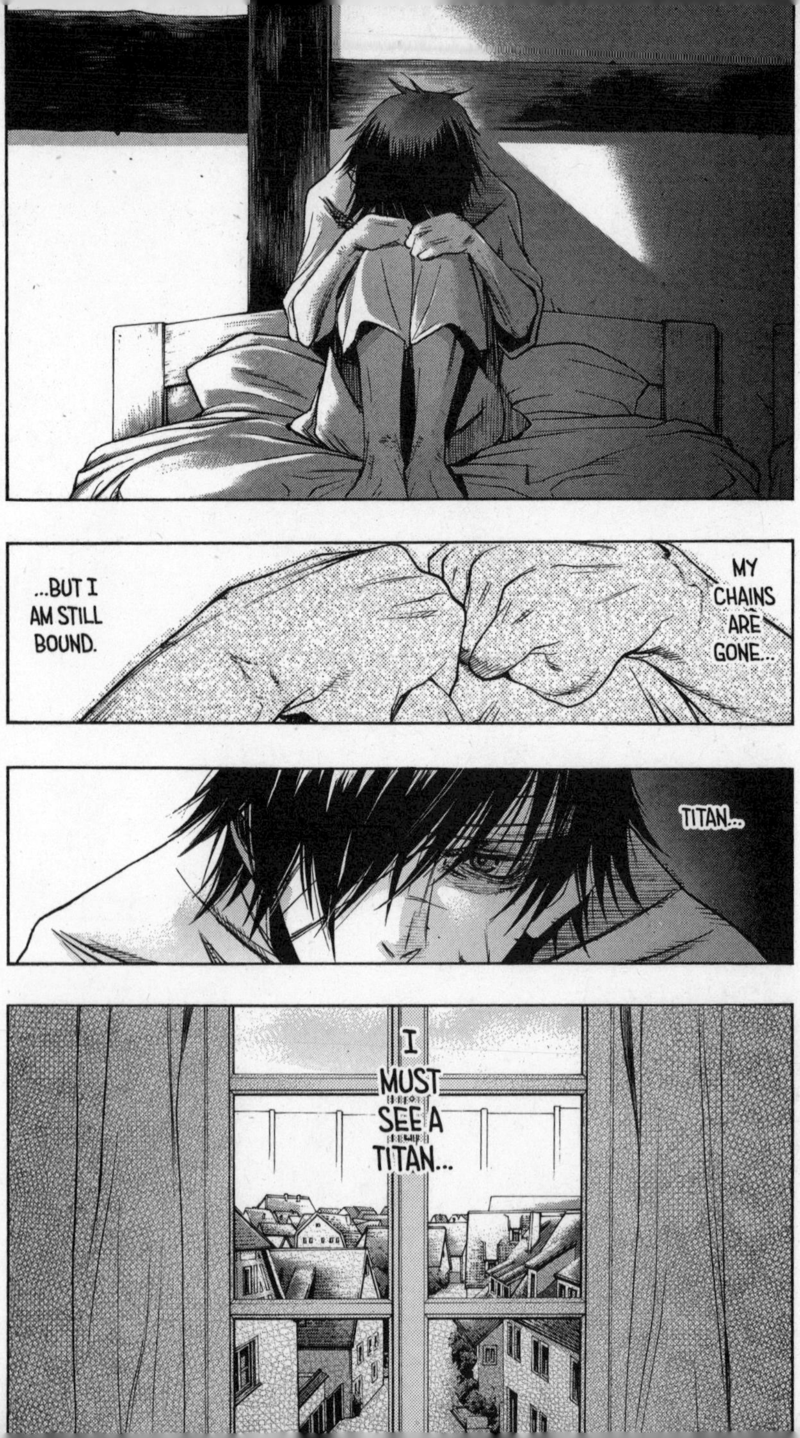
MY CHAINS ARE GONE...
...BUT I AM STILL BOUND.
TITAN...
I MUST SEE A TITAN...

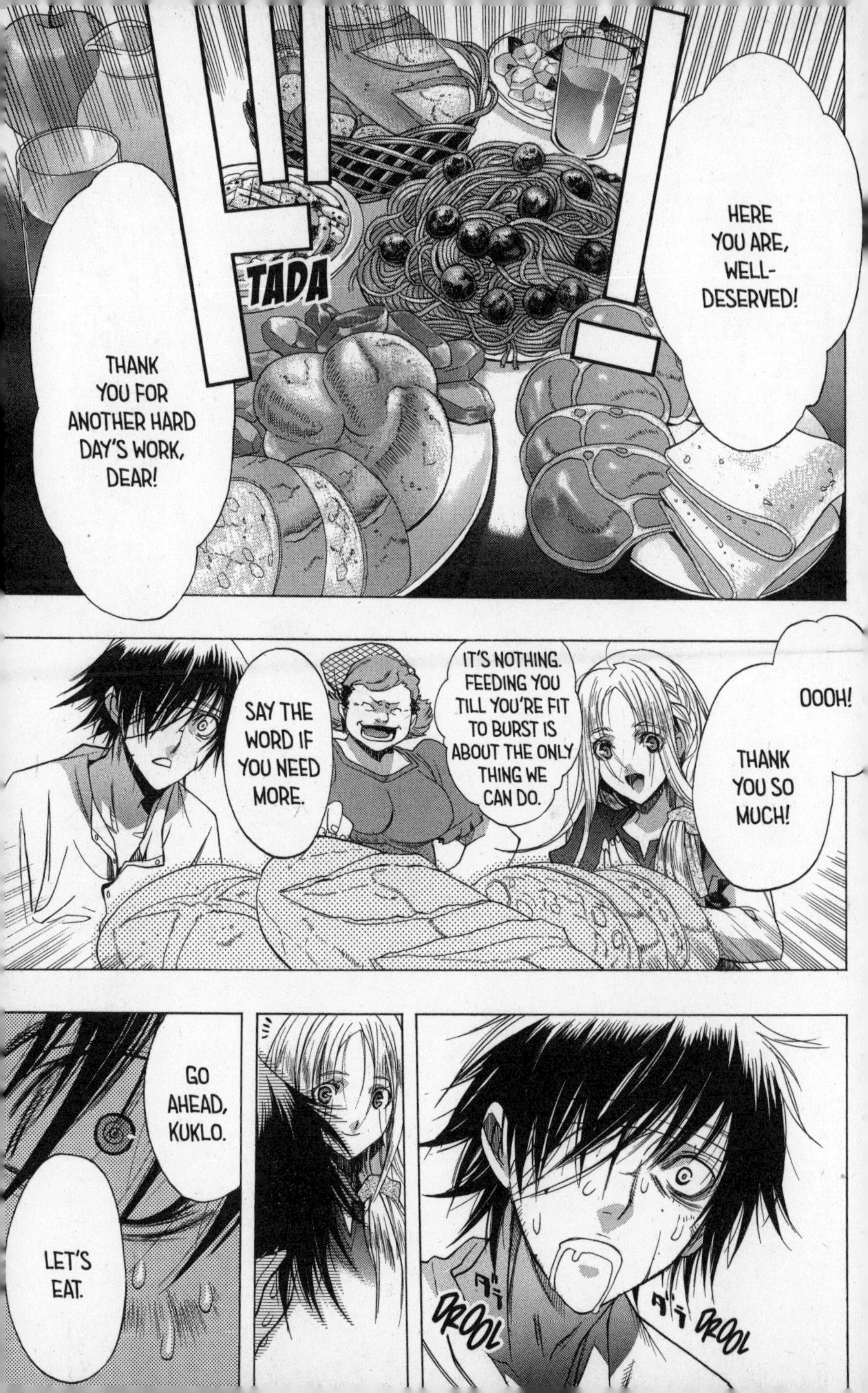
HERE YOU ARE, WELL-DESERVED!
TADA
THANK YOU FOR ANOTHER HARD DAY'S WORK, DEAR!
OOOH!
THANK YOU SO MUCH!
IT'S NOTHING. FEEDING YOU TILL YOU'RE FIT TO BURST IS ABOUT THE ONLY THING WE CAN DO.
SAY THE WORD IF YOU NEED MORE.
DROOL
DROOL
GO AHEAD, KUKLO.
LET'S EAT.

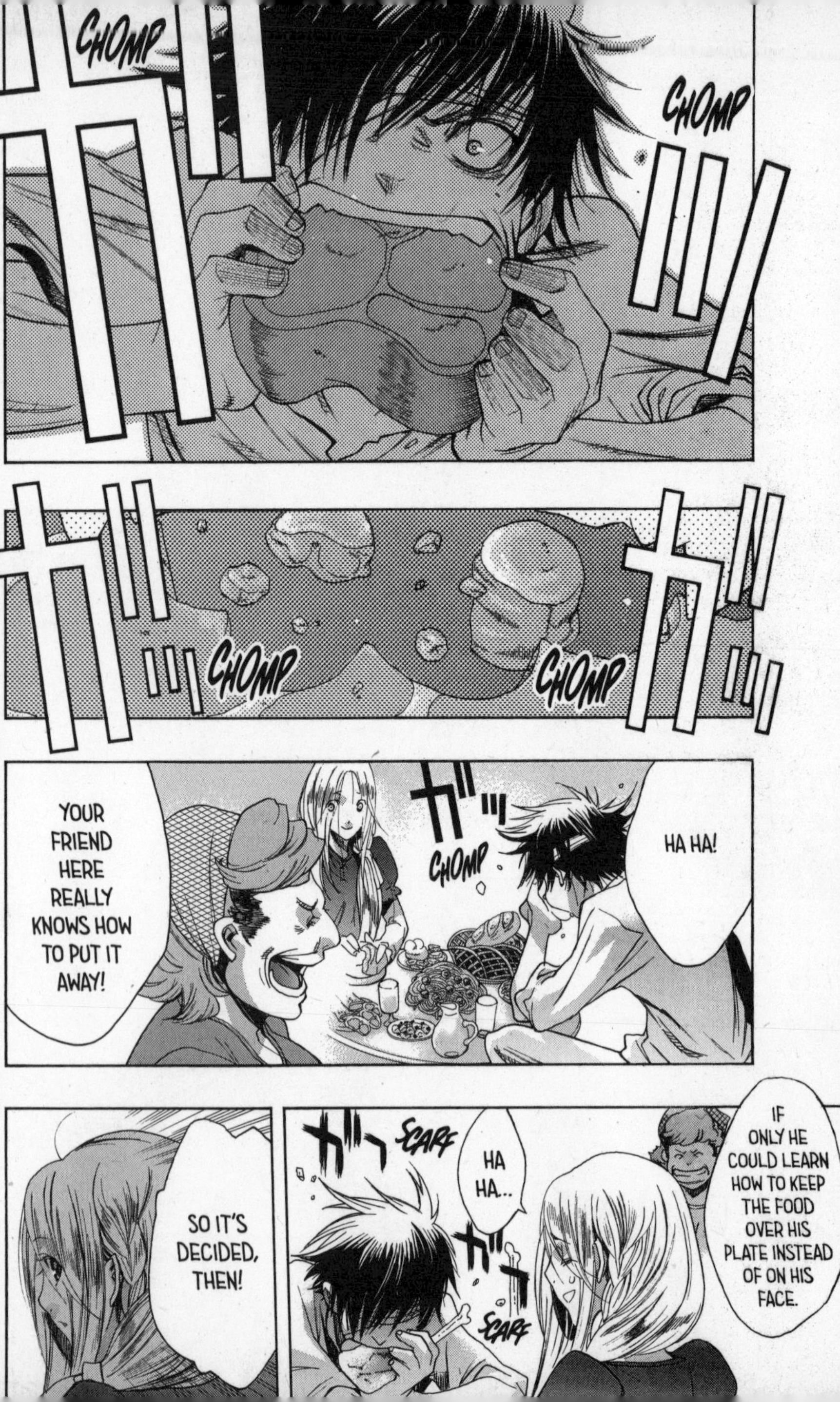
CHOMP
CHOMP
CHOMP
CHOMP
HA HA!
CHOMP
YOUR FRIEND HERE REALLY KNOWS HOW TO PUT IT AWAY!
IF ONLY HE COULD LEARN HOW TO KEEP THE FOOD OVER HIS PLATE INSTEAD OF ON HIS FACE.
HA HA...
SCARF
SCARF
SO IT'S DECIDED, THEN!

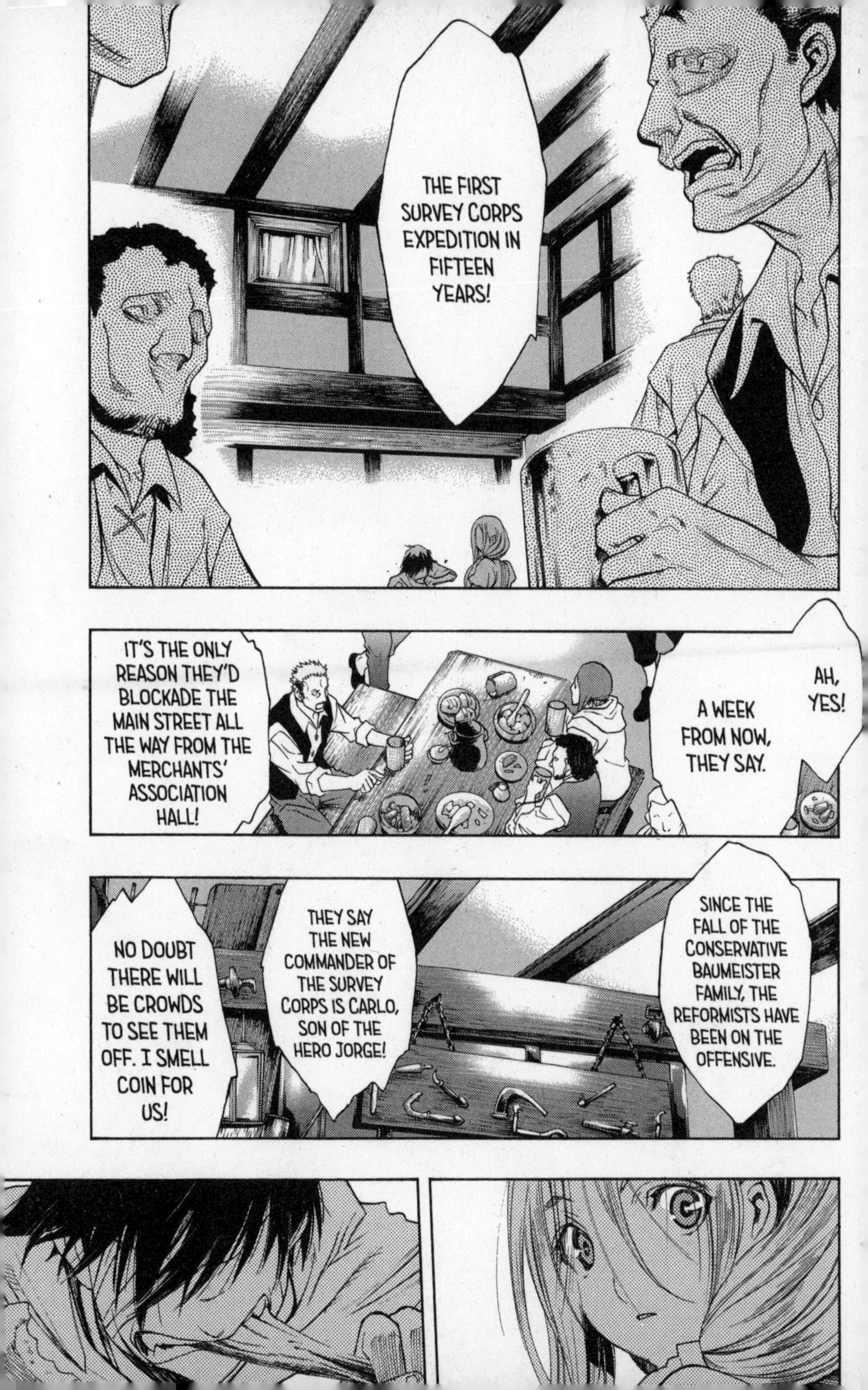
THE FIRST SURVEY CORPS EXPEDITION IN FIFTEEN YEARS!
IT'S THE ONLY REASON THEY'D BLOCKADE THE MAIN STREET ALL THE WAY FROM THE MERCHANTS' ASSOCIATION HALL!
A WEEK FROM NOW, THEY SAY.
AH, YES!
NO DOUBT THERE WILL BE CROWDS TO SEE THEM OFF. I SMELL COIN FOR US!
THEY SAY THE NEW COMMANDER OF THE SURVEY CORPS IS CARLO, SON OF THE HERO JORGE!
SINCE THE FALL OF THE CONSERVATIVE BAUMEISTER FAMILY, THE REFORMISTS HAVE BEEN ON THE OFFENSIVE.

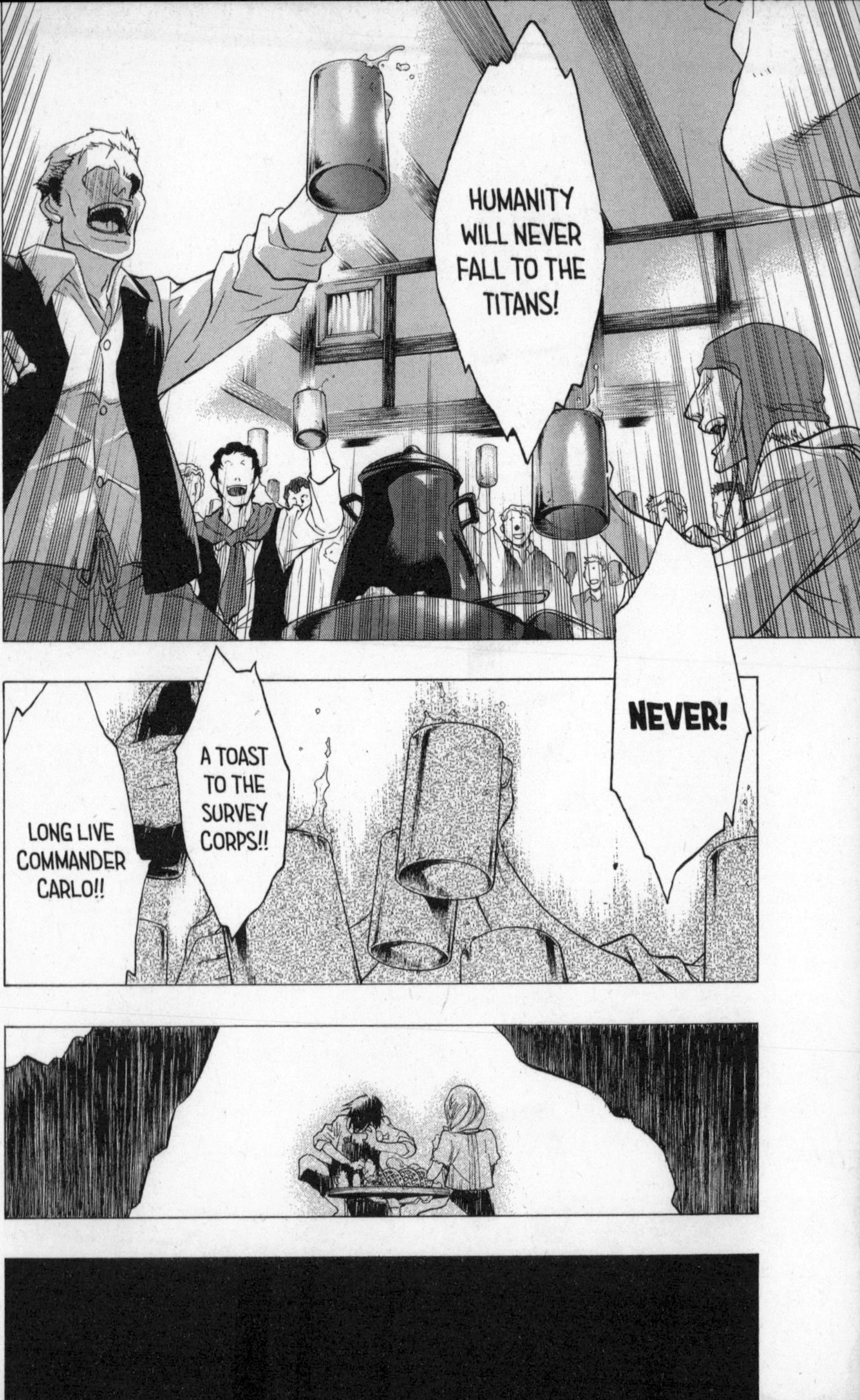
HUMANITY WILL NEVER FALL TO THE TITANS!
NEVER!
LONG LIVE COMMANDER CARLO!!
A TOAST TO THE SURVEY CORPS!!

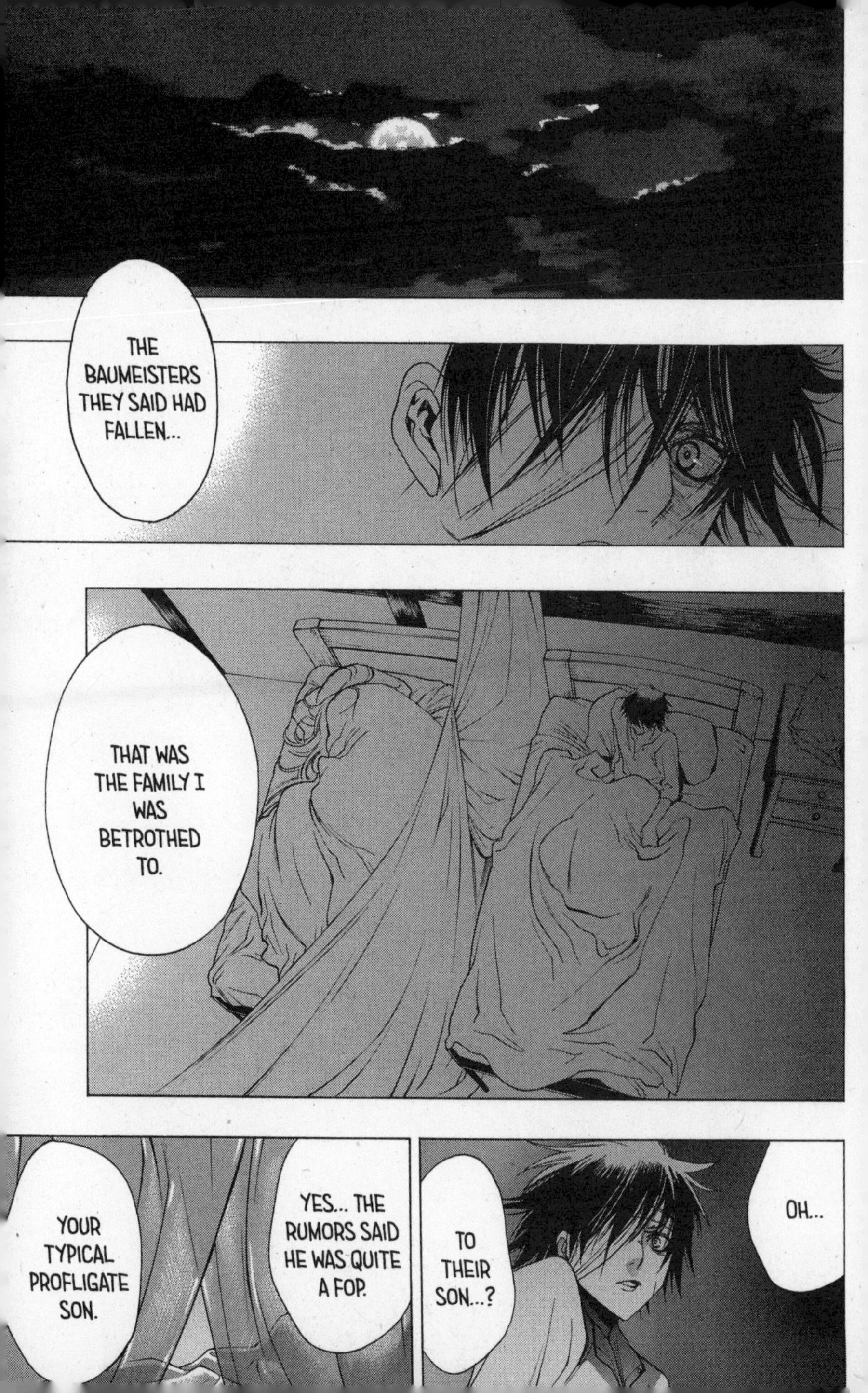
THE BAUMEISTERS THEY SAID HAD FALLEN...
THAT WAS THE FAMILY I WAS BETROTHED TO.
OH...
TO THEIR SON...?
YES... THE RUMORS SAID HE WAS QUITE A FOP.
YOUR TYPICAL PROFLIGATE SON.

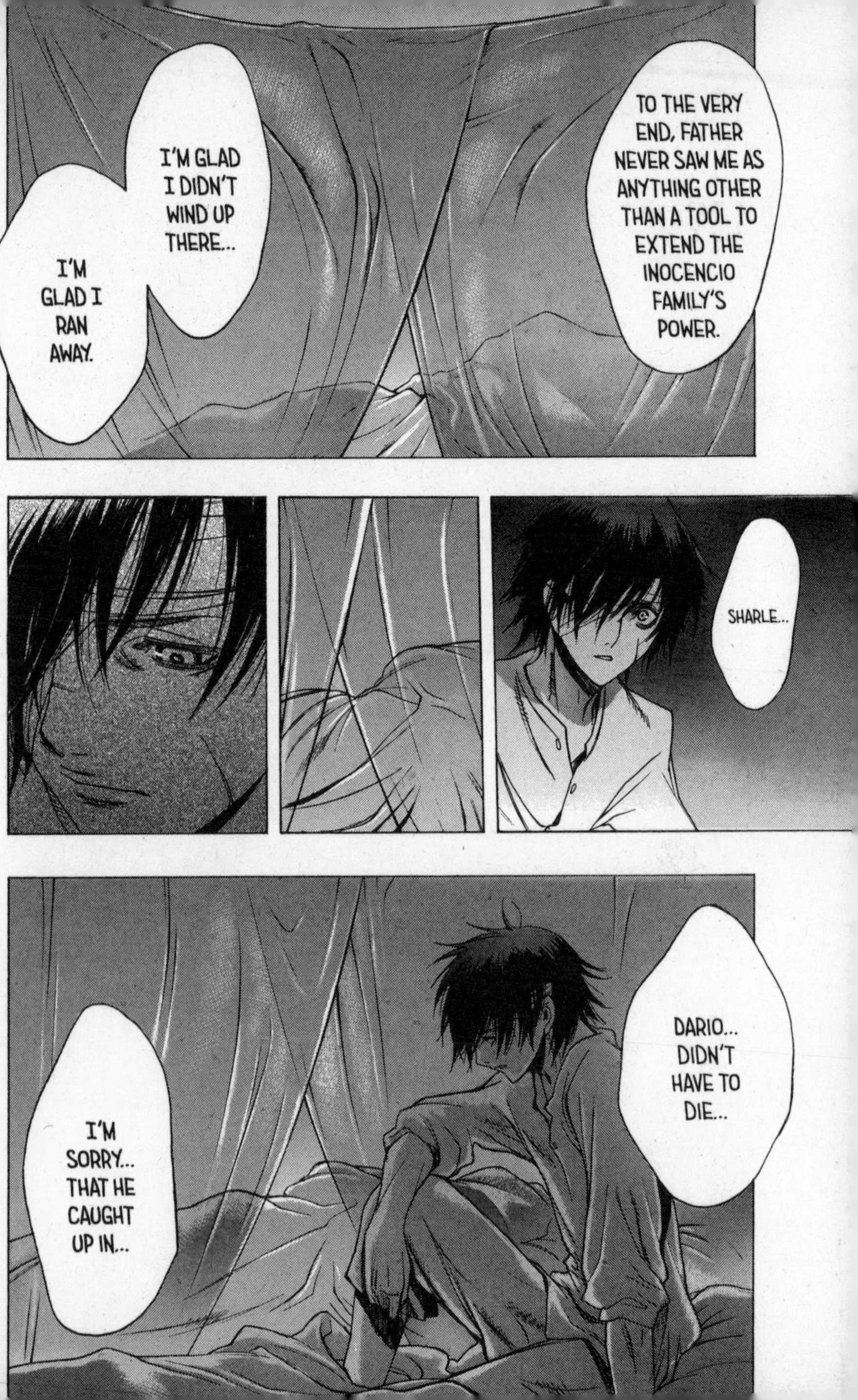
TO THE VERY END, FATHER NEVER SAW ME AS ANYTHING OTHER THAN A TOOL TO EXTEND THE INOCENCIO FAMILY'S POWER.
I'M GLAD I DIDN'T WIND UP THERE...
I'M GLAD I RAN AWAY.
SHARLE...
DARIO... DIDN'T HAVE TO DIE...
I'M SORRY... THAT HE CAUGHT UP IN...

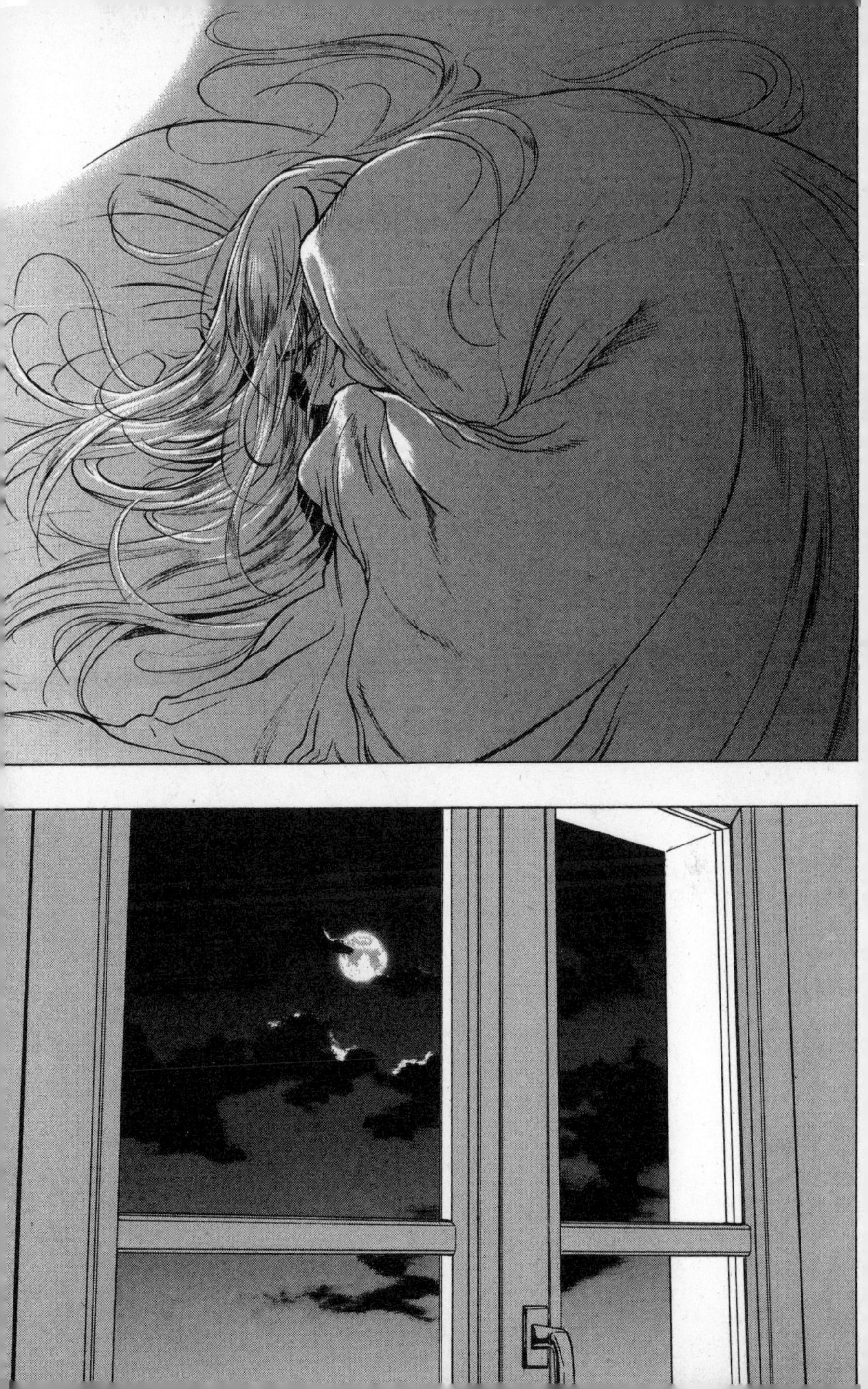

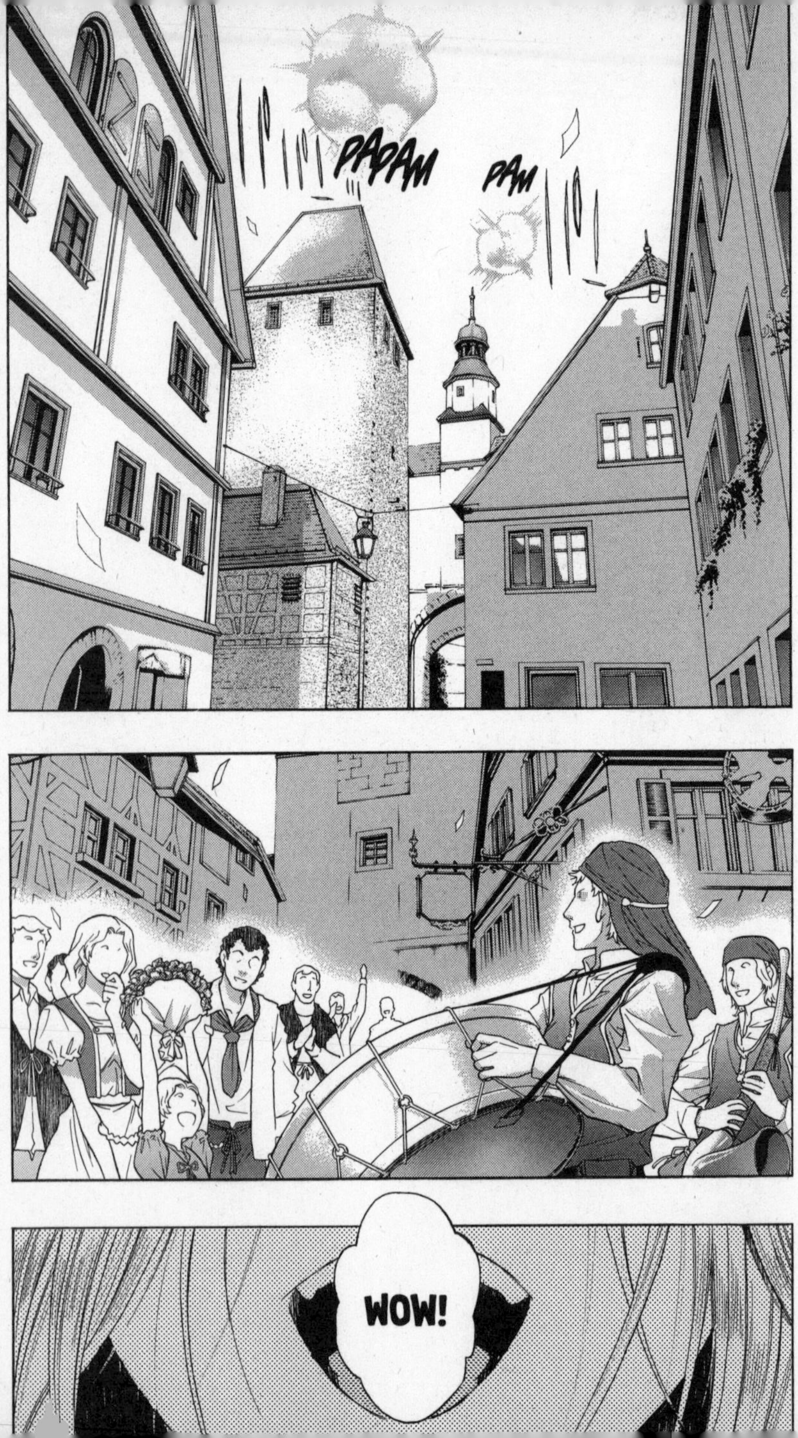
PAPAM
PAM
WOW!

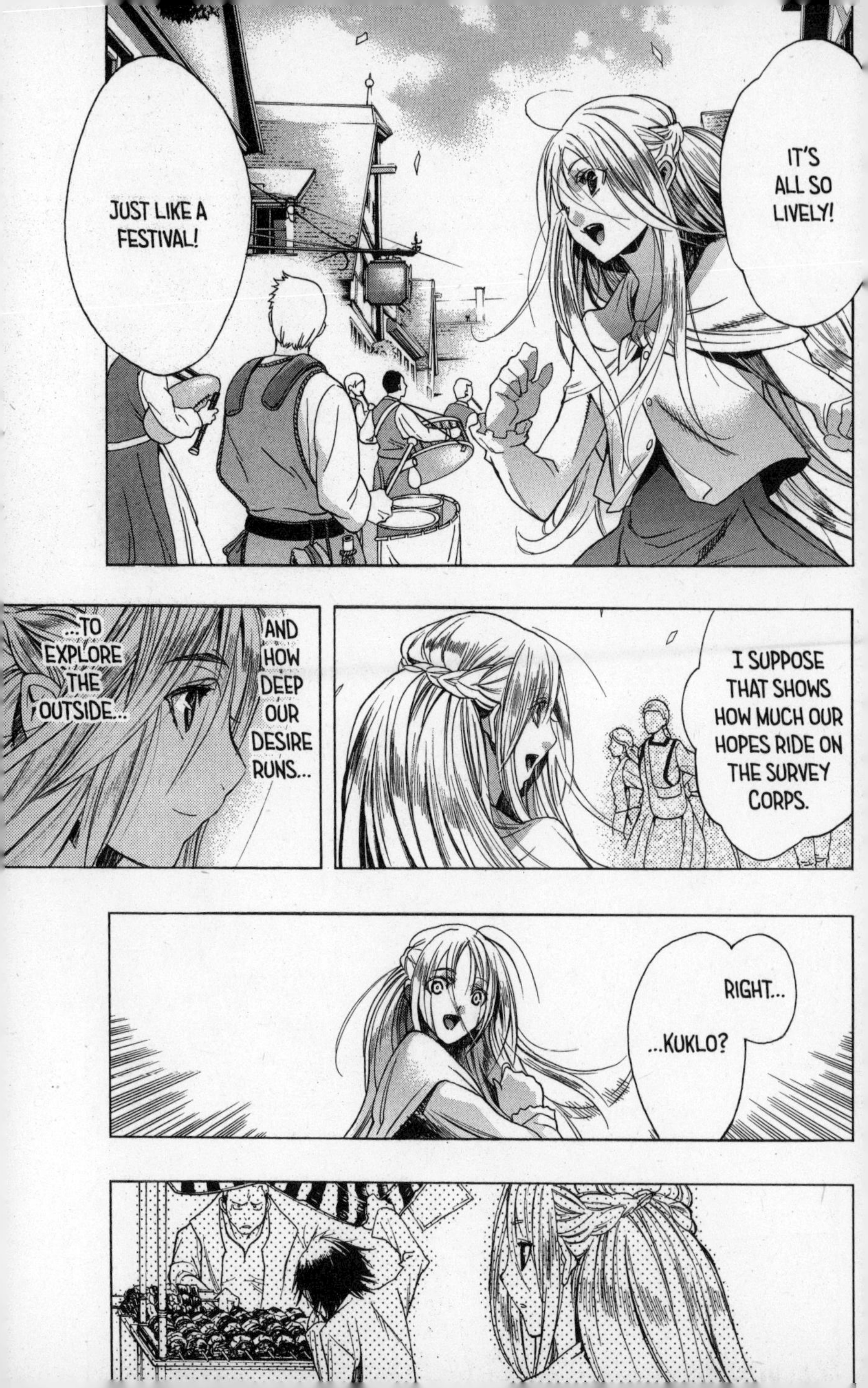
IT'S ALL SO LIVELY!
JUST LIKE A FESTIVAL!
I SUPPOSE THAT SHOWS HOW MUCH OUR HOPES RIDE ON THE SURVEY CORPS.
AND HOW DEEP OUR DESIRE RUNS...
...TO EXPLORE THE OUTSIDE...
RIGHT...
...KUKLO?

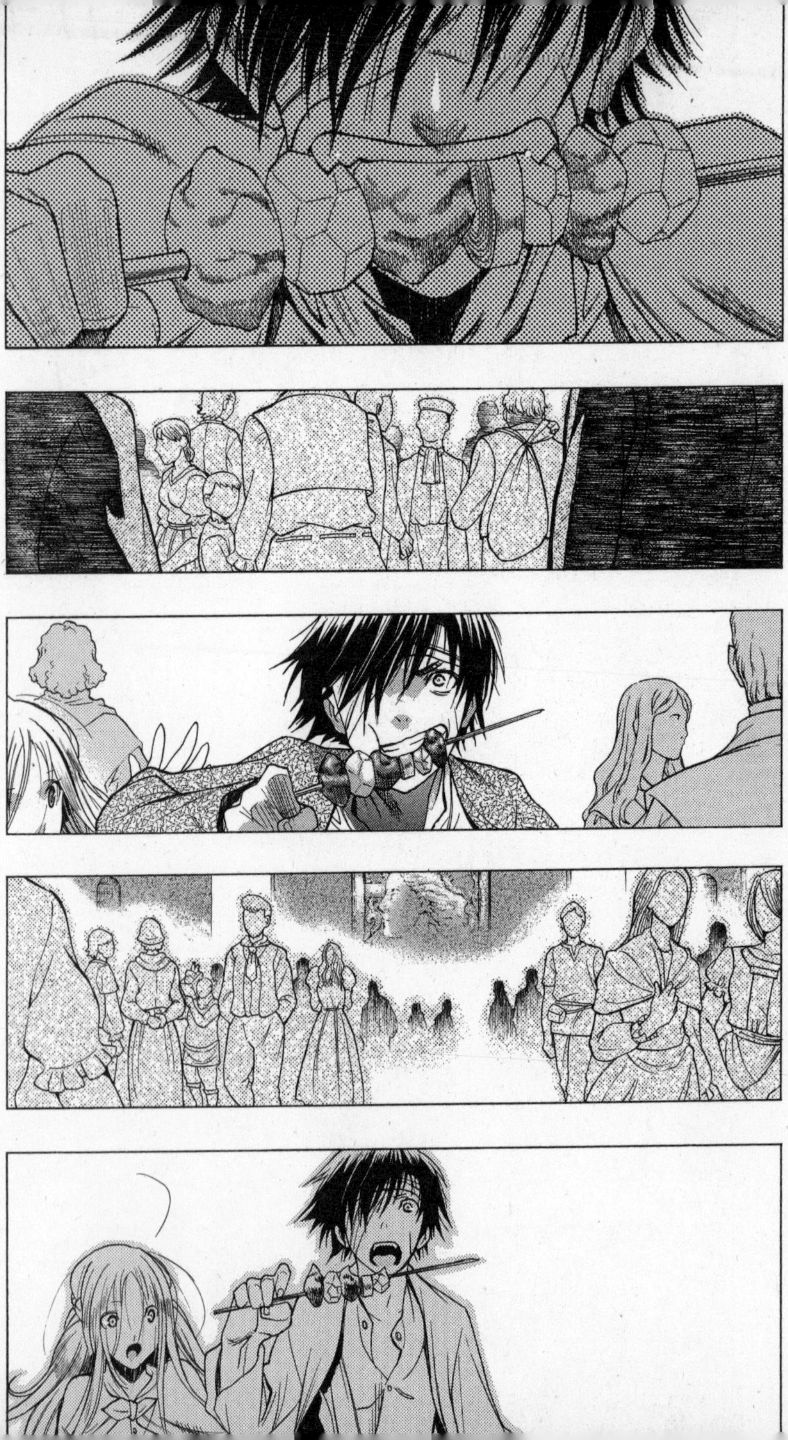

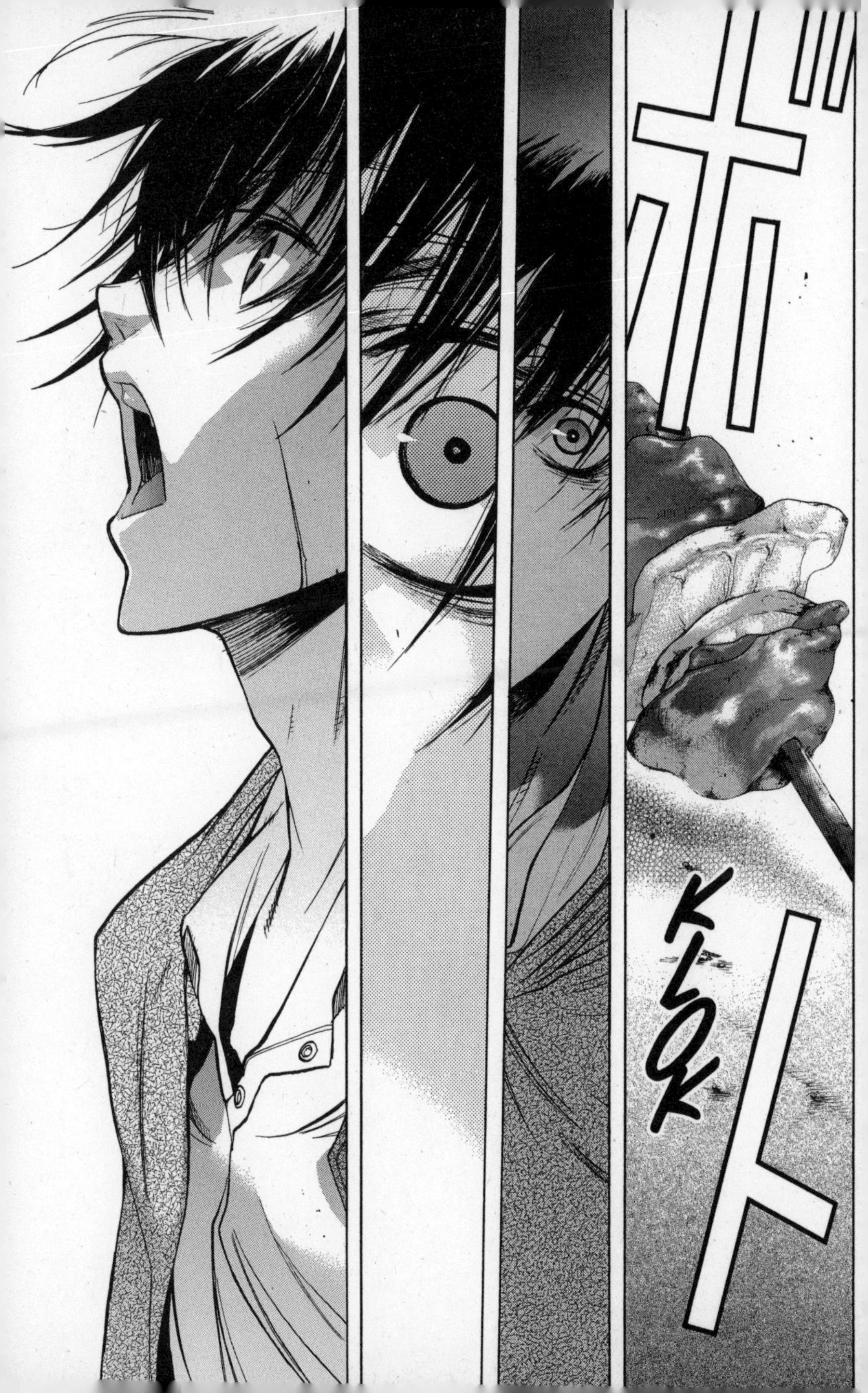

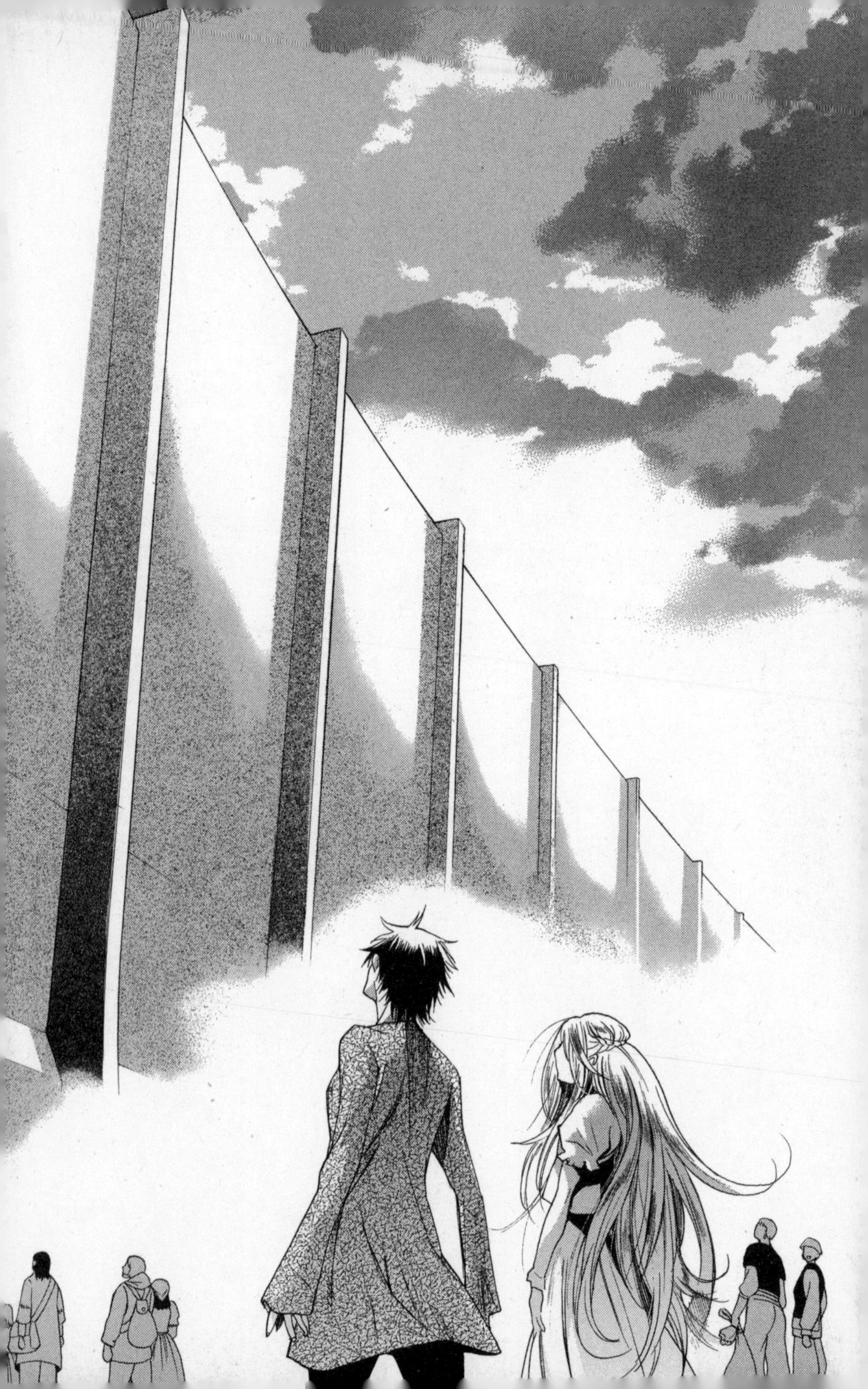

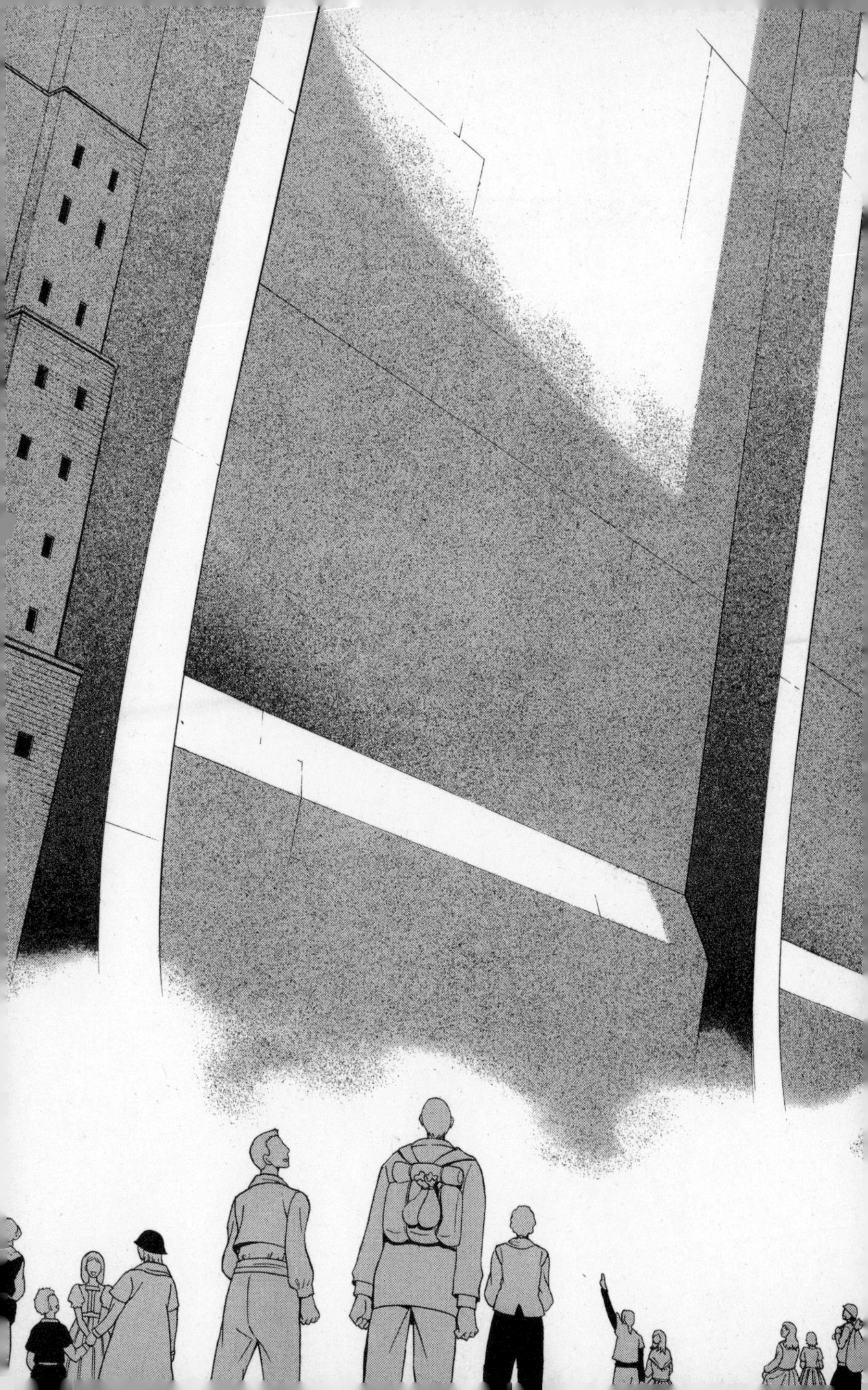

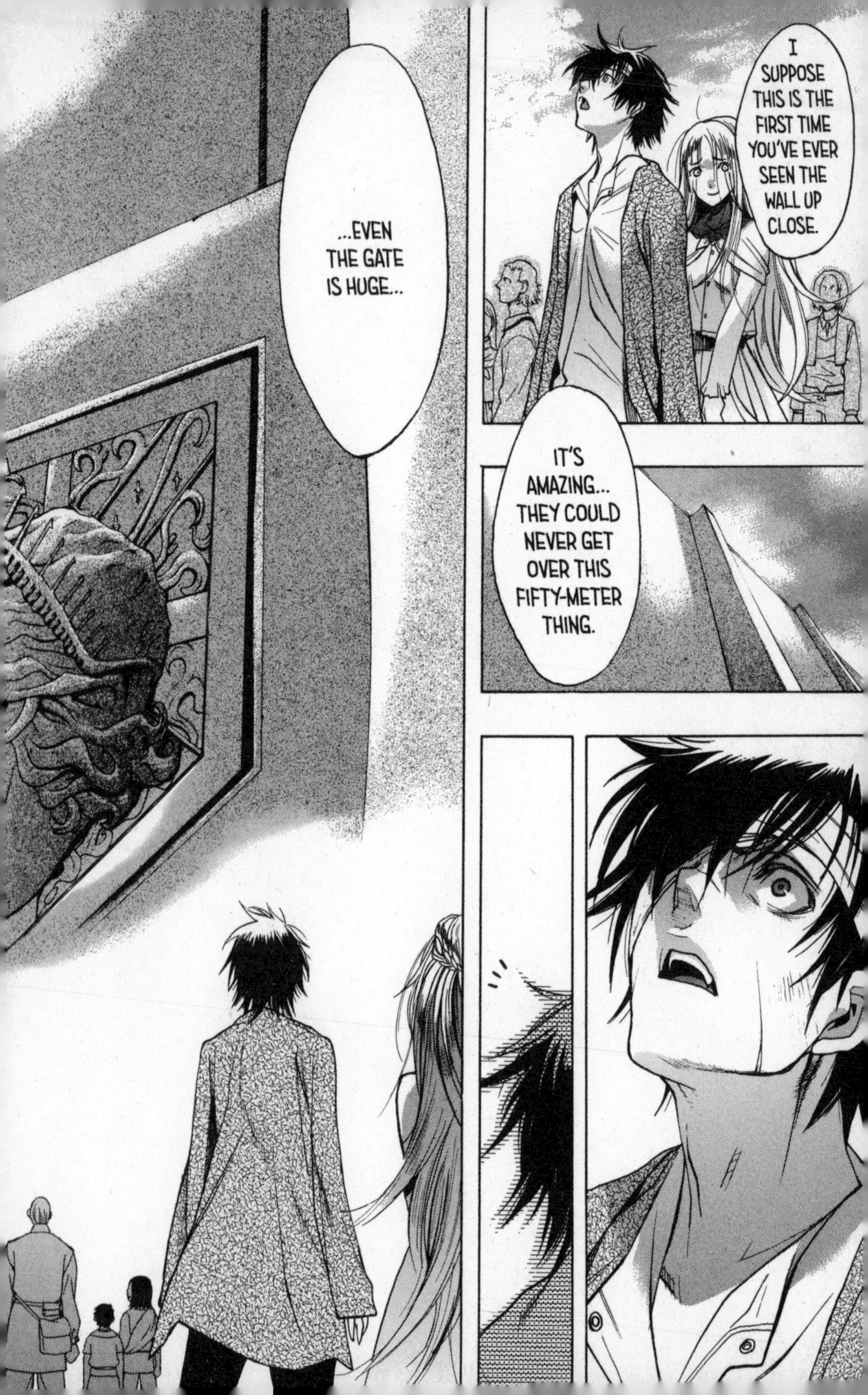
I SUPPOSE THIS IS THE FIRST TIME YOU'VE EVER SEEN THE WALL UP CLOSE.
IT'S AMAZING... THEY COULD NEVER GET OVER THIS FIFTY-METER THING.
...EVEN THE GATE IS HUGE...

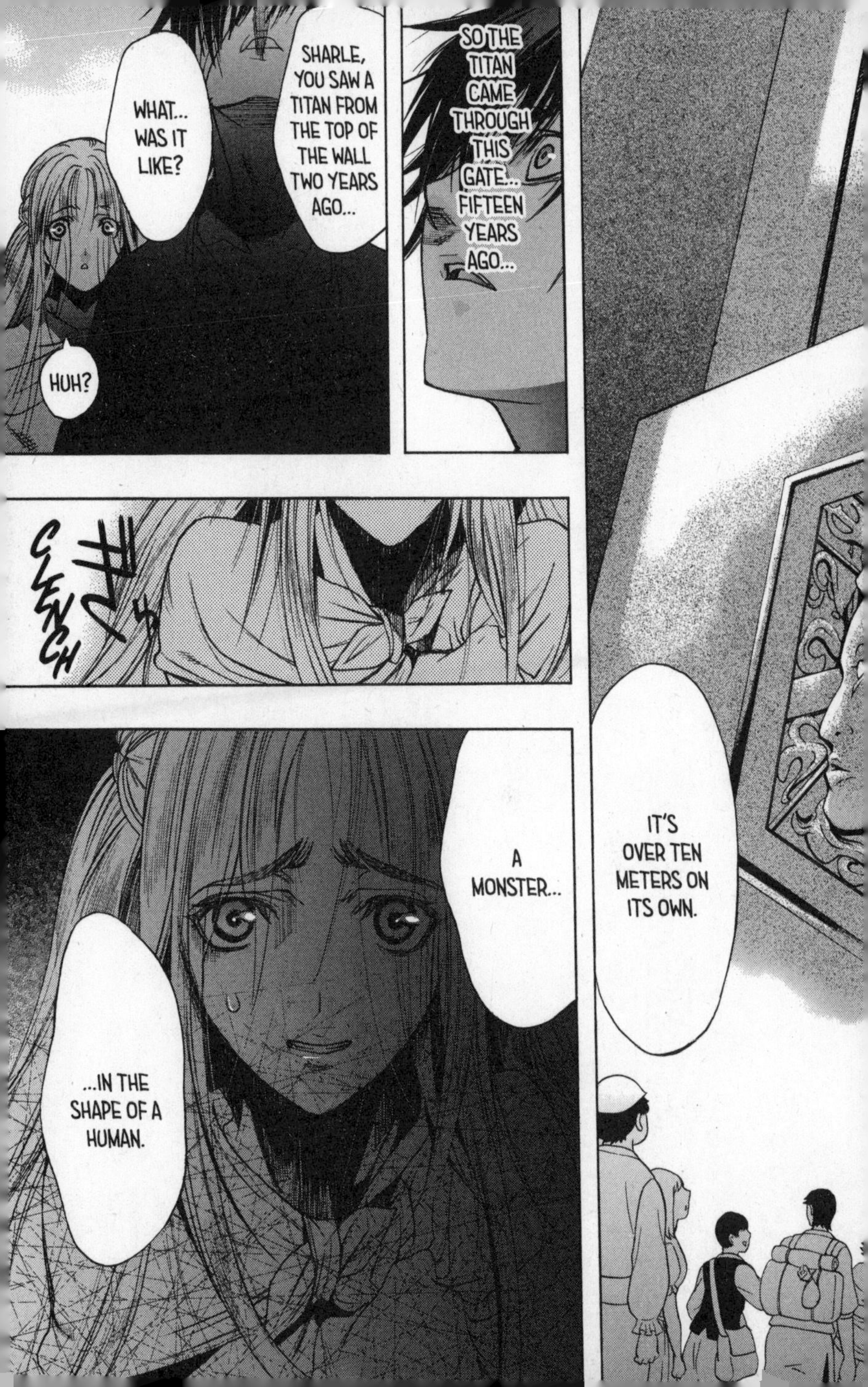
IT'S OVER TEN METERS ON ITS OWN.
SO THE TITAN CAME THROUGH THIS GATE... FIFTEEN YEARS AGO...
SHARLE, YOU SAW A TITAN FROM THE TOP OF THE WALL TWO YEARS AGO...
WHAT... WAS IT LIKE?
HUH?
CLENCH
A MONSTER...
...IN THE SHAPE OF A HUMAN.

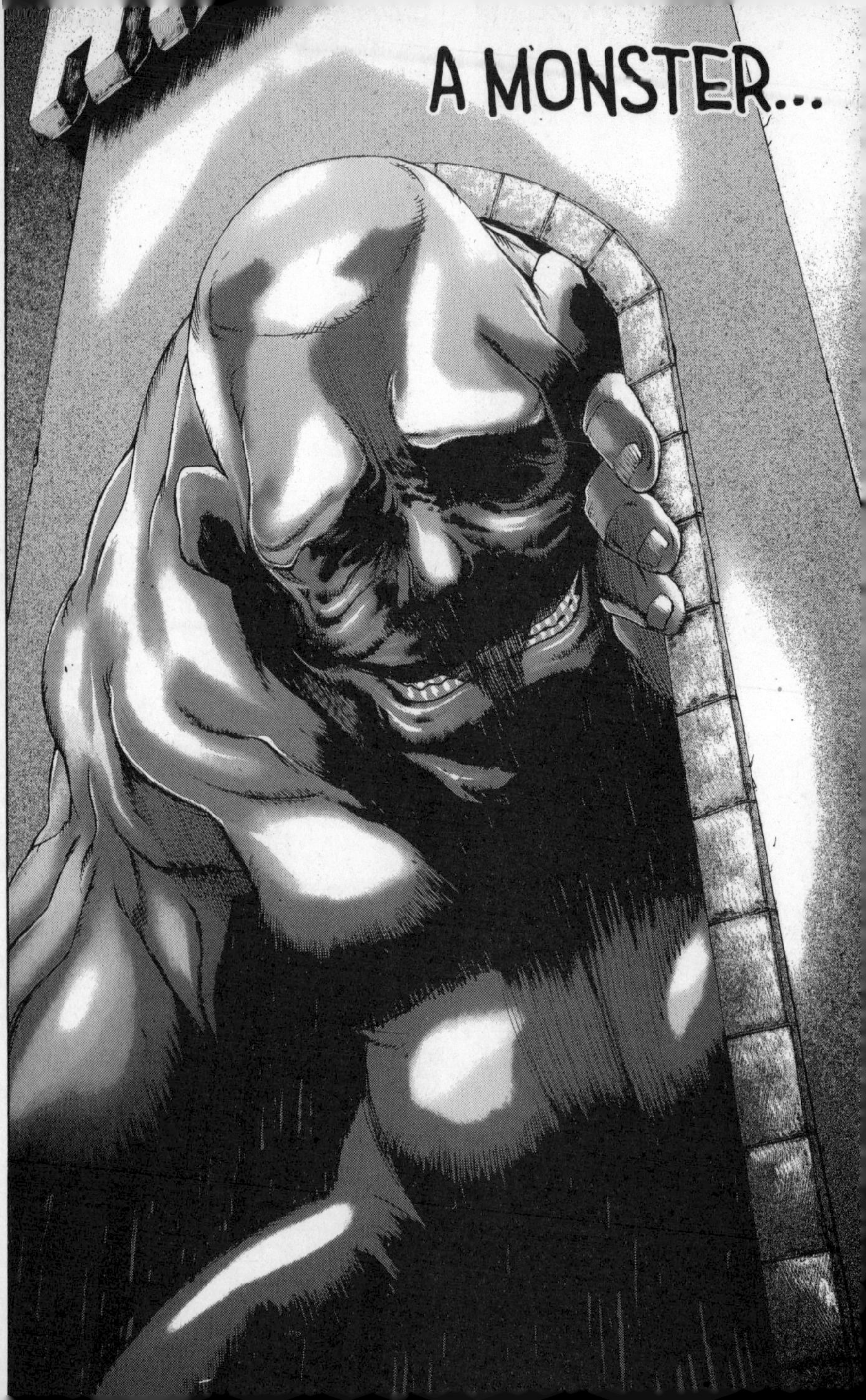
A MONSTER...

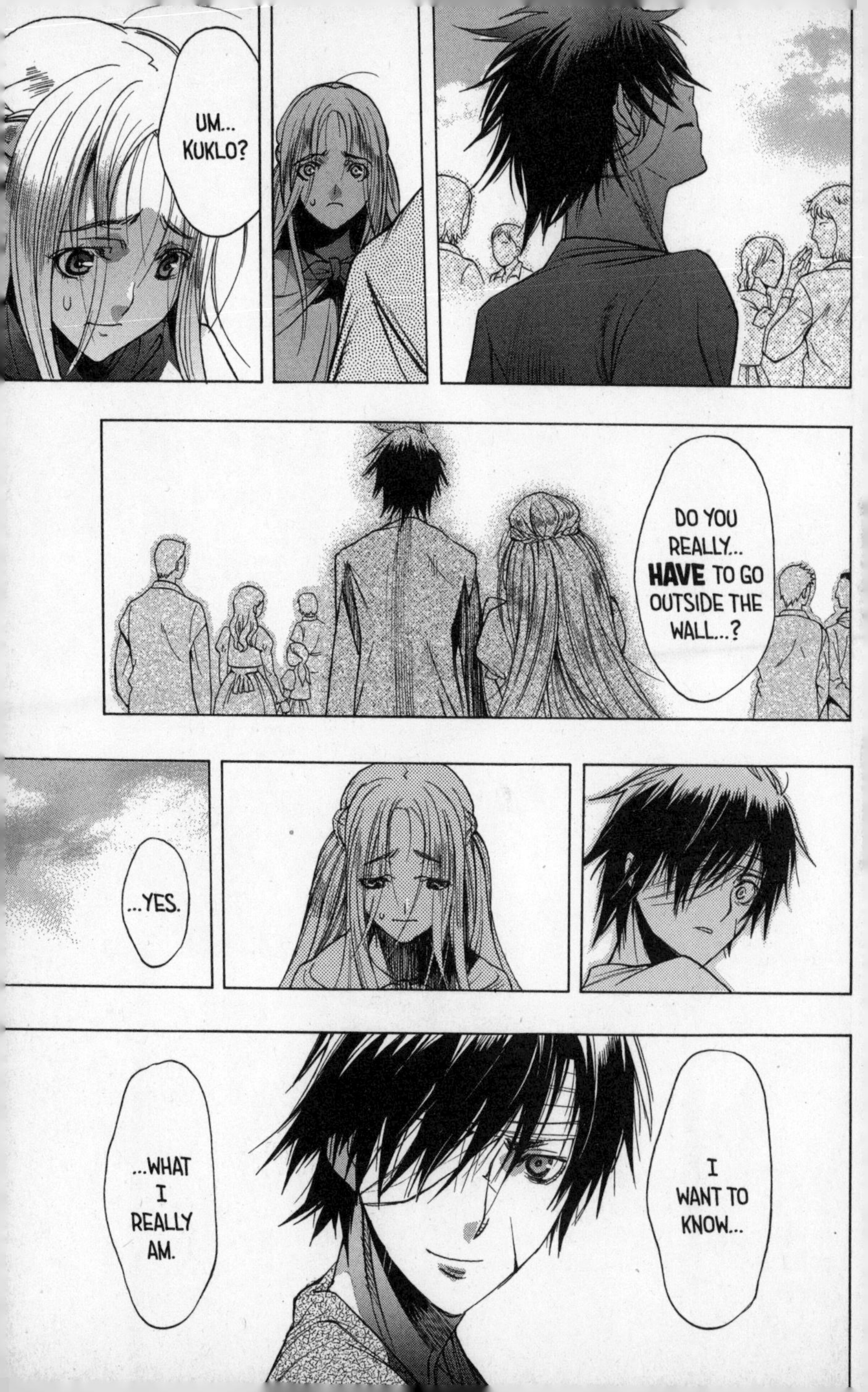
UM... KUKLO?
DO YOU REALLY... **HAVE** TO GO OUTSIDE THE WALL...?
...YES.
I WANT TO KNOW...
...WHAT I REALLY AM.

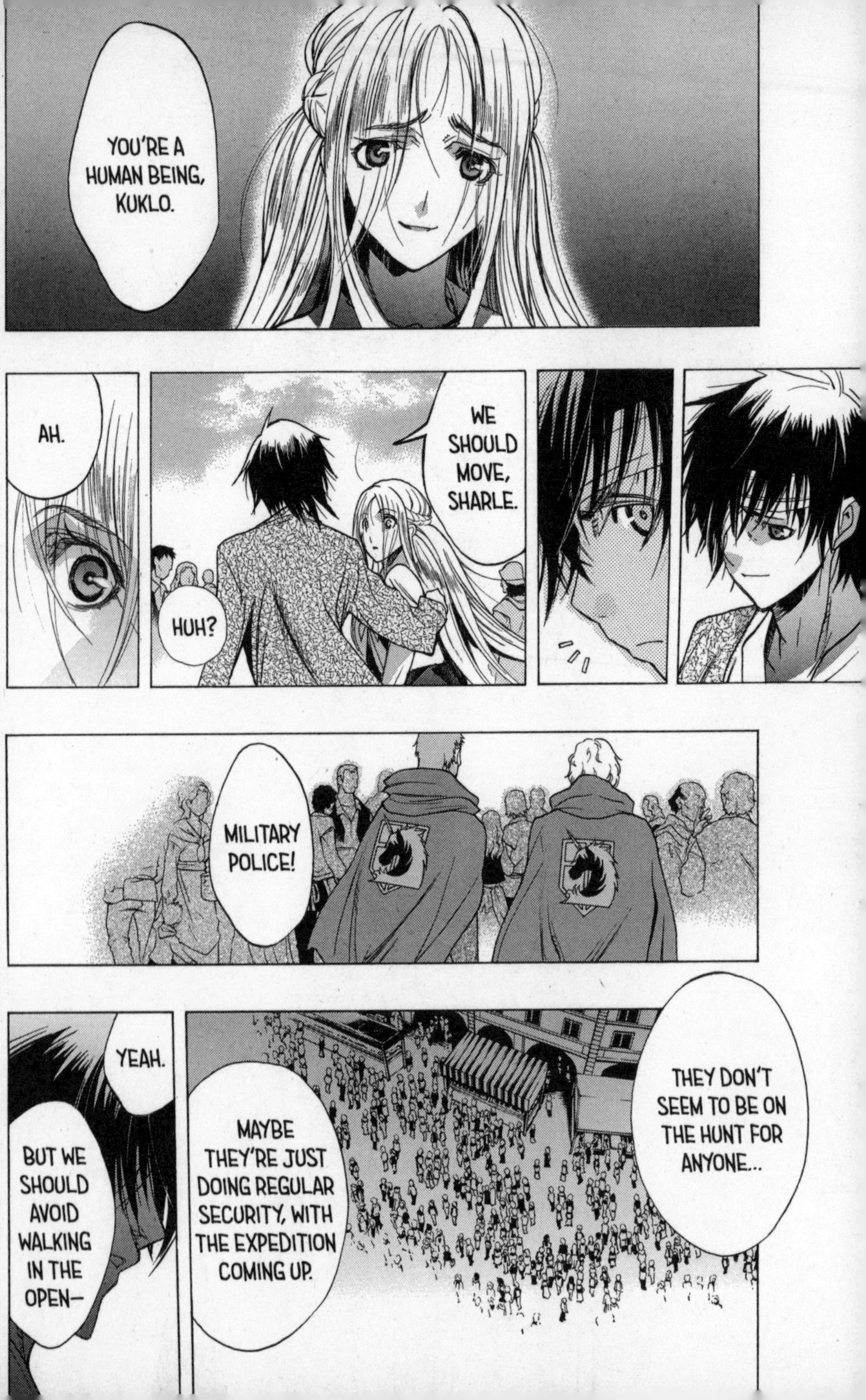
YOU'RE A HUMAN BEING, KUKLO.
WE SHOULD MOVE, SHARLE.
HUH?
AH.
MILITARY POLICE!
THEY DON'T SEEM TO BE ON THE HUNT FOR ANYONE...
MAYBE THEY'RE JUST DOING REGULAR SECURITY, WITH THE EXPEDITION COMING UP.
YEAH.
BUT WE SHOULD AVOID WALKING IN THE OPEN—

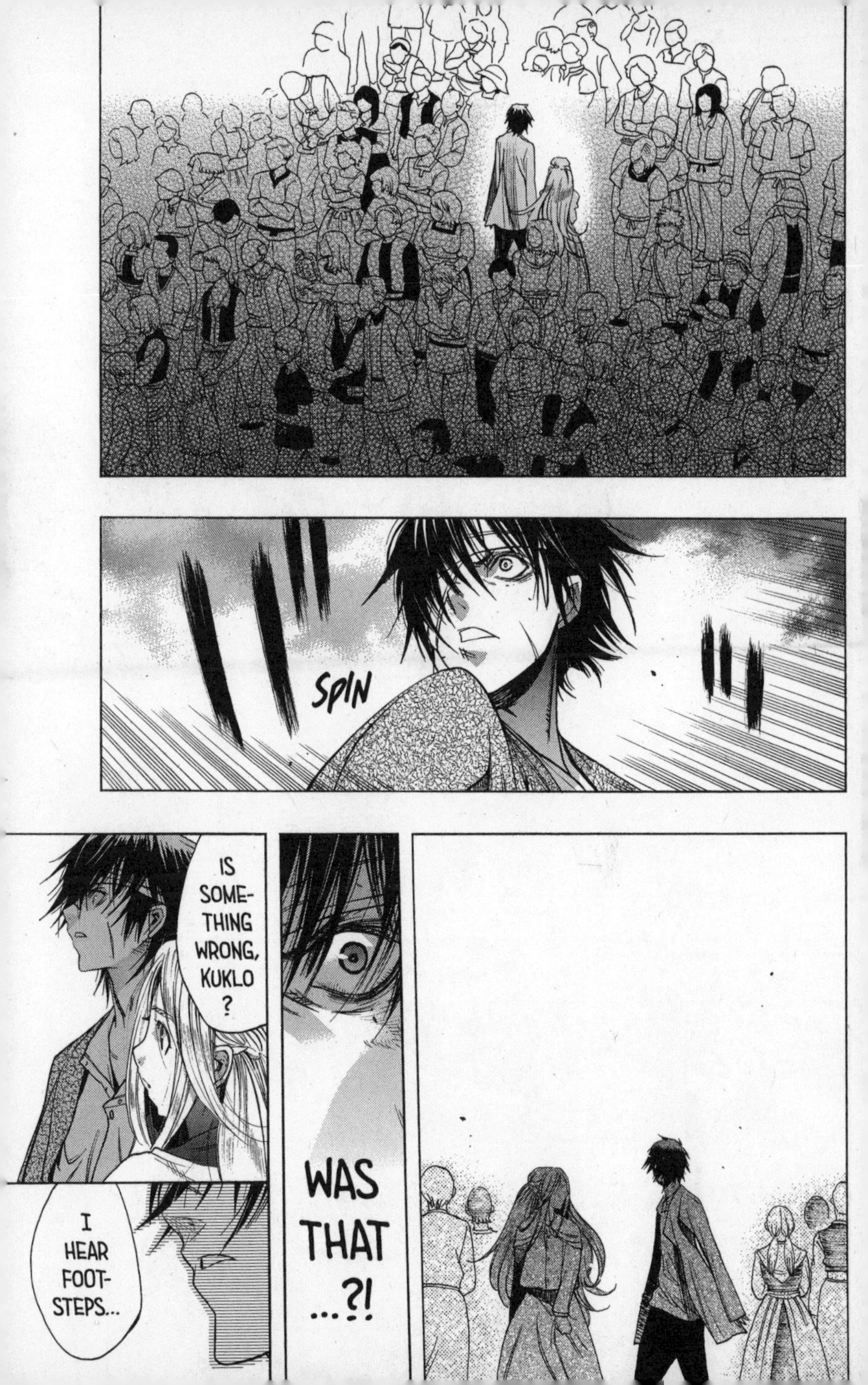
SPIN
IS SOMETHING WRONG, KUKLO ?
WAS THAT ...?!
I HEAR FOOTSTEPS...

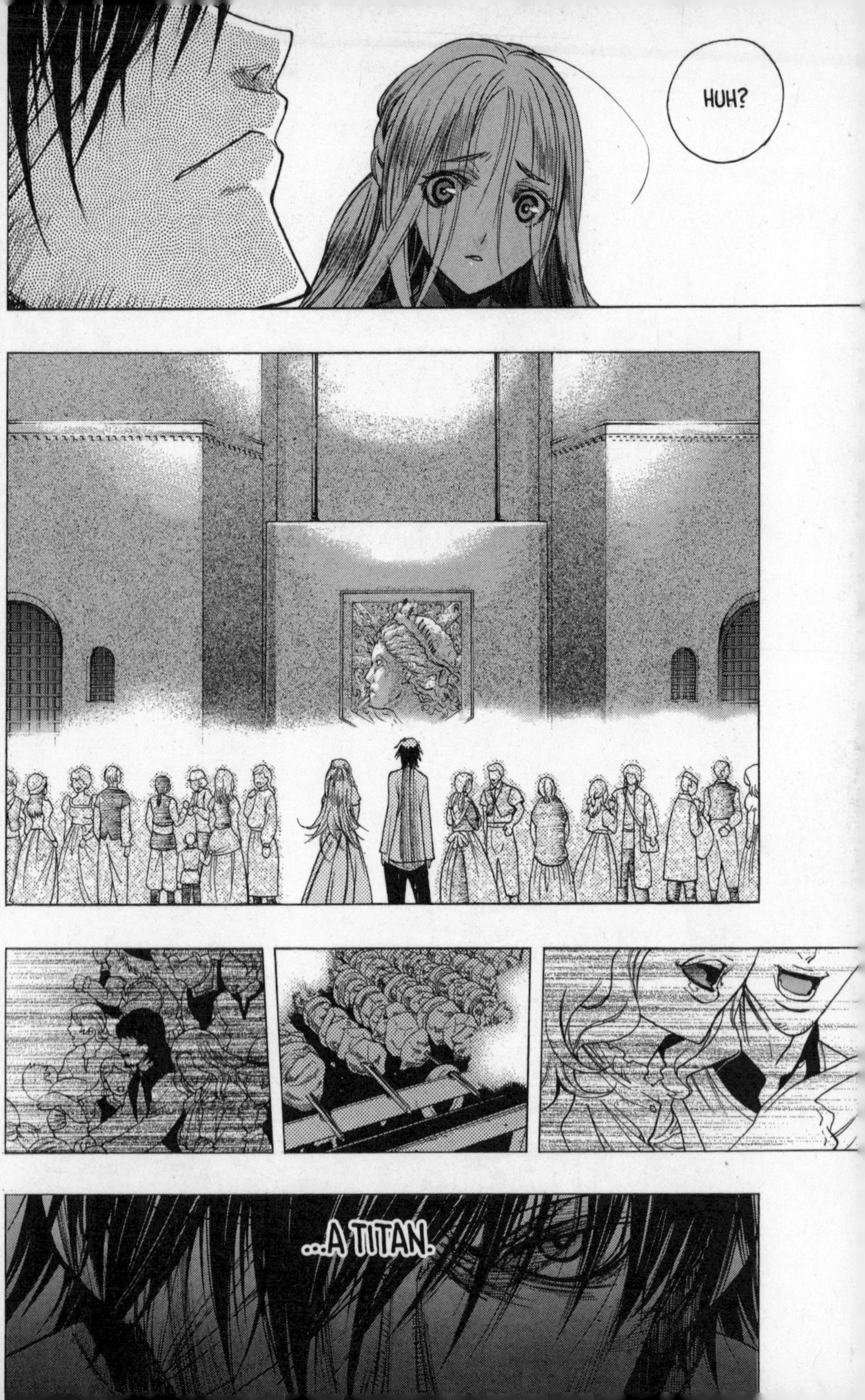
HUH?
...A TITAN.

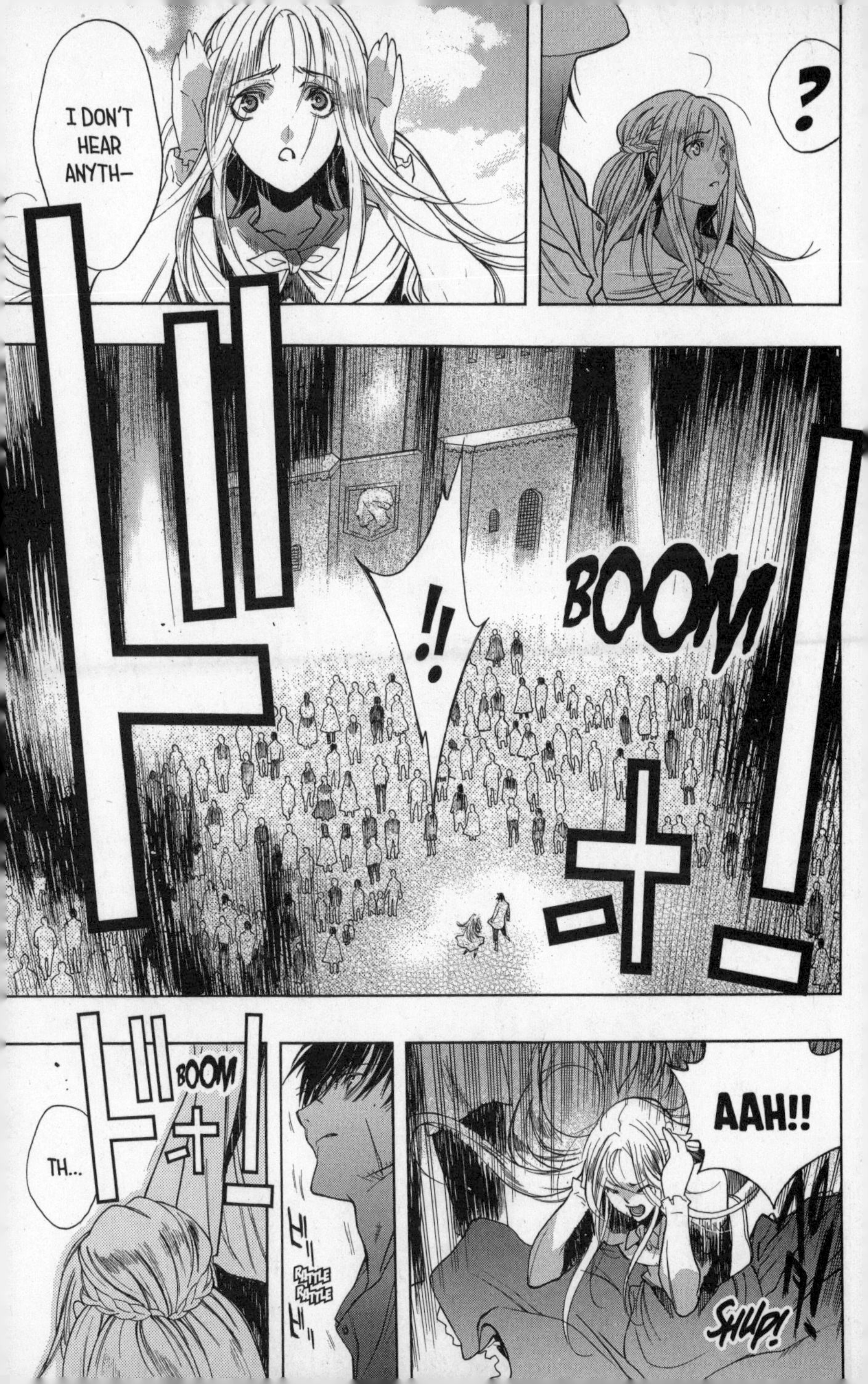
?
I DON'T HEAR ANYTH—
!!
BOOM
AAH!!
SHUP!
RATTLE RATTLE
BOOM
TH...

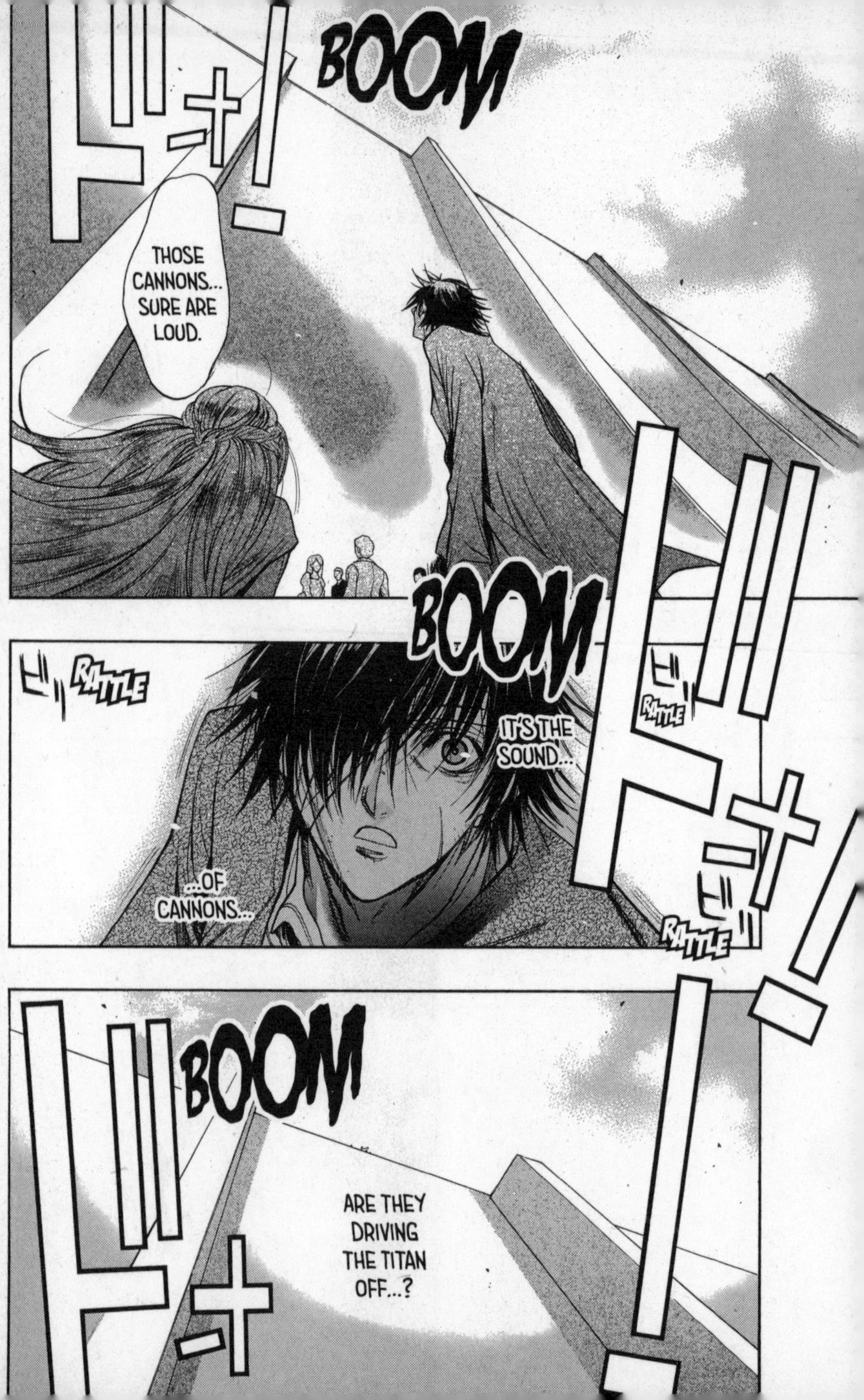
BOOM
THOSE CANNONS... SURE ARE LOUD.
BOOM
RATTLE
IT'S THE SOUND...
...OF CANNONS...
RATTLE
RATTLE
BOOM
ARE THEY DRIVING THE TITAN OFF...?

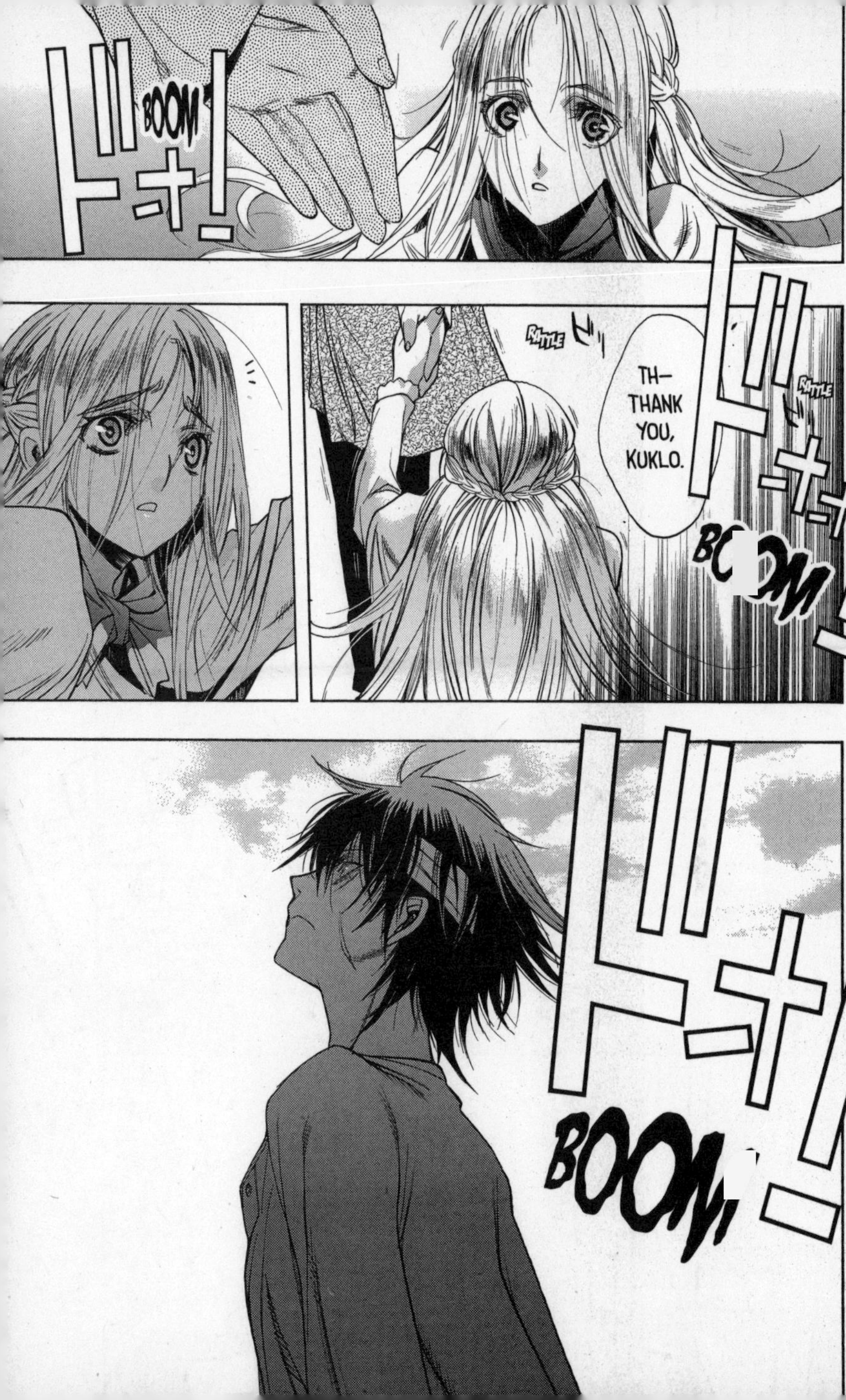
BOOM
RATTLE
TH— THANK YOU, KUKLO.
RATTLE
BOOM

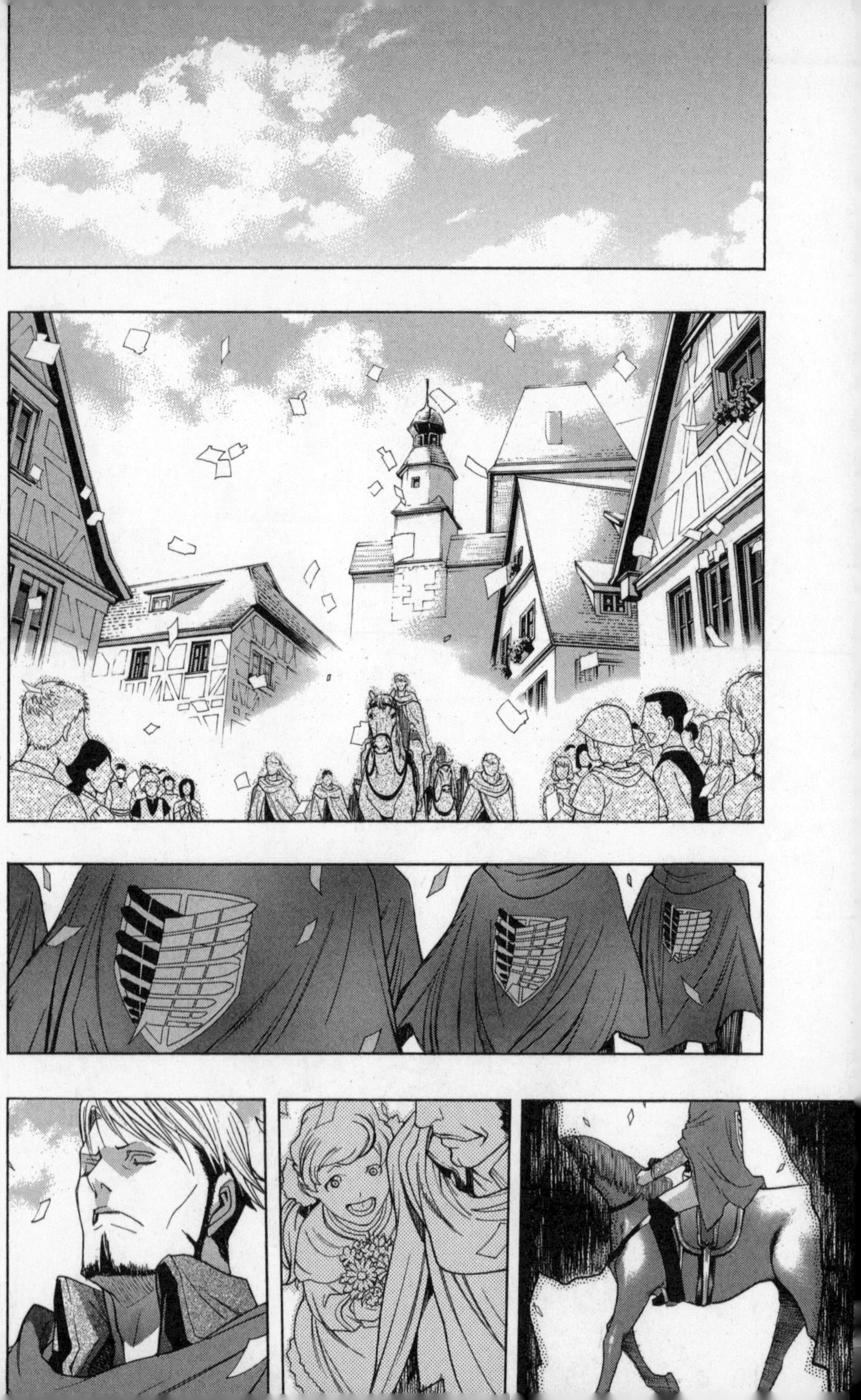

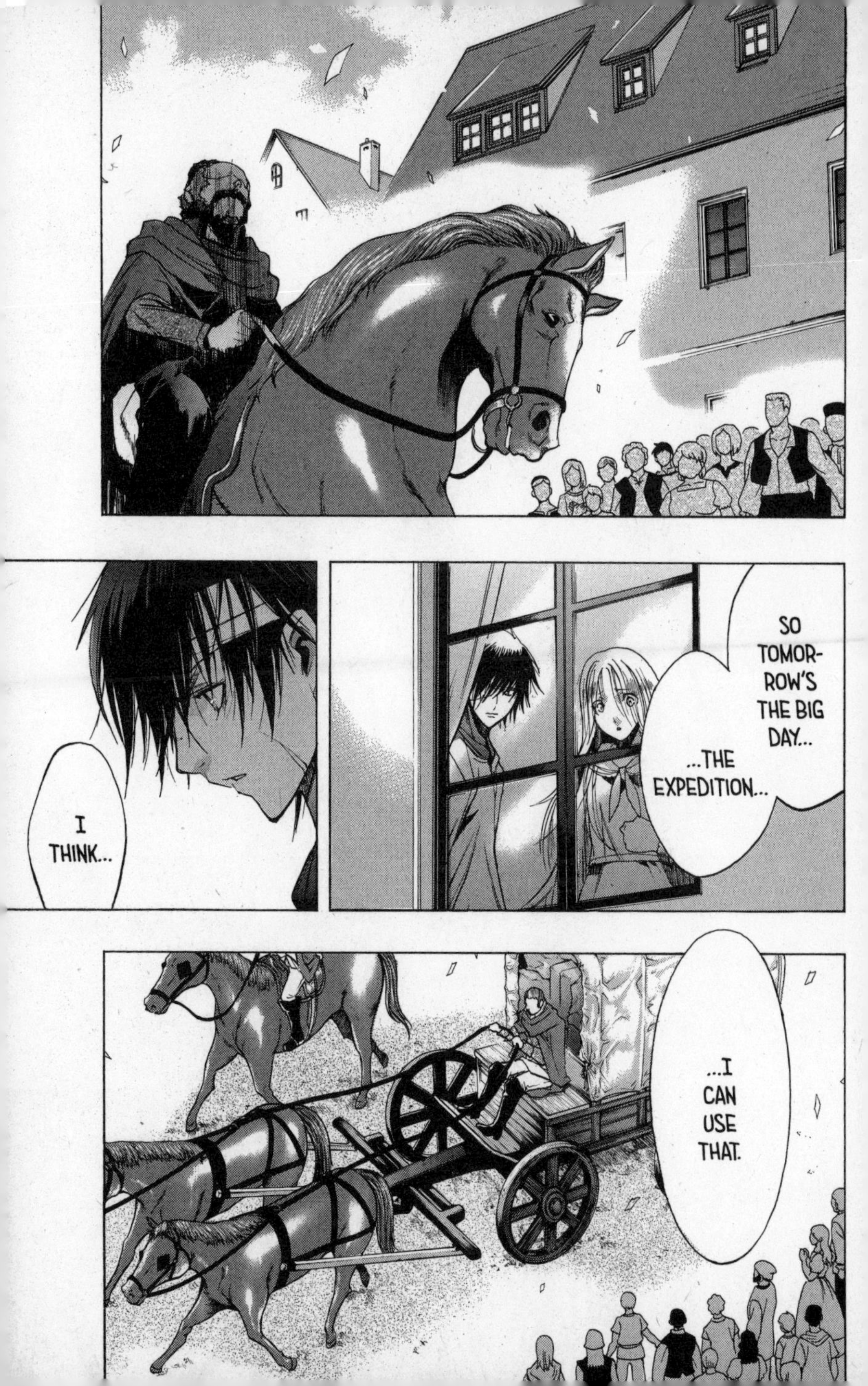
SO TOMORROW'S THE BIG DAY...
...THE EXPEDITION...
I THINK...
...I CAN USE THAT.

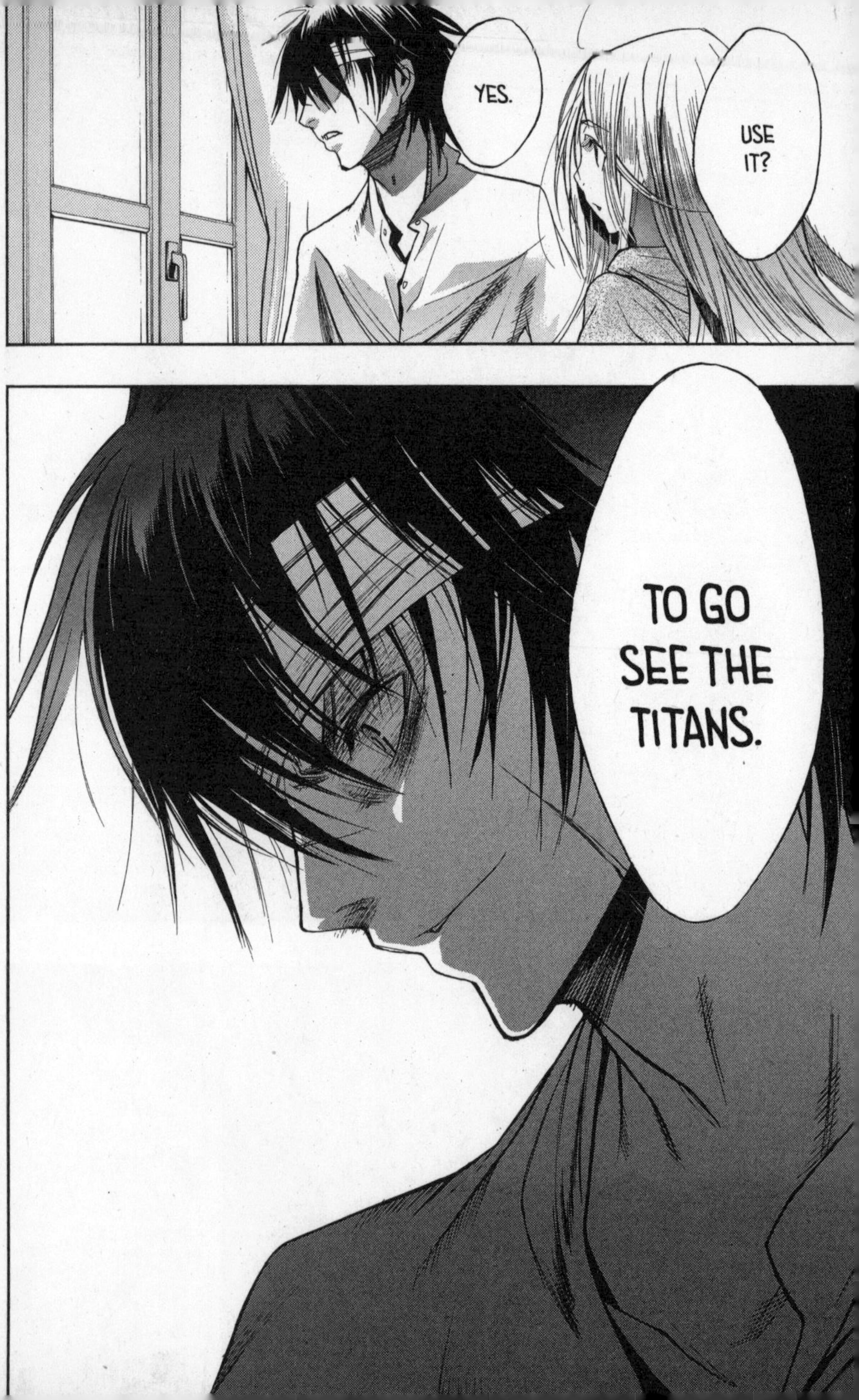
USE IT?
YES.
TO GO SEE THE TITANS.

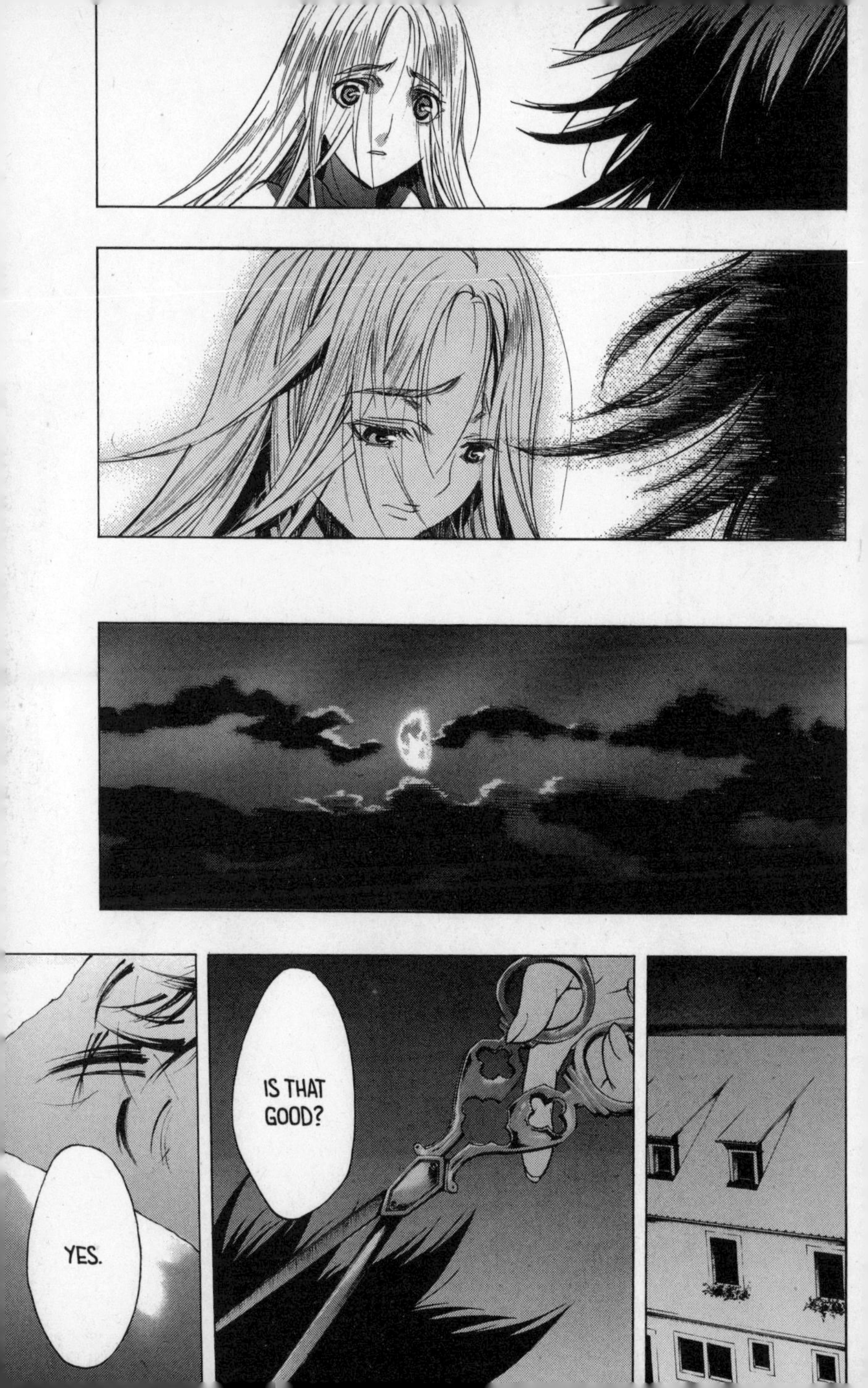
IS THAT GOOD?
YES.

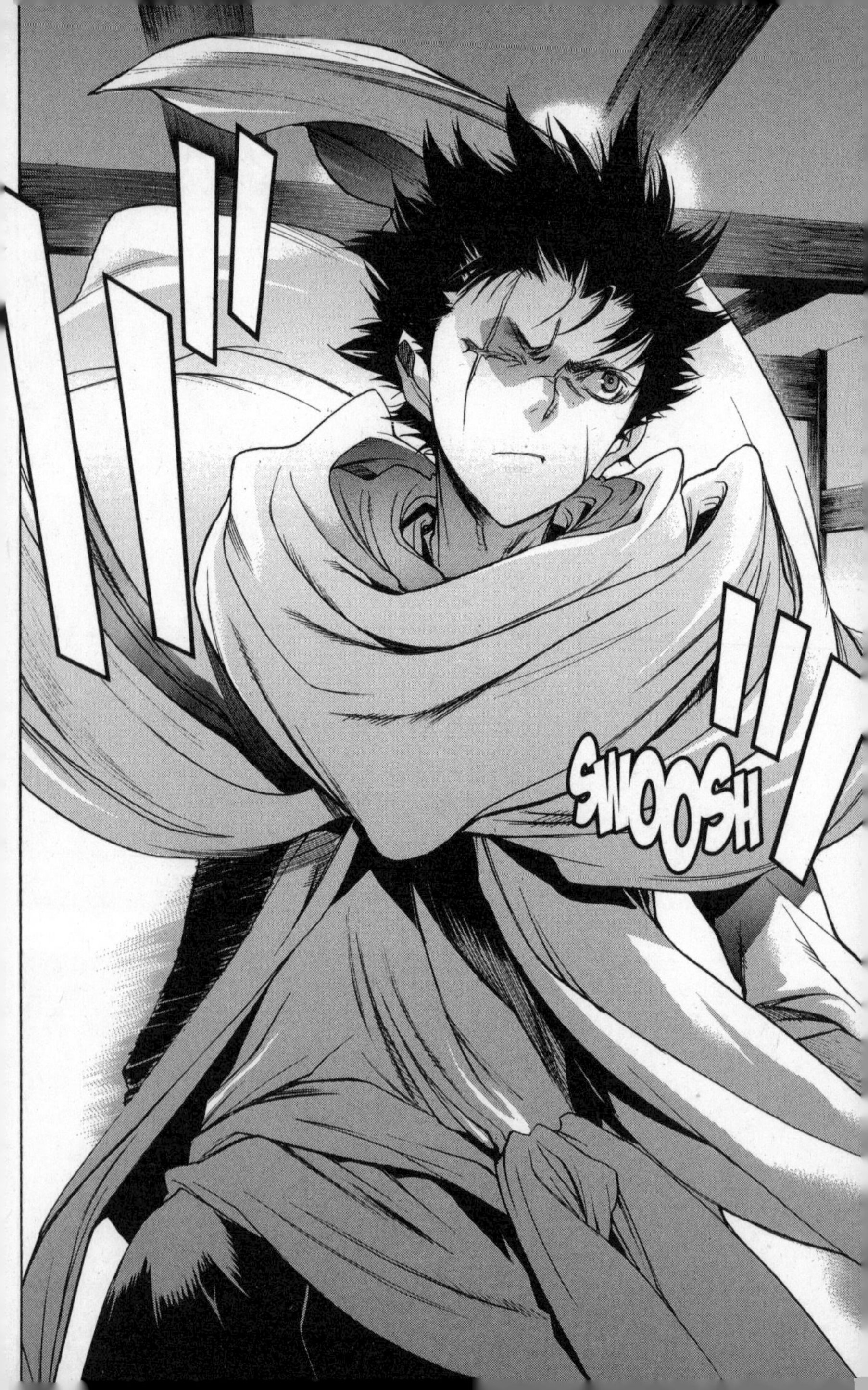
SWOOSH

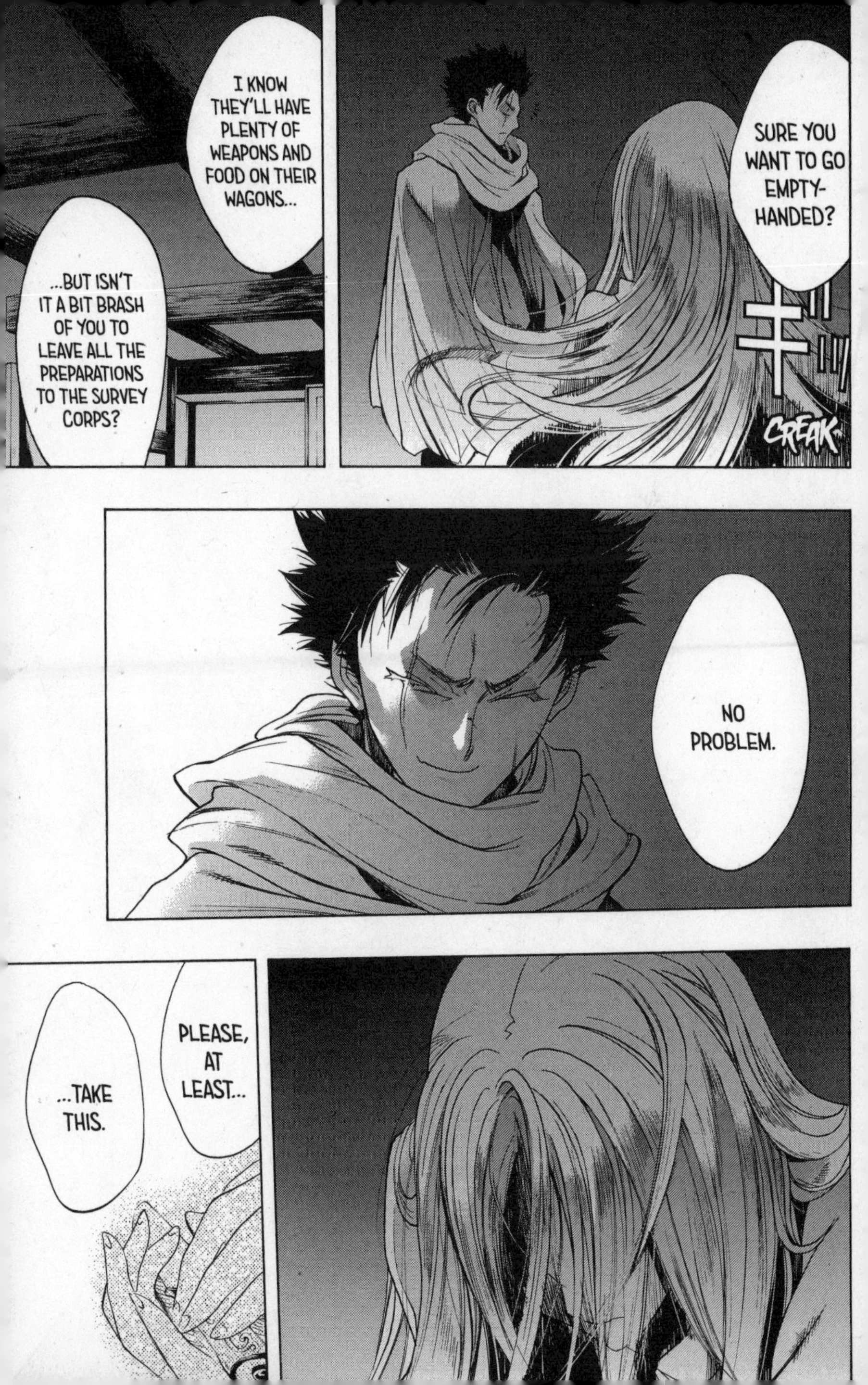
SURE YOU WANT TO GO EMPTY-HANDED?
CREAK
I KNOW THEY'LL HAVE PLENTY OF WEAPONS AND FOOD ON THEIR WAGONS...
...BUT ISN'T IT A BIT BRASH OF YOU TO LEAVE ALL THE PREPARATIONS TO THE SURVEY CORPS?
NO PROBLEM.
PLEASE, AT LEAST...
...TAKE THIS.

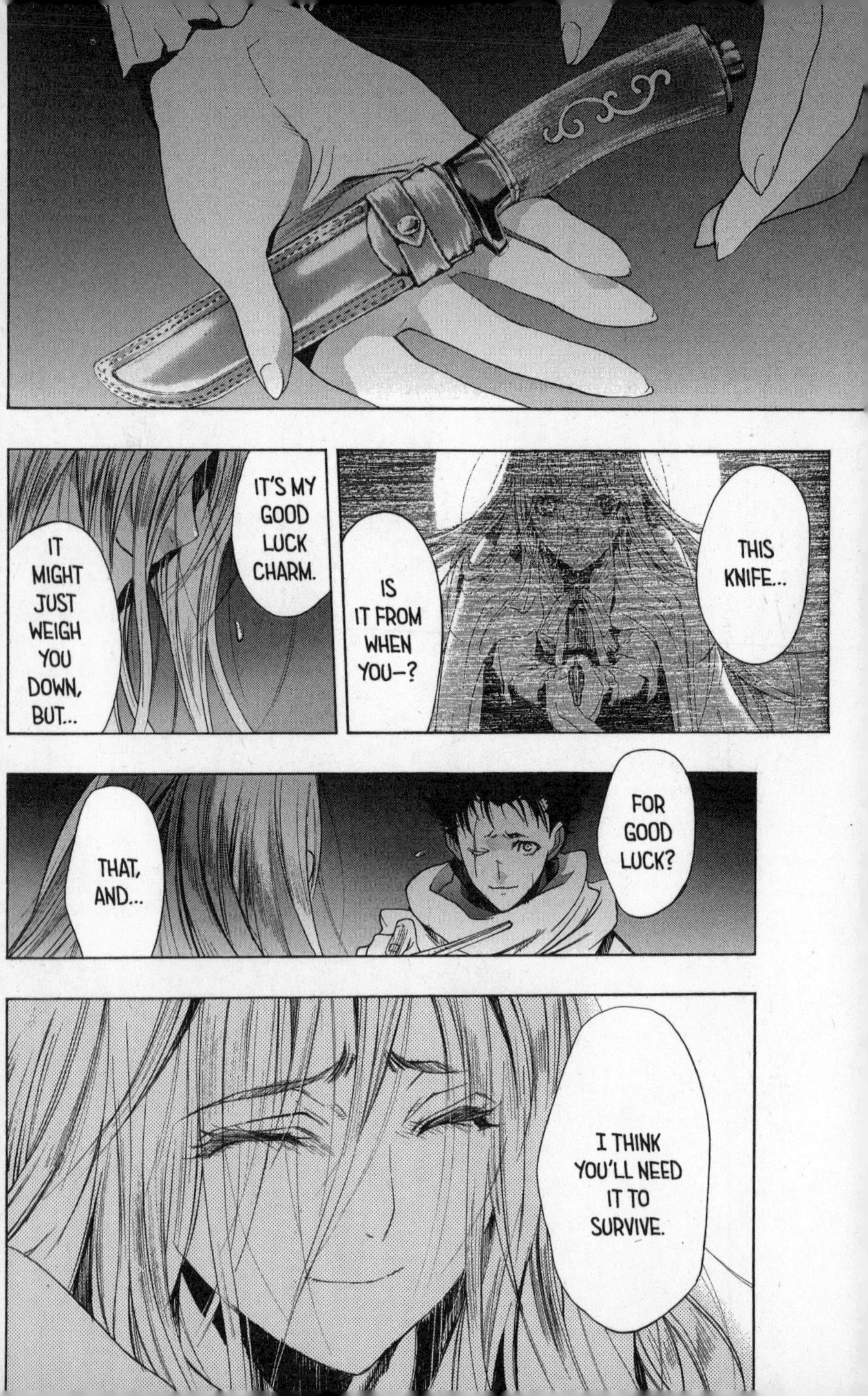
THIS KNIFE...
IS IT FROM WHEN YOU—?
IT'S MY GOOD LUCK CHARM.
IT MIGHT JUST WEIGH YOU DOWN, BUT...
FOR GOOD LUCK?
THAT, AND...
I THINK YOU'LL NEED IT TO SURVIVE.

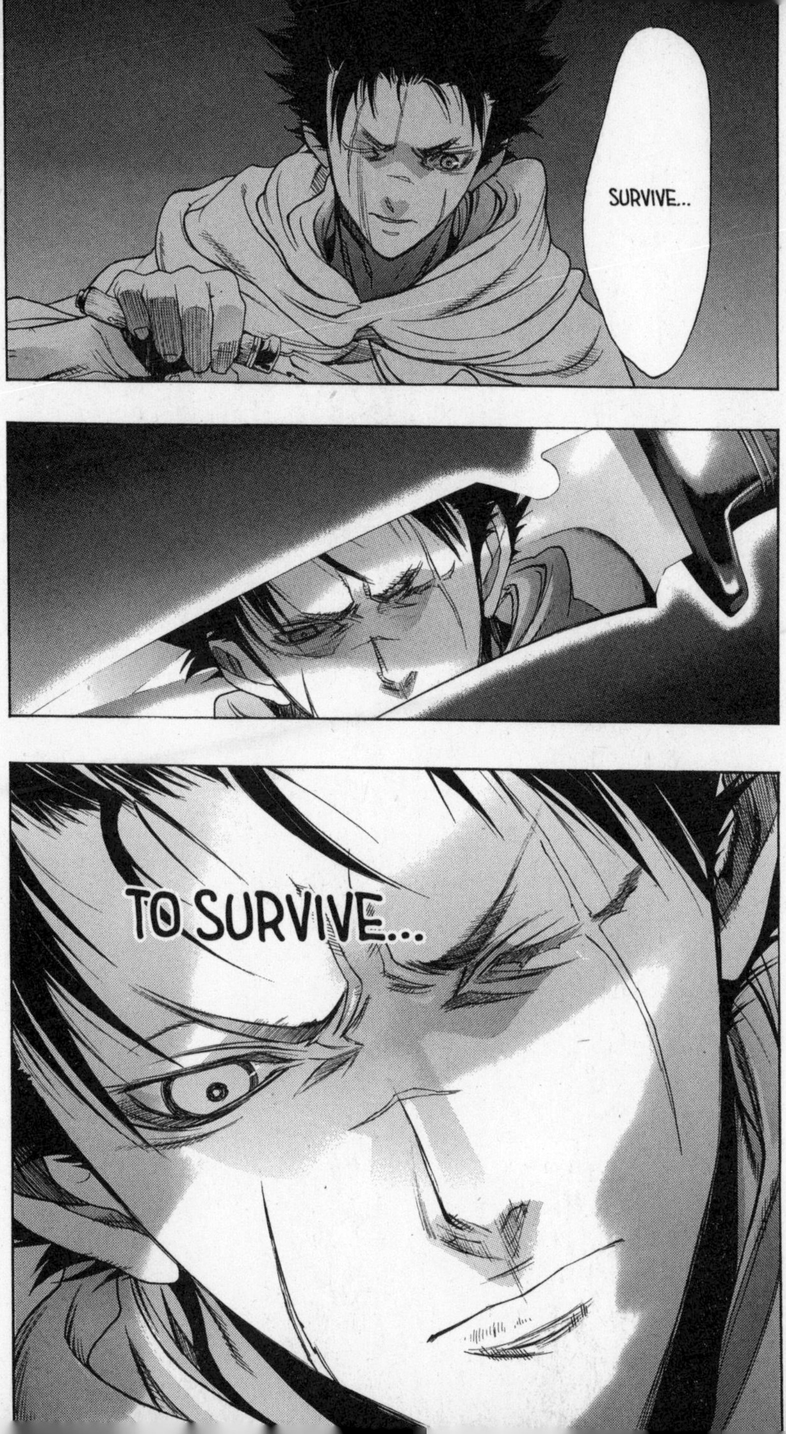
SURVIVE...
TO SURVIVE...

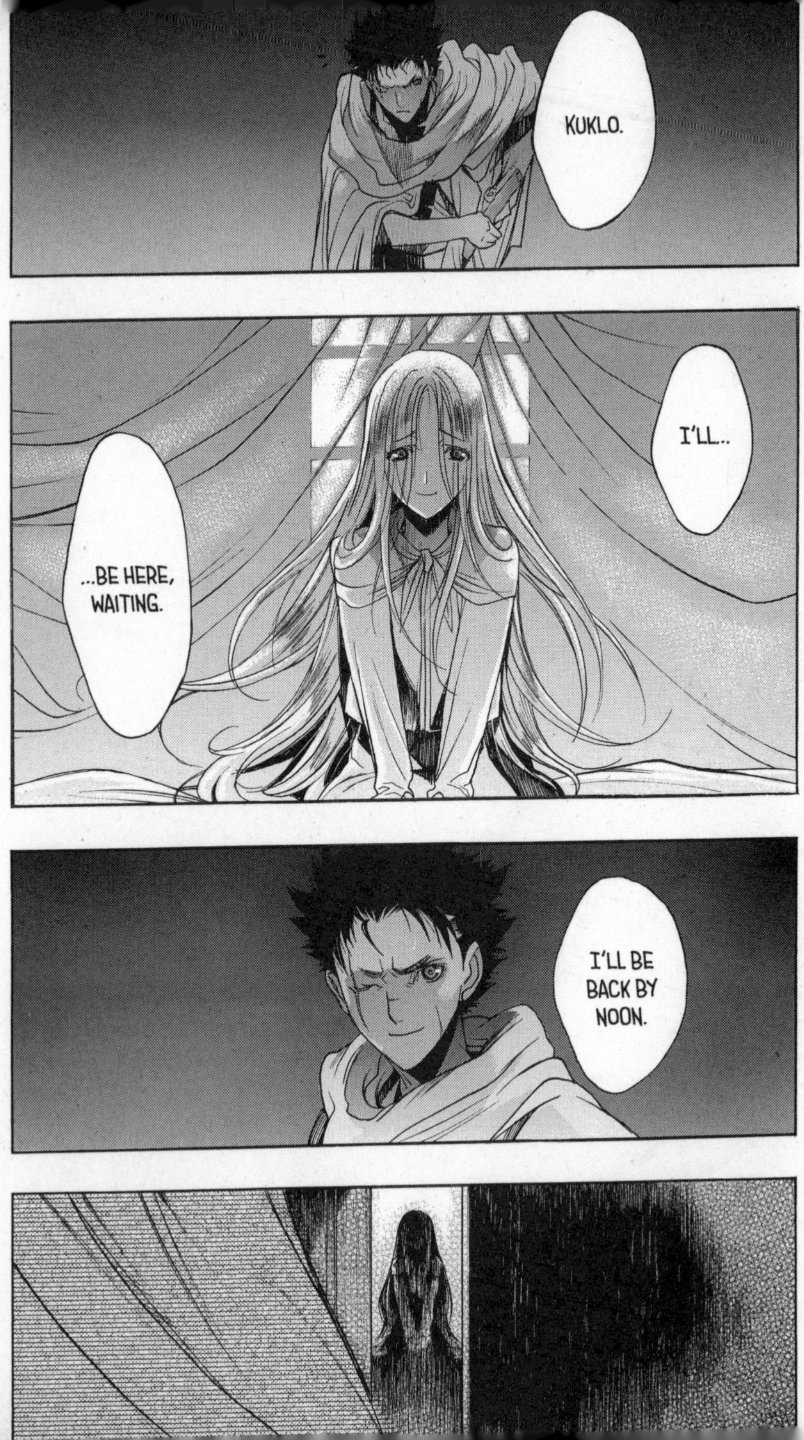
KUKLO.
I'LL...
...BE HERE, WAITING.
I'LL BE BACK BY NOON.

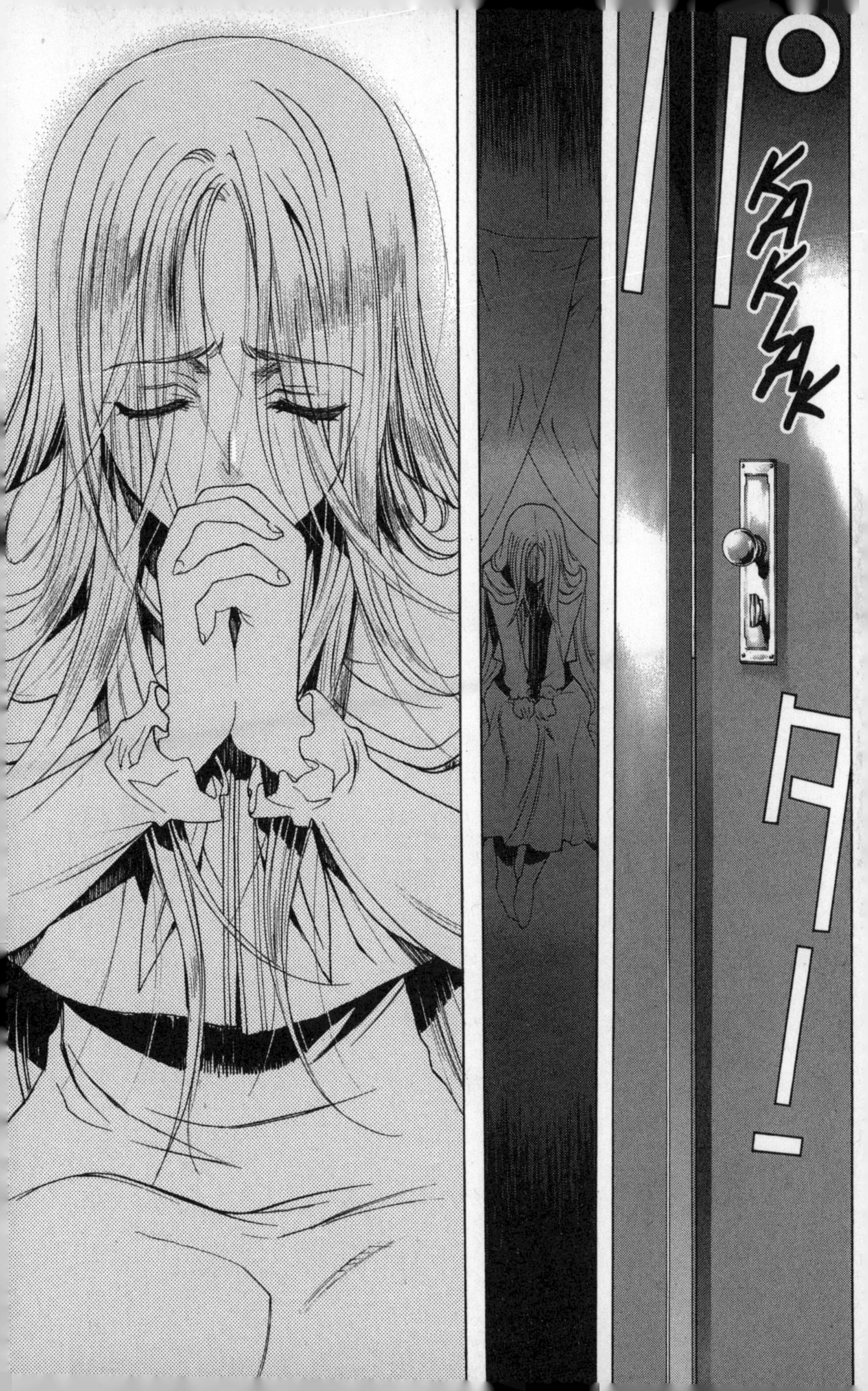
KAKLAK
パタ…

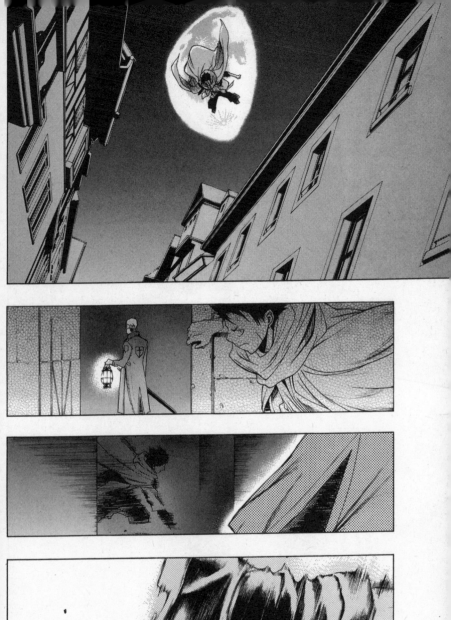
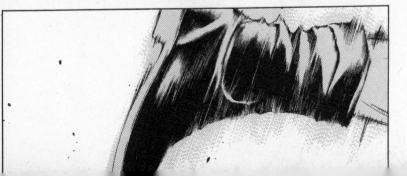

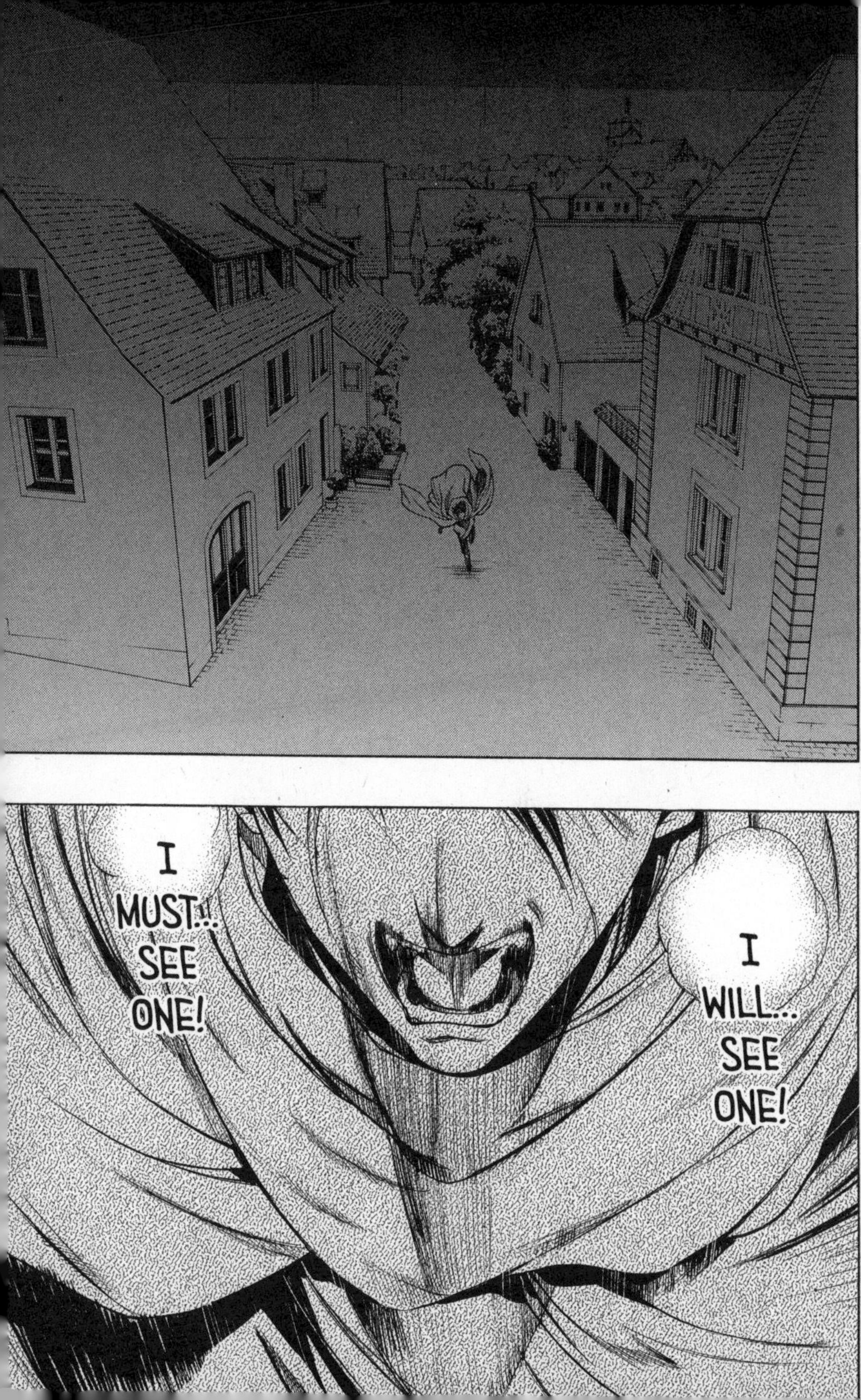
I WILL... SEE ONE!
I MUST...! SEE ONE!

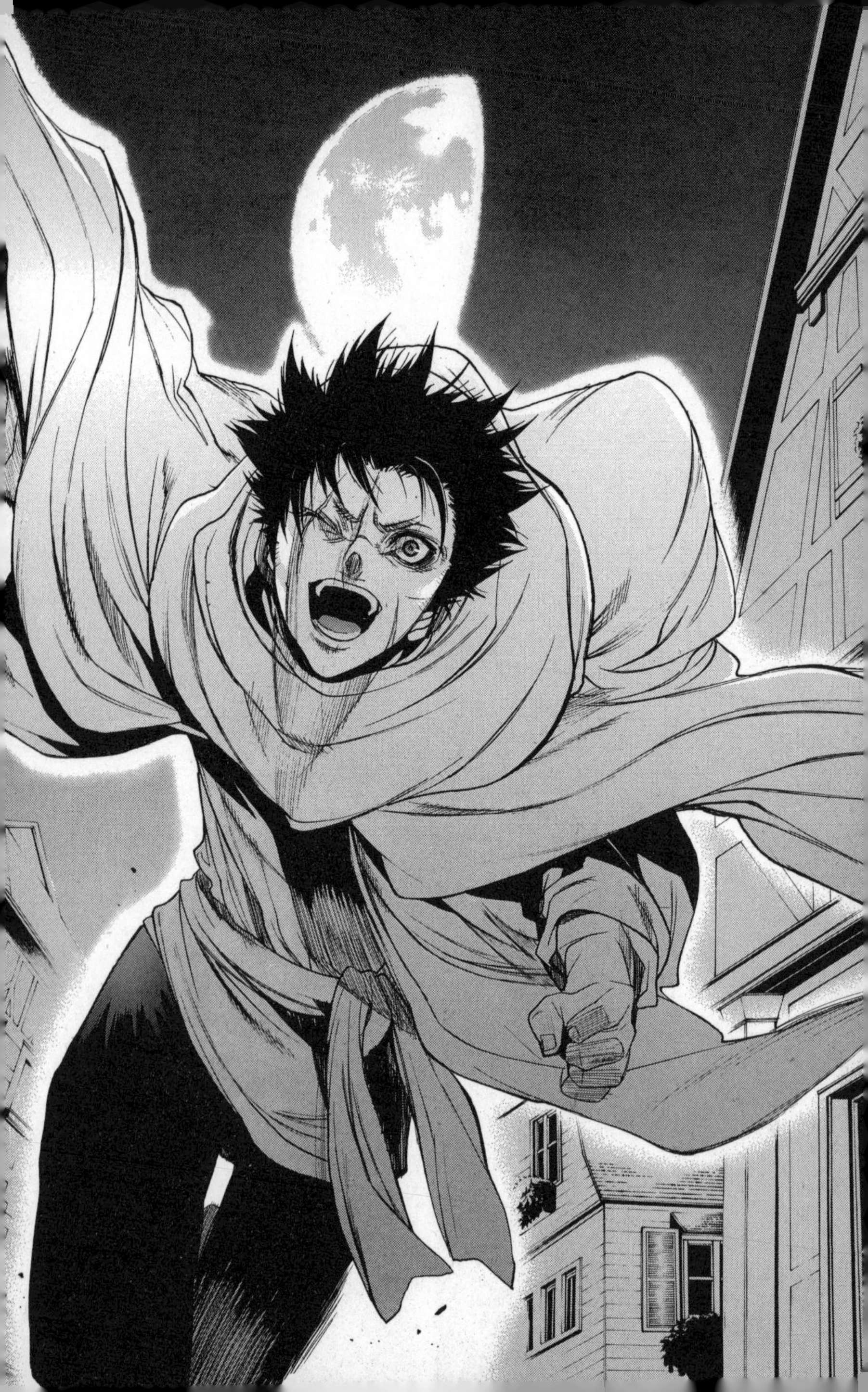

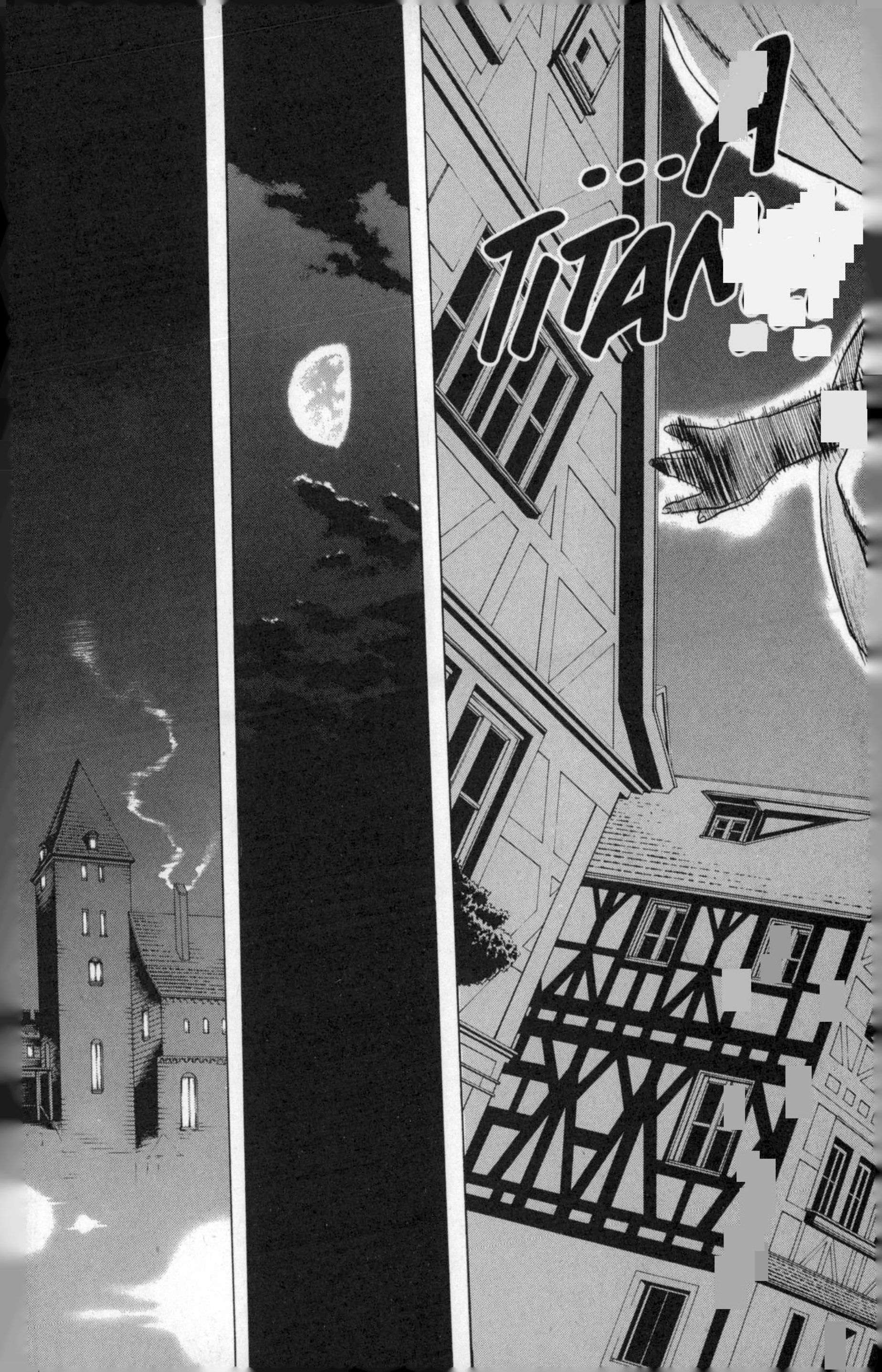
...A TITA

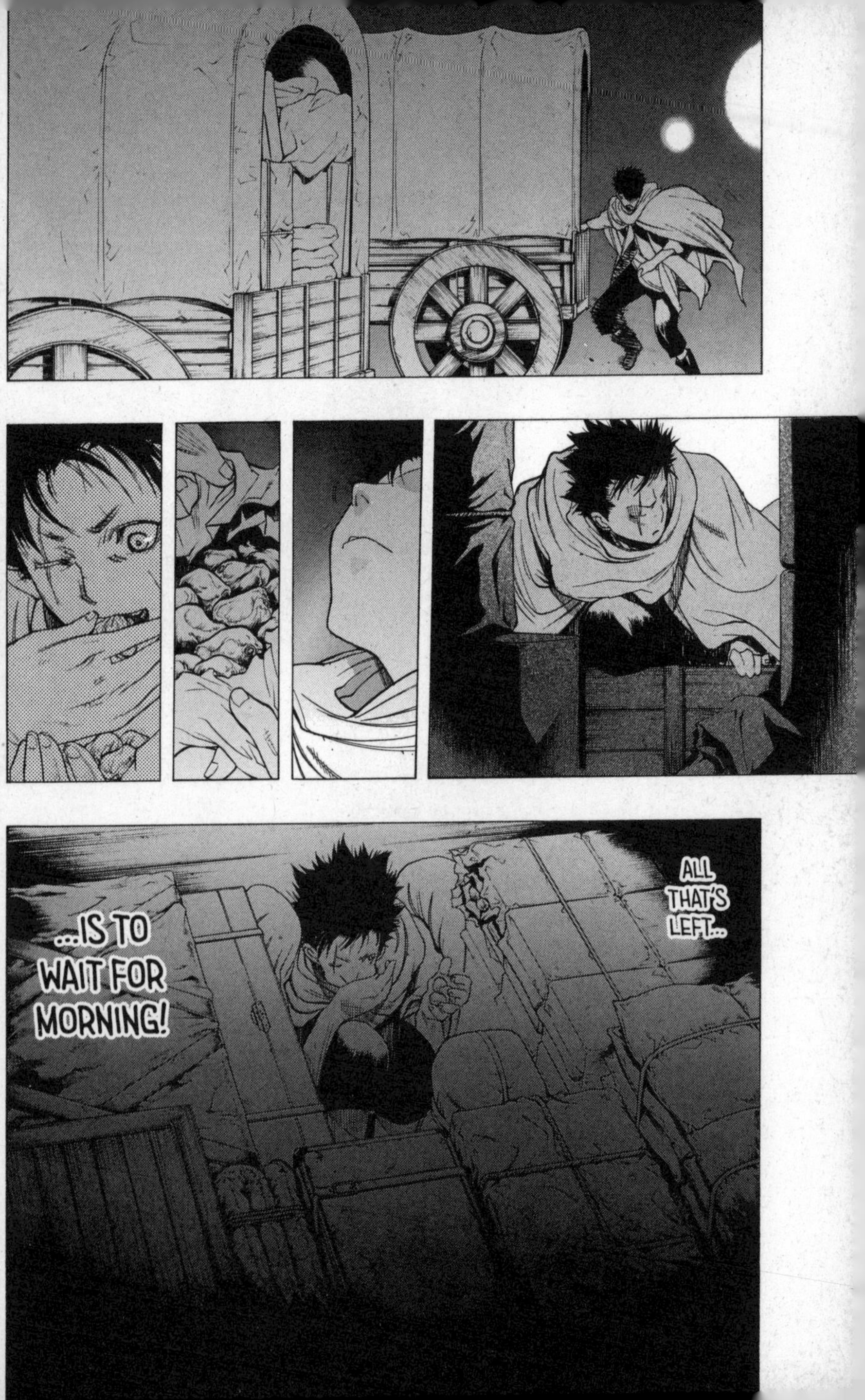
ALL THAT'S LEFT...
...IS TO WAIT FOR MORNING!

Chapter 5: Predawn Departure - End

ATTACK on TITAN

BEFORE THE FALL

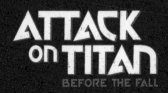

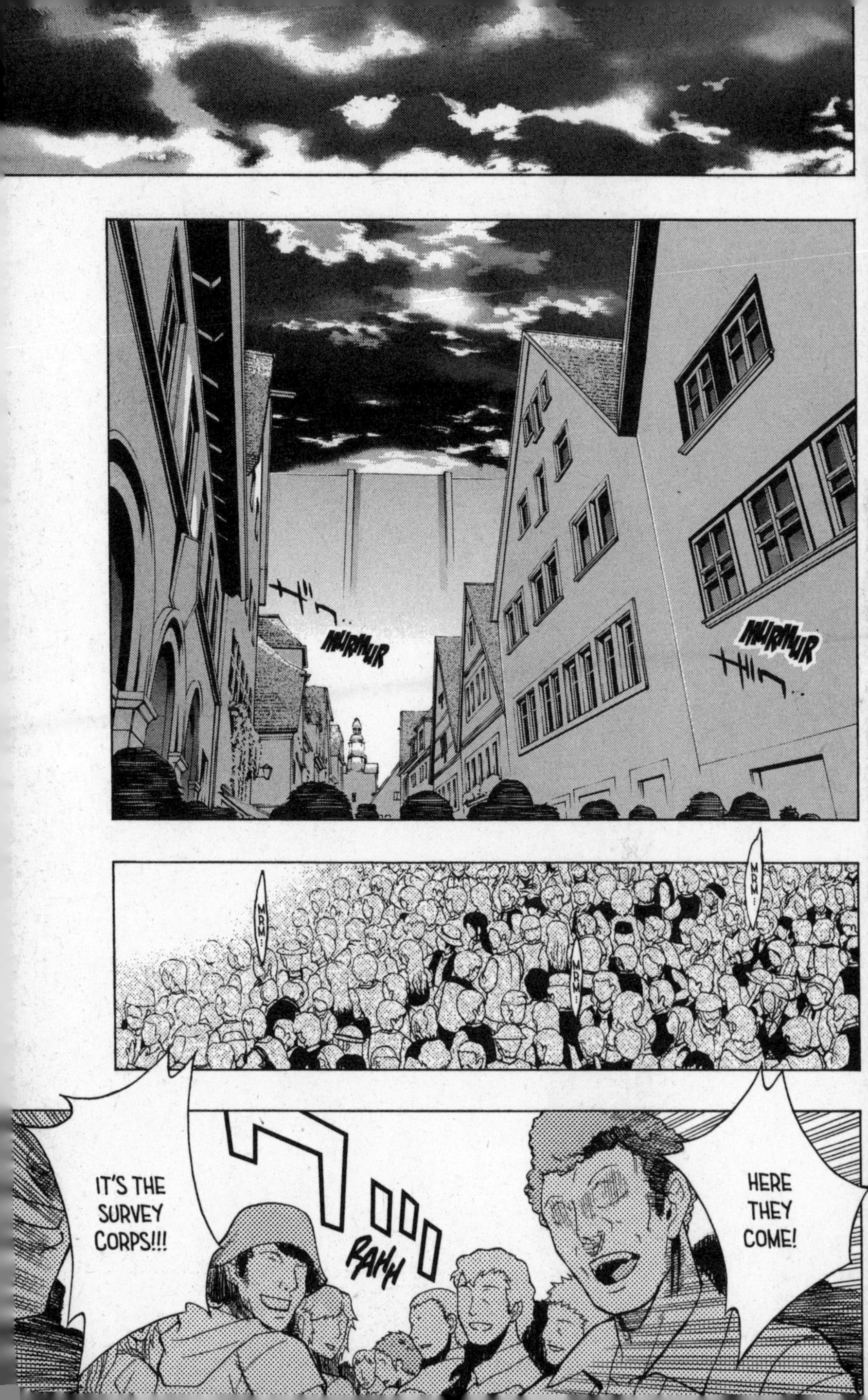

MURMUR
MURMUR
MRM!
MRM!
MRM!
HERE THEY COME!
RAHH
IT'S THE SURVEY CORPS!!!

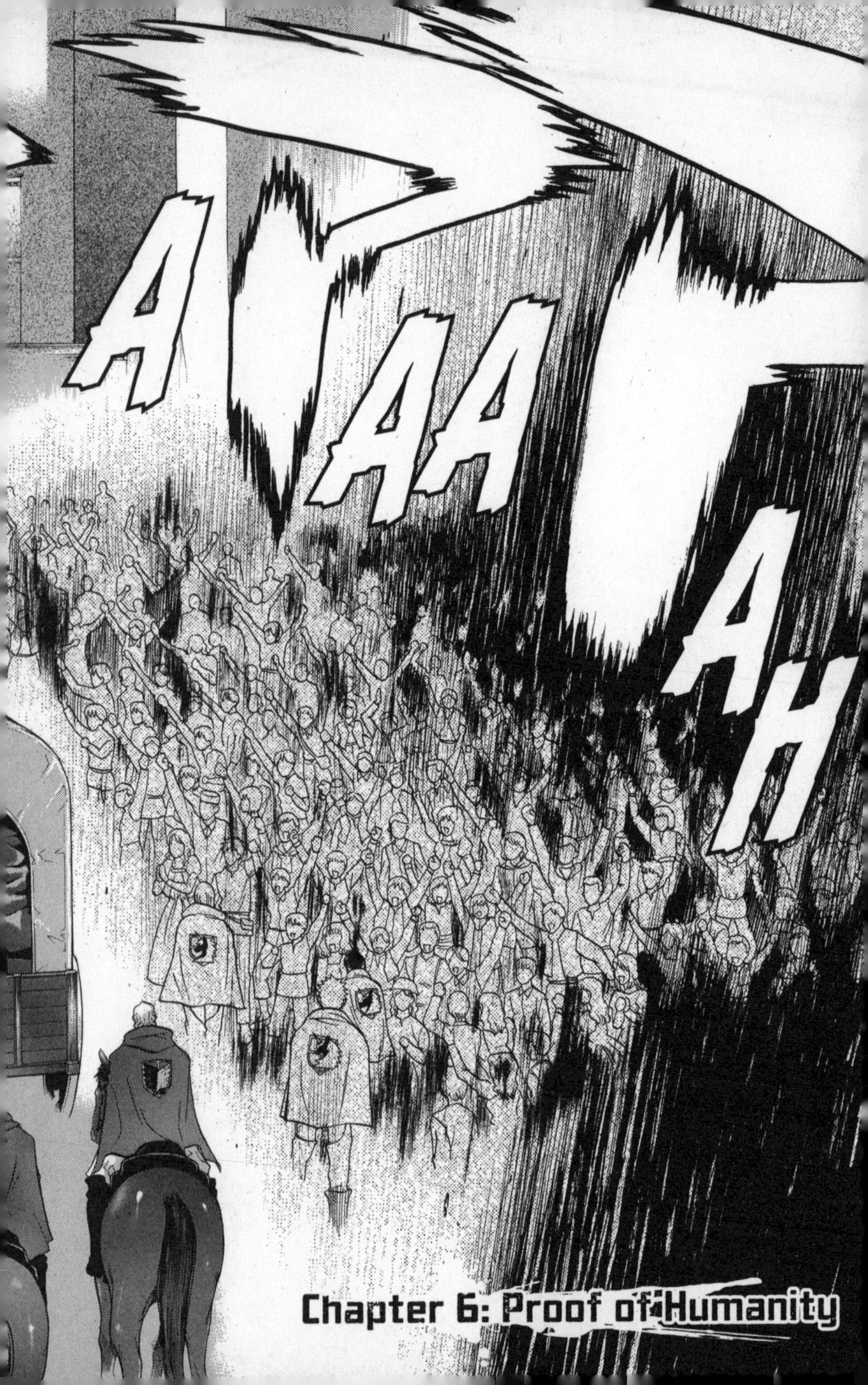
AAAAAH
Chapter 6: Proof of Humanity

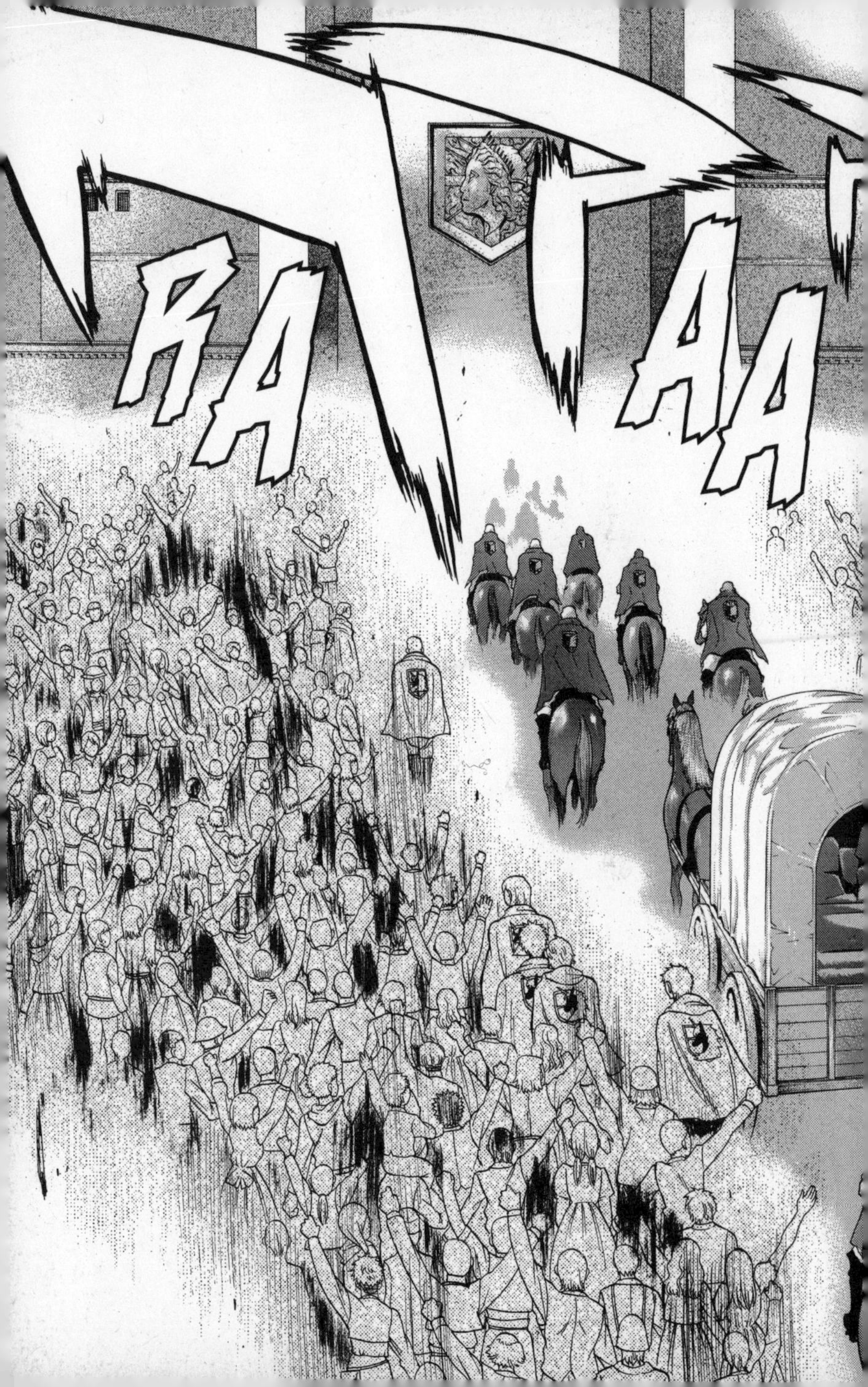

VRATTRAAAT

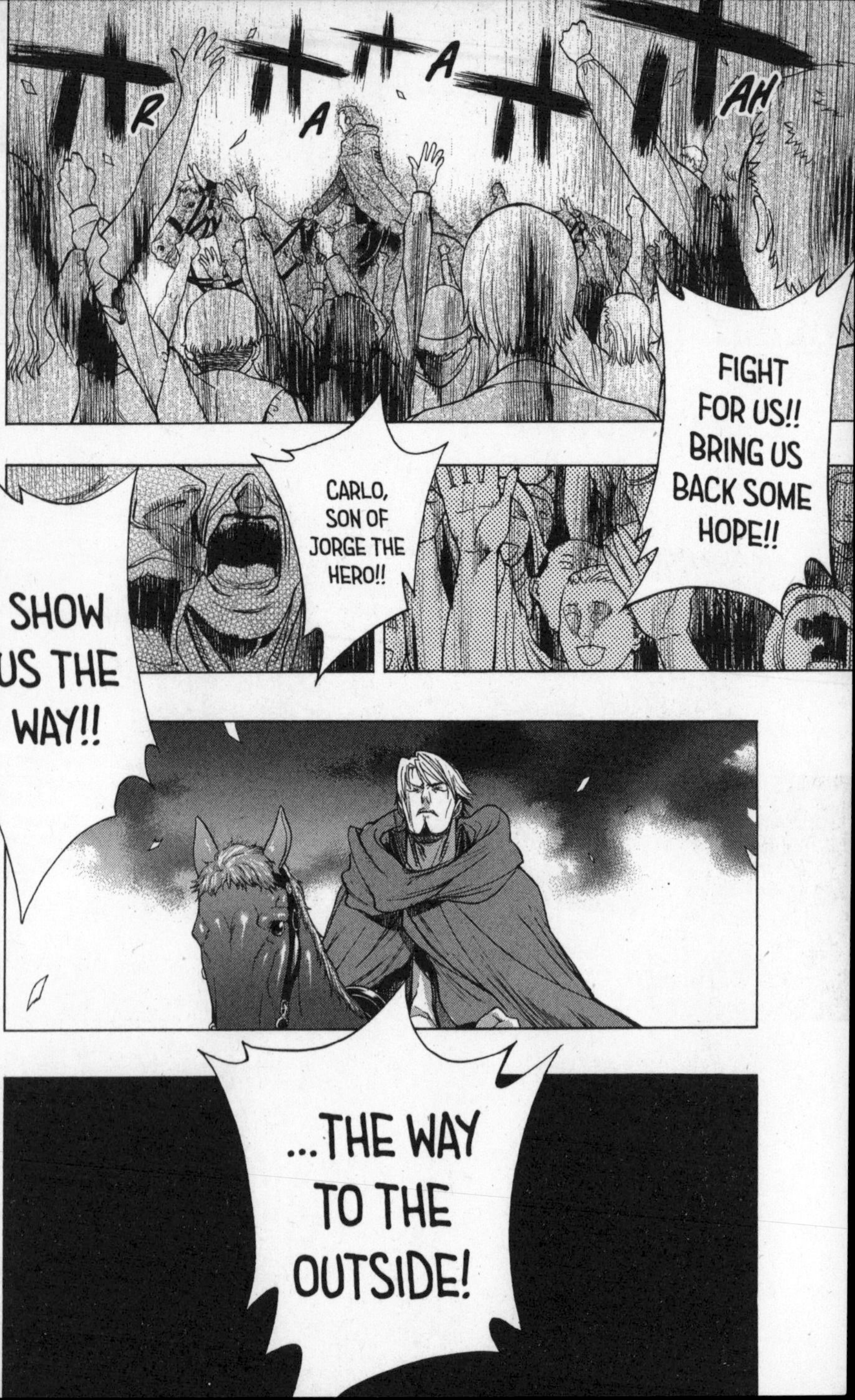
R
A
A
AH
FIGHT FOR US!! BRING US BACK SOME HOPE!!
CARLO, SON OF JORGE THE HERO!!
SHOW US THE WAY!!
...THE WAY TO THE OUTSIDE!

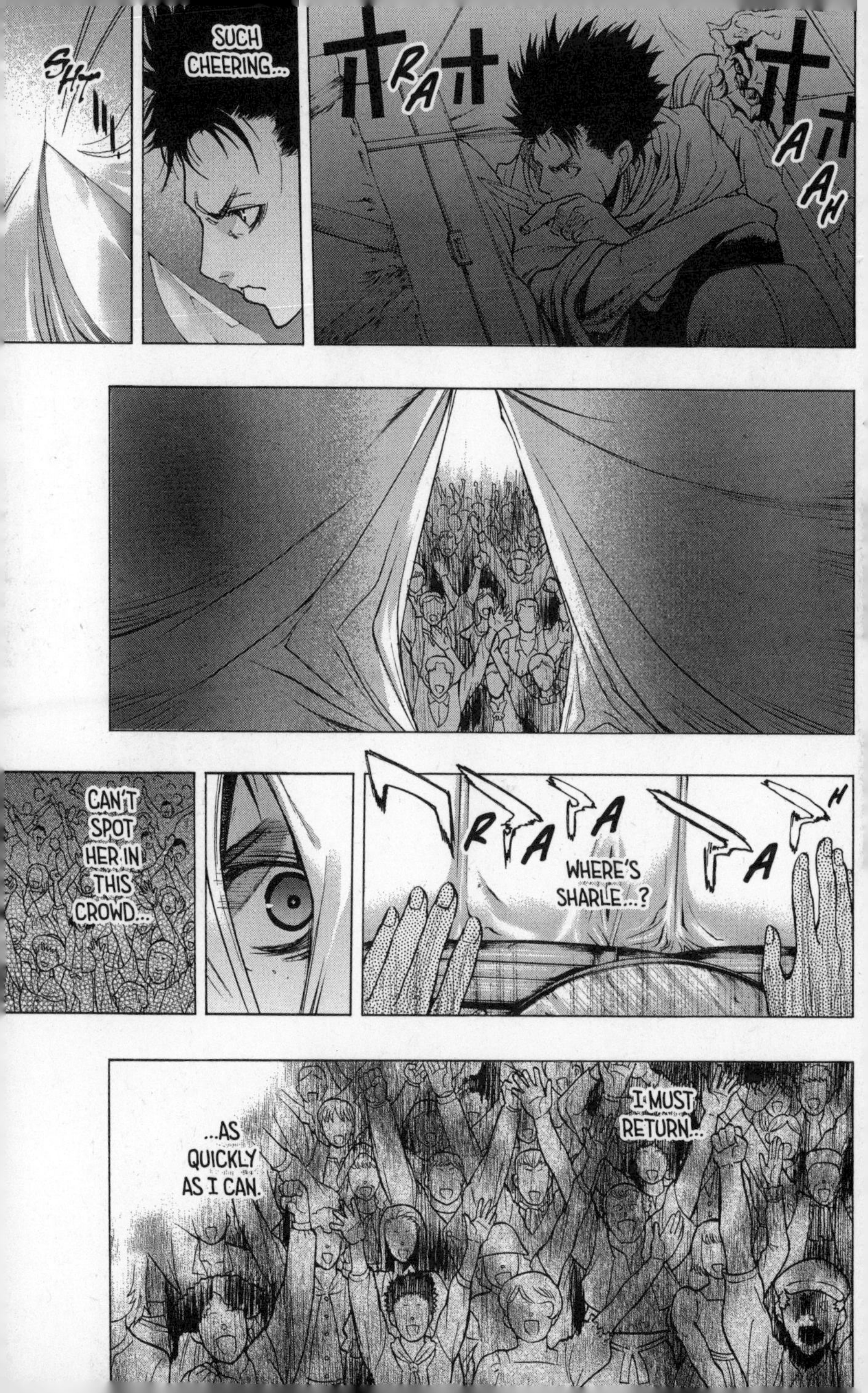

SUCH CHEERING...
WHERE'S SHARLE...?
CAN'T SPOT HER IN THIS CROWD...
I MUST RETURN...
...AS QUICKLY AS I CAN.

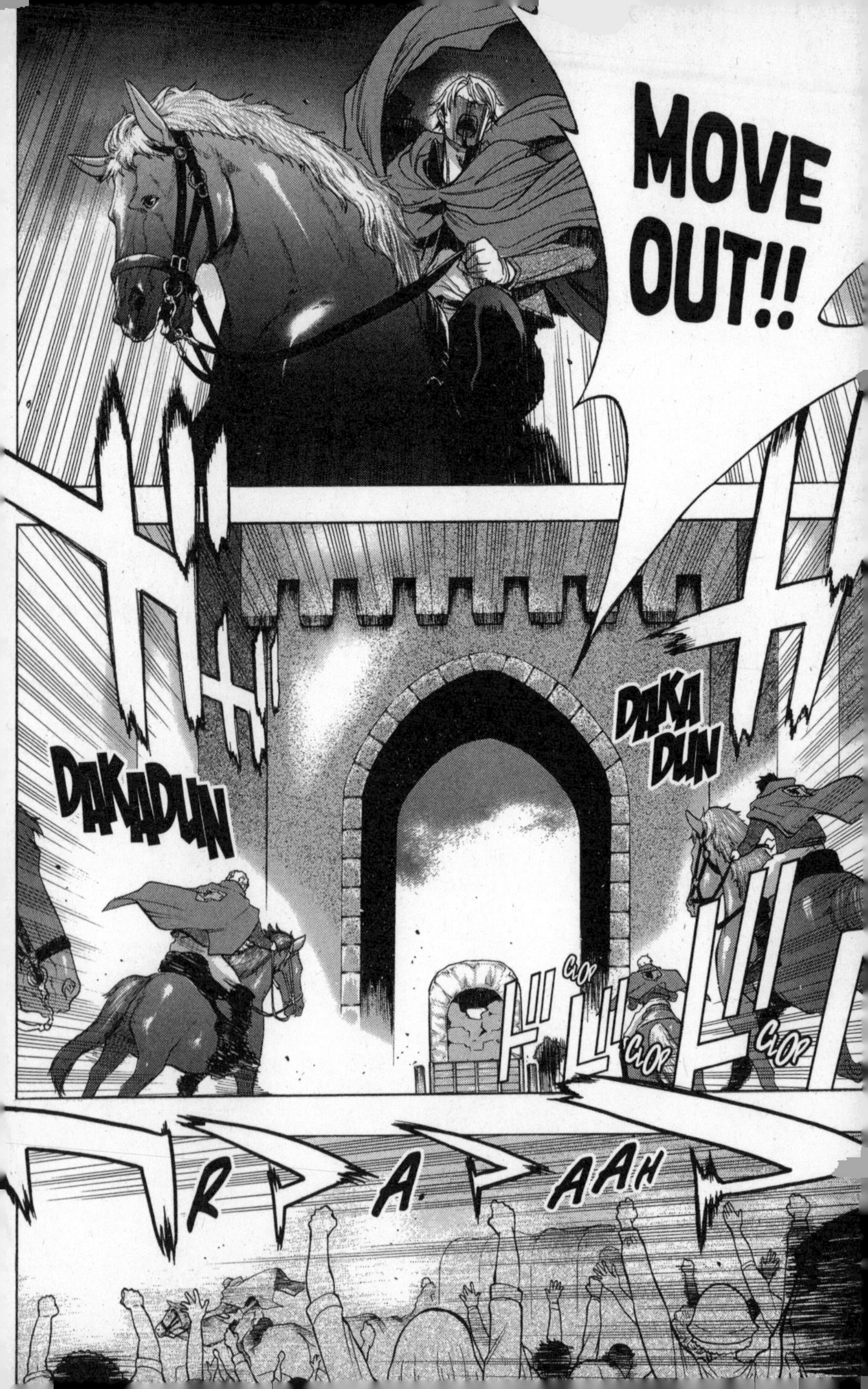
MOVE OUT!!
DAKA DUN
DAKADUN
CLOP
CLOP
CLOP
R A AAH

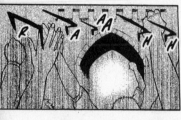

R A A H H

HE'LL
BE ALL
RIGHT...
WON'T
HE?

GR R RR MM M

STILL...

...I CAN'T
HELP BUT
FEEL HE
SHOULDN'T
HAVE
GONE...

ZUH-

DMM

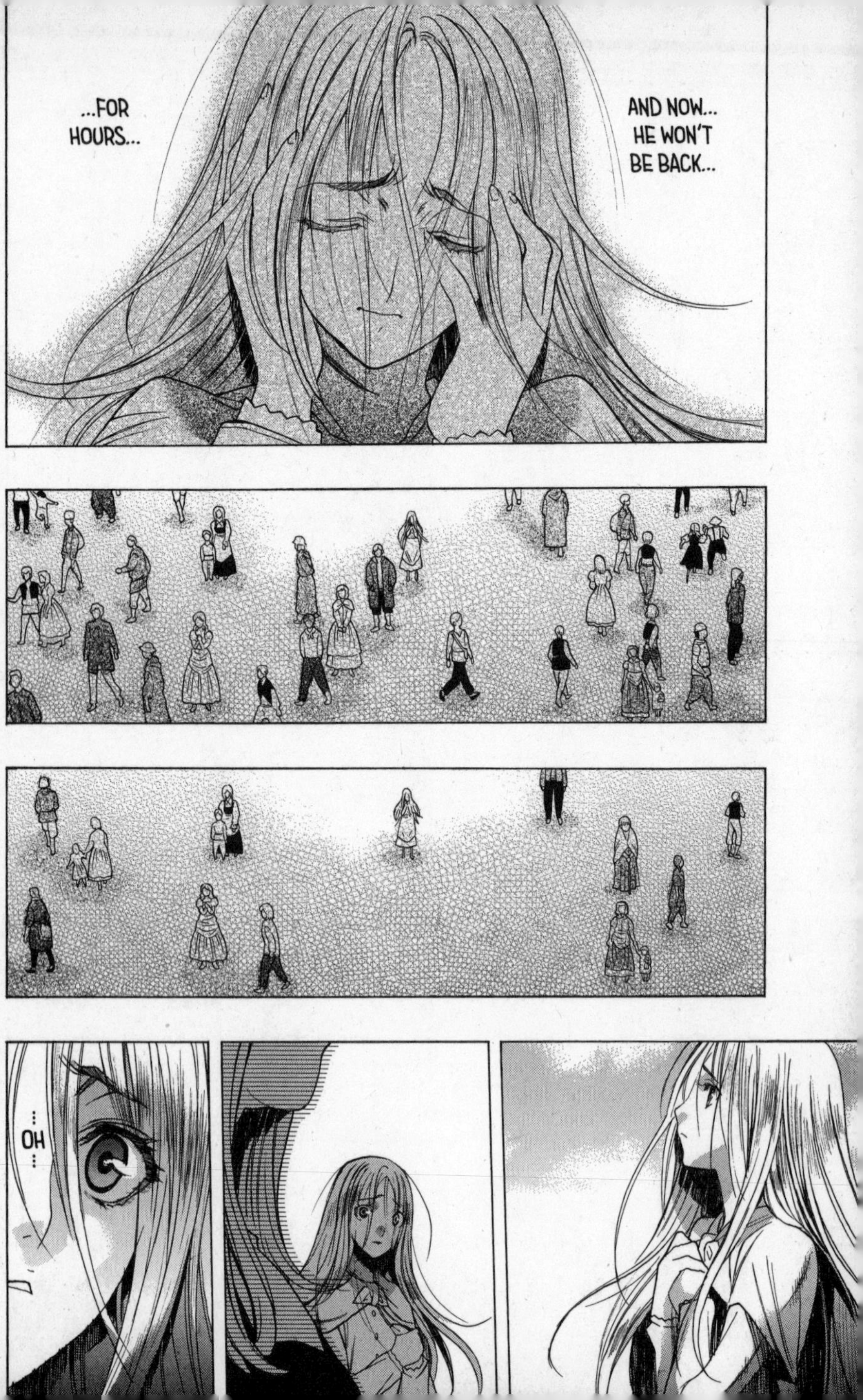
AND NOW... HE WON'T BE BACK...
...FOR HOURS...
...OH...

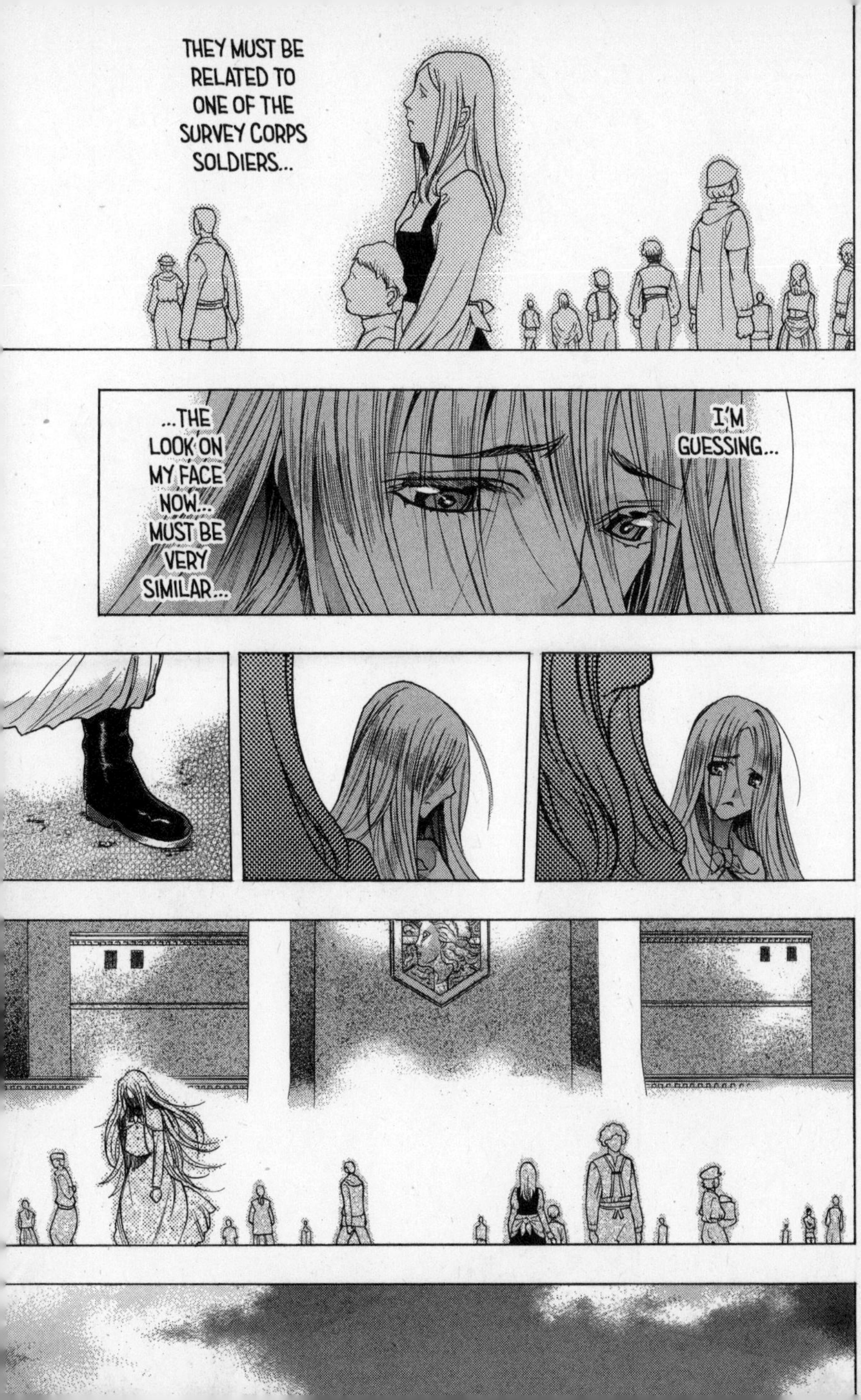
THEY MUST BE RELATED TO ONE OF THE SURVEY CORPS SOLDIERS...
I'M GUESSING...
...THE LOOK ON MY FACE NOW... MUST BE VERY SIMILAR...

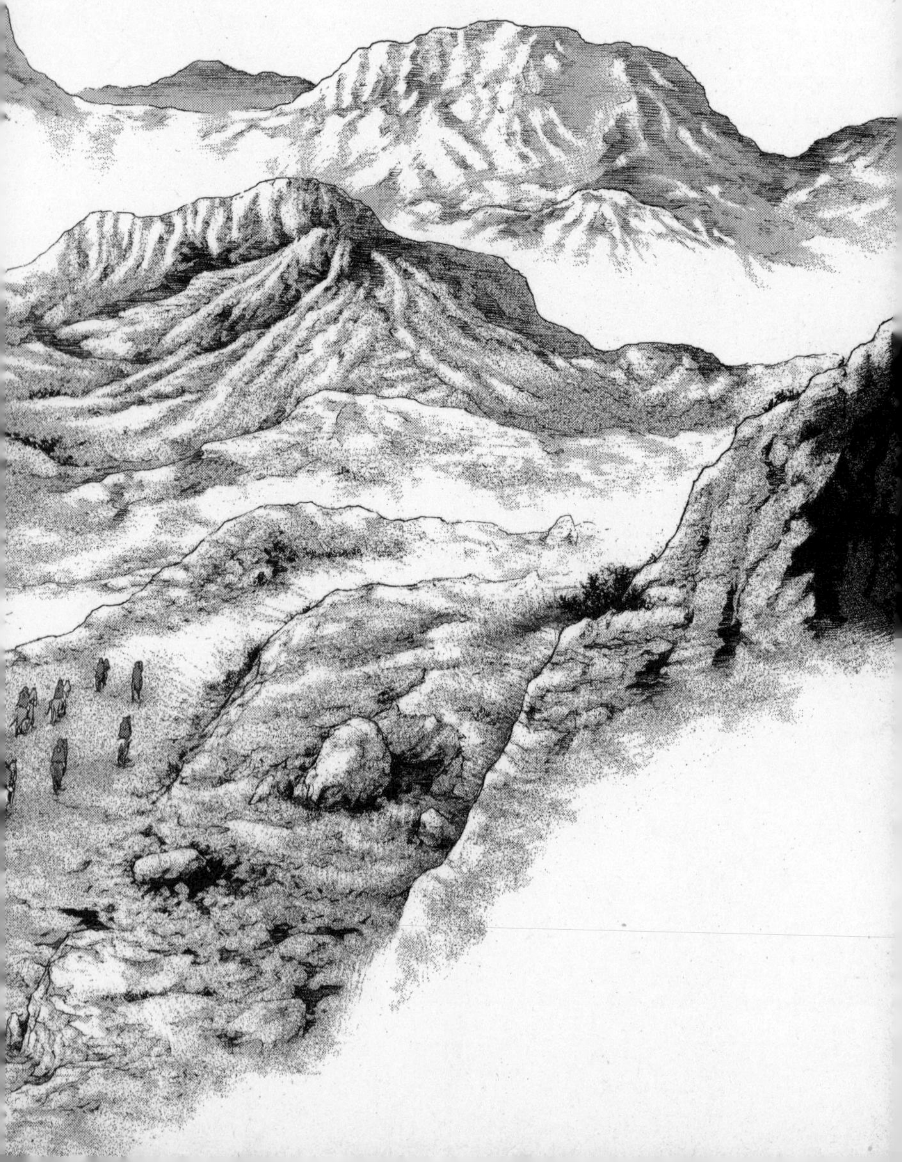

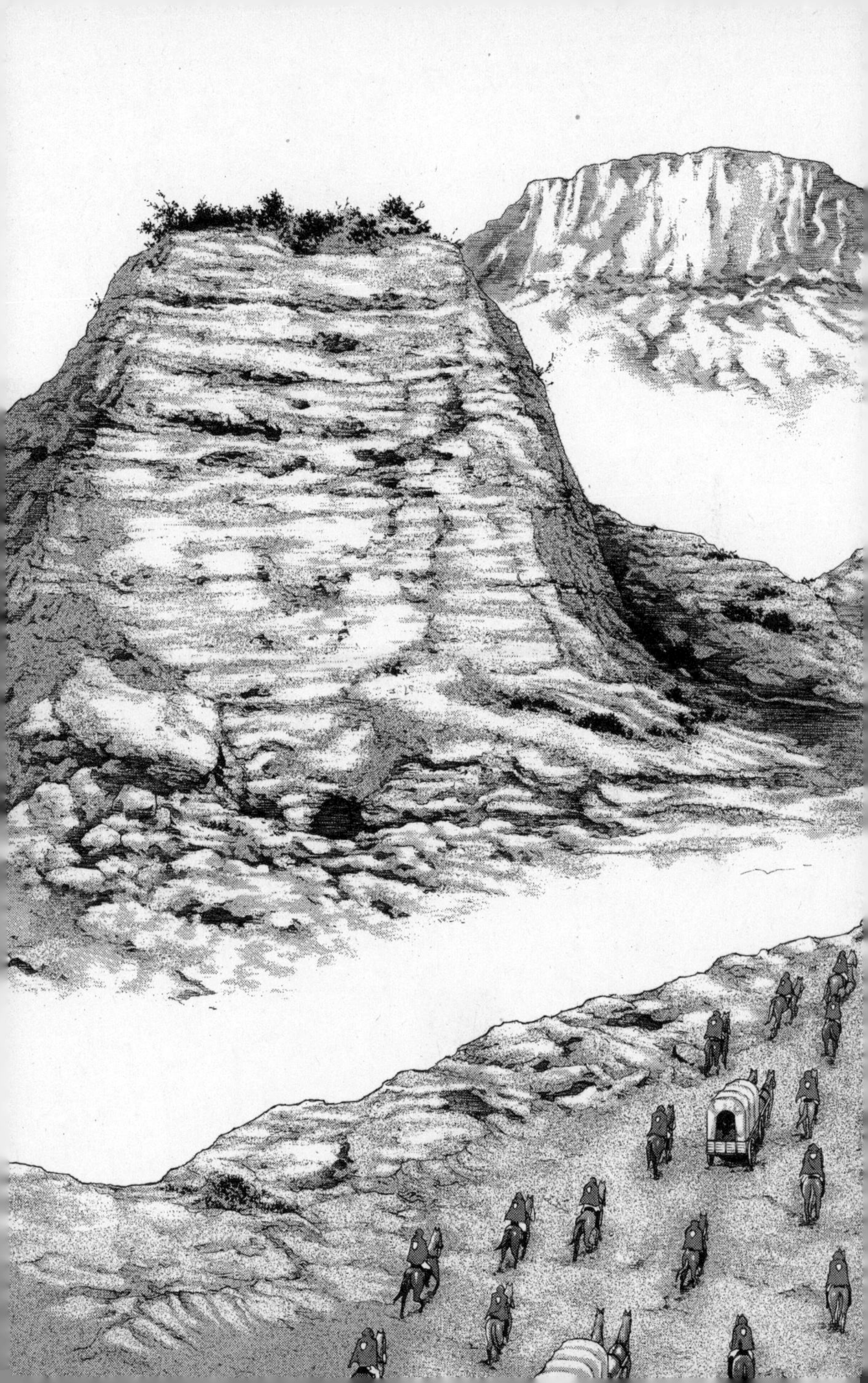

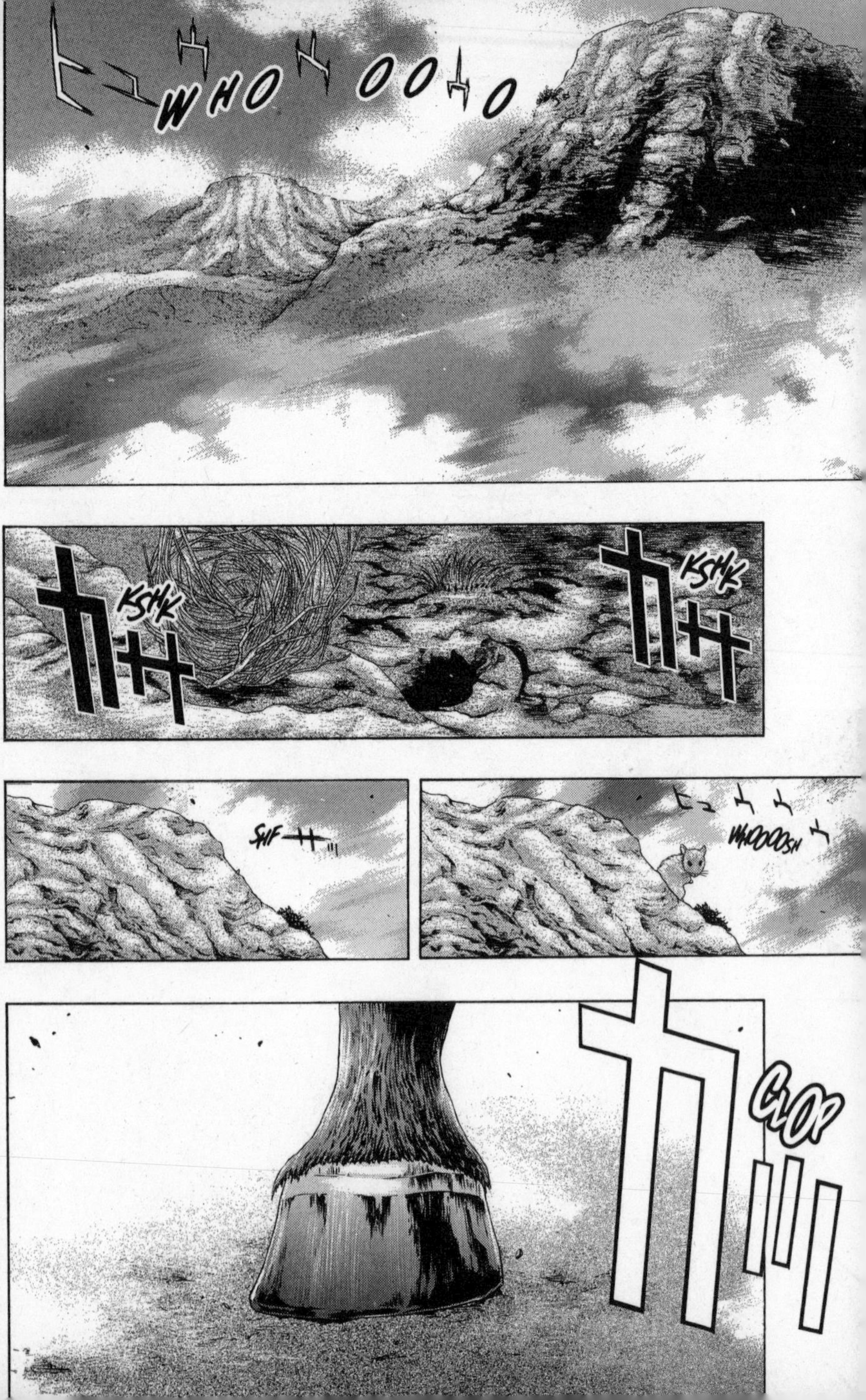
WHOOOO
KSHK
KSHK
WHOOOOSH
SHF
CLOP

KACLOP

KACLOP

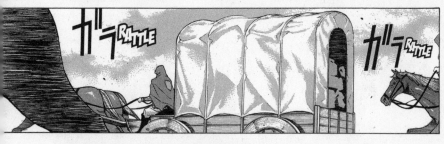

RATTLE

RATTLE

WE HAVEN'T SEEN ANY TITANS...

IS THAT... A GUN...?

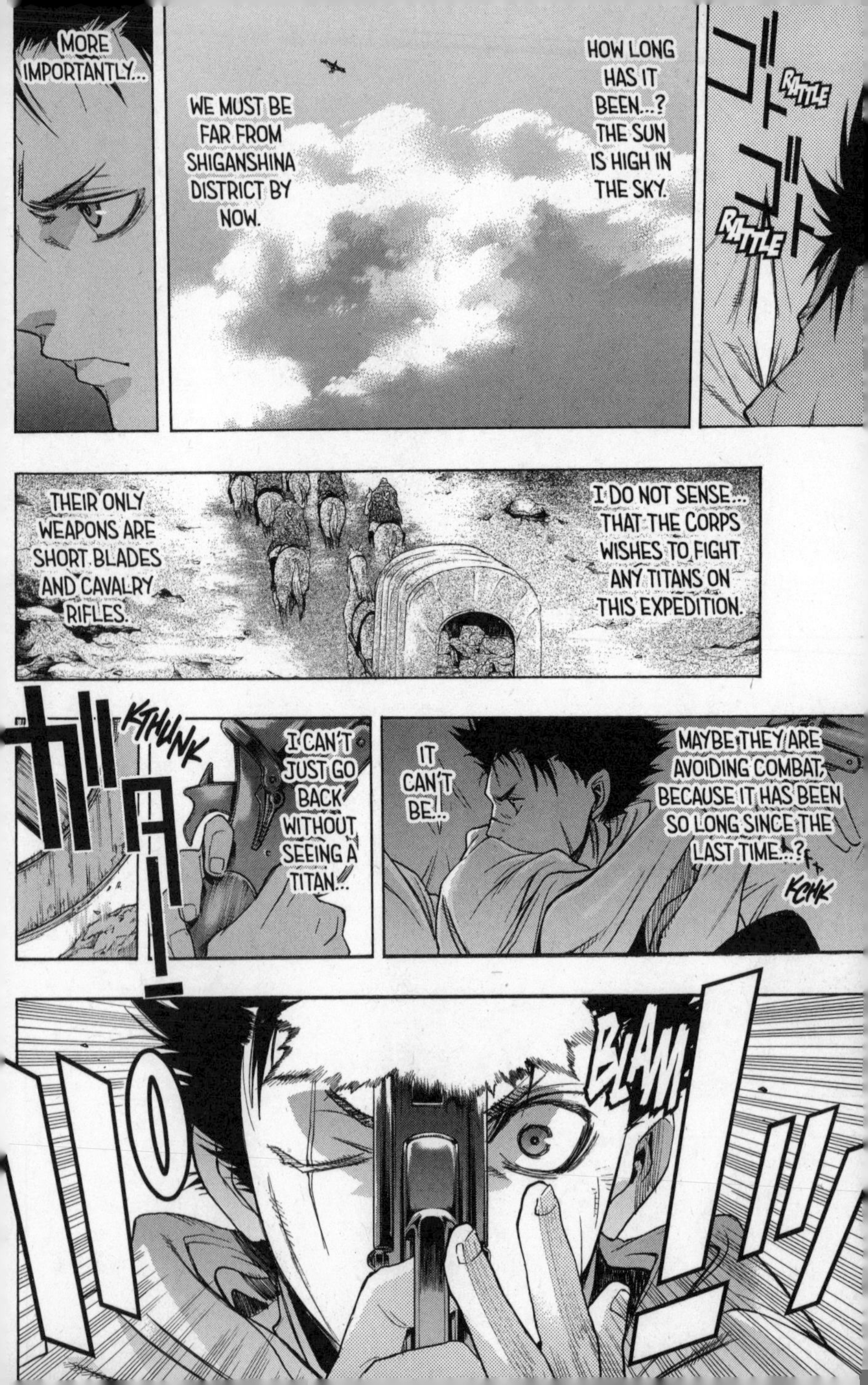
RATTLE
RATTLE
HOW LONG HAS IT BEEN...? THE SUN IS HIGH IN THE SKY.
WE MUST BE FAR FROM SHIGANSHINA DISTRICT BY NOW.
MORE IMPORTANTLY...
I DO NOT SENSE... THAT THE CORPS WISHES TO FIGHT ANY TITANS ON THIS EXPEDITION.
THEIR ONLY WEAPONS ARE SHORT BLADES AND CAVALRY RIFLES.
MAYBE THEY ARE AVOIDING COMBAT, BECAUSE IT HAS BEEN SO LONG SINCE THE LAST TIME...?
KCHK
IT CAN'T BE...
I CAN'T JUST GO BACK WITHOUT SEEING A TITAN...
KTHUNK
BLAM

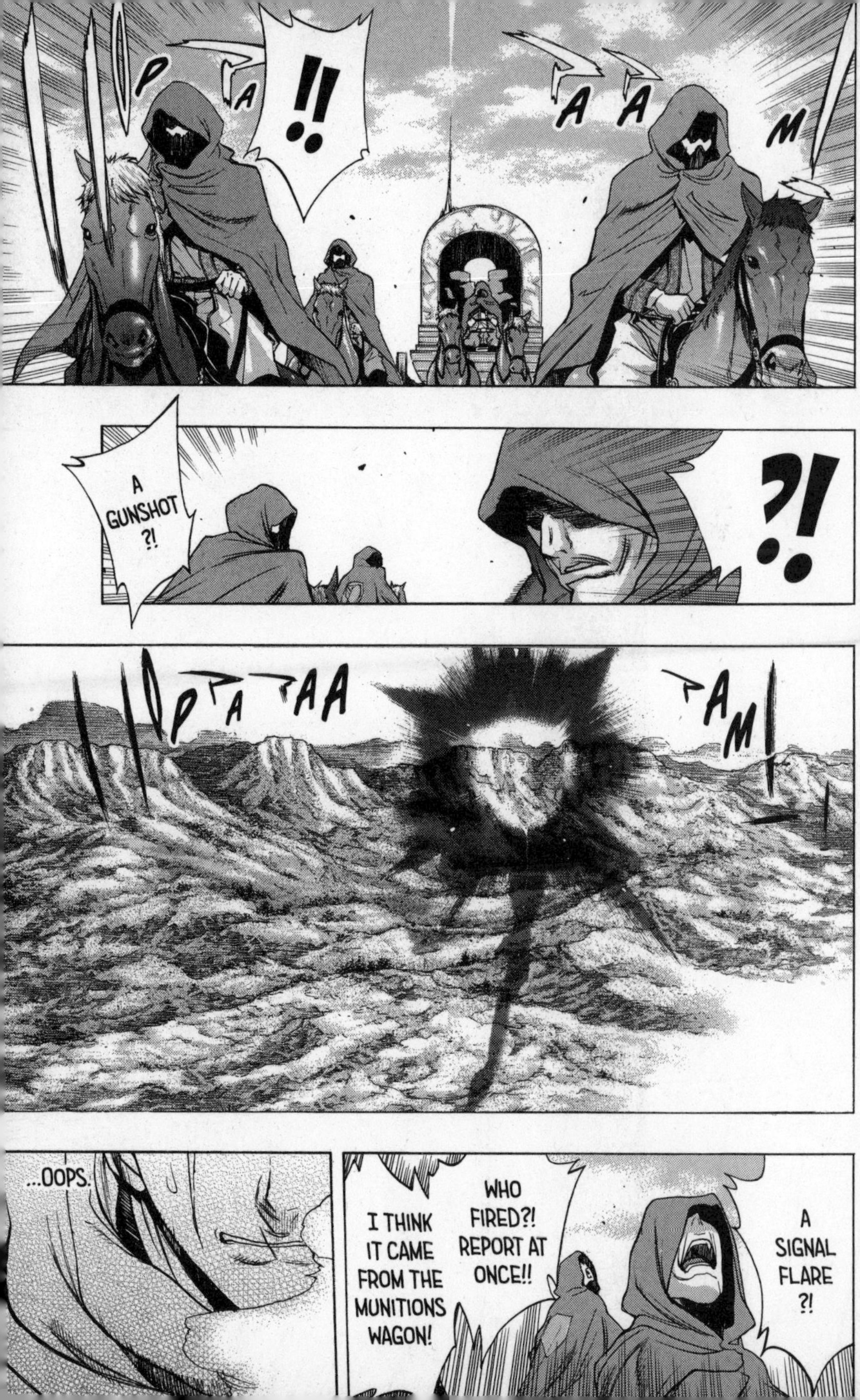

PA
!!
AAM
?!
A GUNSHOT ?!
PPAAA
AM
A SIGNAL FLARE ?!
WHO FIRED?! REPORT AT ONCE!!
I THINK IT CAME FROM THE MUNITIONS WAGON!
...OOPS.

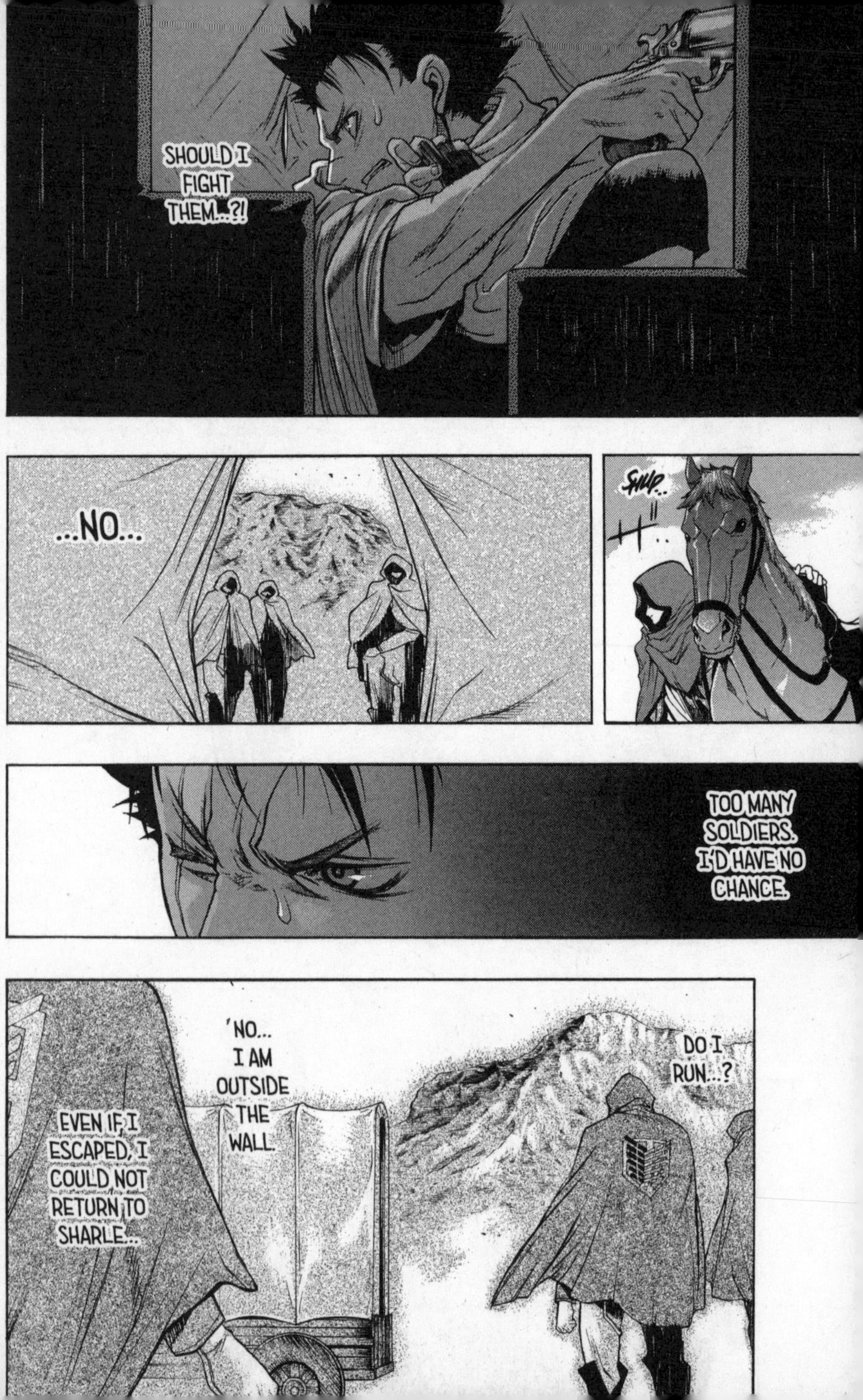
SHOULD I FIGHT THEM...?!
SHUP...
...NO...
TOO MANY SOLDIERS. I'D HAVE NO CHANCE.
DO I RUN...?
NO... I AM OUTSIDE THE WALL.
EVEN IF I ESCAPED, I COULD NOT RETURN TO SHARLE...

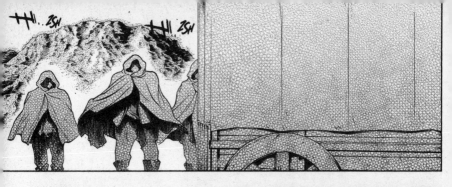

IF I'M GOING TO BE CAUGHT ANYWAY, THEN...

HOP

!

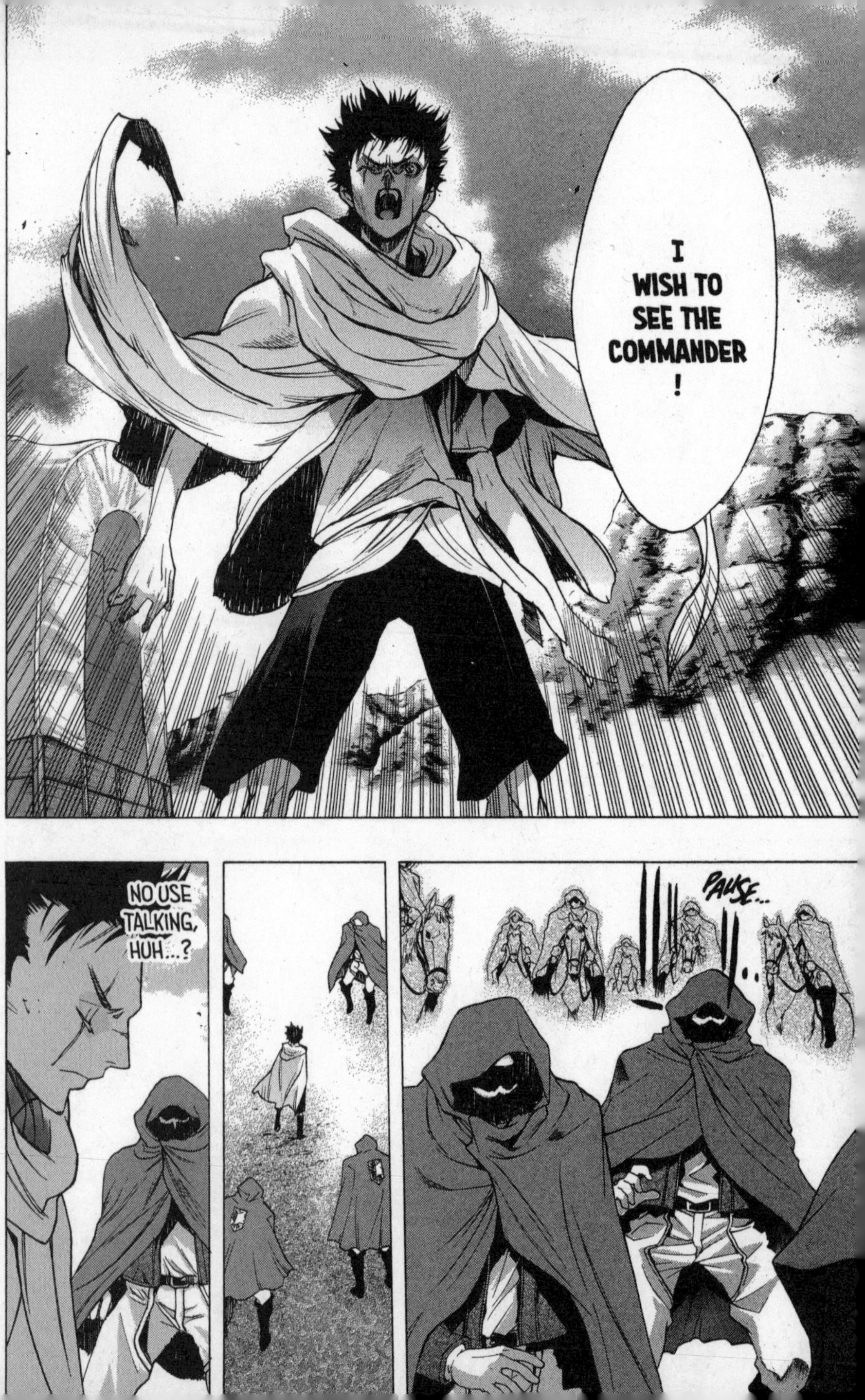
I WISH TO SEE THE COMMANDER !
PAUSE...
...
NO USE TALKING, HUH...?

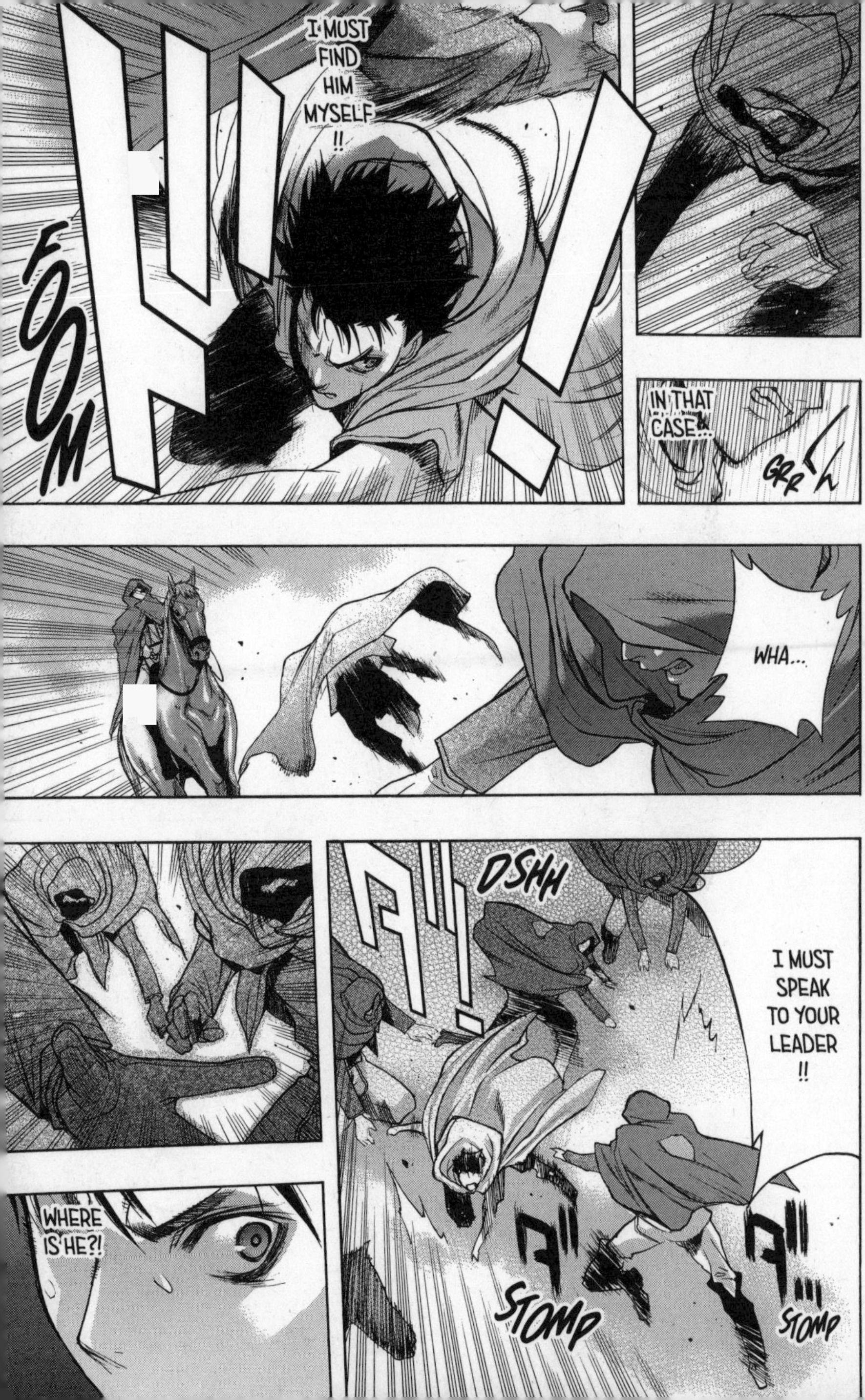
IN THAT CASE...
GRR
I MUST FIND HIM MYSELF!!
FOOM
WHA...
DSHH
I MUST SPEAK TO YOUR LEADER!!
STOMP
STOMP
WHERE IS HE?!

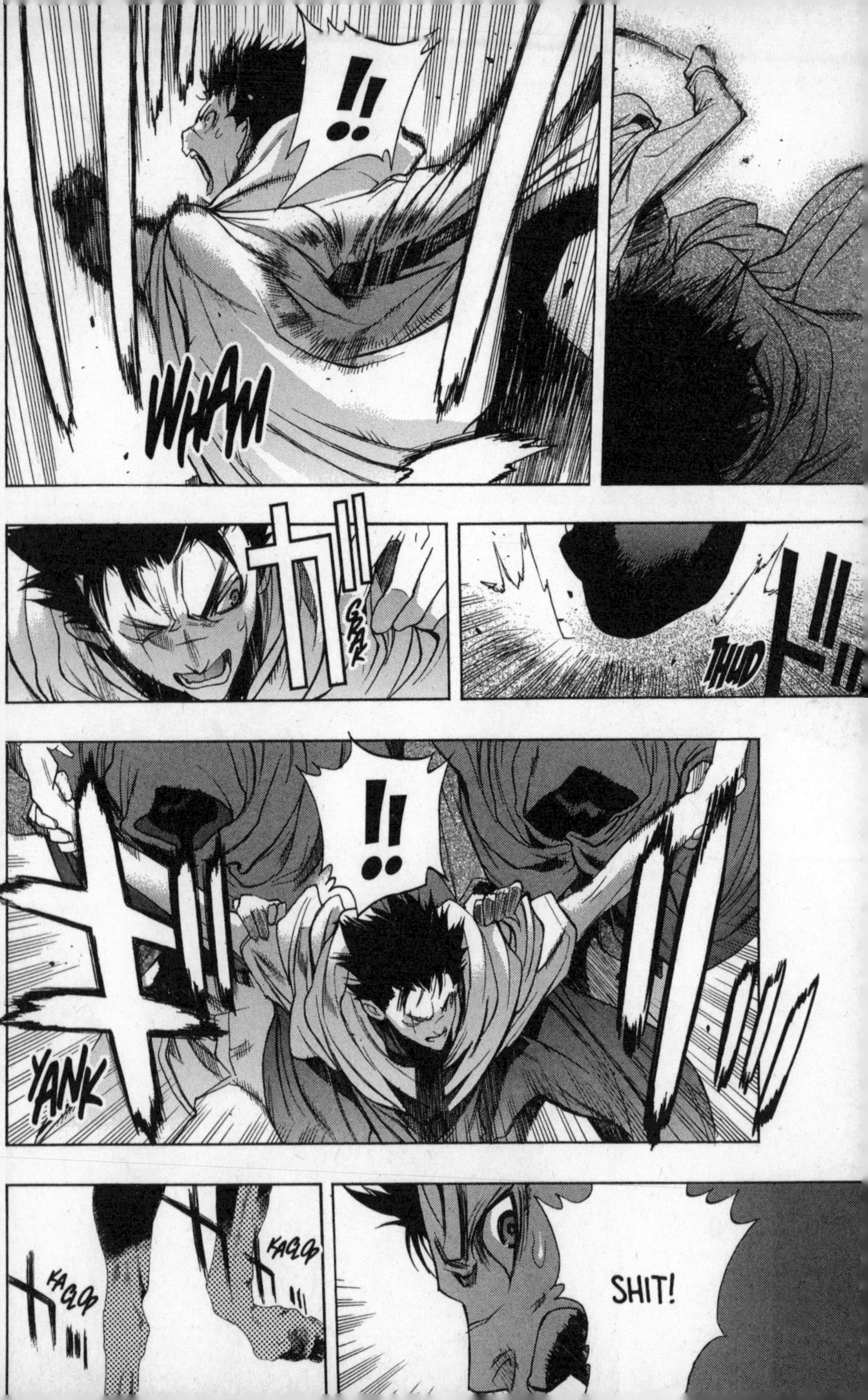
!!
WHAM
THUD
GRAB
!!
YANK
SHIT!
KACLOP
KACLOP

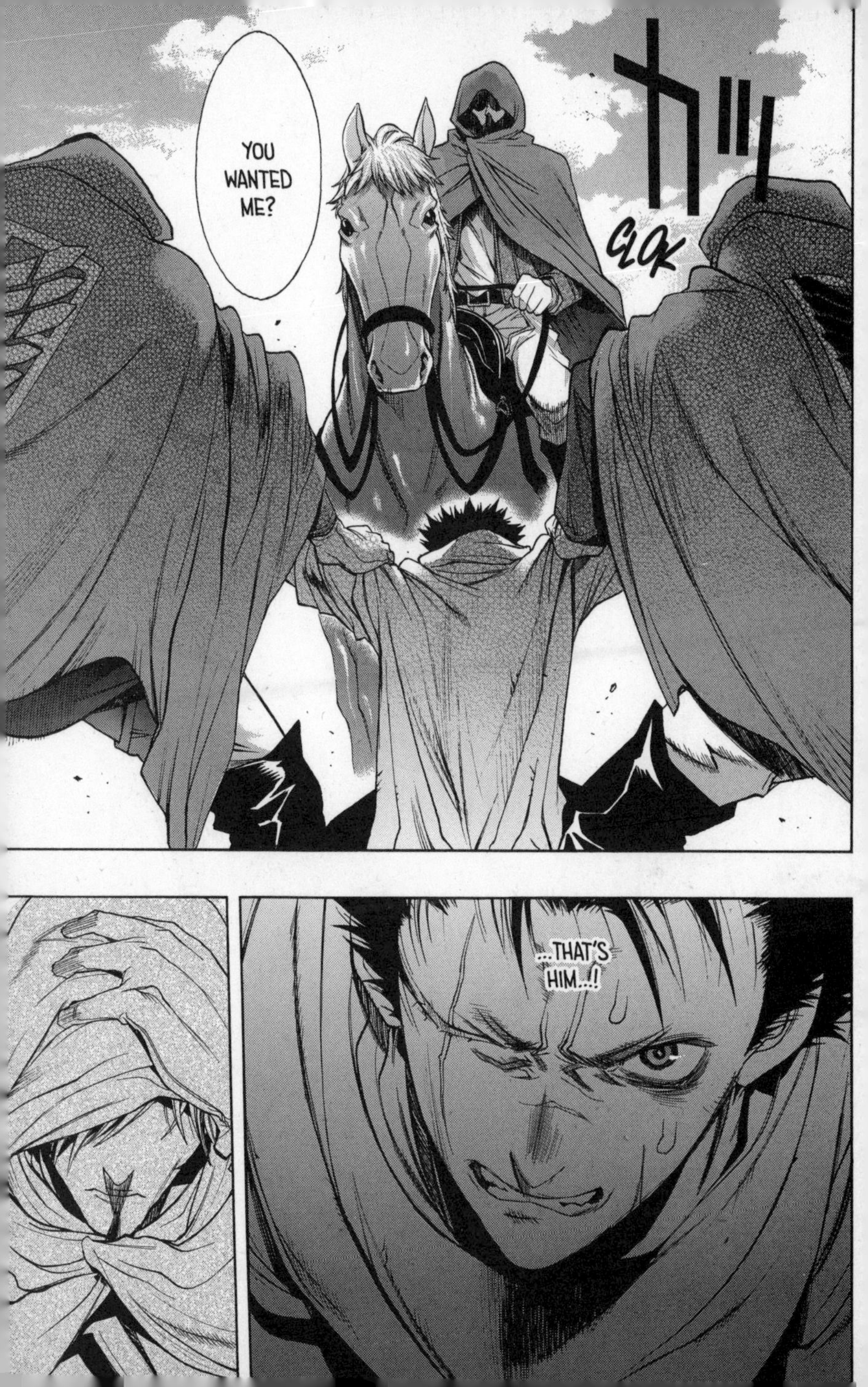
ガッ
CLOK
YOU WANTED ME?
...THAT'S HIM...!

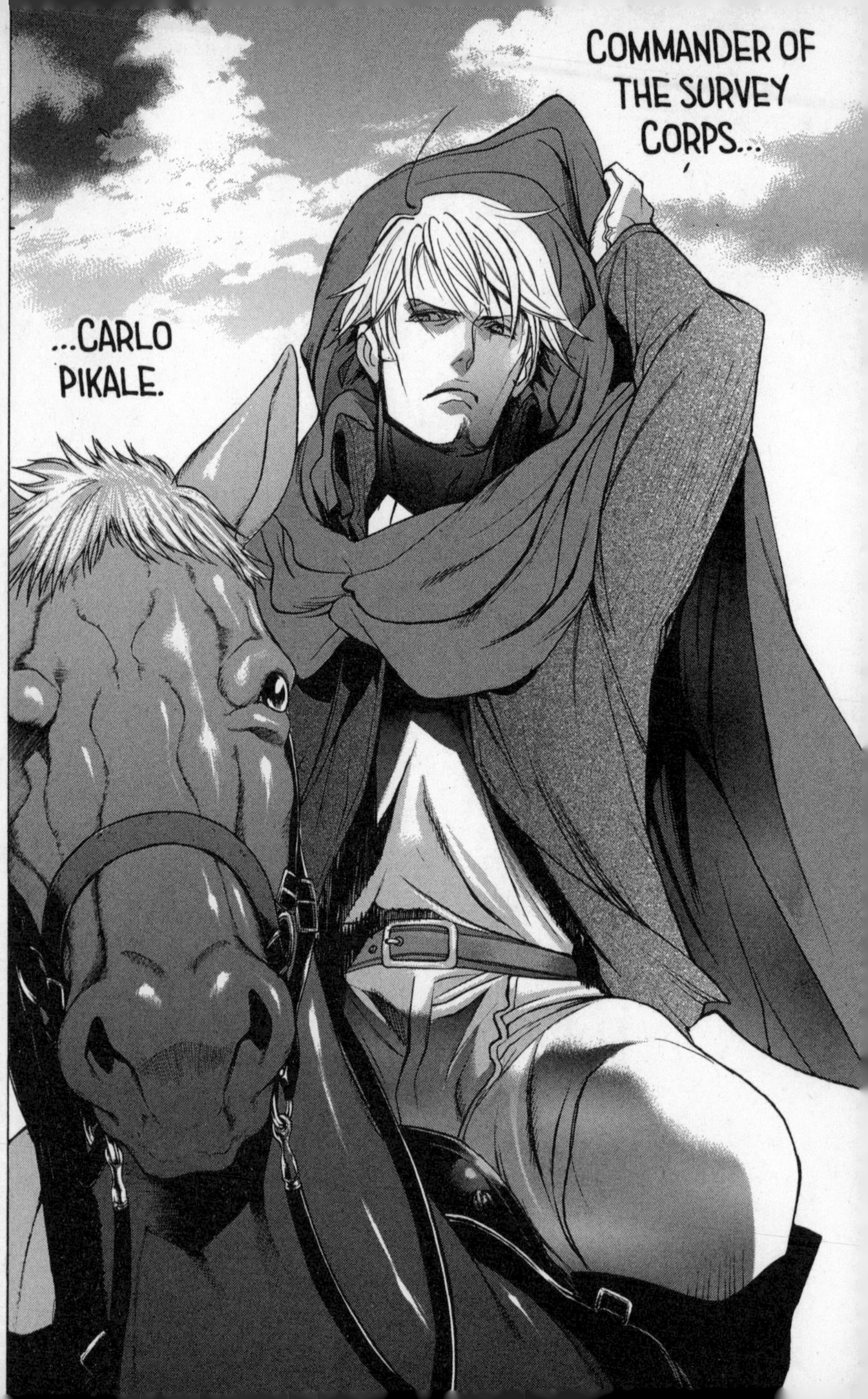
COMMANDER OF THE SURVEY CORPS...
...CARLO PIKALE.

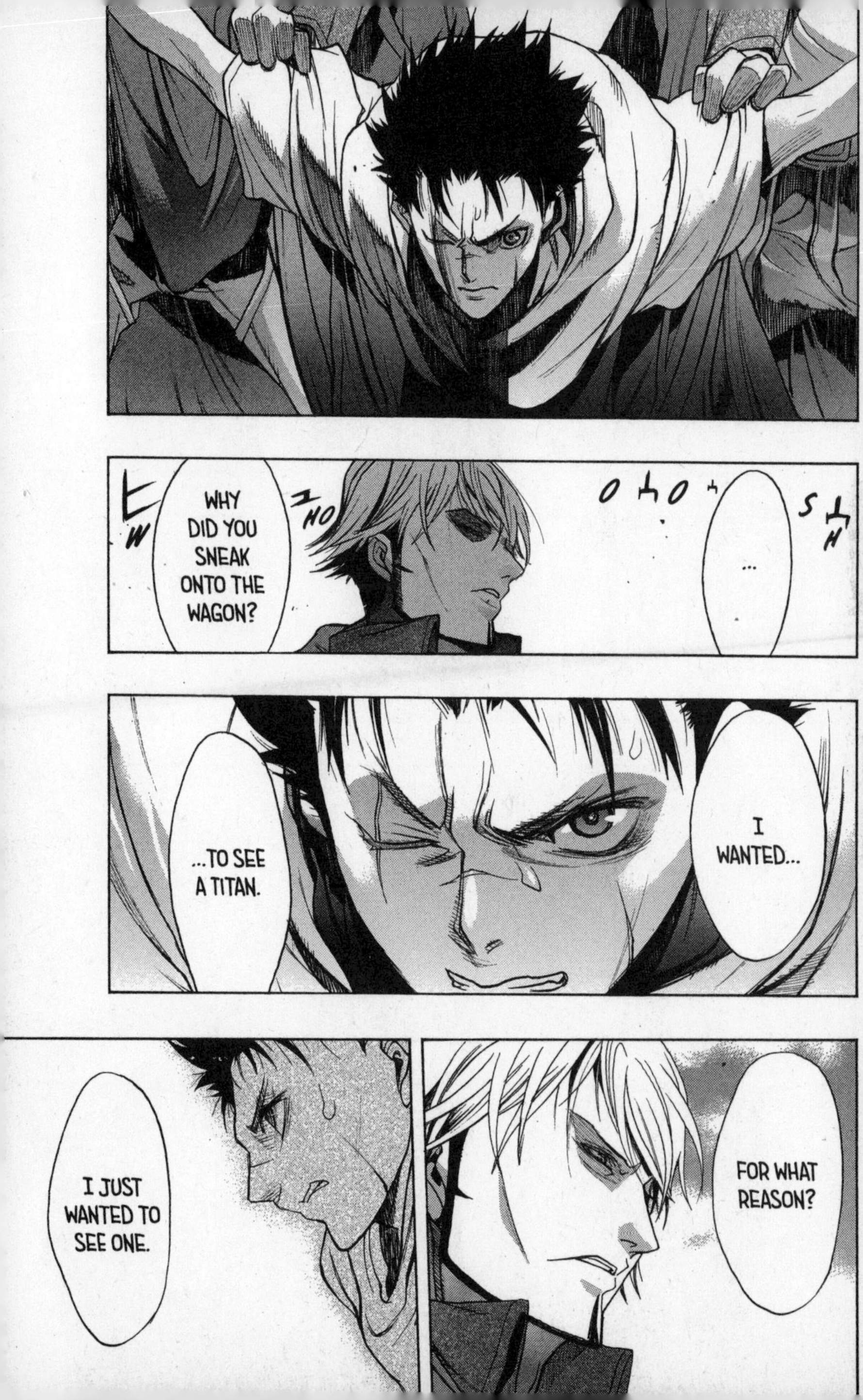
...
WHY DID YOU SNEAK ONTO THE WAGON?
I WANTED...
...TO SEE A TITAN.
FOR WHAT REASON?
I JUST WANTED TO SEE ONE.

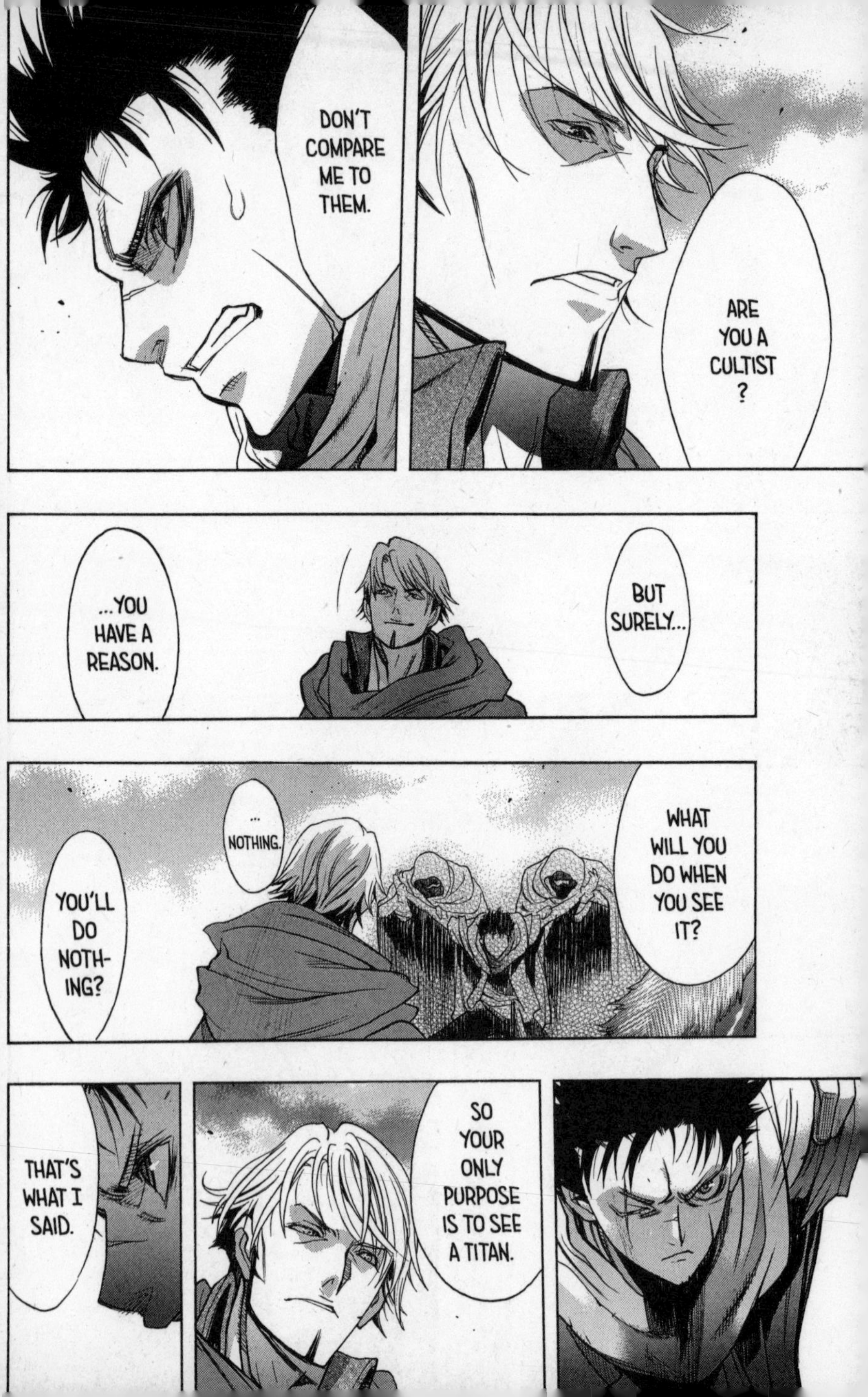

ARE YOU A CULTIST?
DON'T COMPARE ME TO THEM.
BUT SURELY...
...YOU HAVE A REASON.
WHAT WILL YOU DO WHEN YOU SEE IT?
... NOTHING.
YOU'LL DO NOTH-ING?
SO YOUR ONLY PURPOSE IS TO SEE A TITAN.
THAT'S WHAT I SAID.

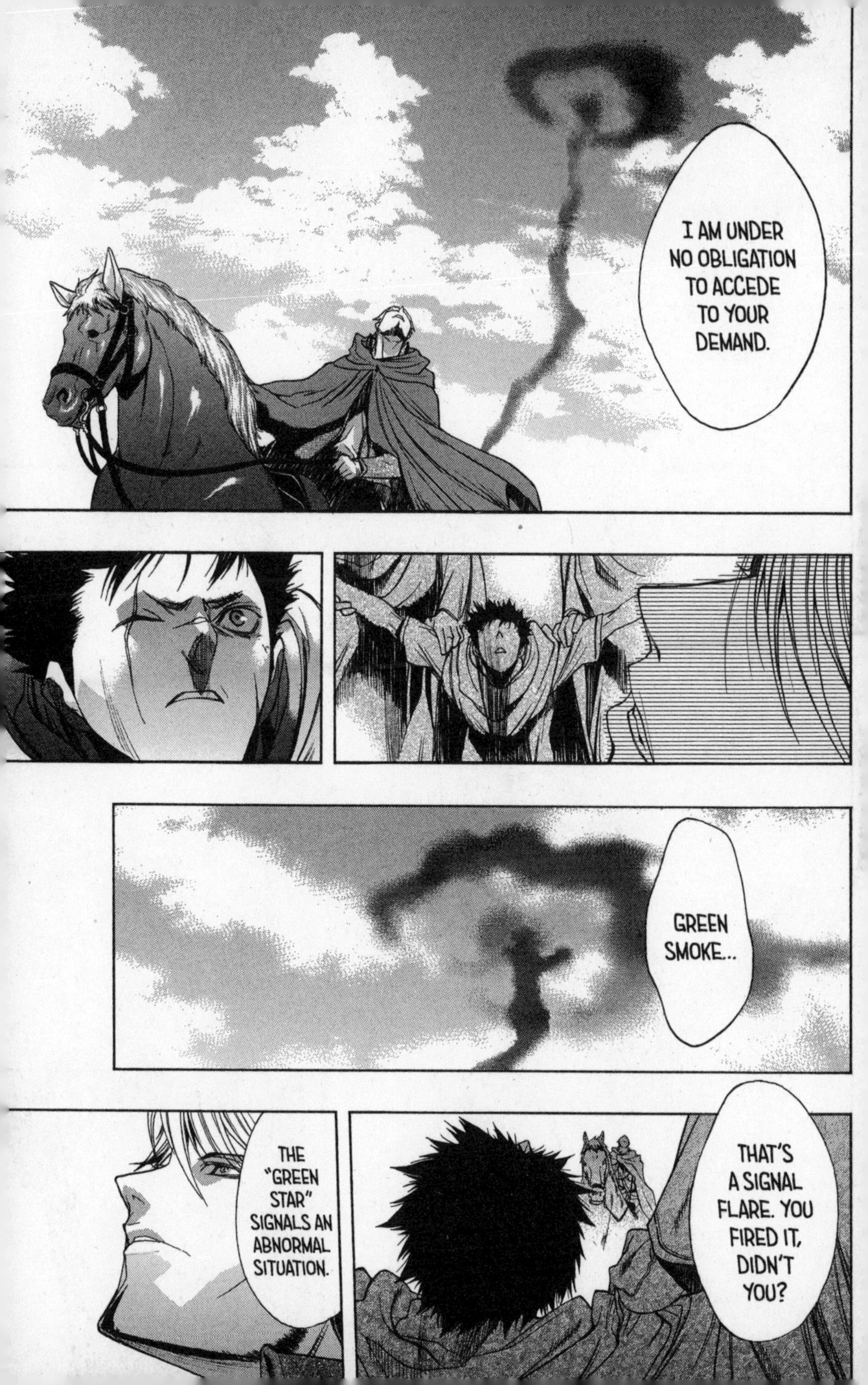
I AM UNDER NO OBLIGATION TO ACCEDE TO YOUR DEMAND.
GREEN SMOKE...
THAT'S A SIGNAL FLARE. YOU FIRED IT, DIDN'T YOU?
THE "GREEN STAR" SIGNALS AN ABNORMAL SITUATION.

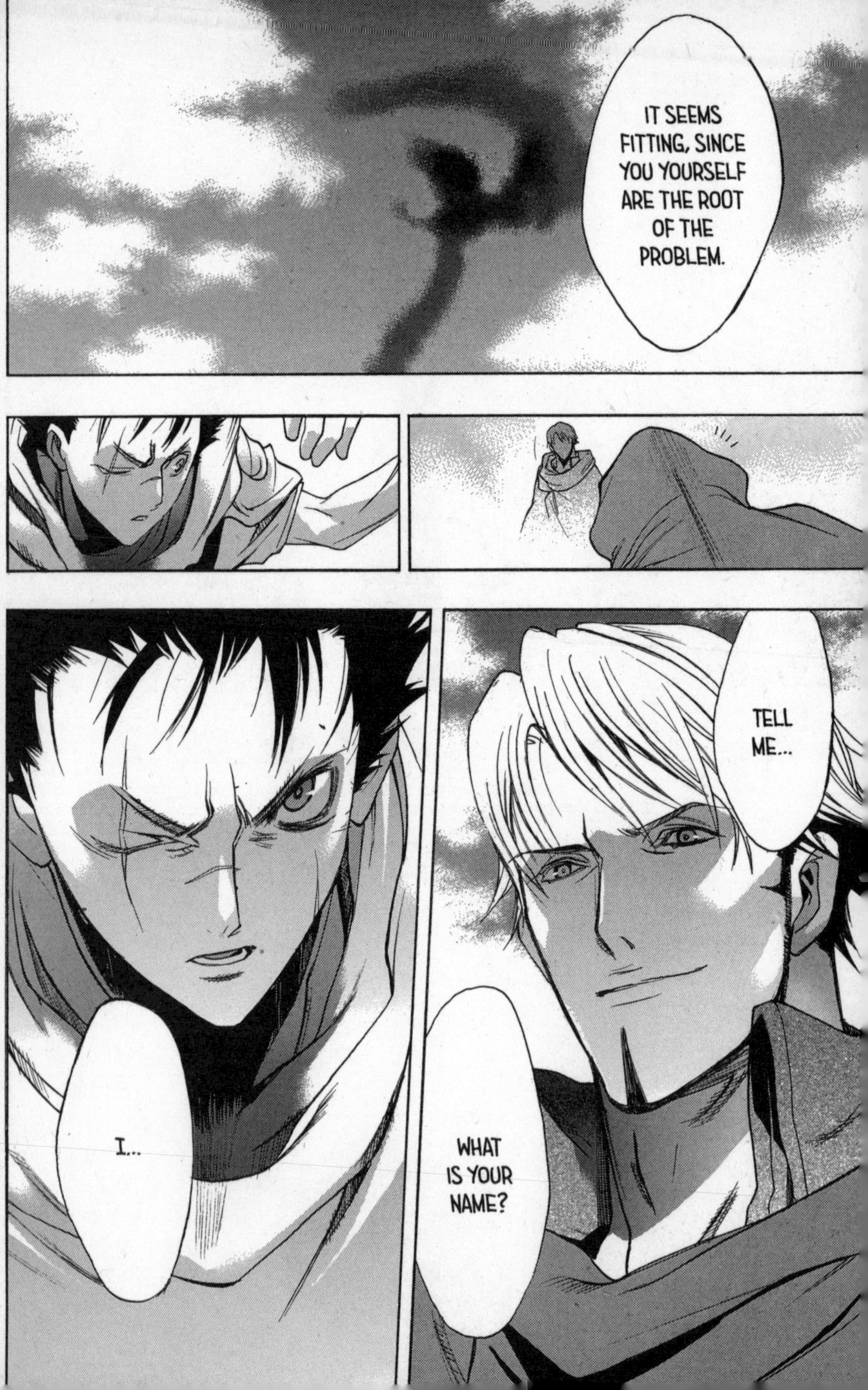
IT SEEMS FITTING, SINCE YOU YOURSELF ARE THE ROOT OF THE PROBLEM.
TELL ME...
WHAT IS YOUR NAME?
I...

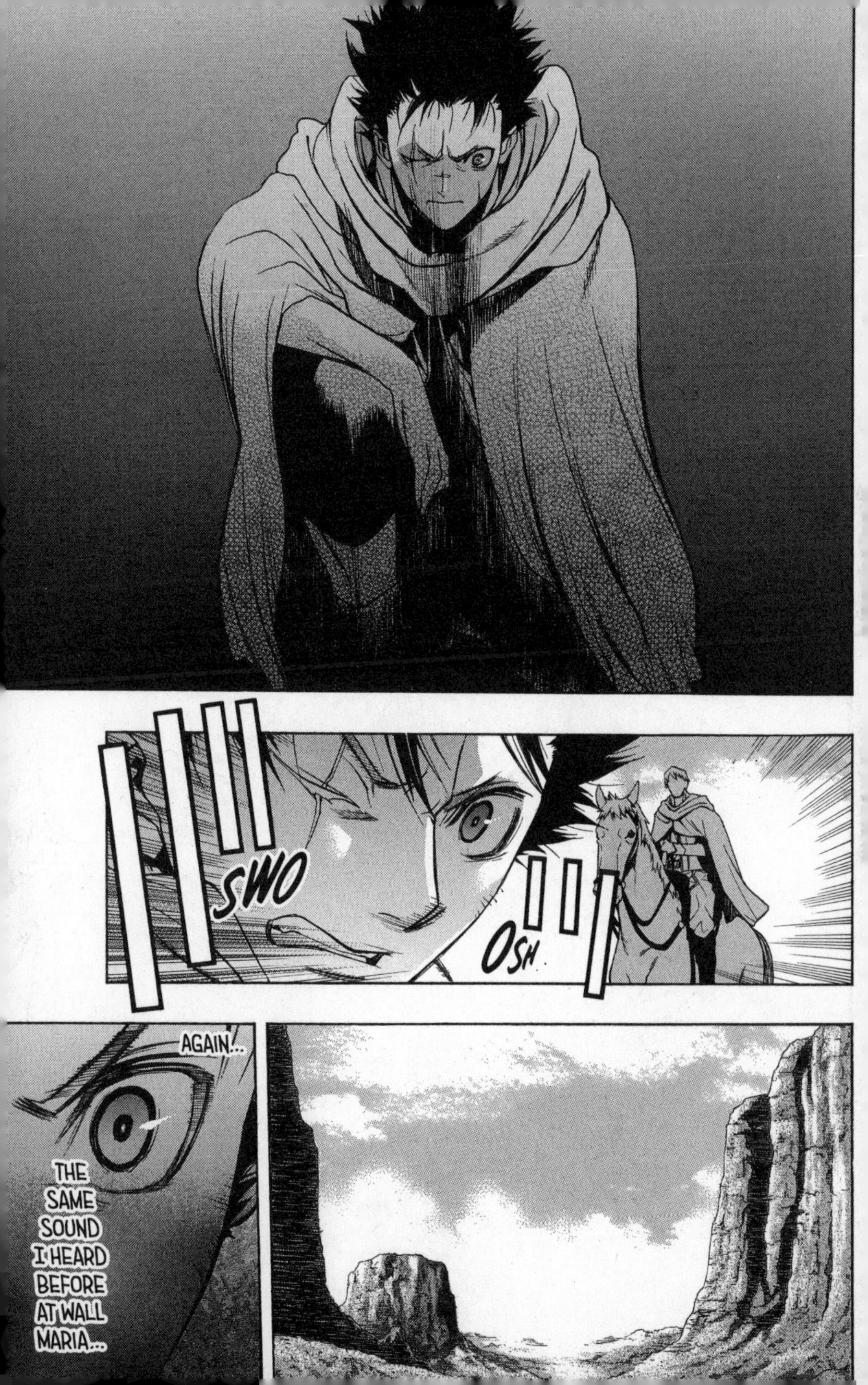
SWO
OSH.
AGAIN...
THE SAME SOUND I HEARD BEFORE AT WALL MARIA...

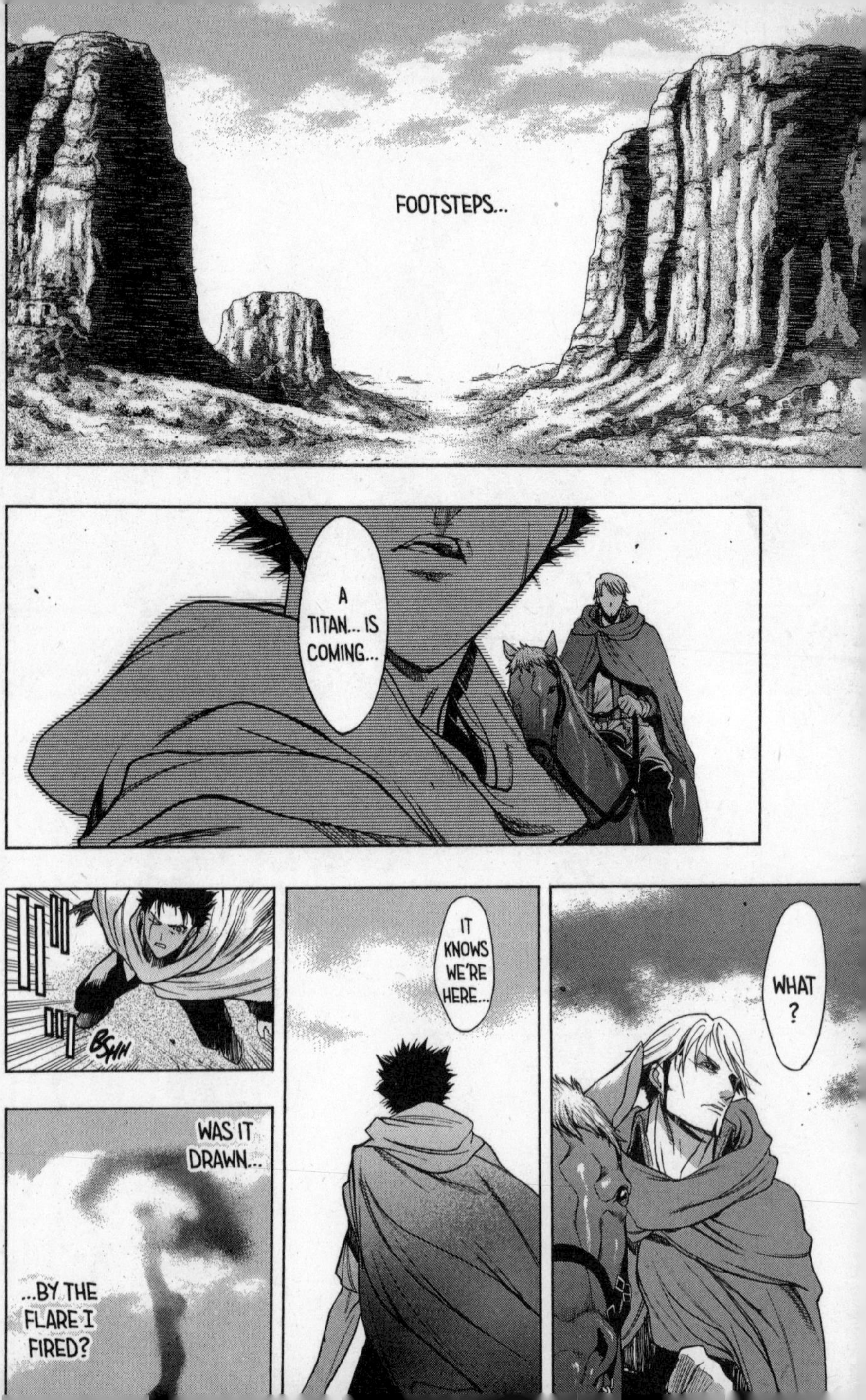
FOOTSTEPS...
A TITAN... IS COMING...
WHAT?
IT KNOWS WE'RE HERE...
BSHH
WAS IT DRAWN...
...BY THE FLARE I FIRED?

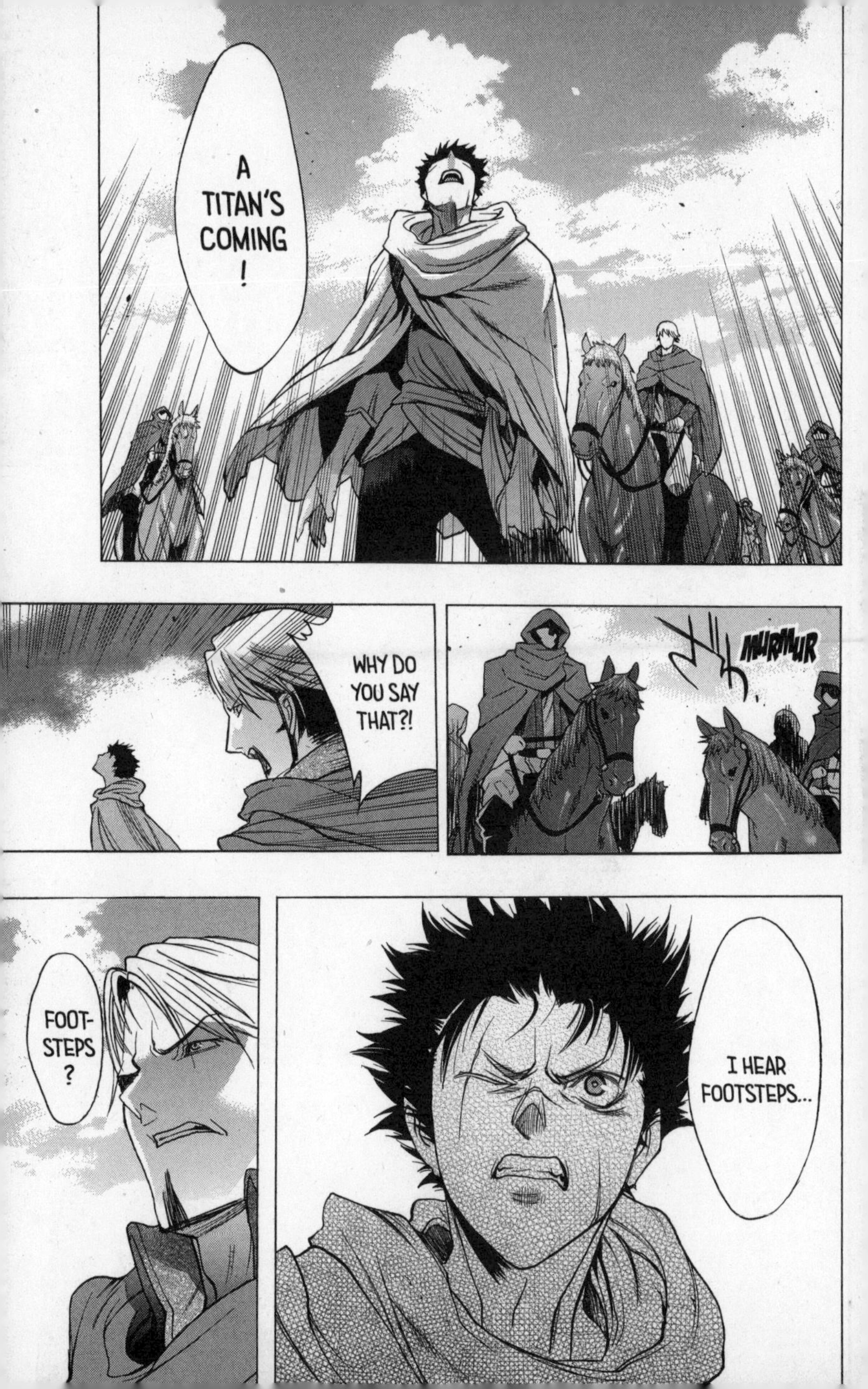
A TITAN'S COMING!
WHY DO YOU SAY THAT?!
MURMUR
I HEAR FOOTSTEPS...
FOOT-STEPS?

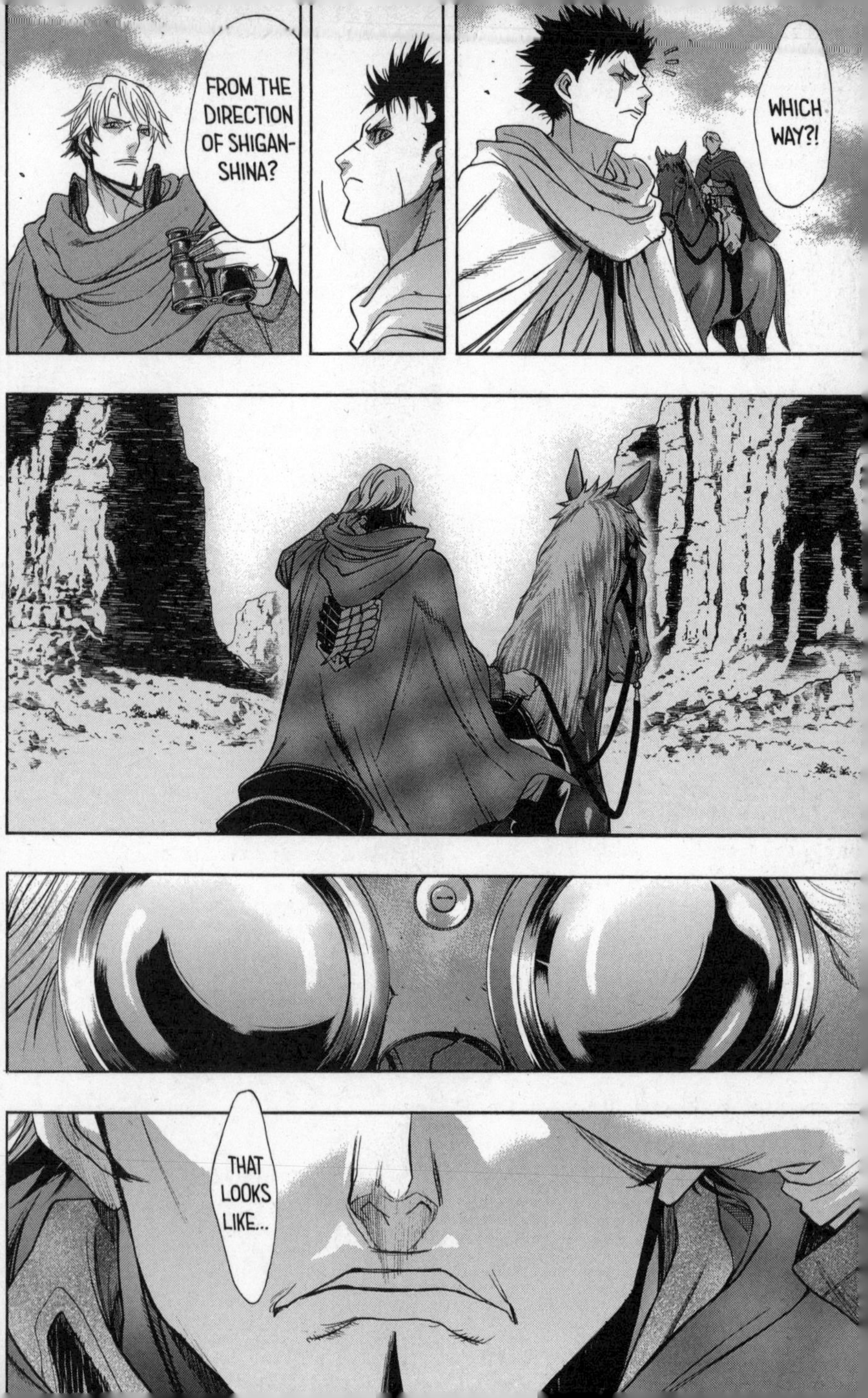
WHICH WAY?!
FROM THE DIRECTION OF SHIGAN-SHINA?
THAT LOOKS LIKE...

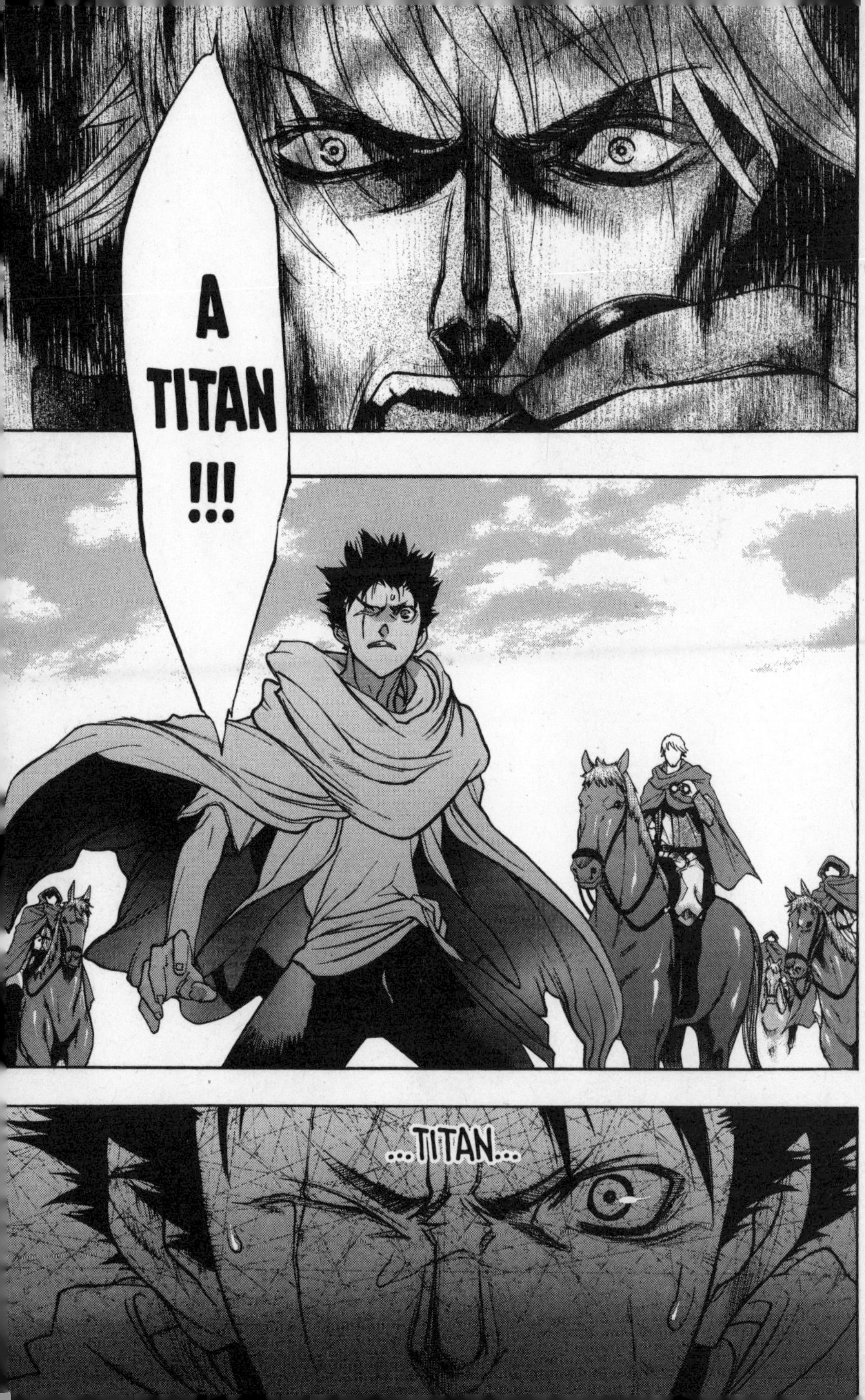
A TITAN !!!
...TITAN...

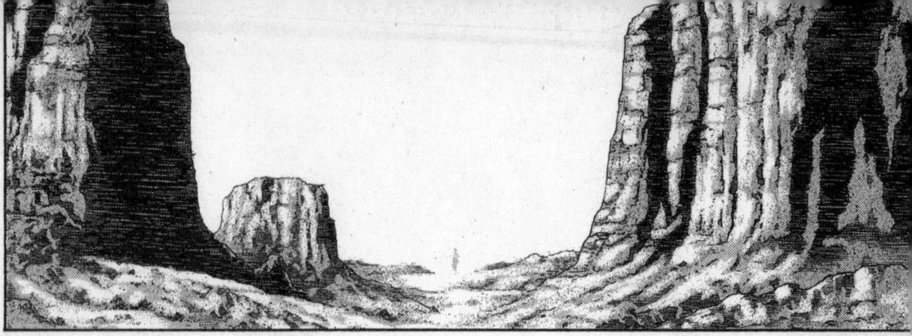

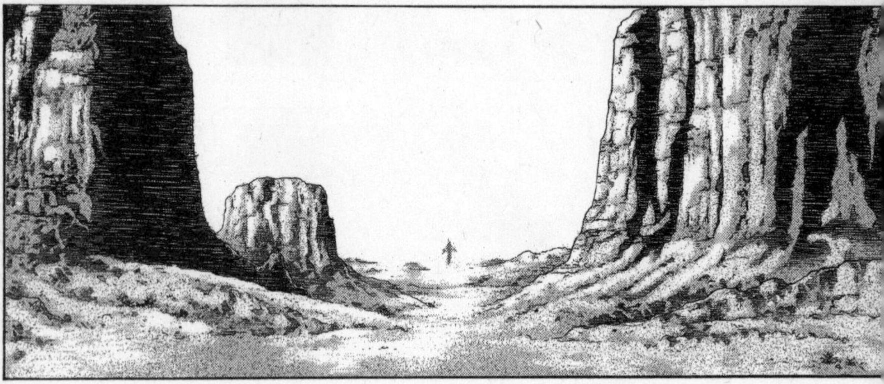

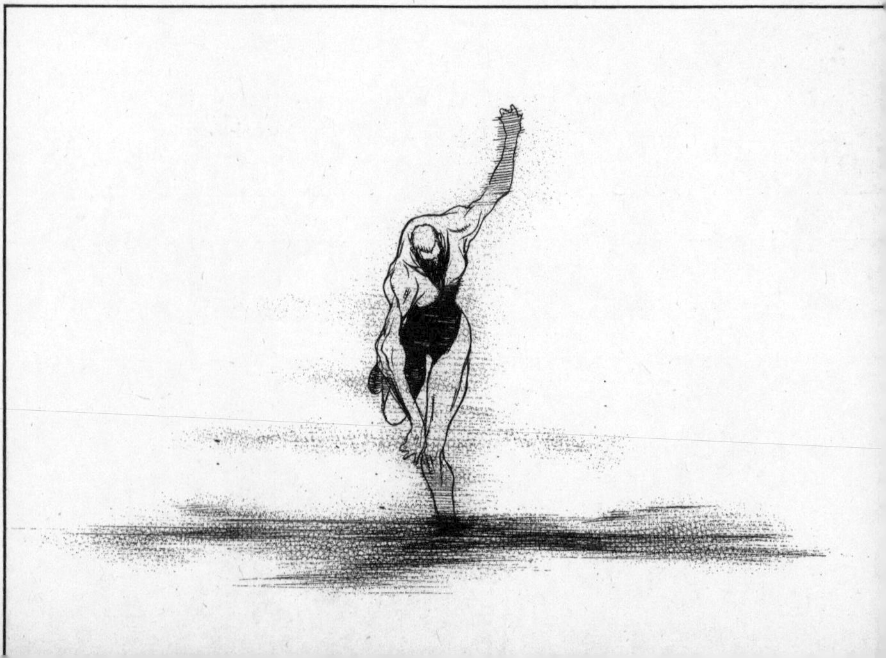

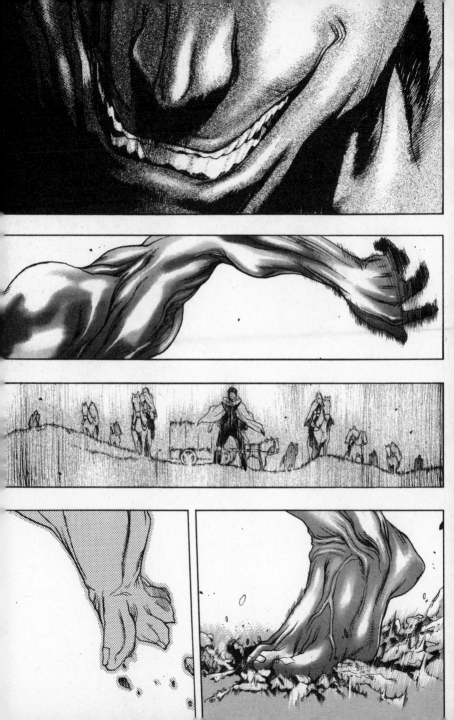

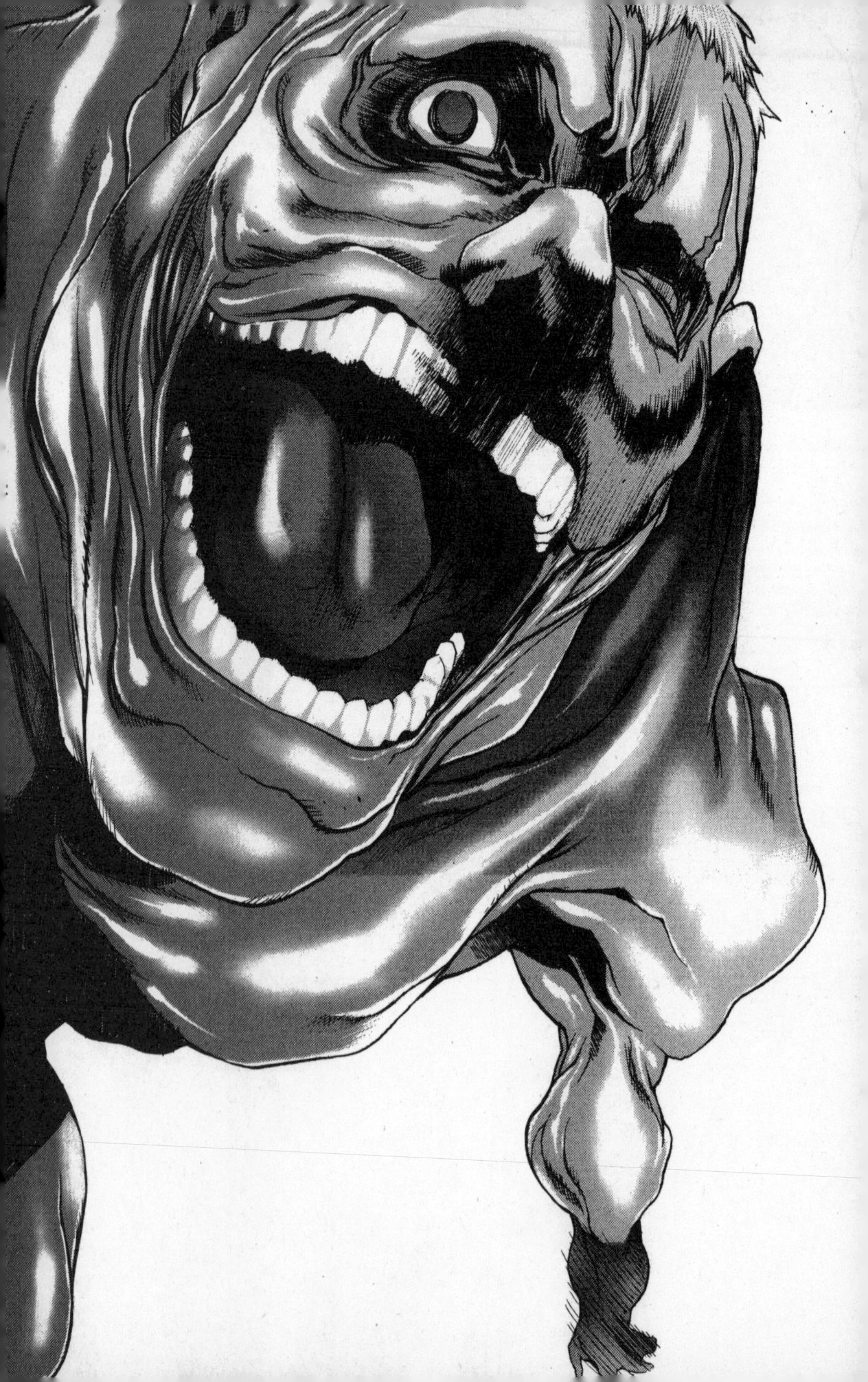

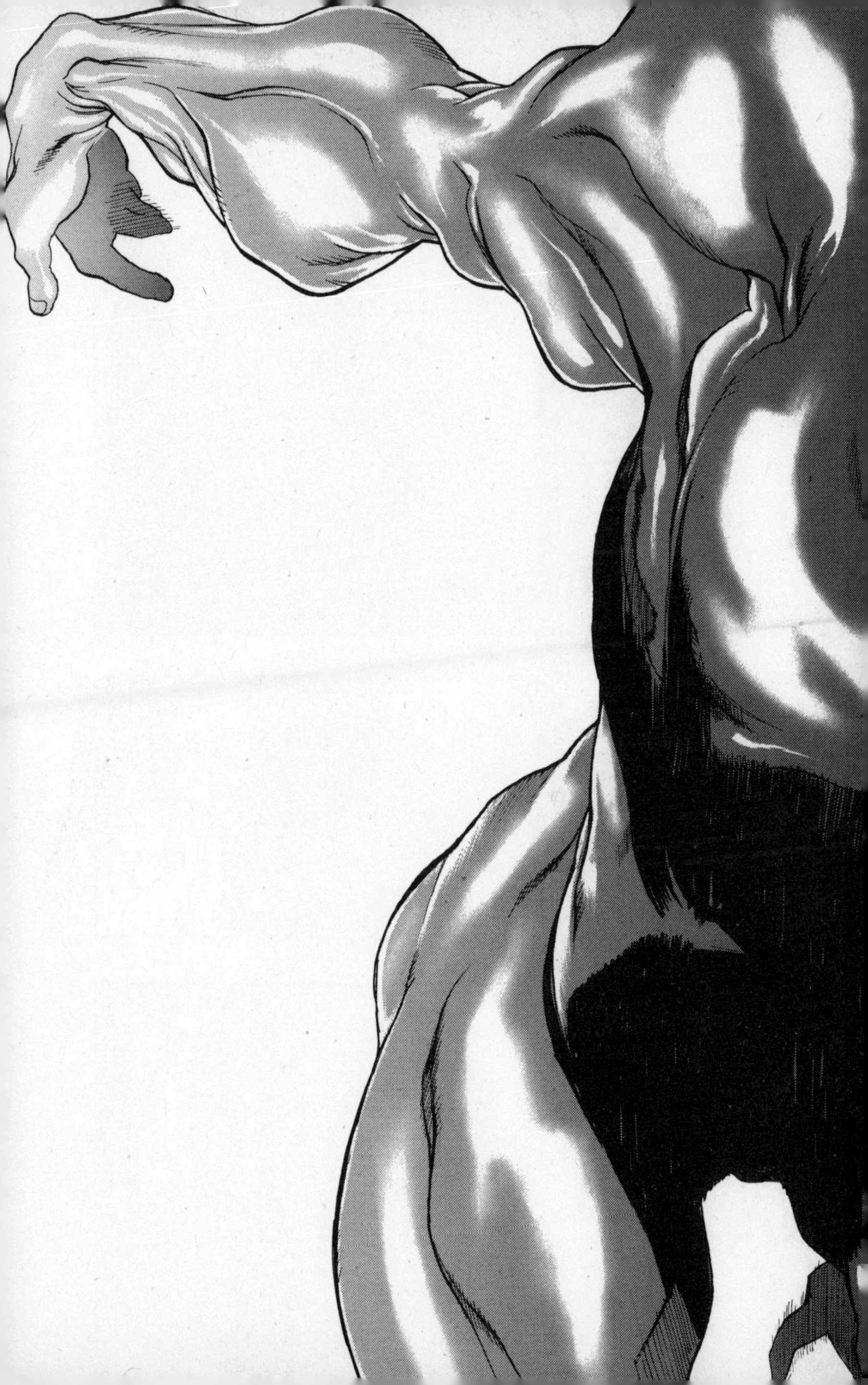

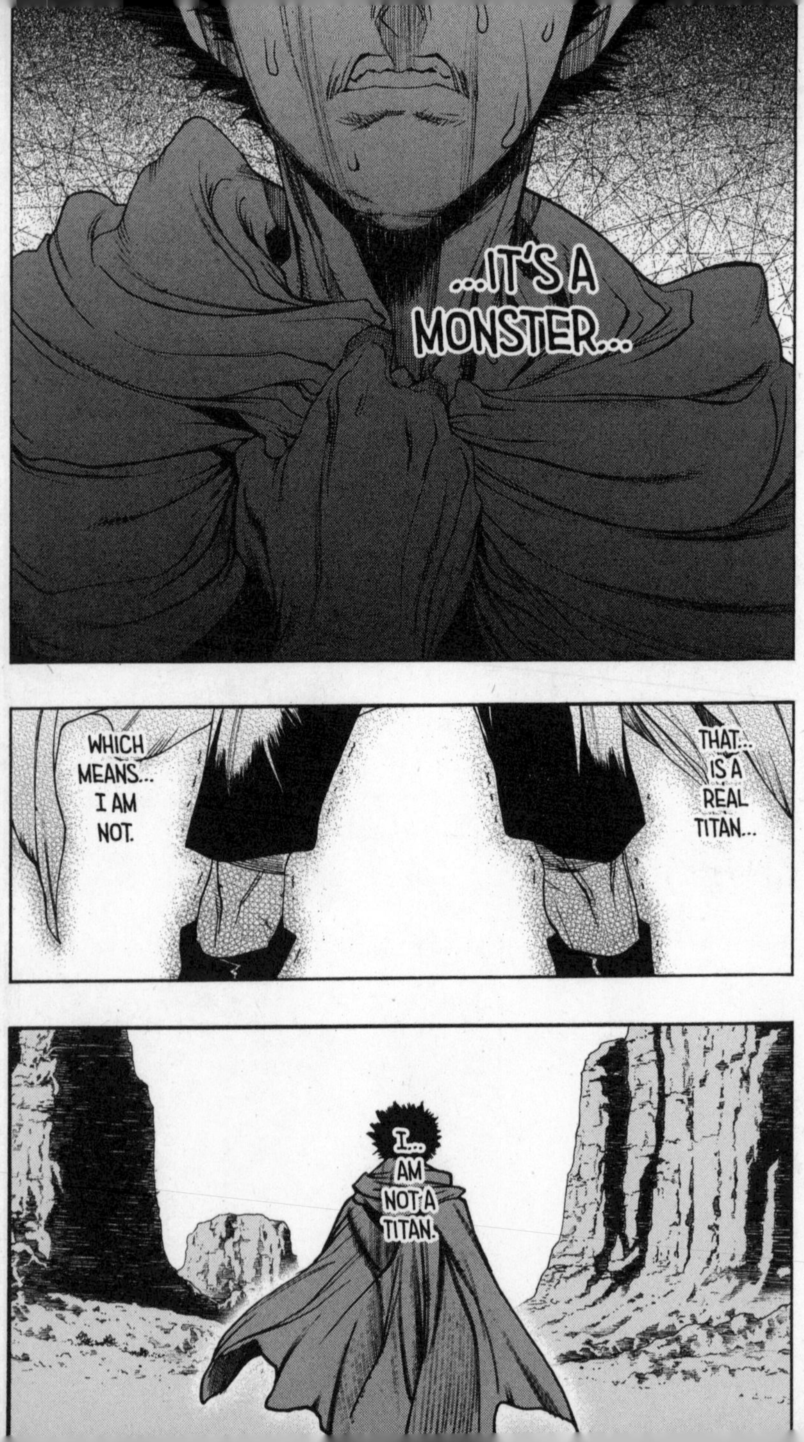
...IT'S A MONSTER...
THAT... IS A REAL TITAN...
WHICH MEANS... I AM NOT.
I... AM NOT A TITAN.

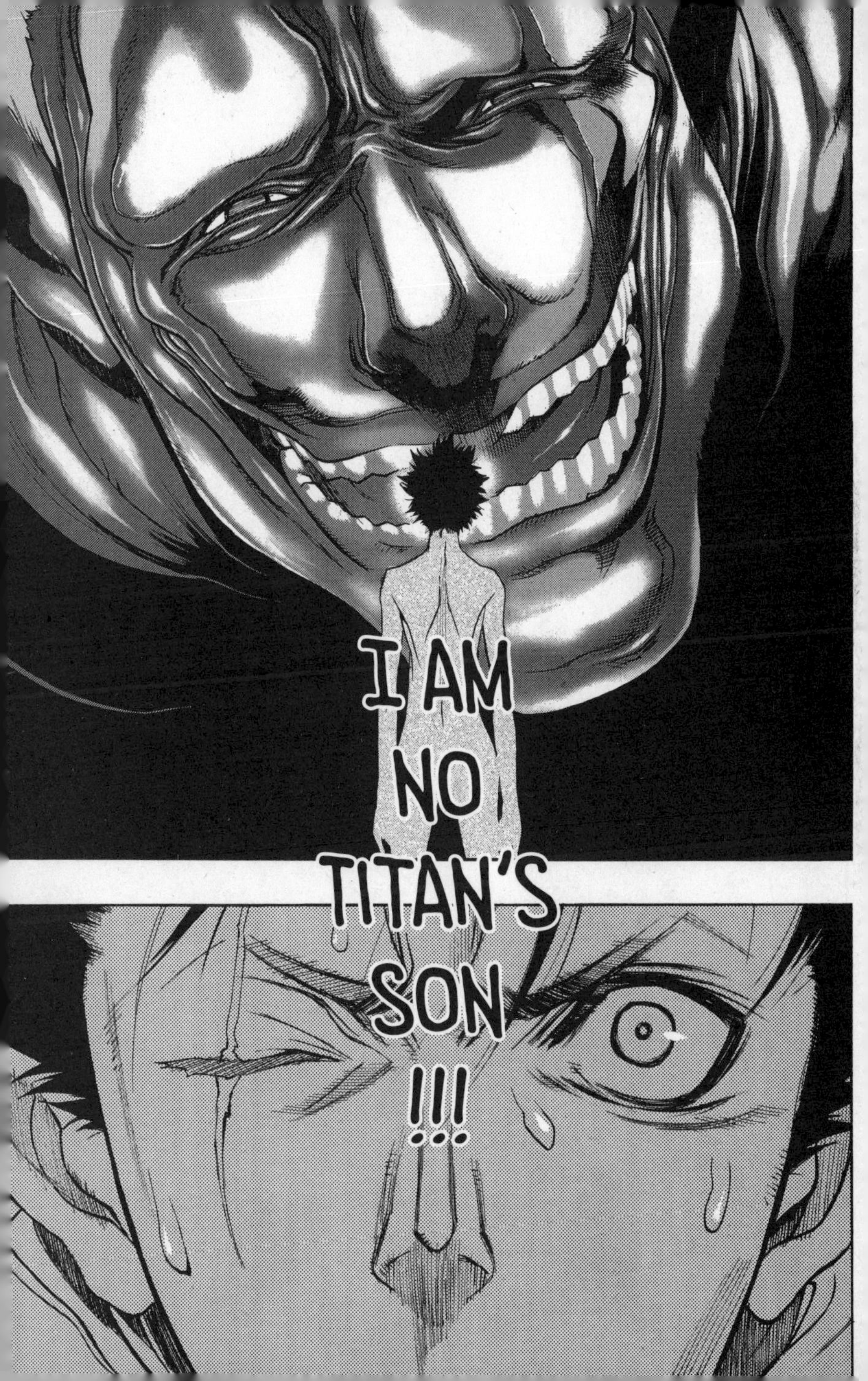
I AM NO TITAN'S SON !!!

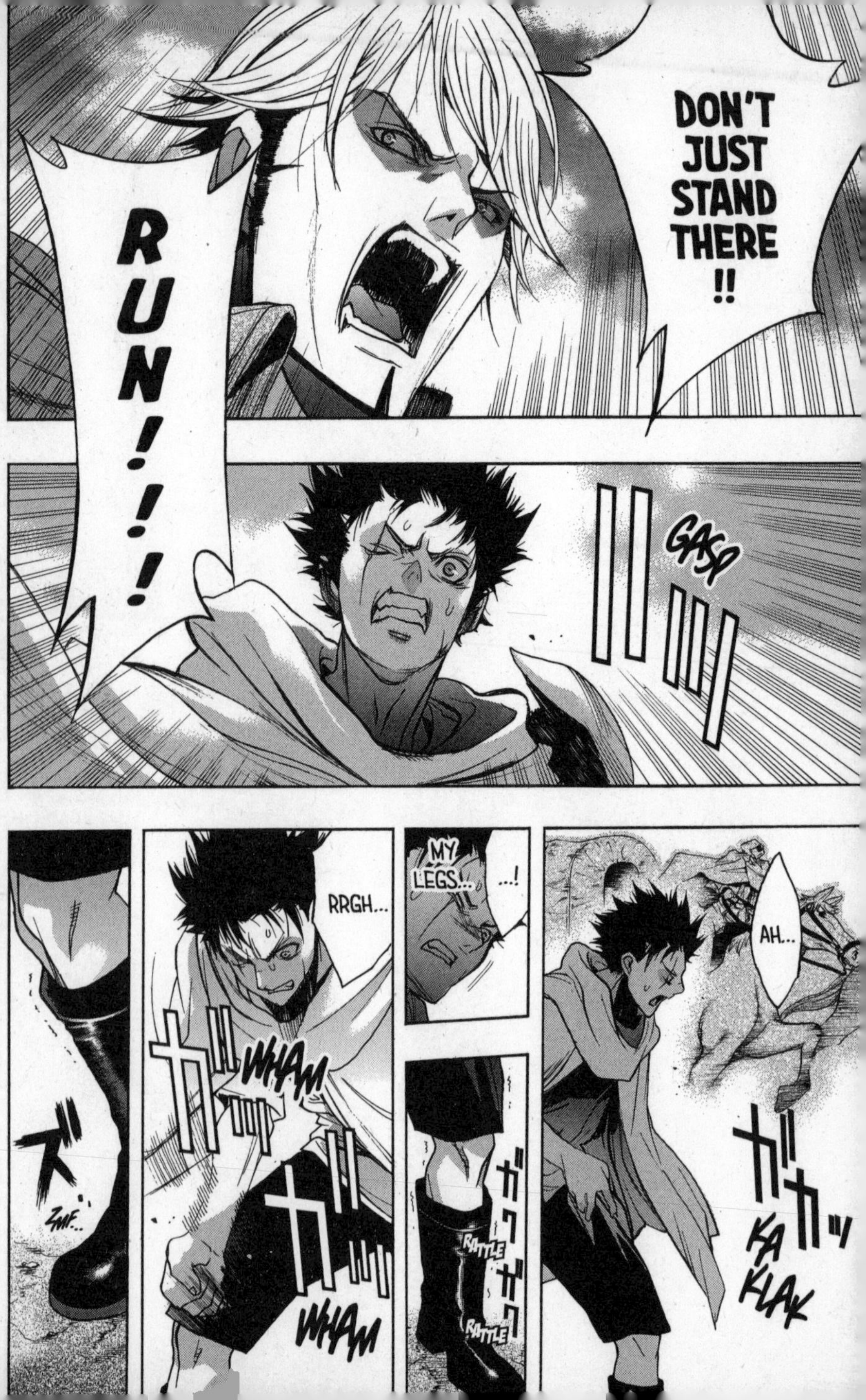
DON'T JUST STAND THERE!!
RUN!!!!
GASP
RRGH...
WHAM
WHAM
ZMF...
MY LEGS...
...!
RATTLE
RATTLE
AH...
KA-KLAK

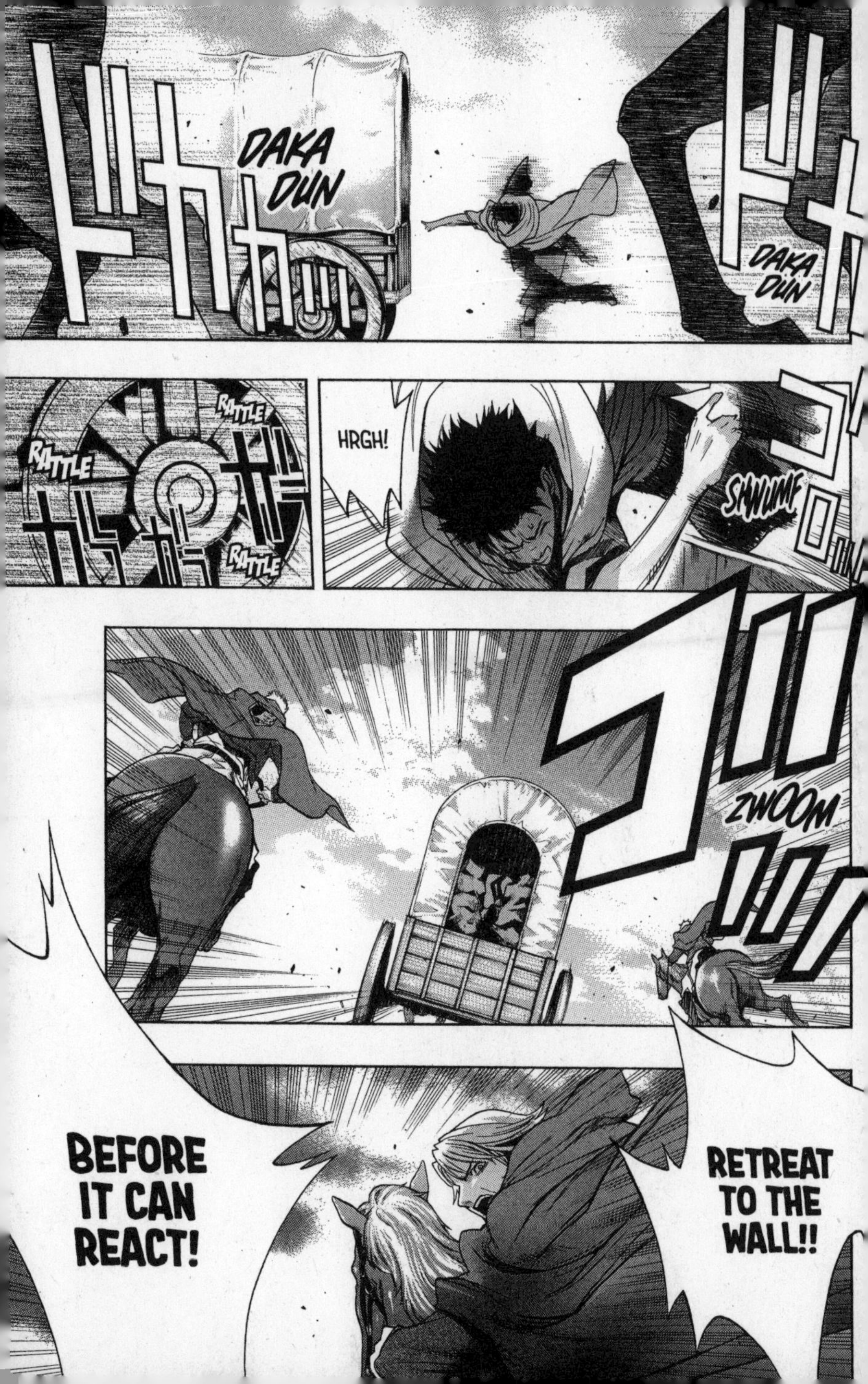
DAKA DUN
DAKA DUN
HRGH!
SHWUMF
RATTLE
RATTLE
RATTLE
ZWOOM
RETREAT TO THE WALL!!
BEFORE IT CAN REACT!

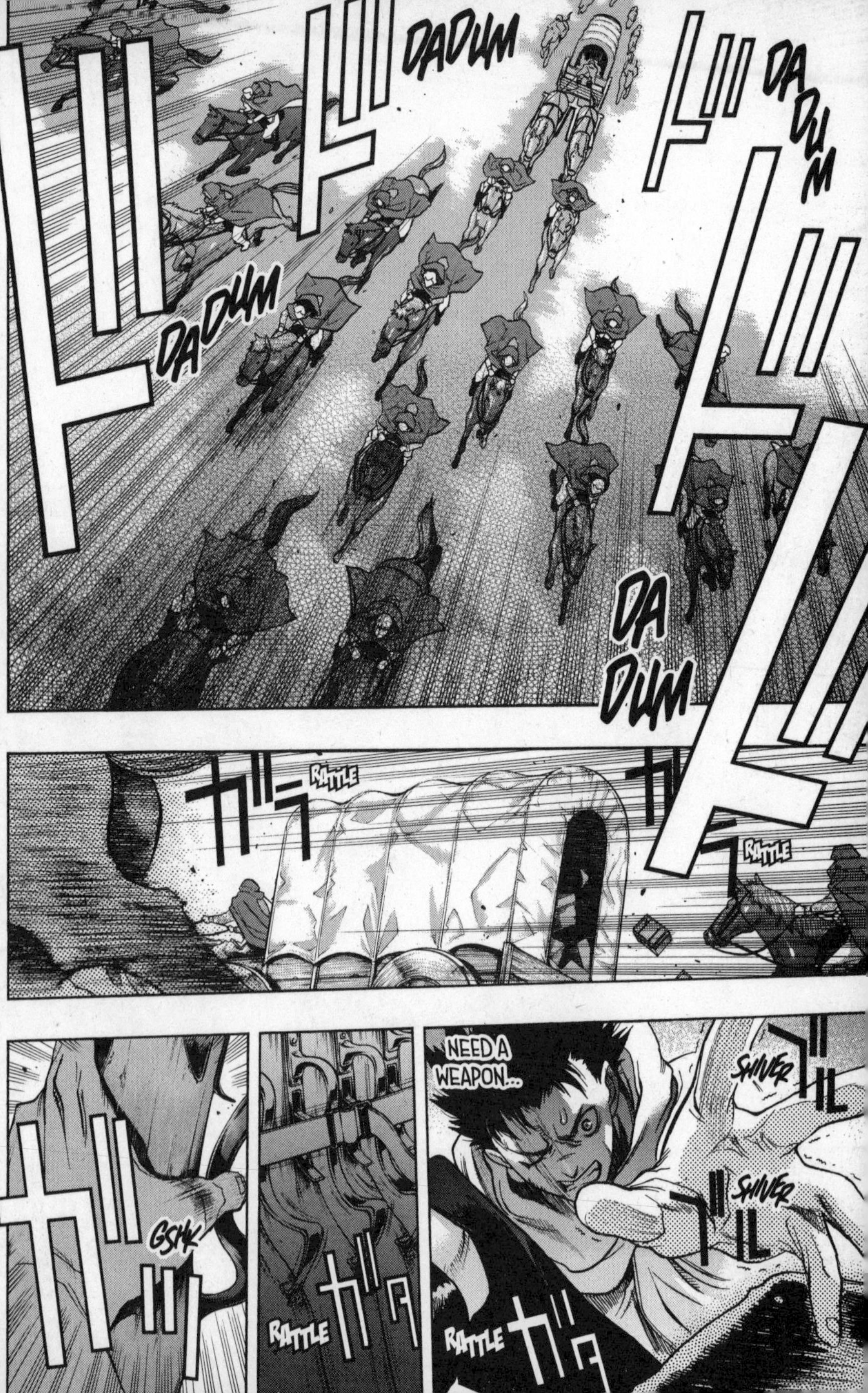
DADUM
DADUM
DADUM
DA DUM
RATTLE
RATTLE
NEED A WEAPON...
SHIVER
SHIVER
RATTLE
RATTLE
GSHK

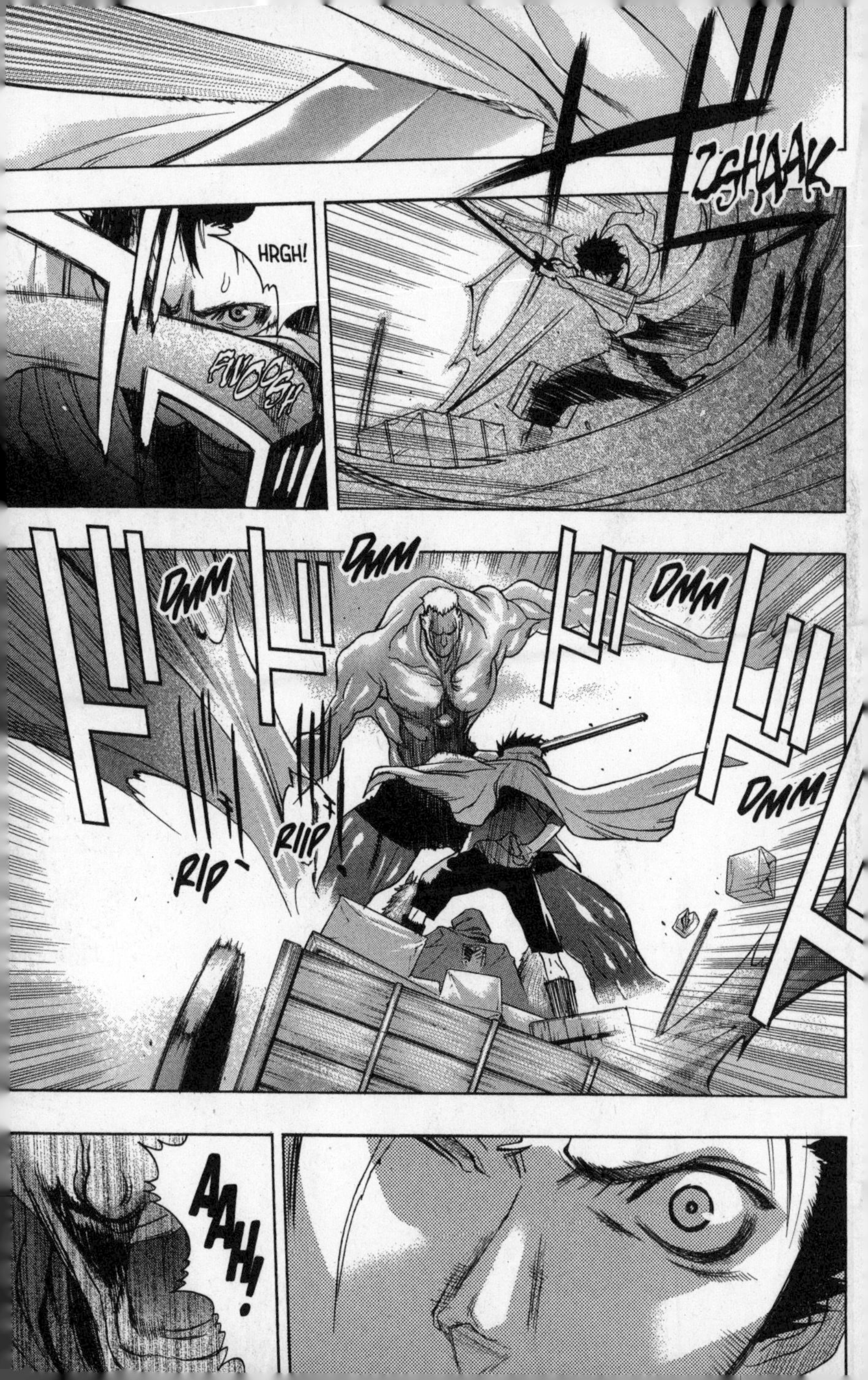
ZSHAAK
HRGH!
FWOOSH
DMM
DMM
DMM
DMM
RIIP
RIP
AAAH!

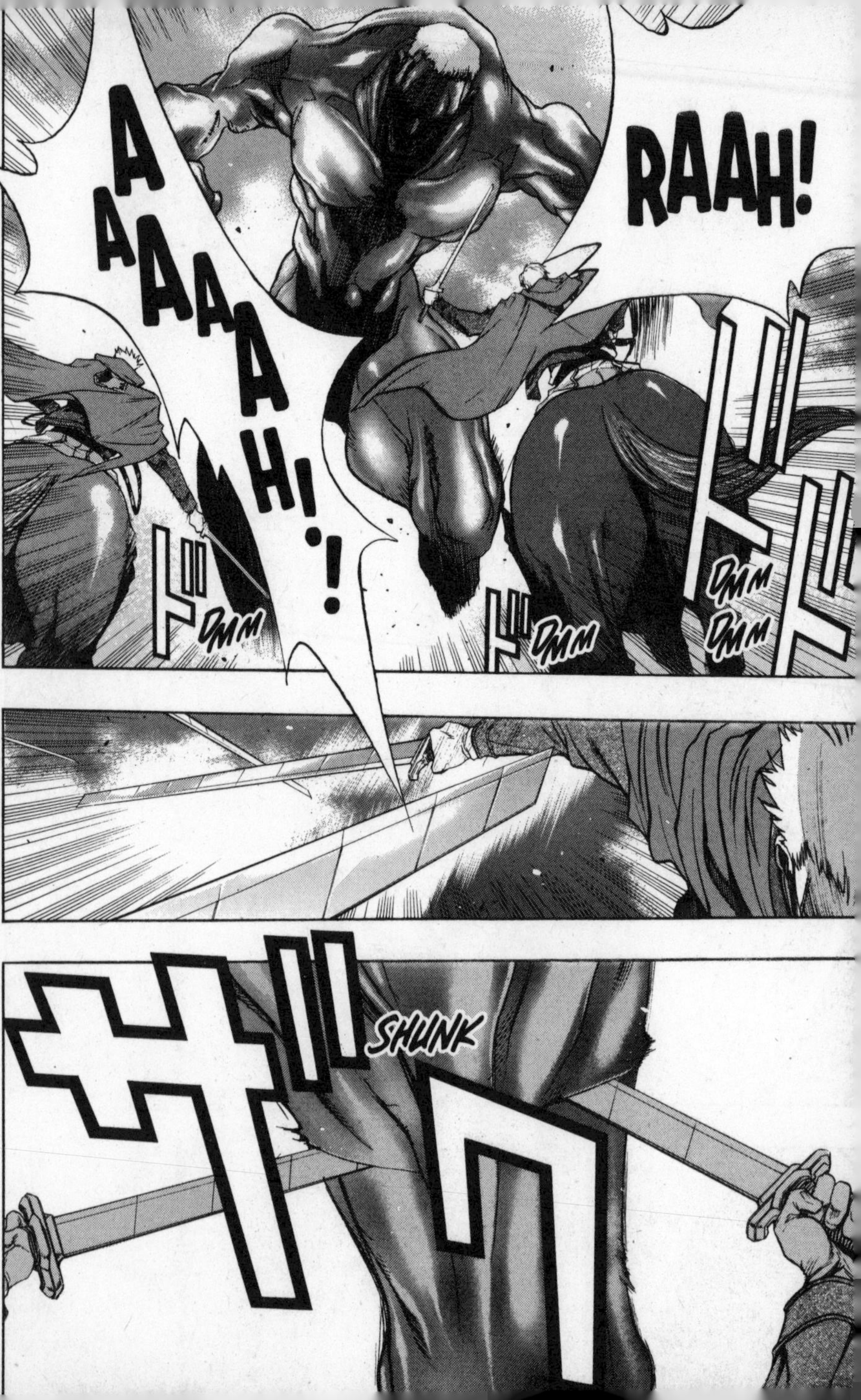
RAAH!
AAAAAAAH!!
DMM
DMM
DMM DMM
SHUNK

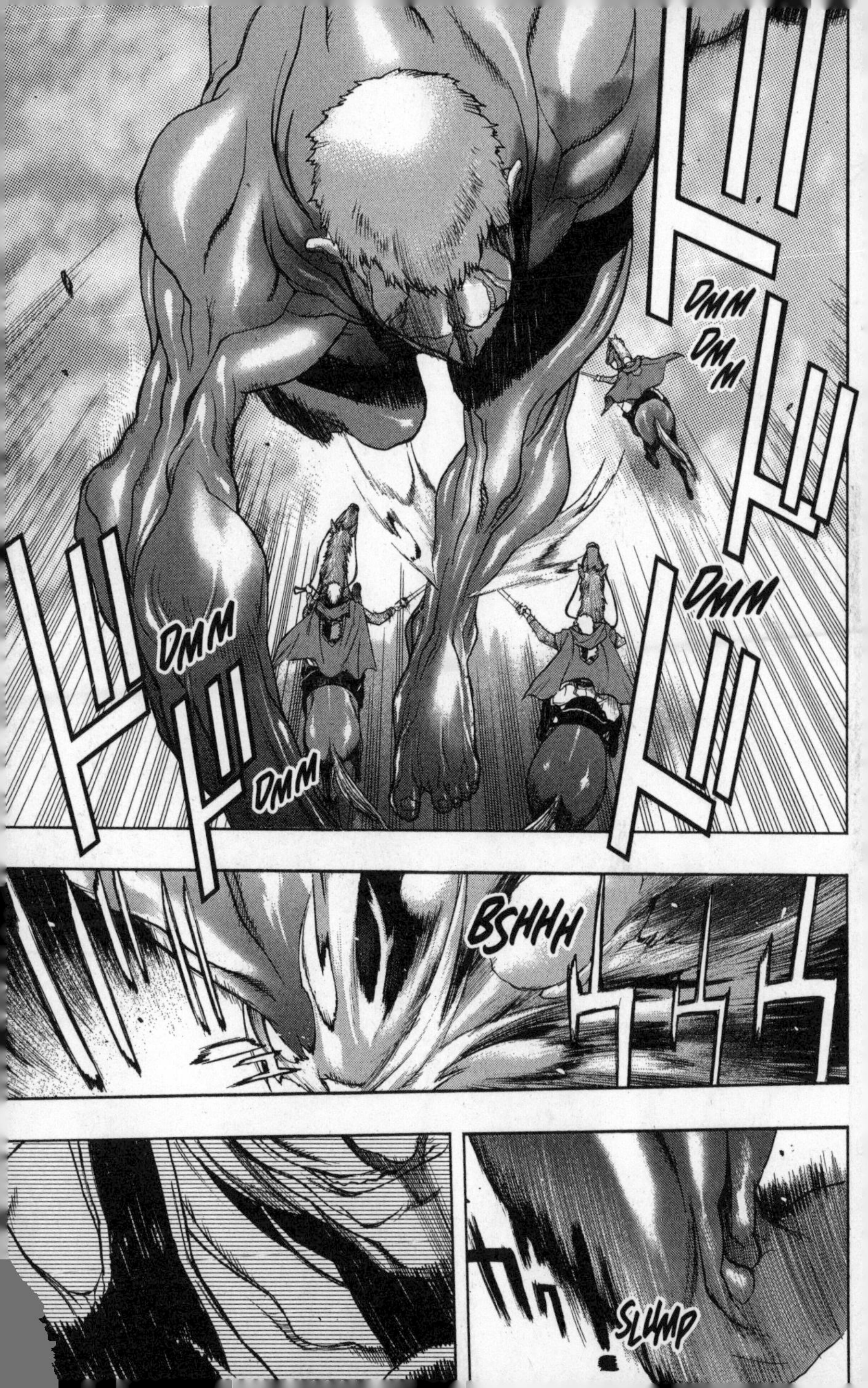
DMM DMM
DMM
DMM
DMM
BSHHH
SLUMP

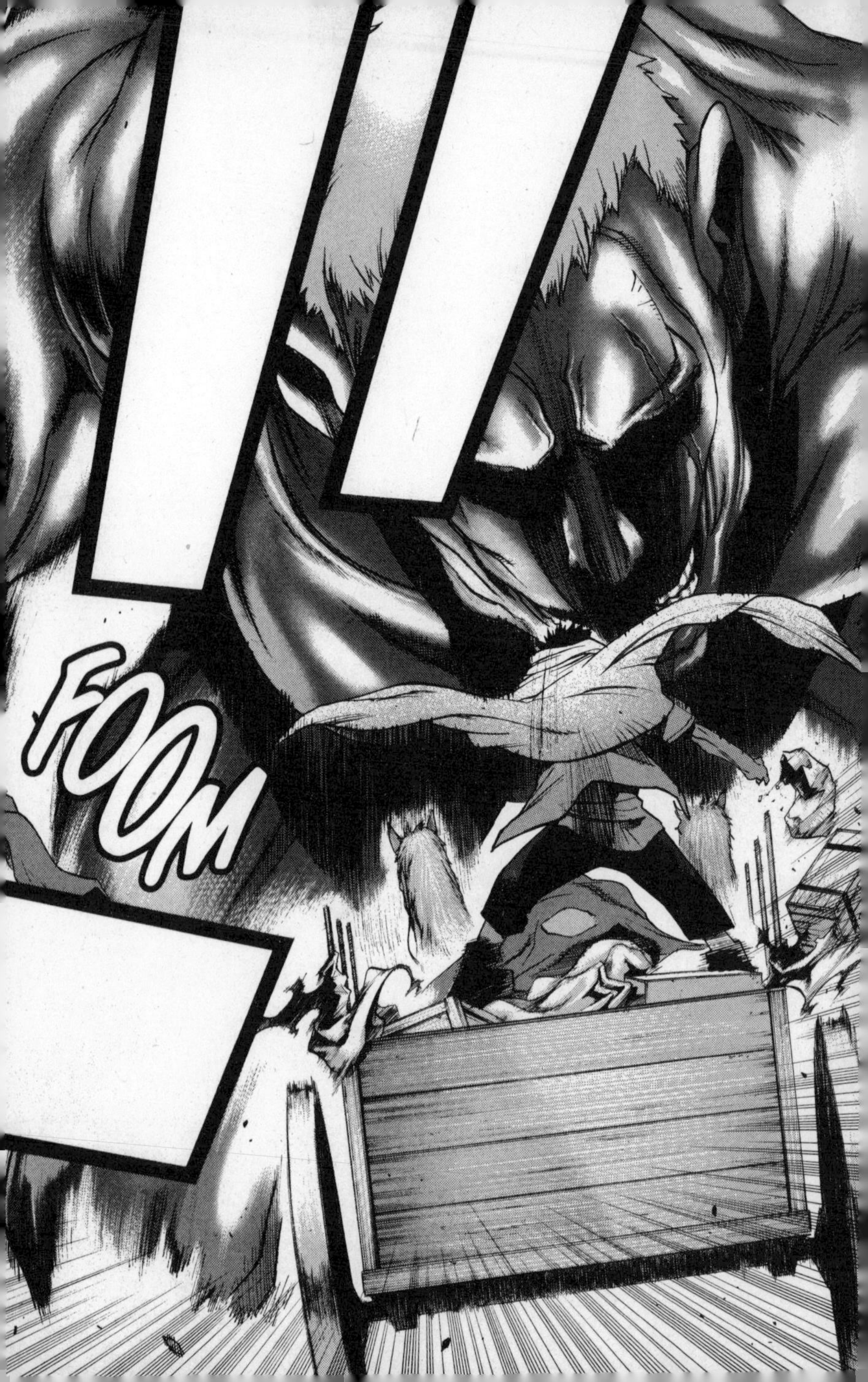
FOOM

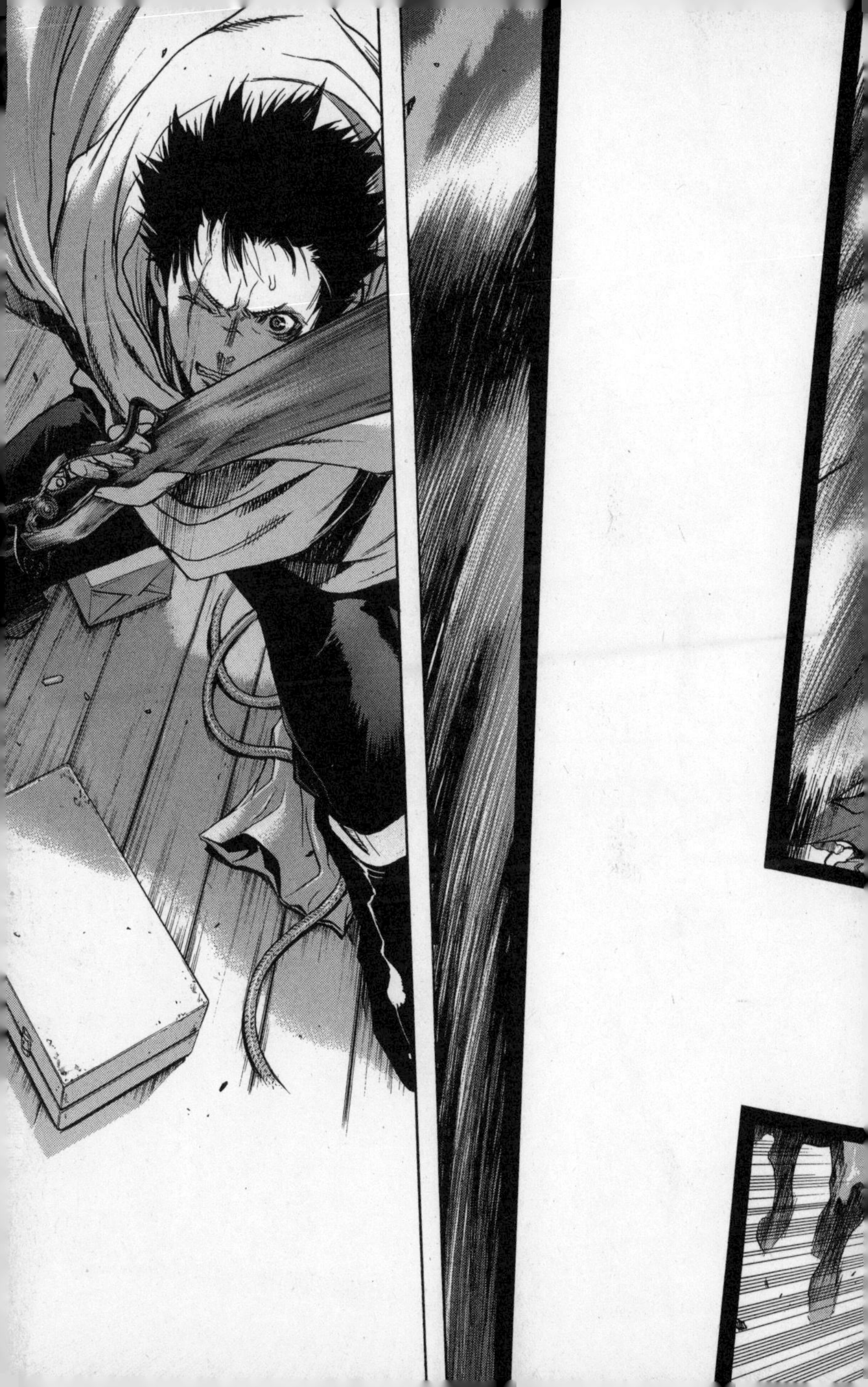

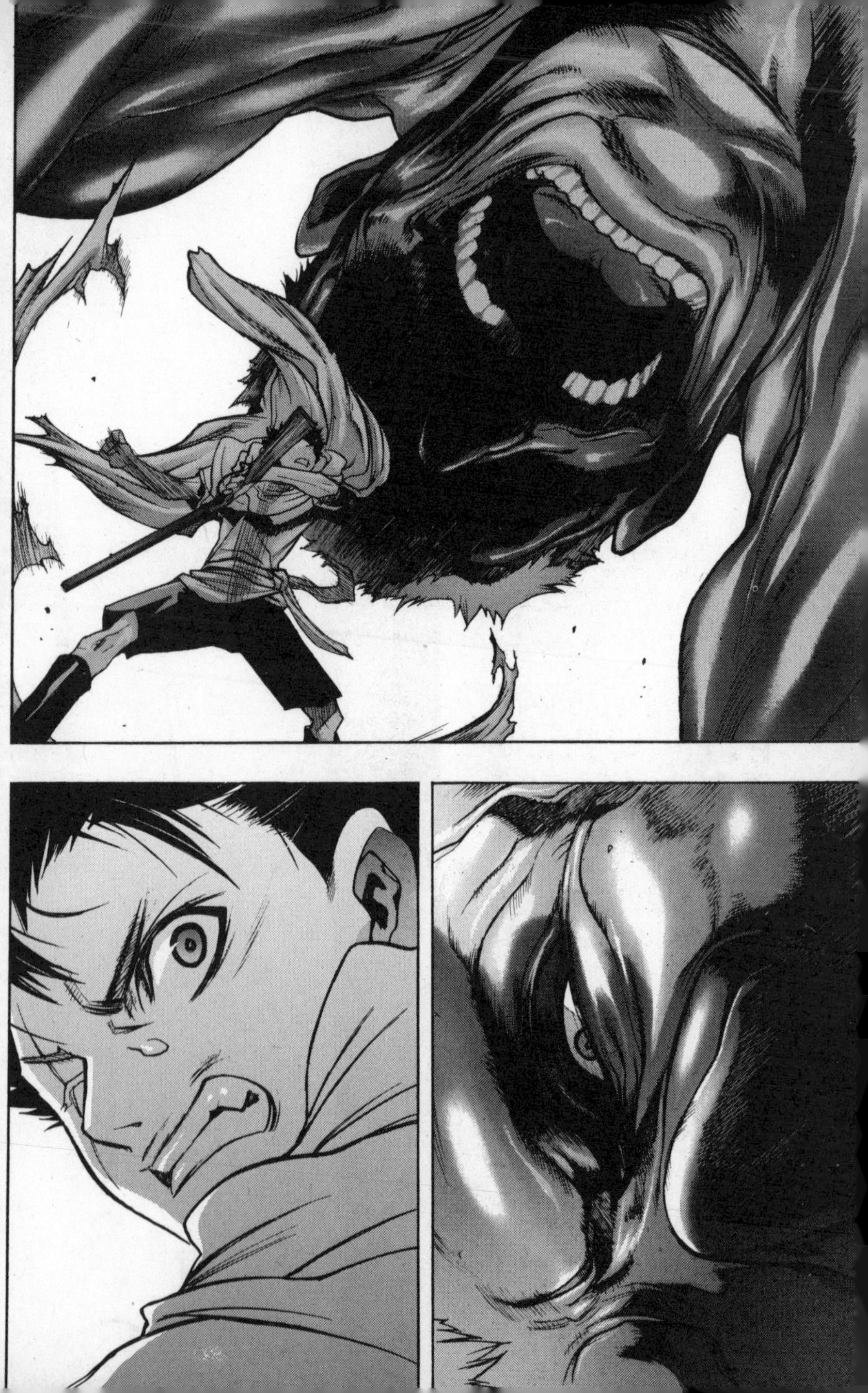

DMM DMM DMM DMM

...SO FAR AWAY... IT'S STILL...

DMM DMM DMM DMM DMM

CAN WE ACTUALLY ESCAPE

...?!

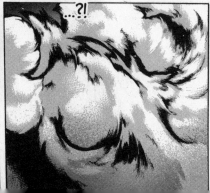

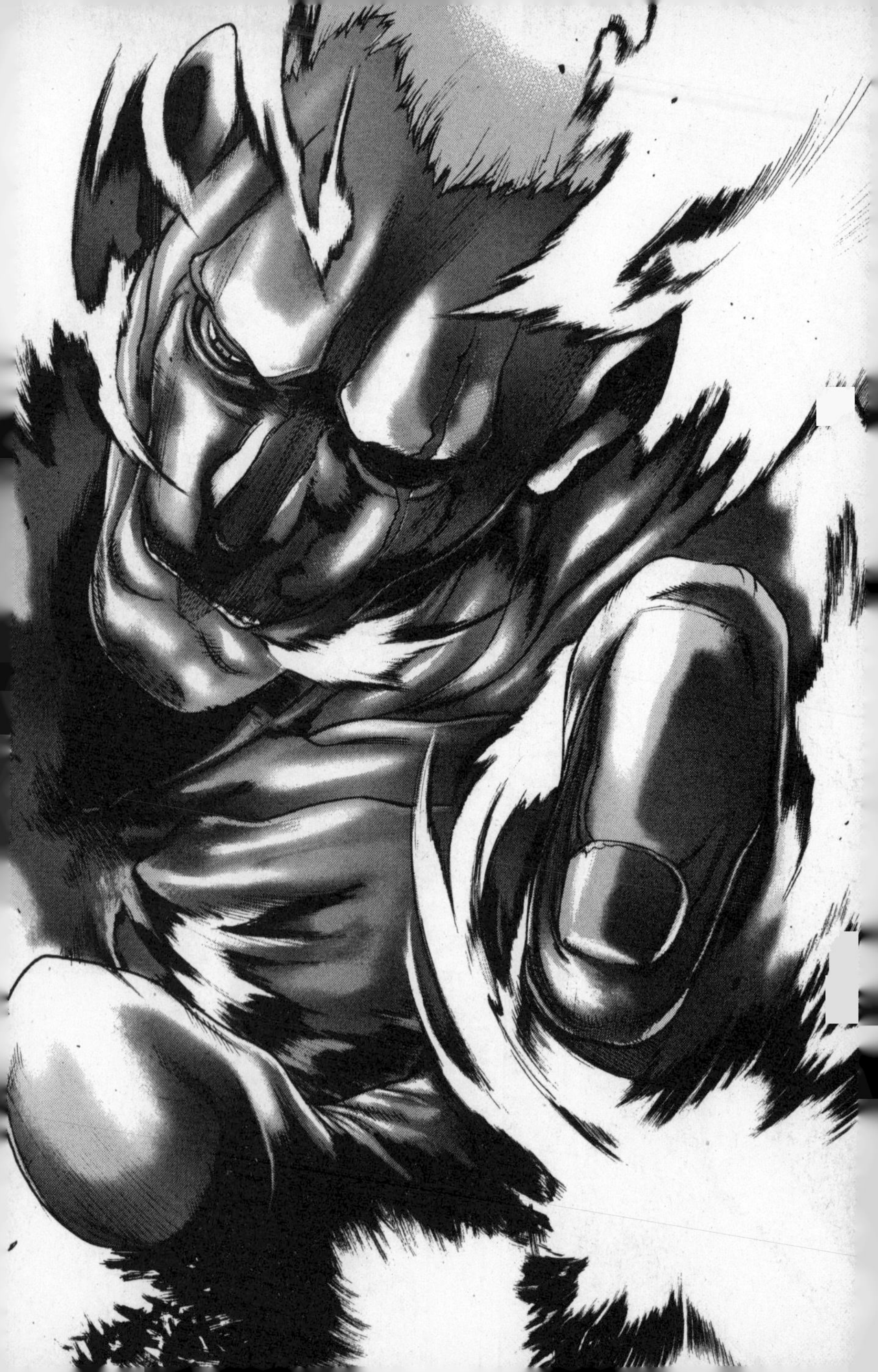

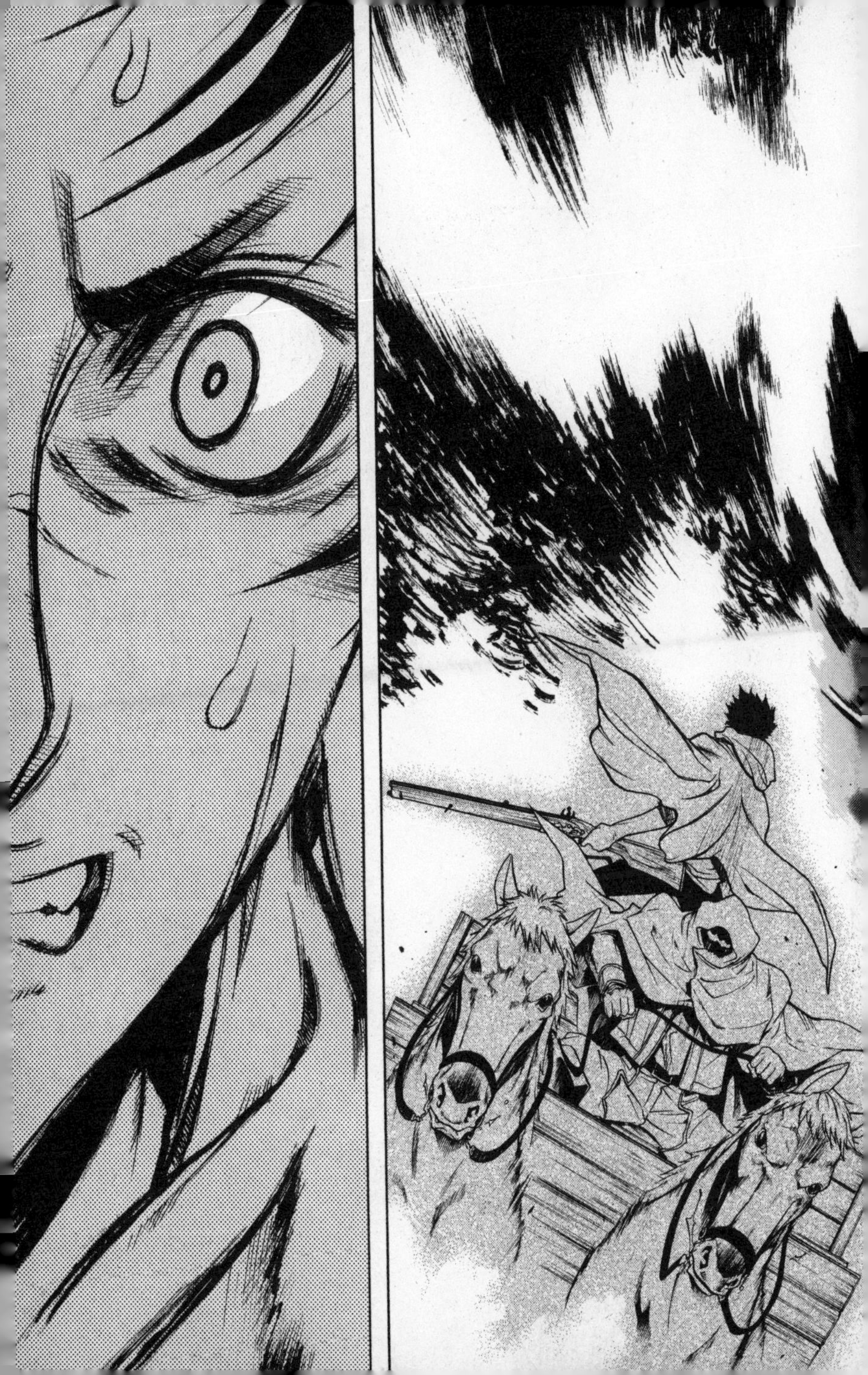

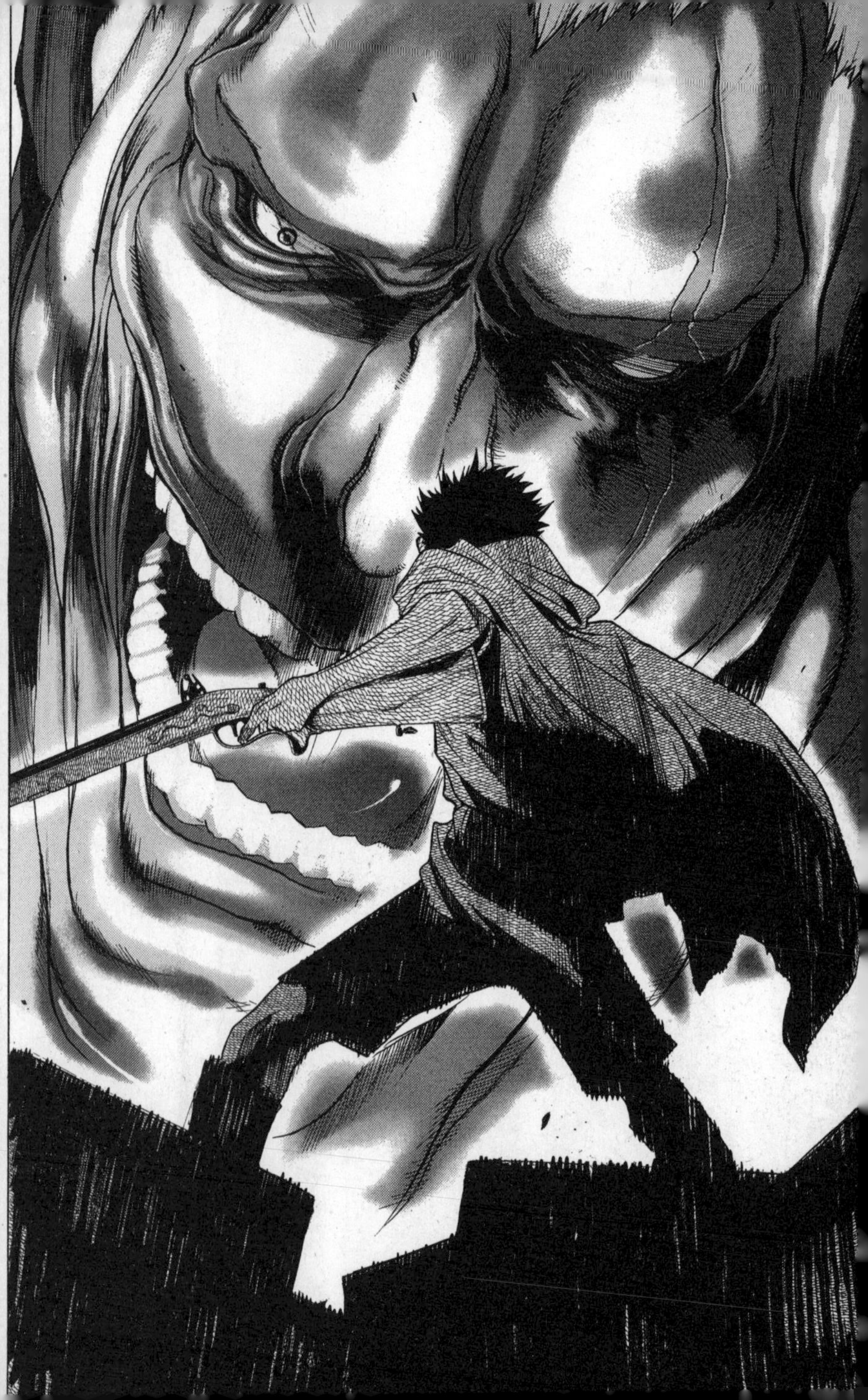

Chapter 6: Proof of Humanity - End

ATTACK
on TITAN
BEFORE THE FALL

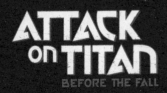

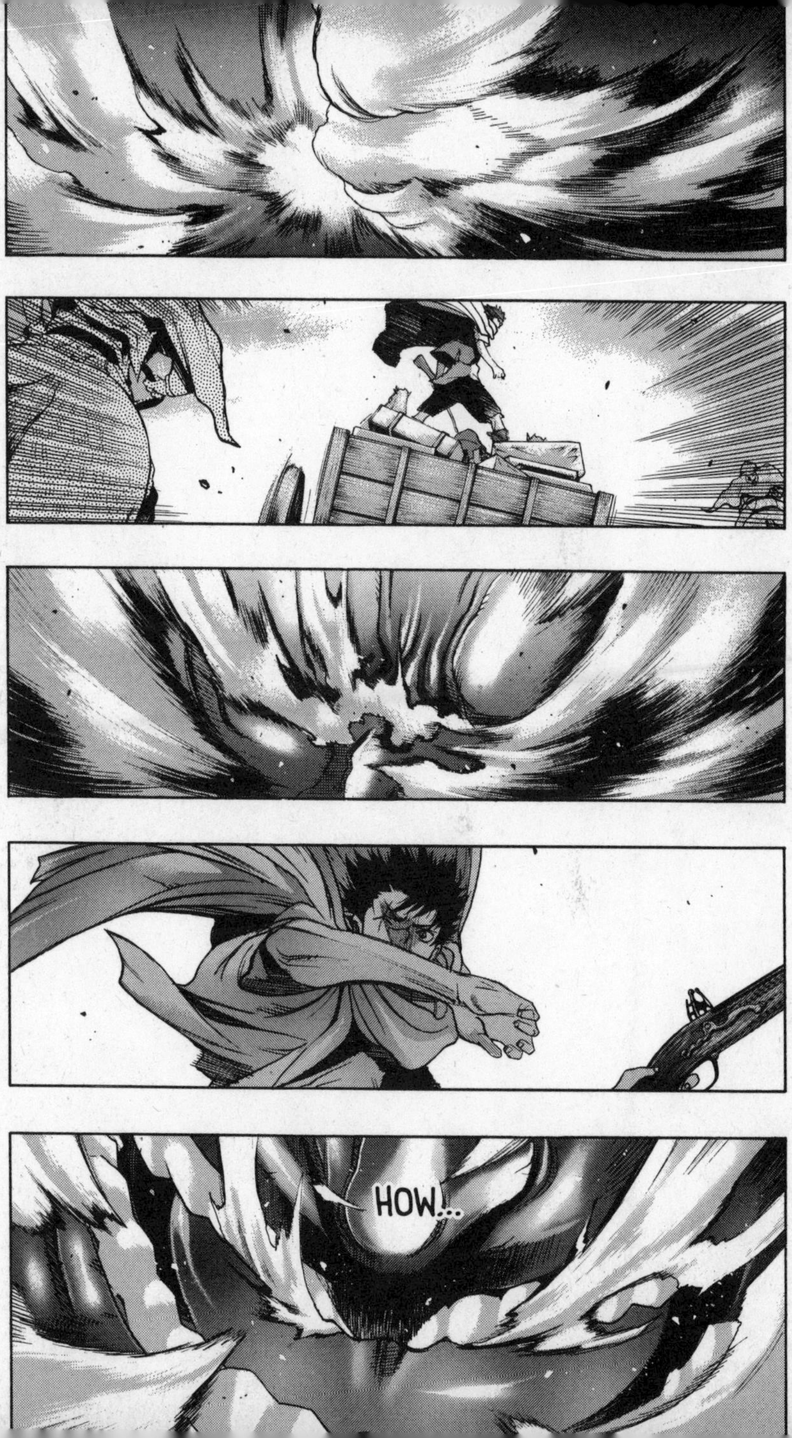
HOW...

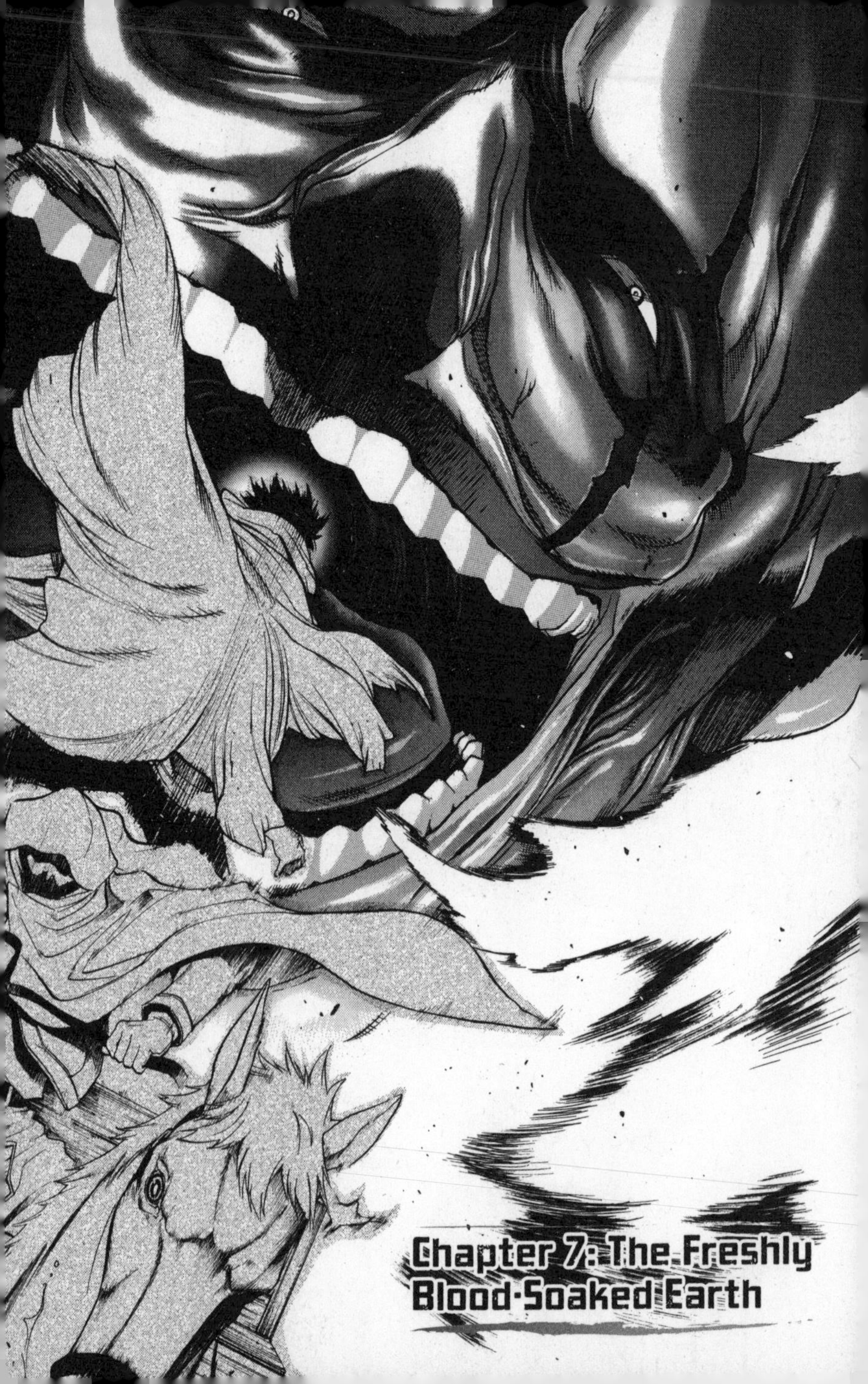
Chapter 7: The Freshly
Blood-Soaked Earth

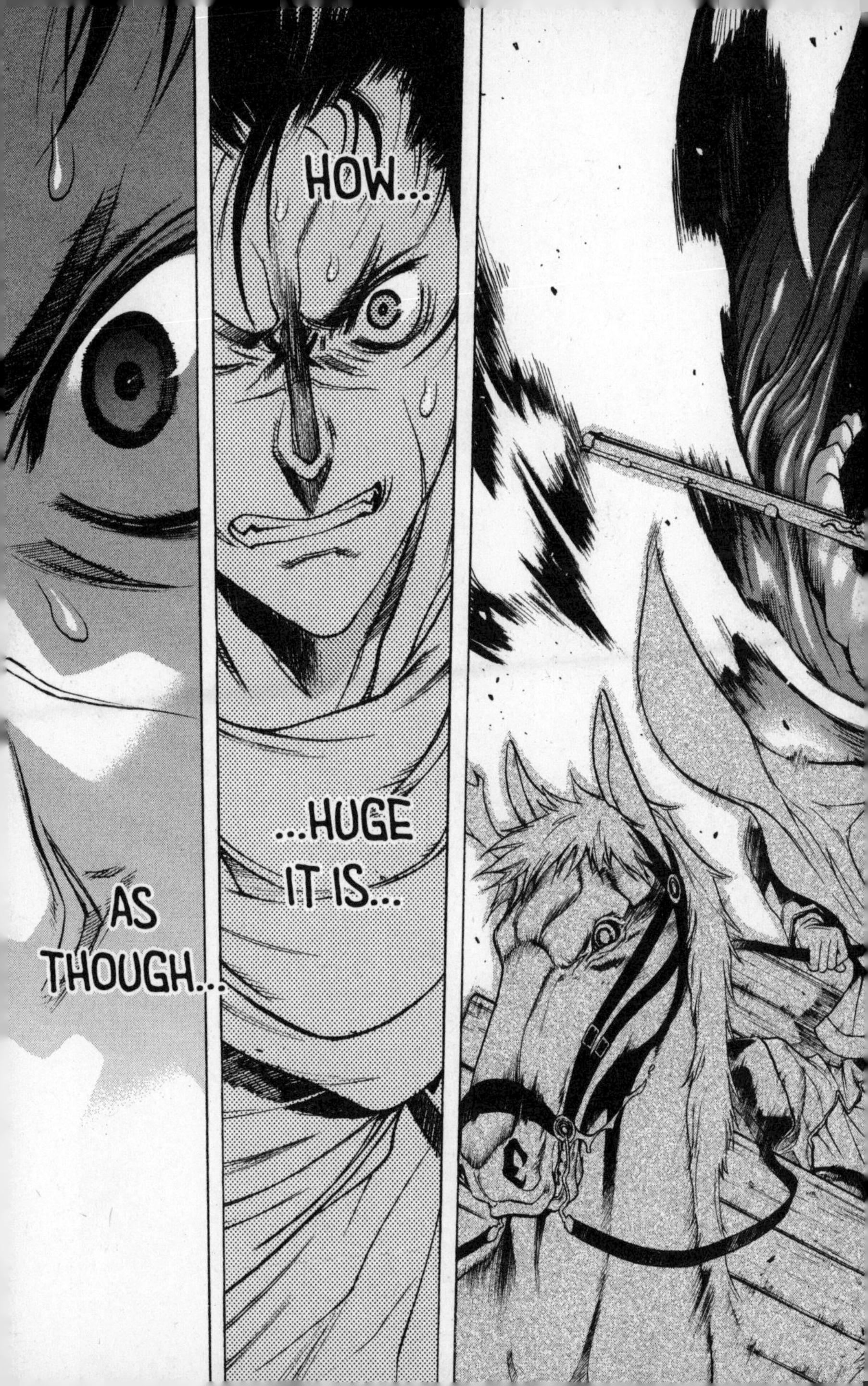
HOW...
...HUGE IT IS...
AS THOUGH...

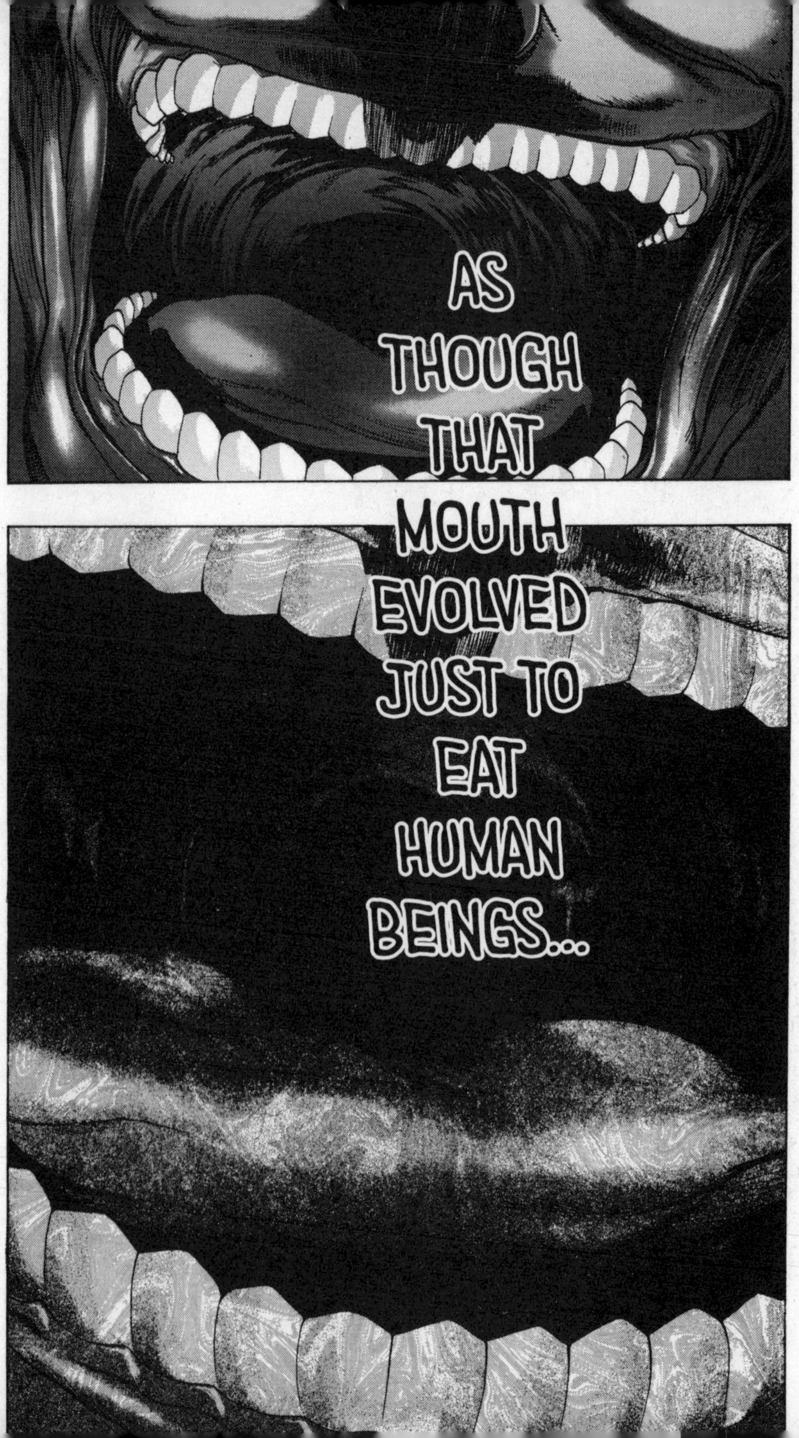
AS THOUGH THAT MOUTH EVOLVED JUST TO EAT HUMAN BEINGS...

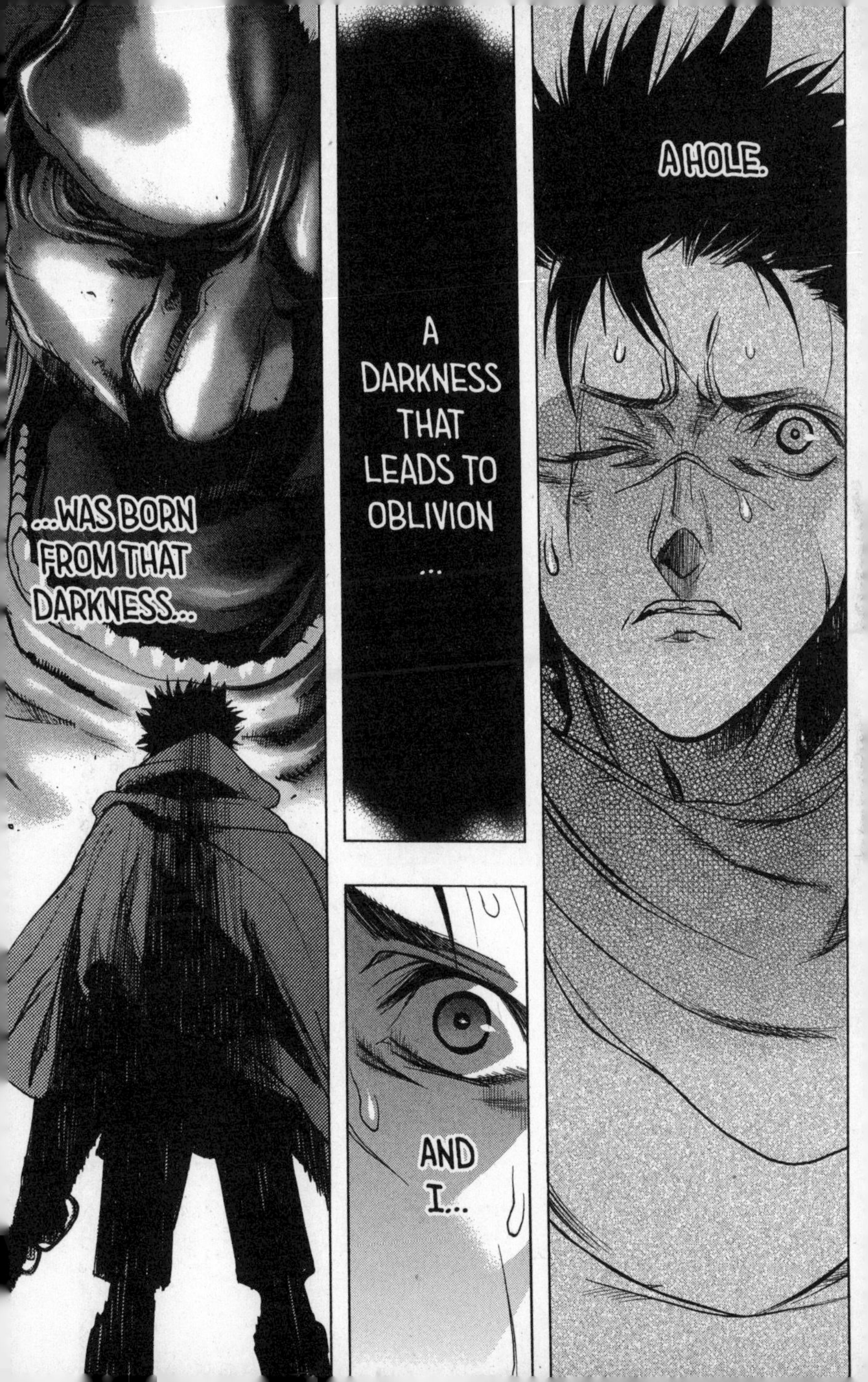
A HOLE.
A DARKNESS THAT LEADS TO OBLIVION ...
AND I...
...WAS BORN FROM THAT DARKNESS...

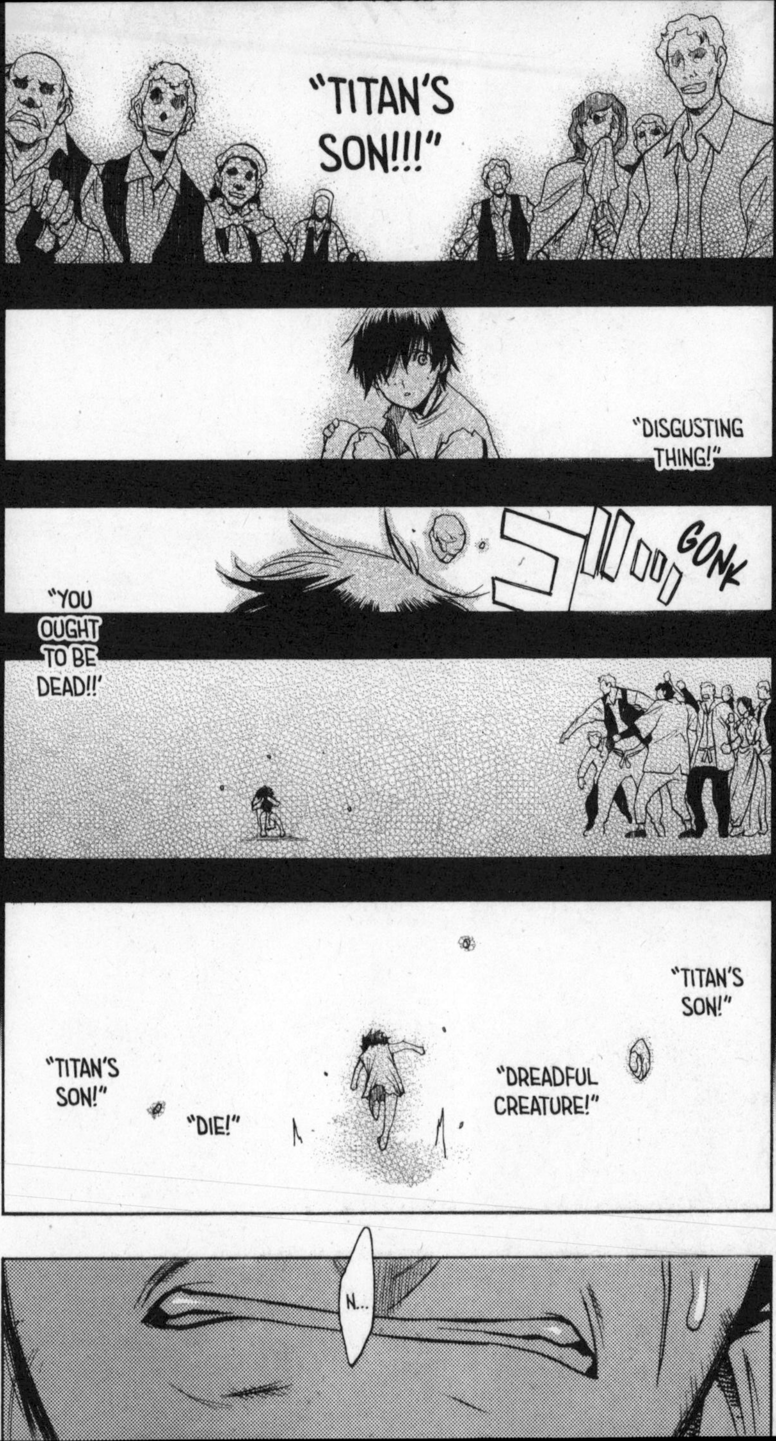
"TITAN'S SON!!!"
"DISGUSTING THING!"
GONK
"YOU OUGHT TO BE DEAD!!"
"TITAN'S SON!"
"DREADFUL CREATURE!"
"DIE!"
"TITAN'S SON!"
N...

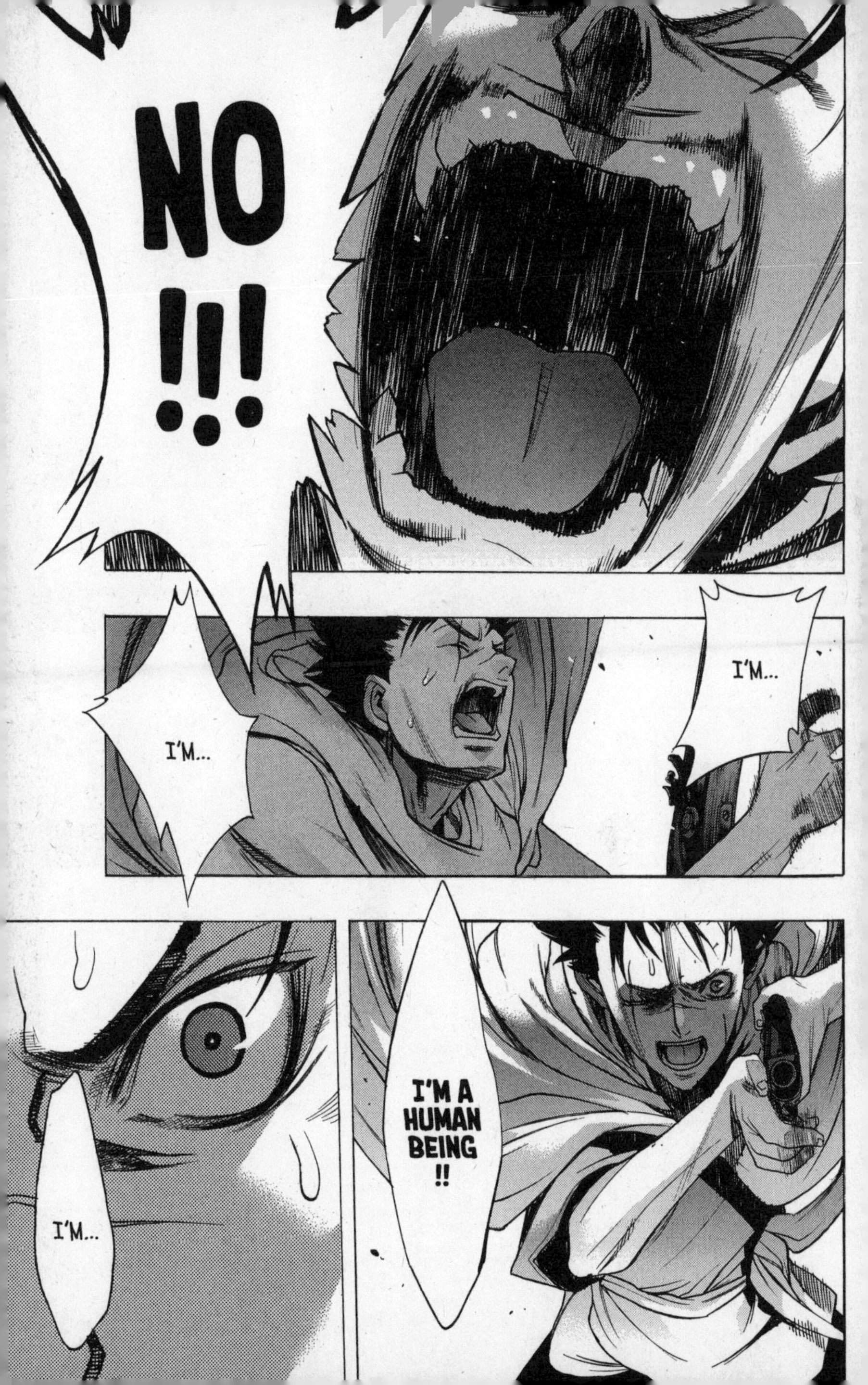
NO!!!
I'M...
I'M...
I'M A HUMAN BEING!!
I'M...

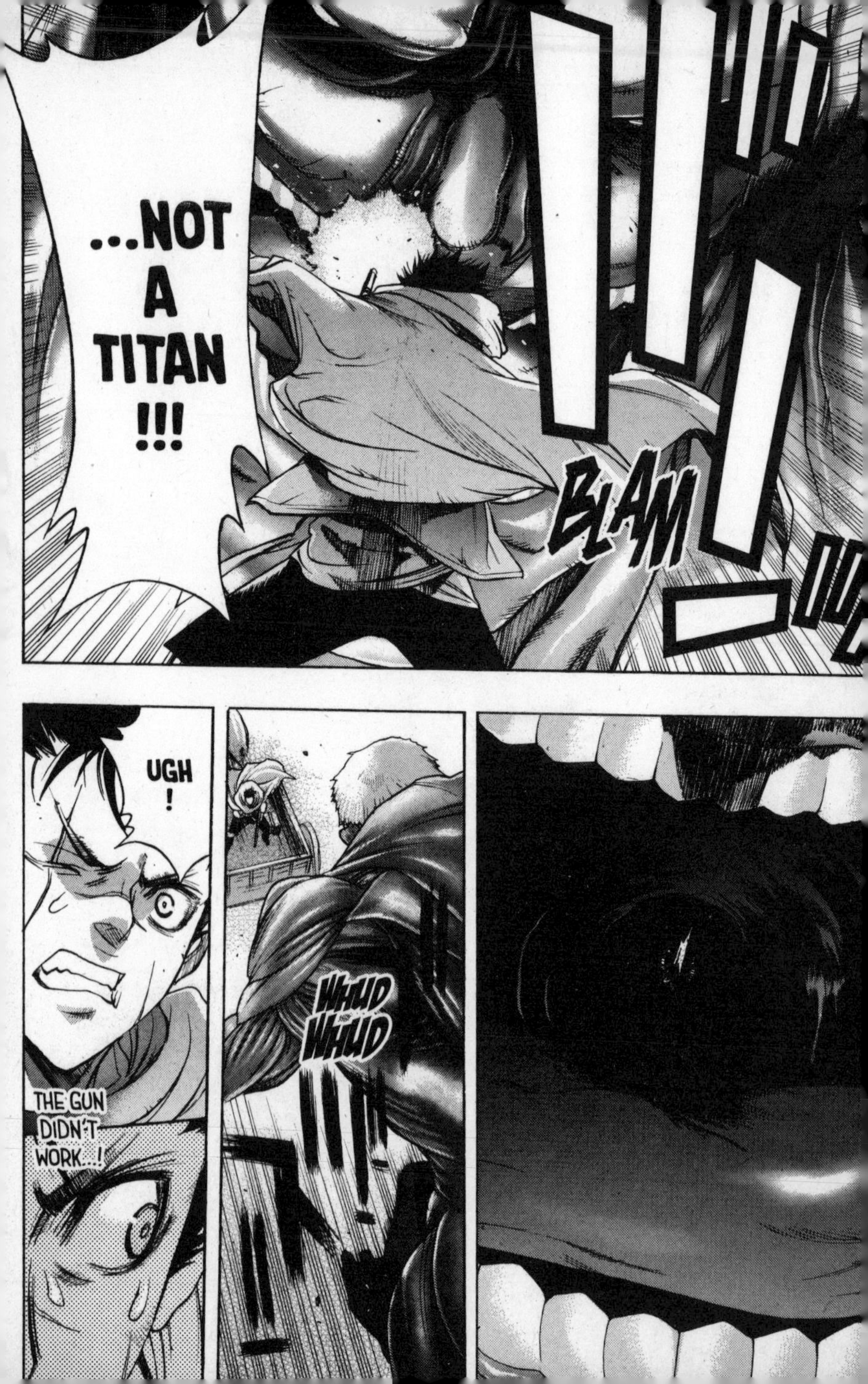
...NOT A TITAN!!!
BLAM
WHUD
WHUD
UGH!
THE GUN DIDN'T WORK...!

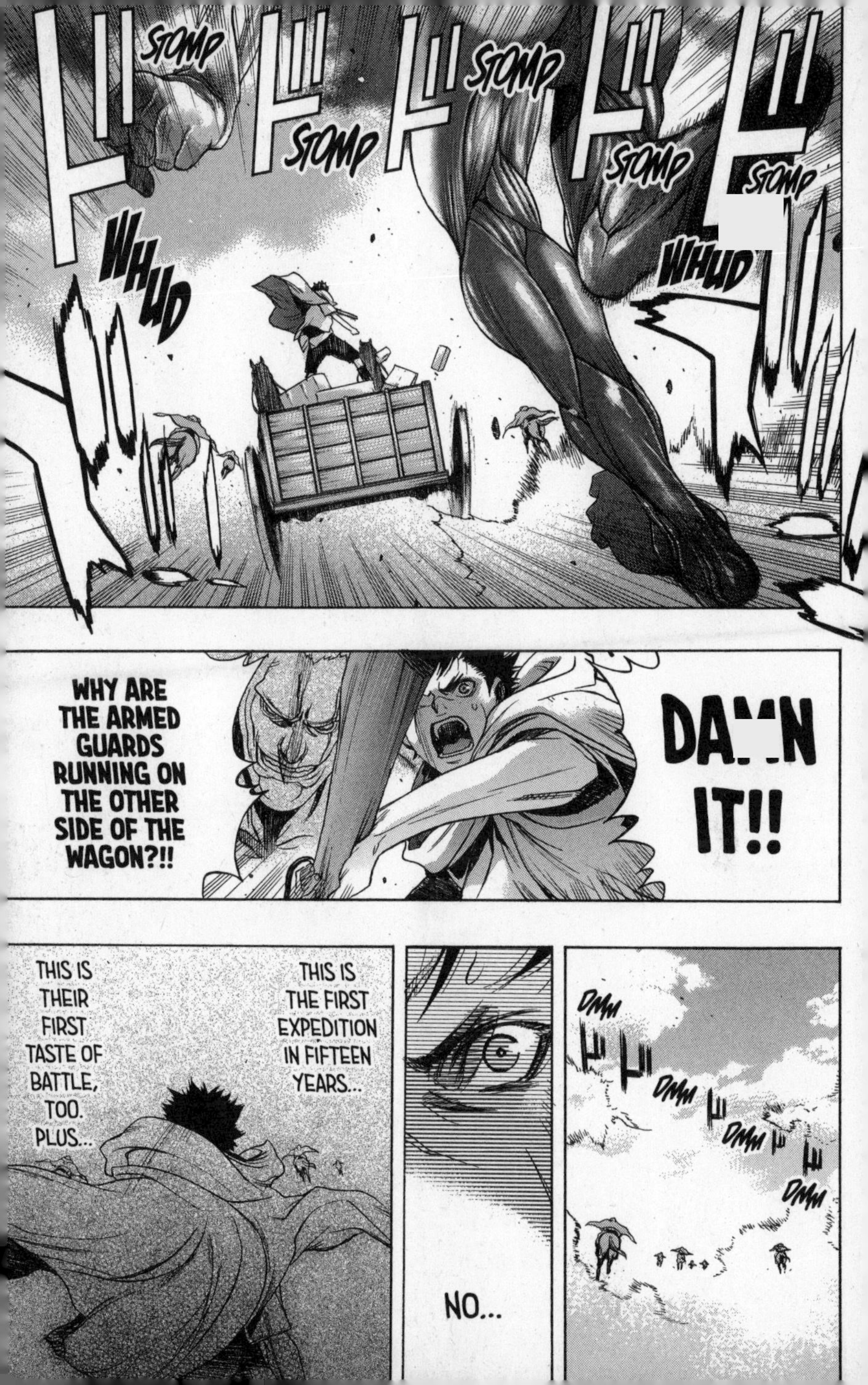
STOMP
STOMP
STOMP
STOMP
STOMP
WHUD
WHUD
DAMN IT!!
WHY ARE THE ARMED GUARDS RUNNING ON THE OTHER SIDE OF THE WAGON?!!
DMM
DMM
DMM
DMM
NO...
THIS IS THE FIRST EXPEDITION IN FIFTEEN YEARS...
THIS IS THEIR FIRST TASTE OF BATTLE, TOO. PLUS...

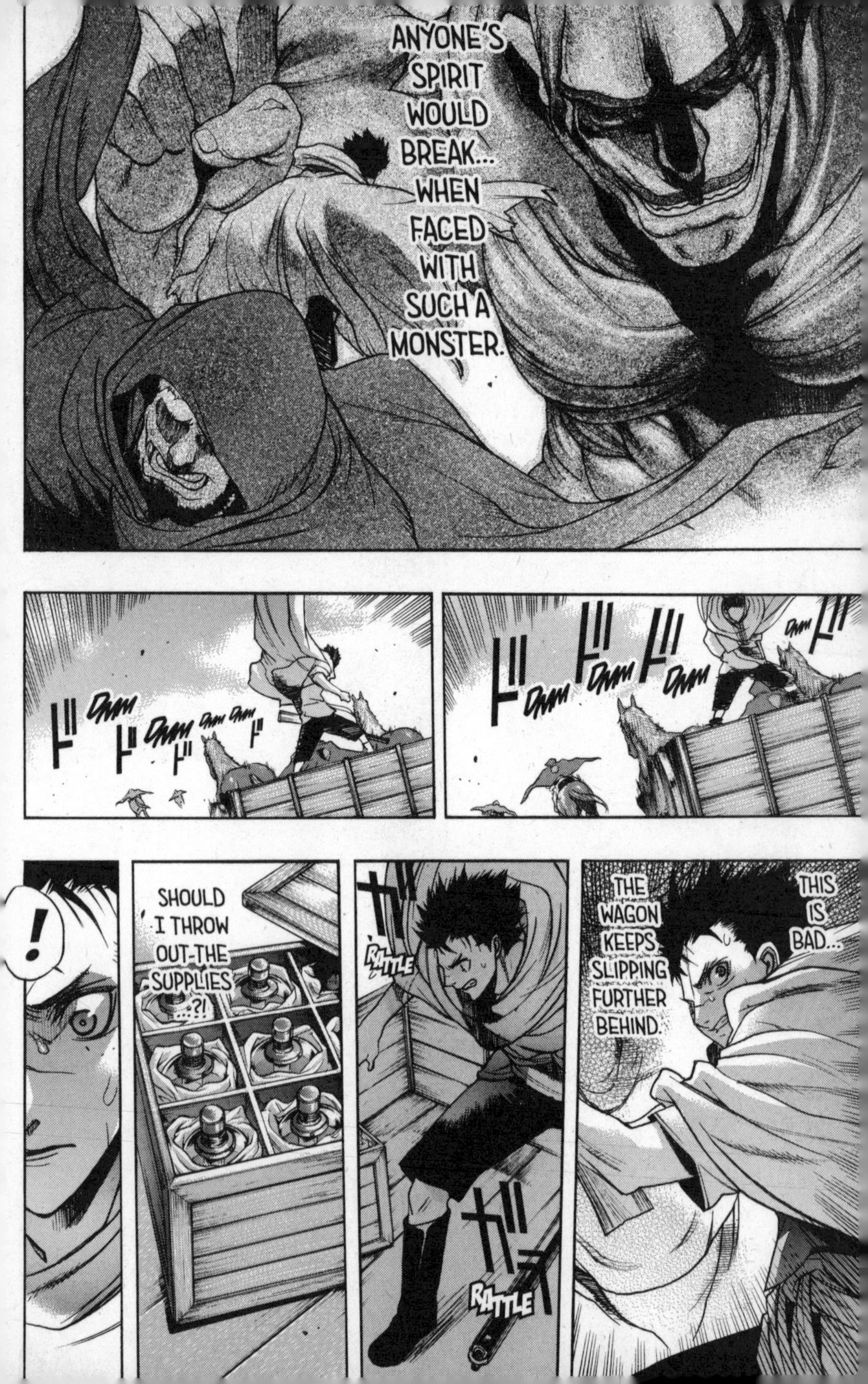
ANYONE'S SPIRIT WOULD BREAK... WHEN FACED WITH SUCH A MONSTER.
DMM DMM DMM DMM
DMM DMM DMM DMM DMM
THIS IS BAD...
THE WAGON KEEPS SLIPPING FURTHER BEHIND.
RATTLE
RATTLE
SHOULD I THROW OUT THE SUPPLIES...?!
!

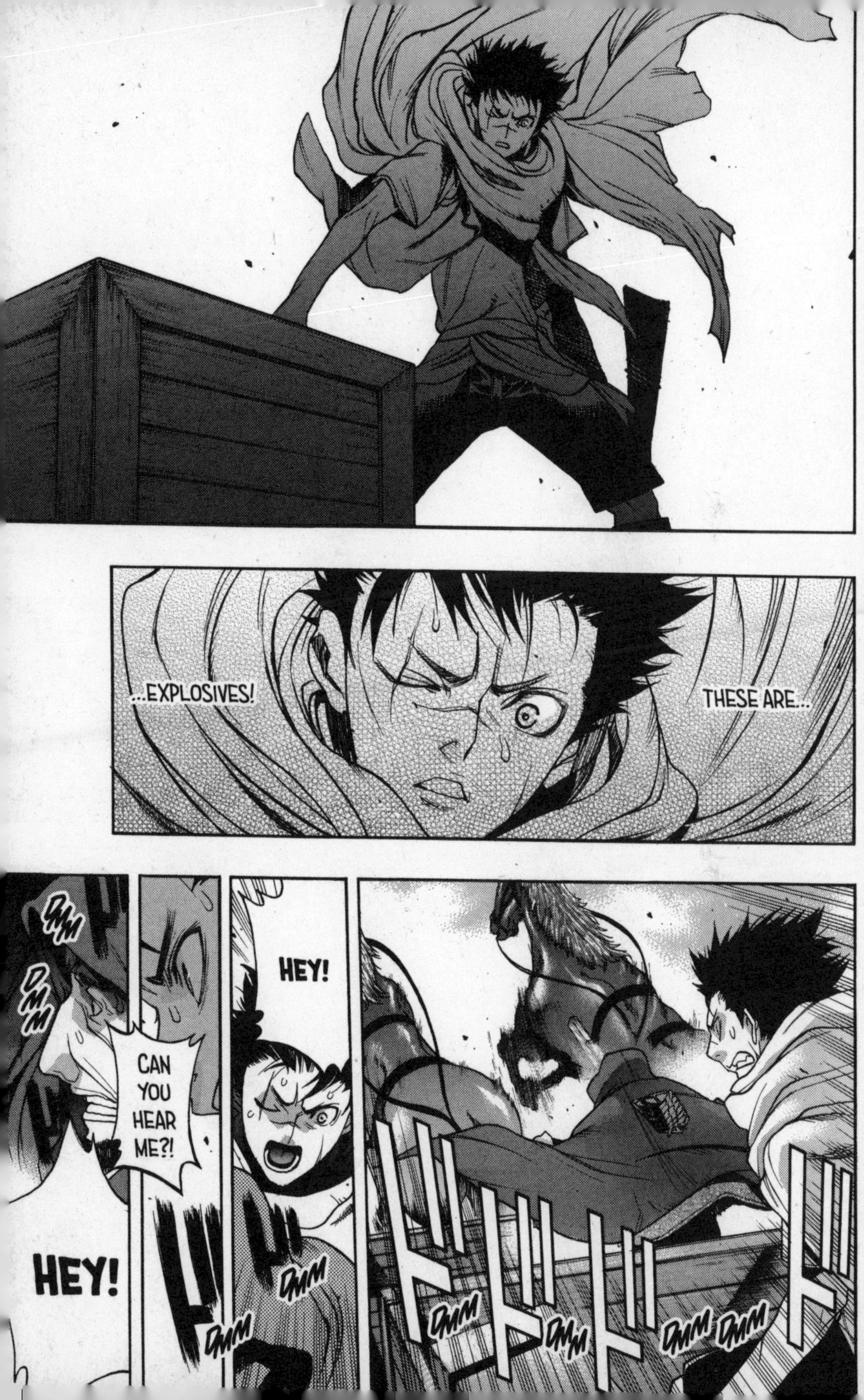
THESE ARE...
...EXPLOSIVES!
HEY!
CAN YOU HEAR ME?!
HEY!
DMM
DMM
DMM
DMM
DMM
DMM
DMM
DMM
DMM

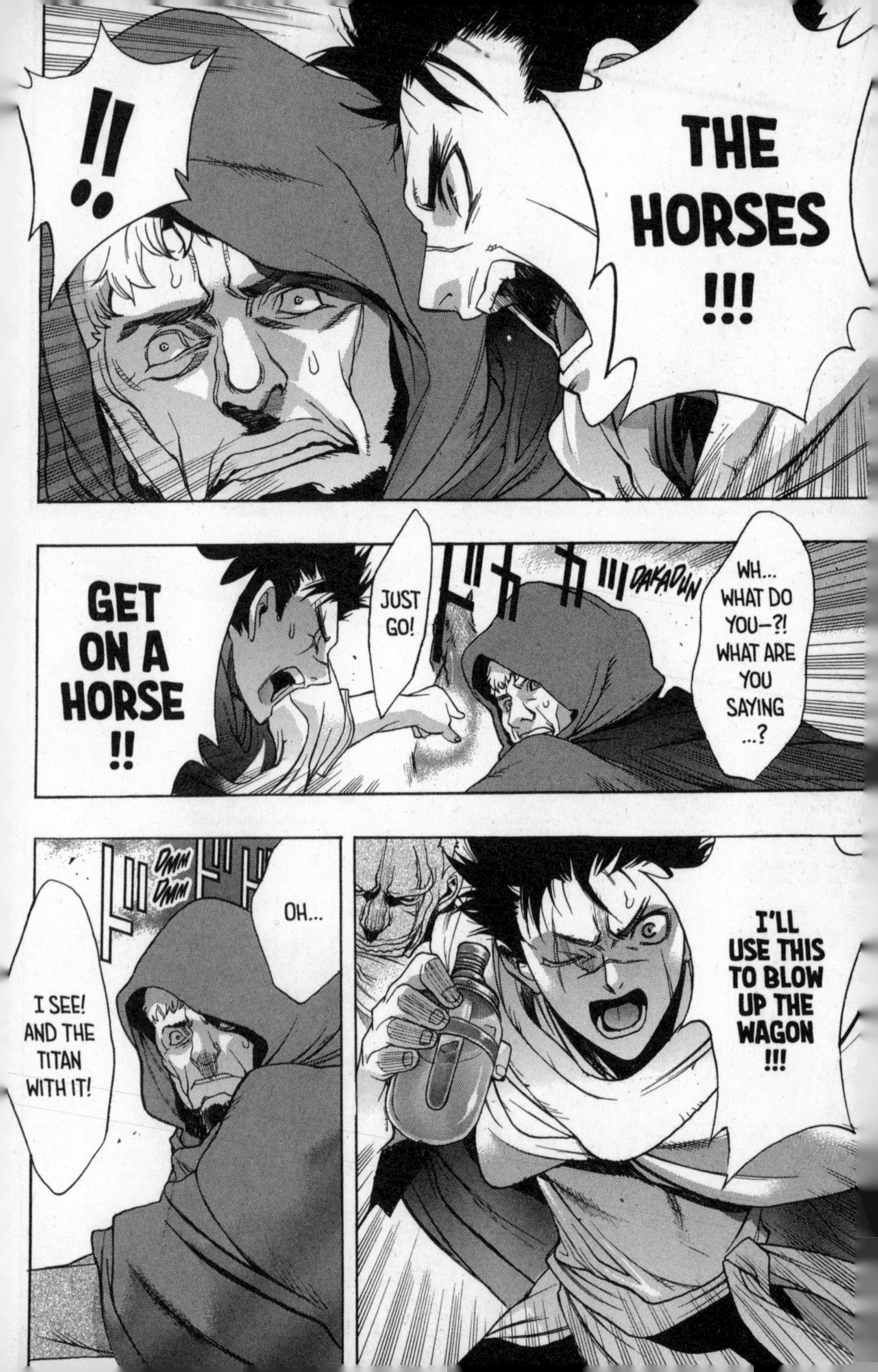
THE HORSES !!!
!!
WH... WHAT DO YOU—?! WHAT ARE YOU SAYING ...?
DAKADUN
JUST GO!
GET ON A HORSE !!
I'LL USE THIS TO BLOW UP THE WAGON !!!
OH...
DMM DMM
I SEE! AND THE TITAN WITH IT!

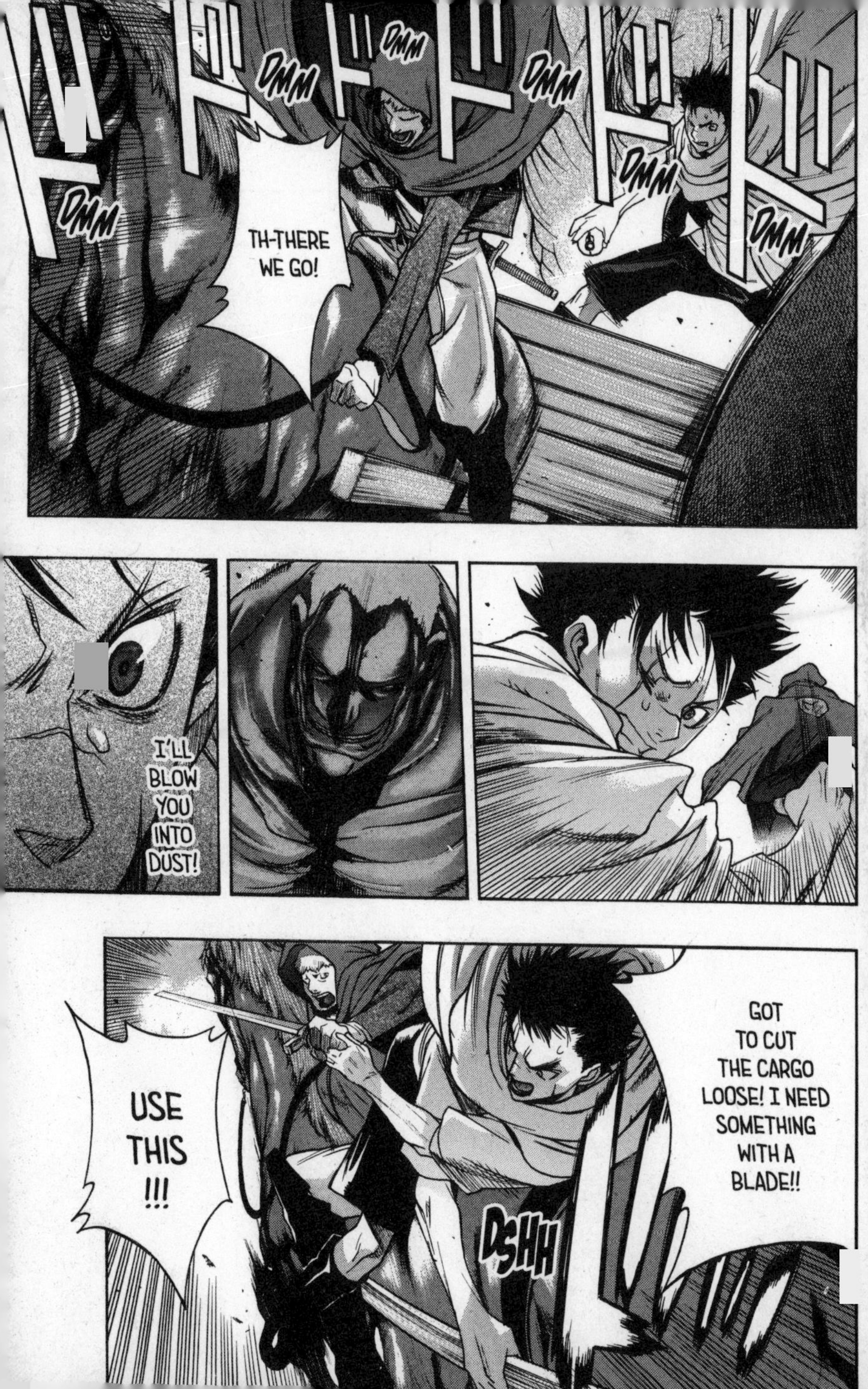
DMM
DMM
DMM
DMM
DMM
DMM
TH-THERE WE GO!
I'LL BLOW YOU INTO DUST!
GOT TO CUT THE CARGO LOOSE! I NEED SOMETHING WITH A BLADE!!
USE THIS !!!
DSHH

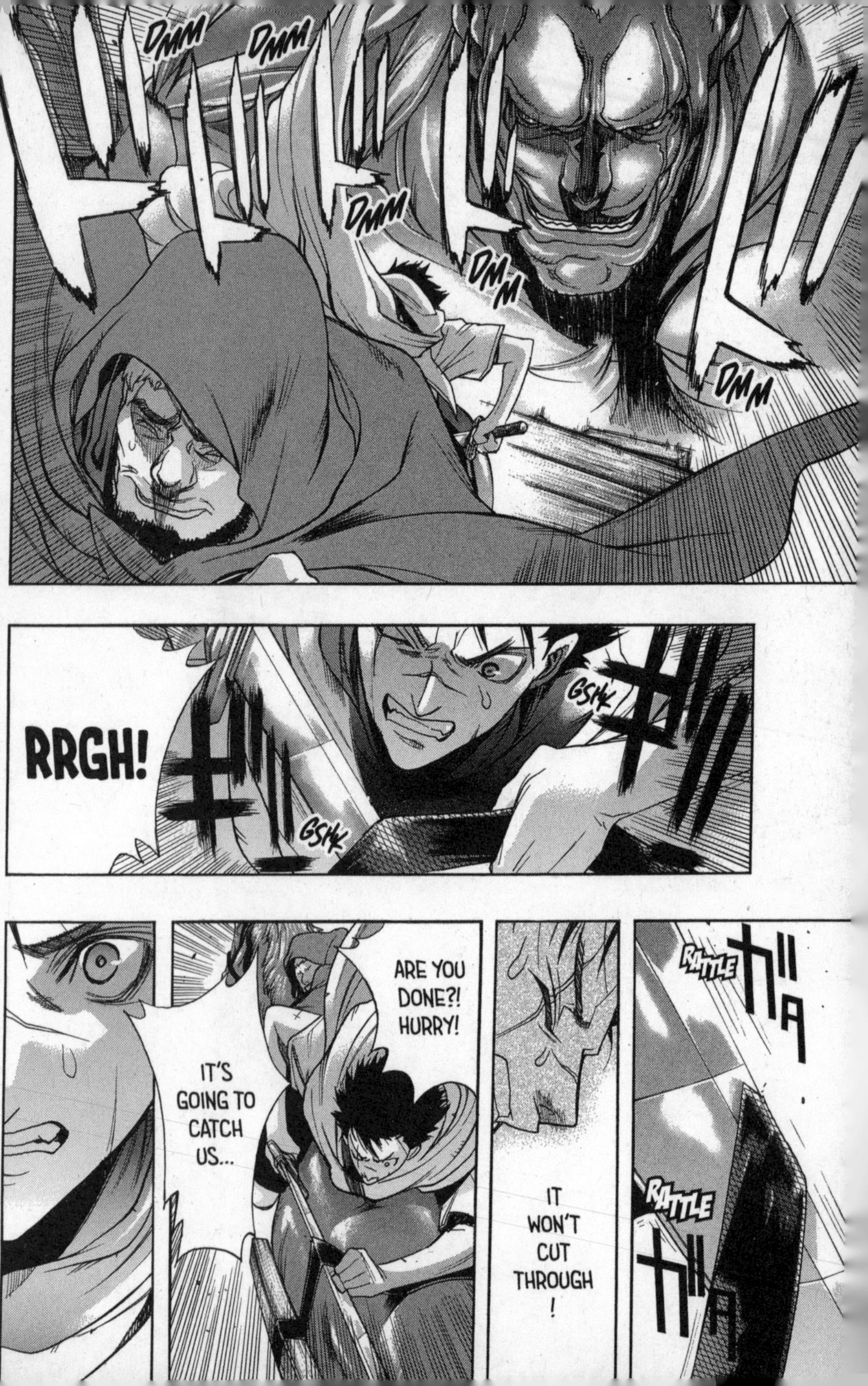
DMM
DMM
DMM
DMM
DMM
RRGH!
GSHK
GSHK
RATTLE
ARE YOU DONE?! HURRY!
IT'S GOING TO CATCH US...
IT WON'T CUT THROUGH!
RATTLE

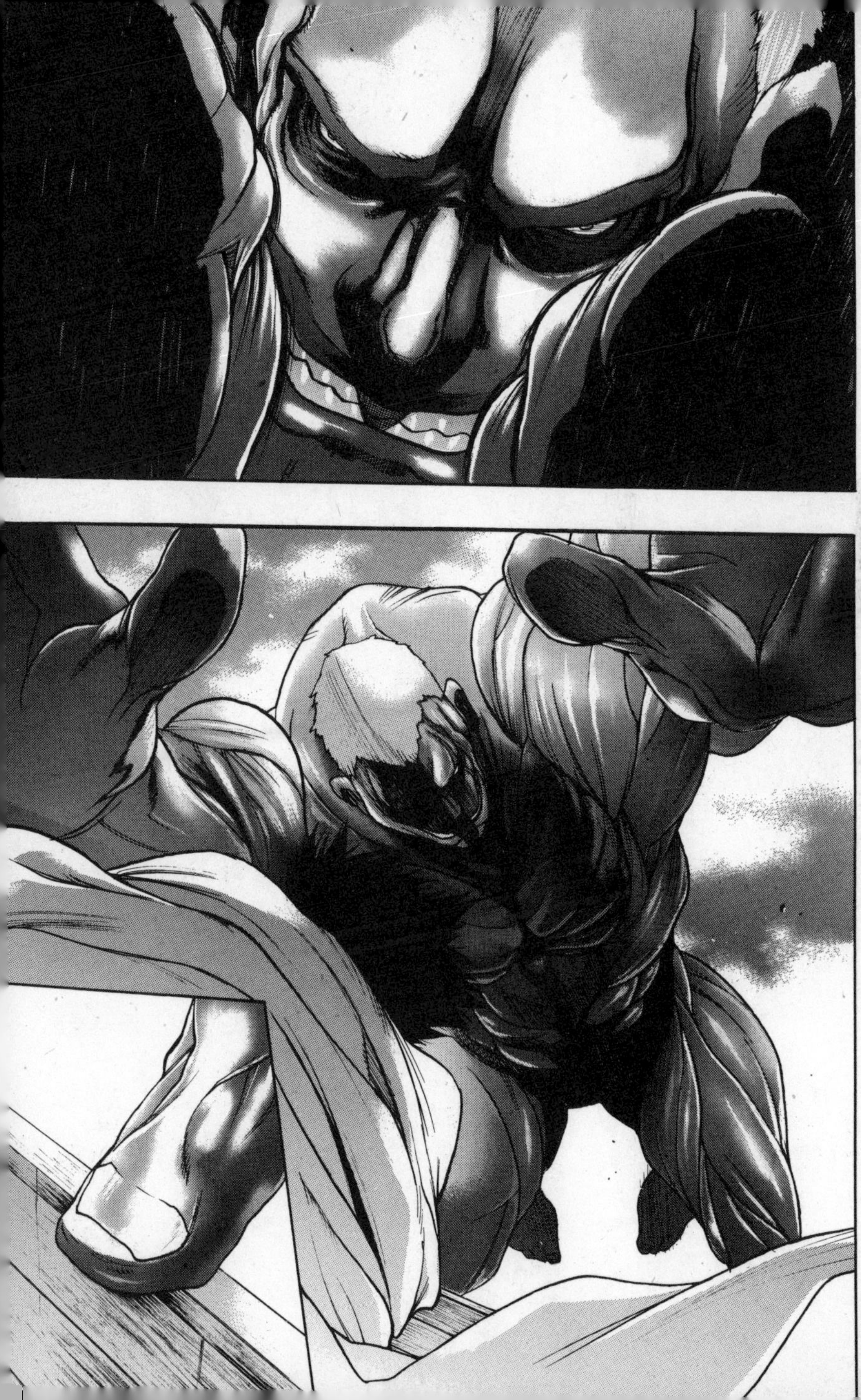

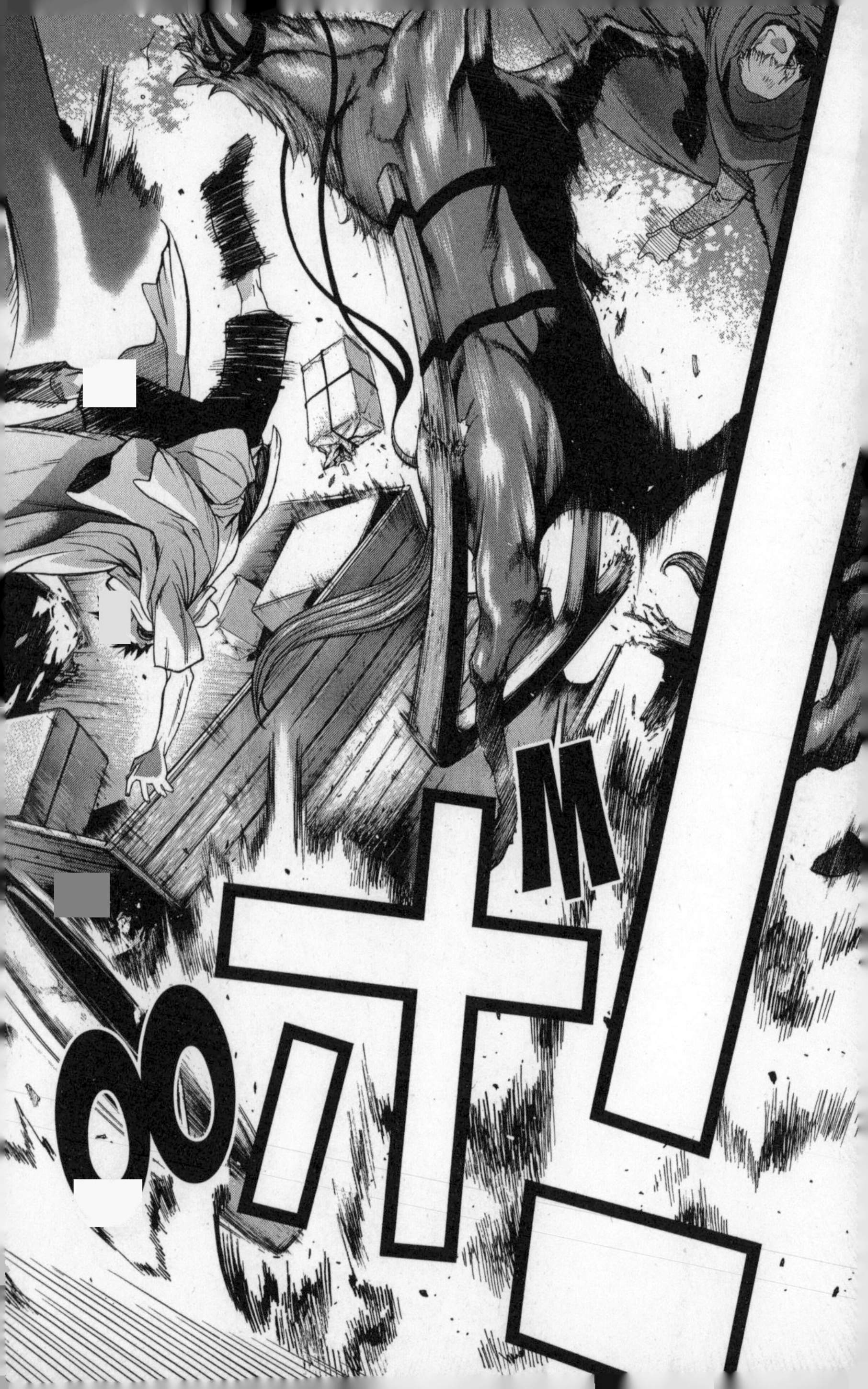

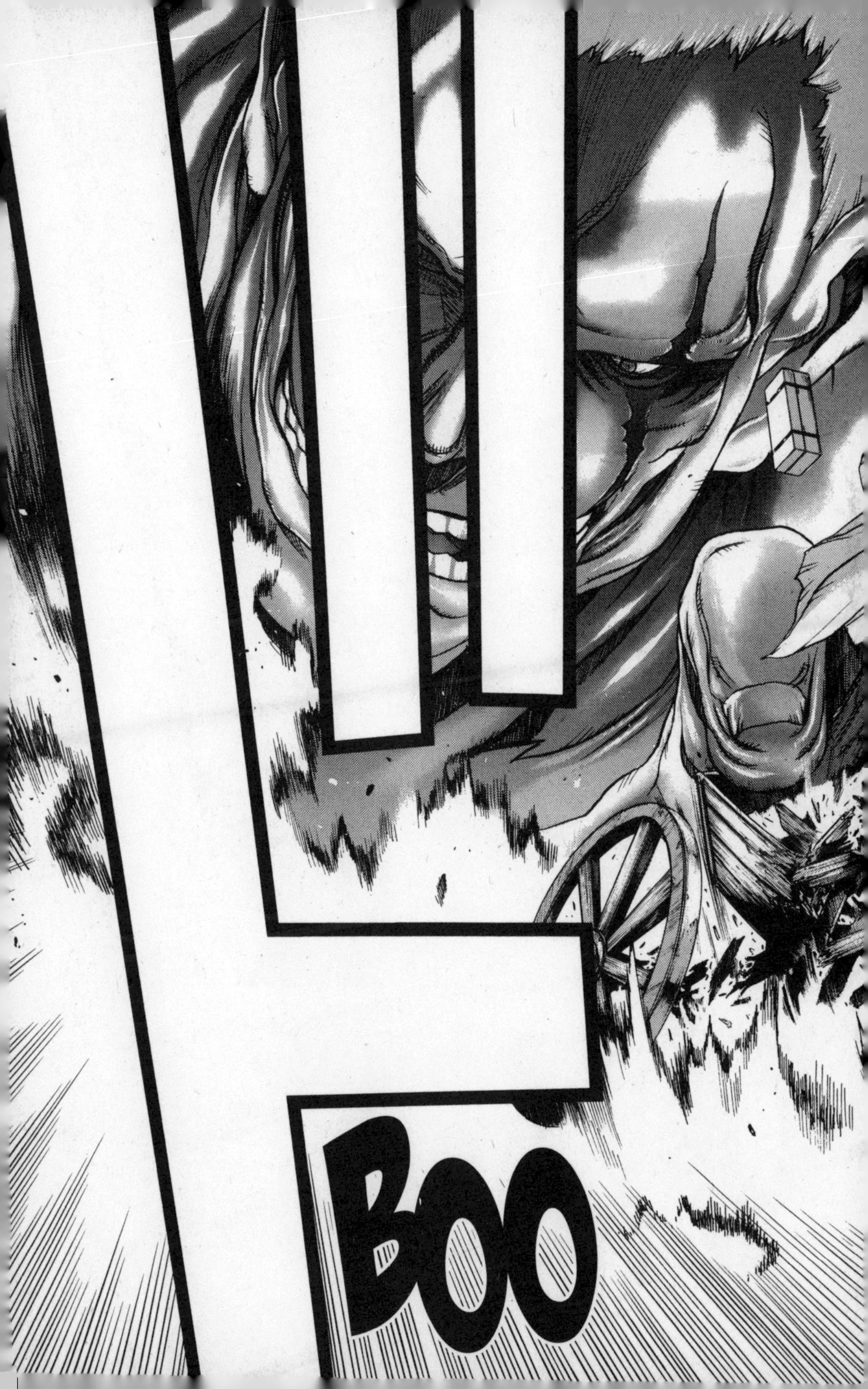
BOO

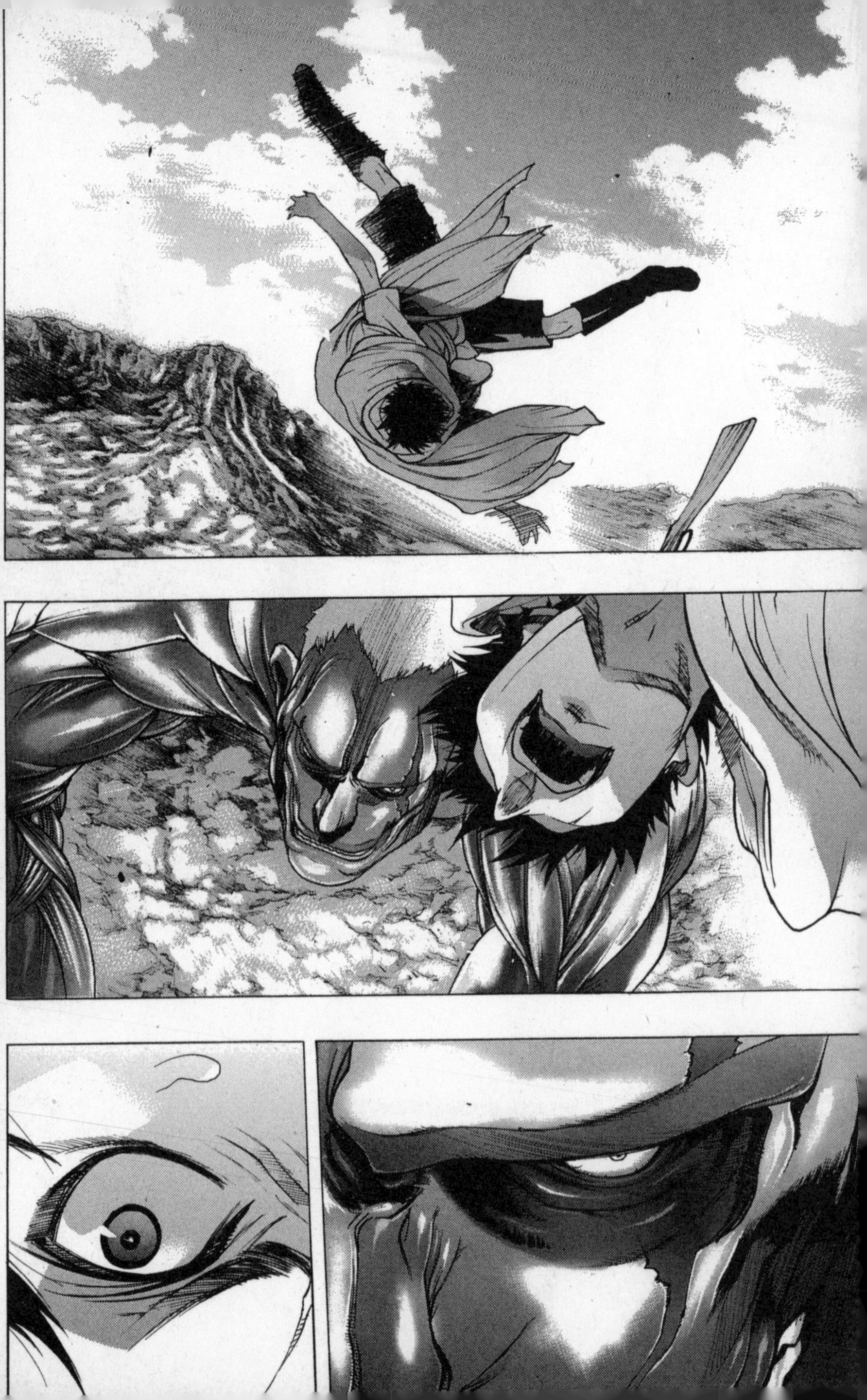

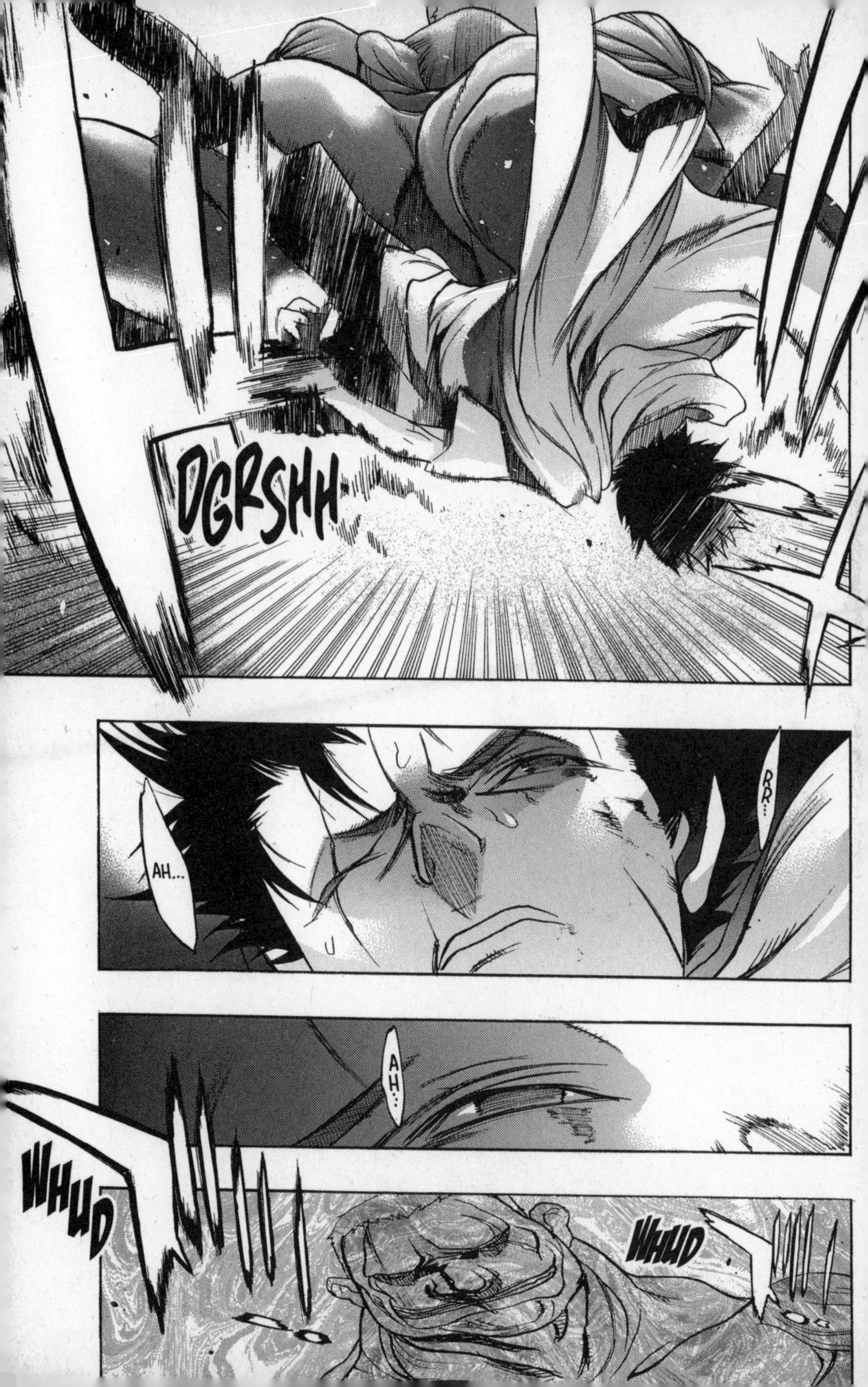
DGRSHH
RR...
AH...
AH...
WHUD
WHUD

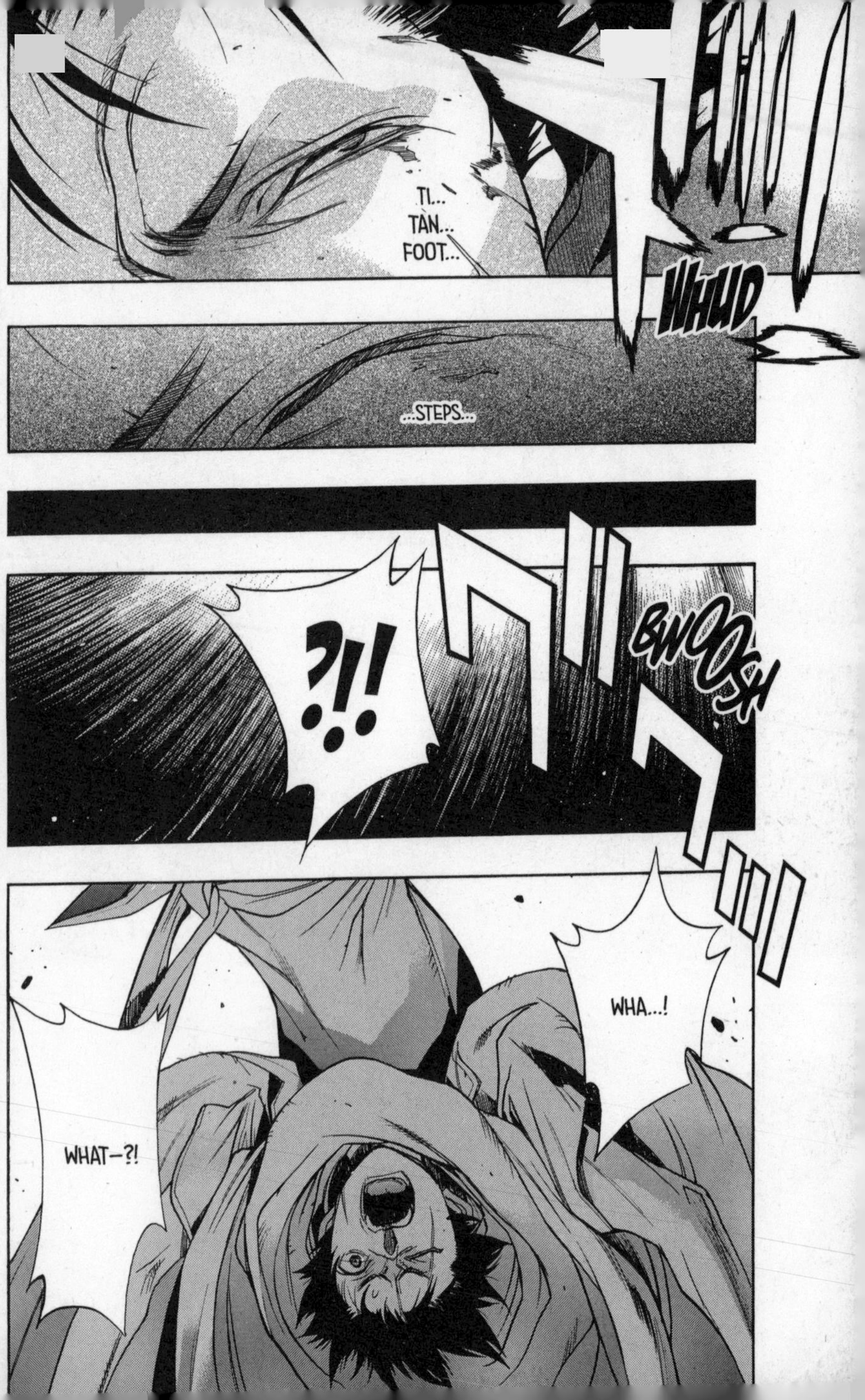
TI...
TAN...
FOOT...
WHUD
...STEPS...
?!!
BWOOSH
WHA...!
WHAT—?!

WHA—

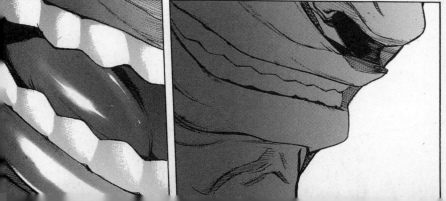

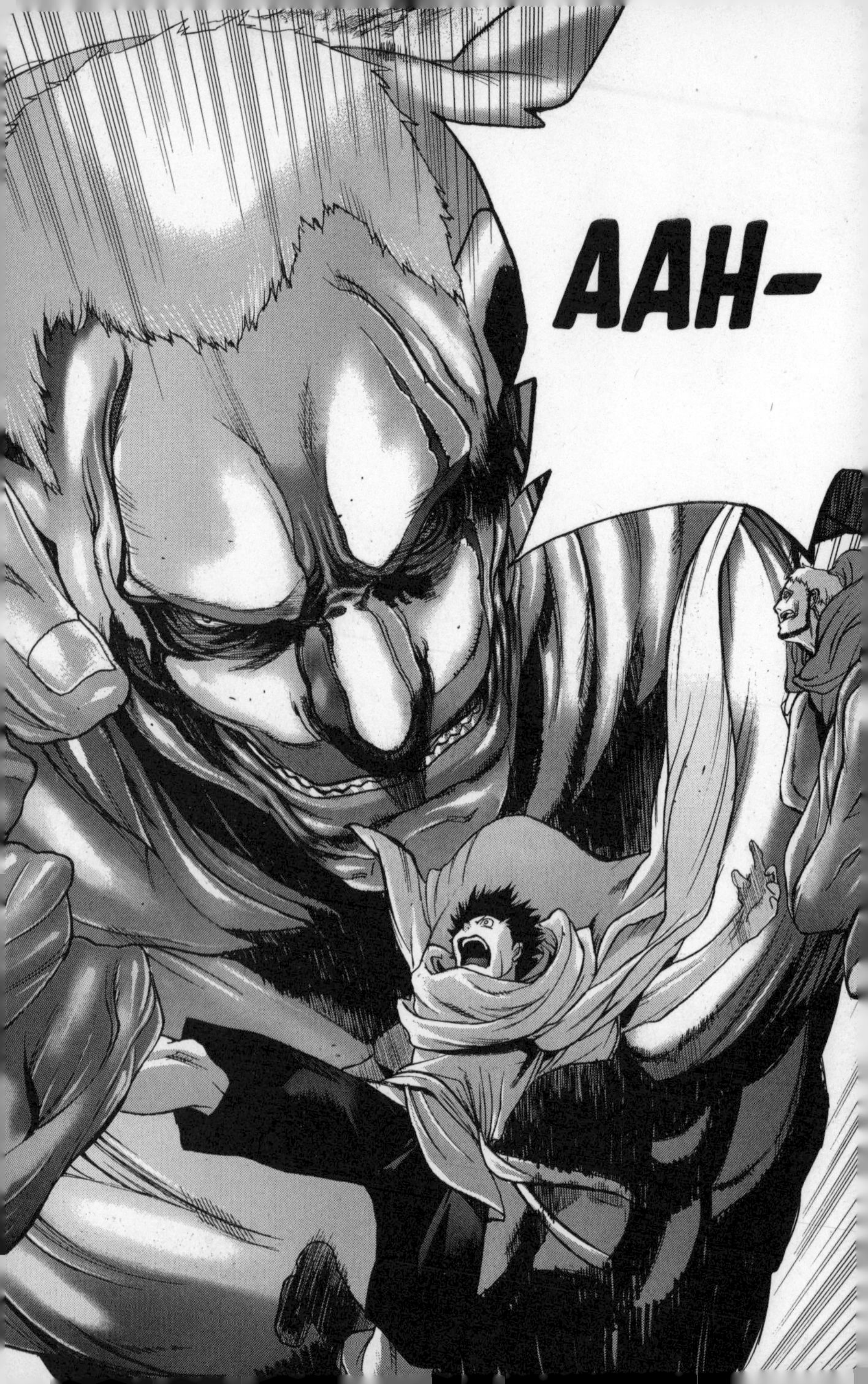
AAH-

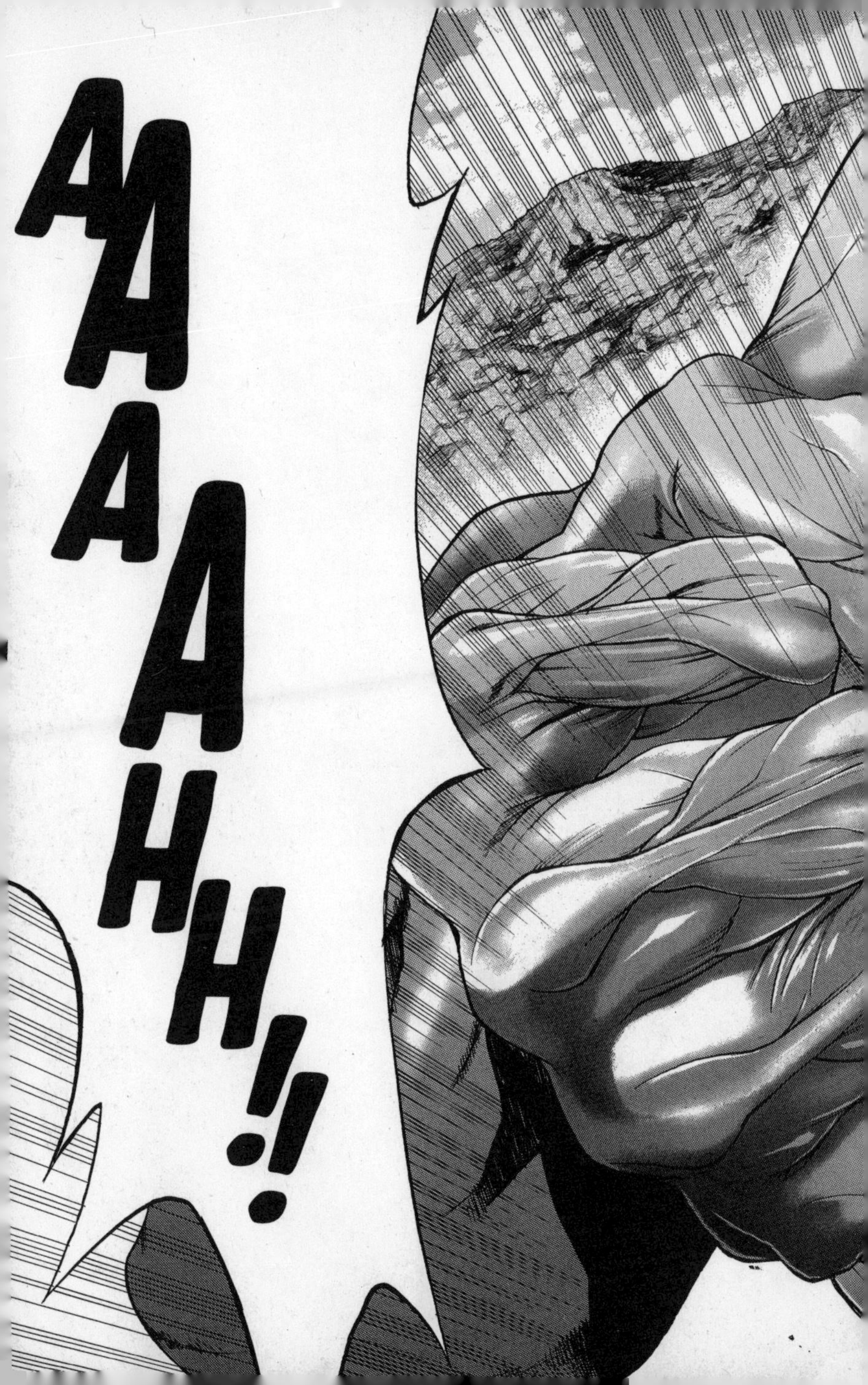
AAAAAHH!!

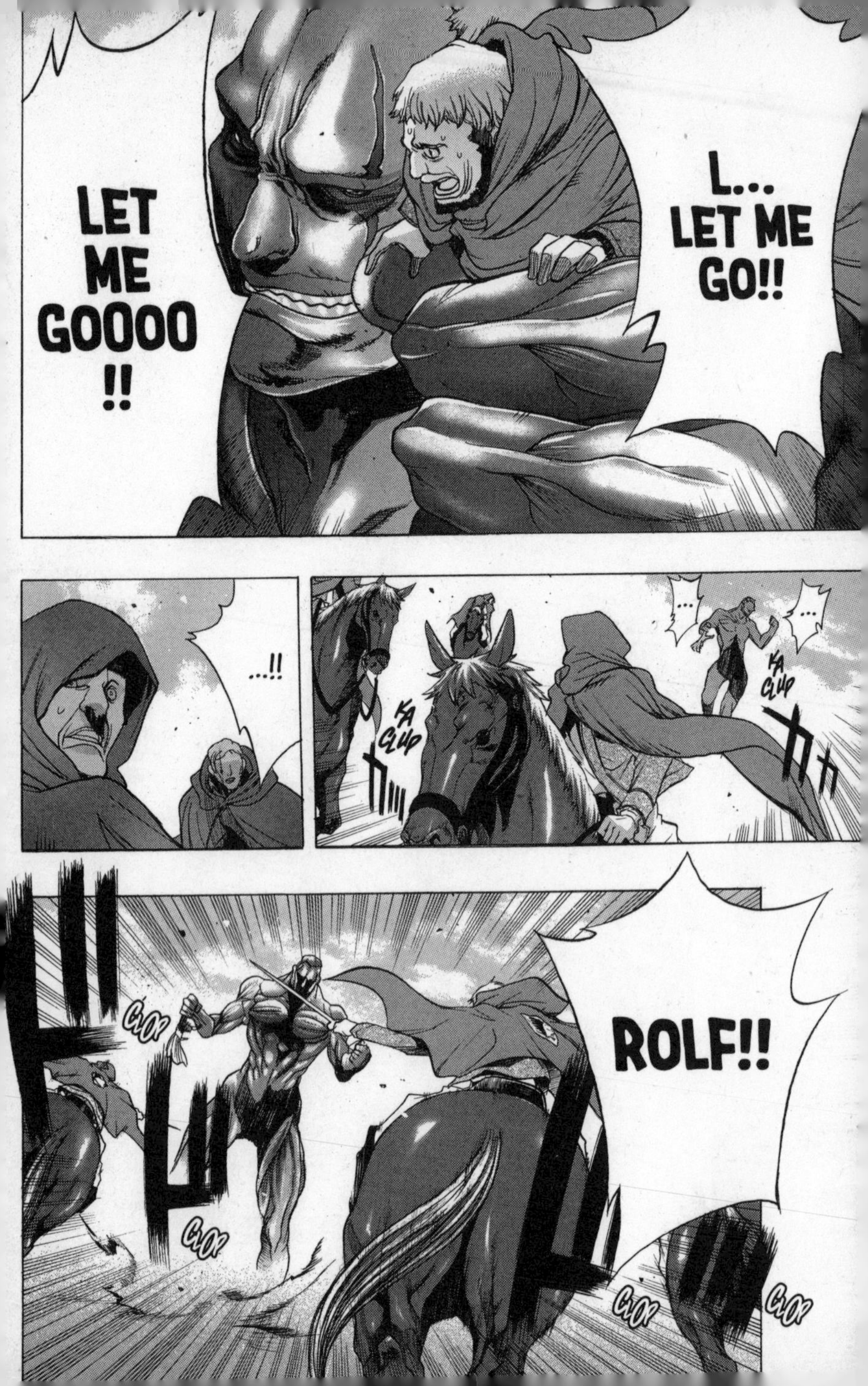
L... LET ME GO!!
LET ME GOOOO!!
...!!
...
...
KA CLUP
KA CLUP
ROLF!!
CLOP
CLOP
CLOP
CLOP

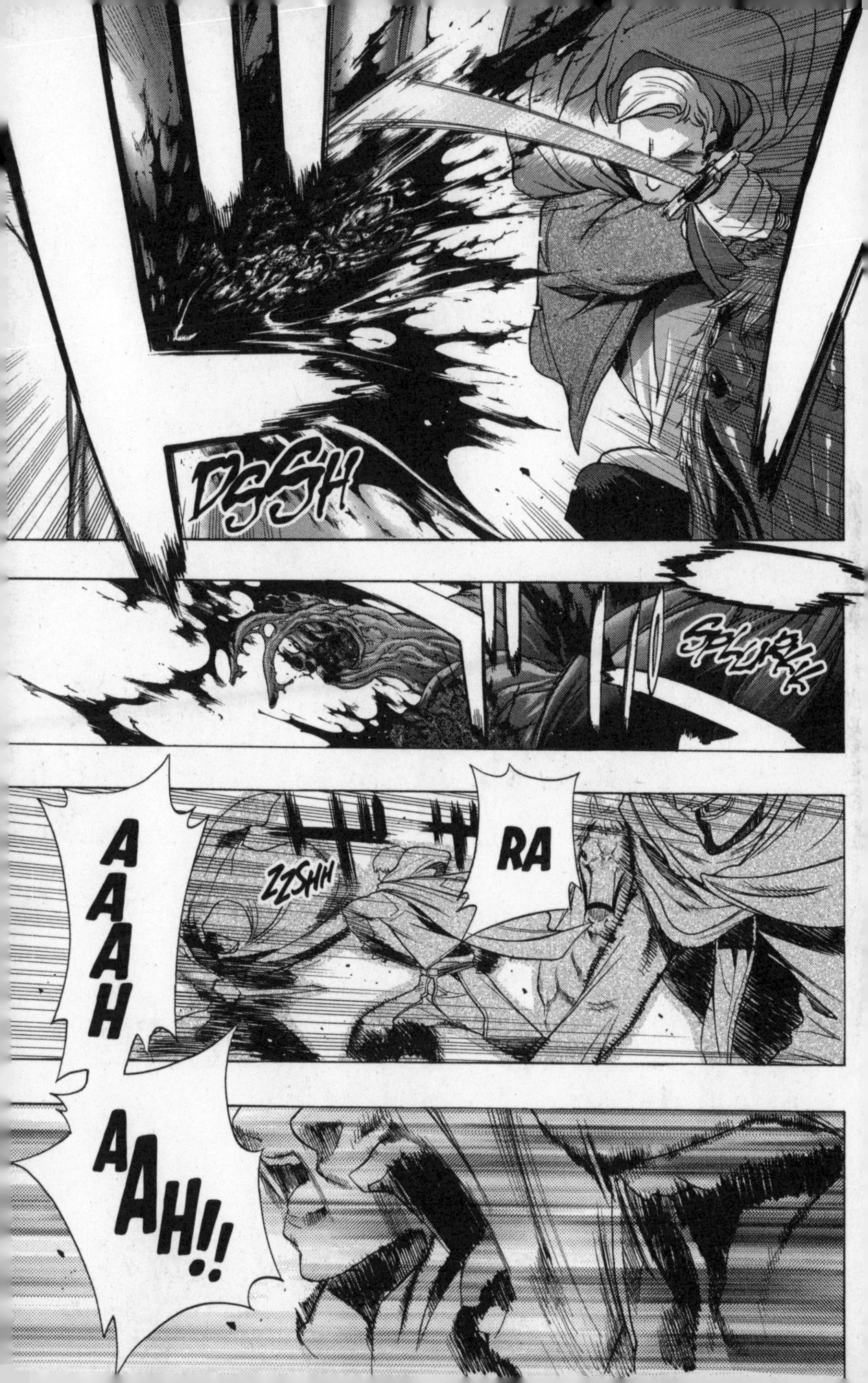
DGSH
RA
ZZSHH
AAAAH
AAH!!

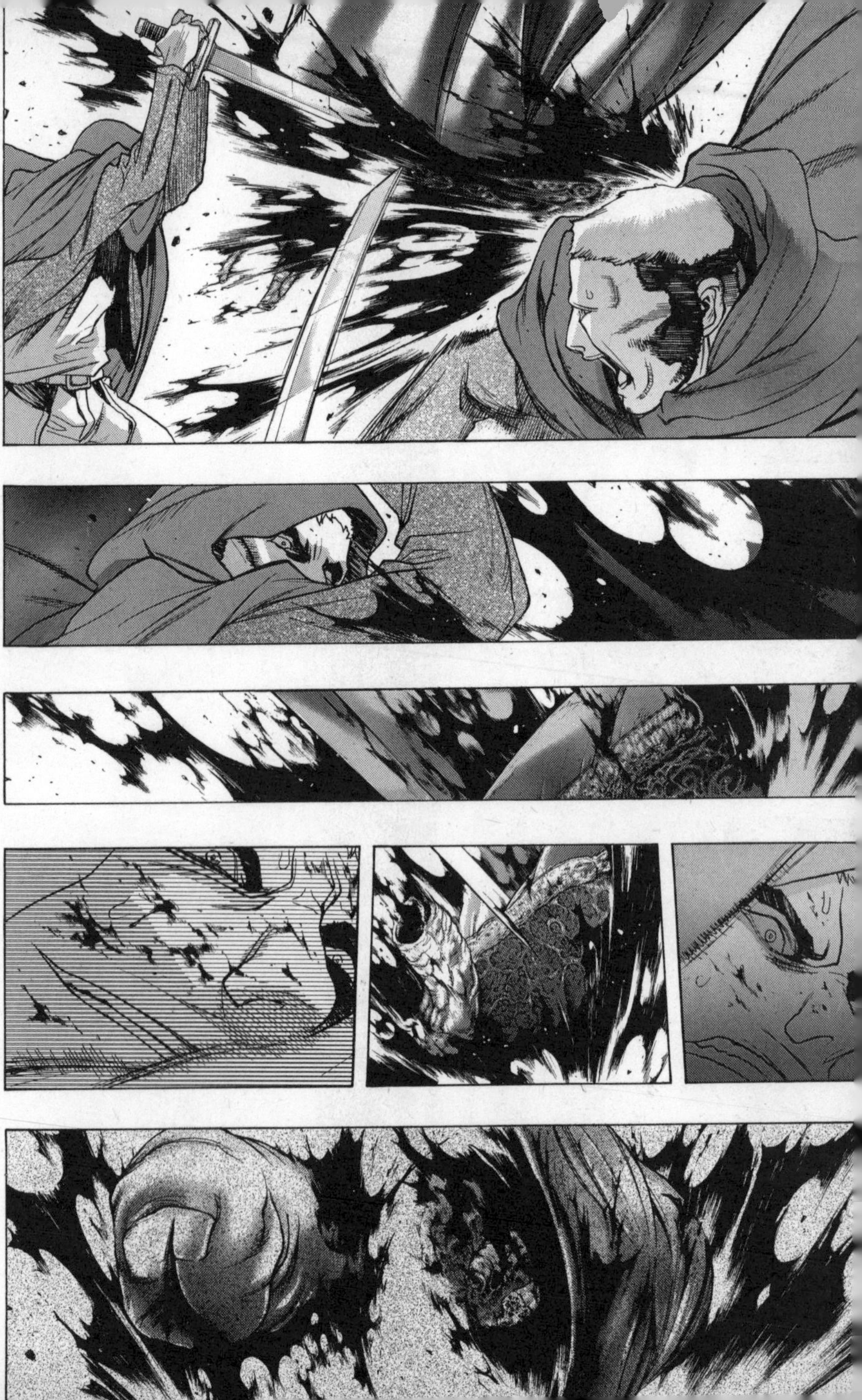

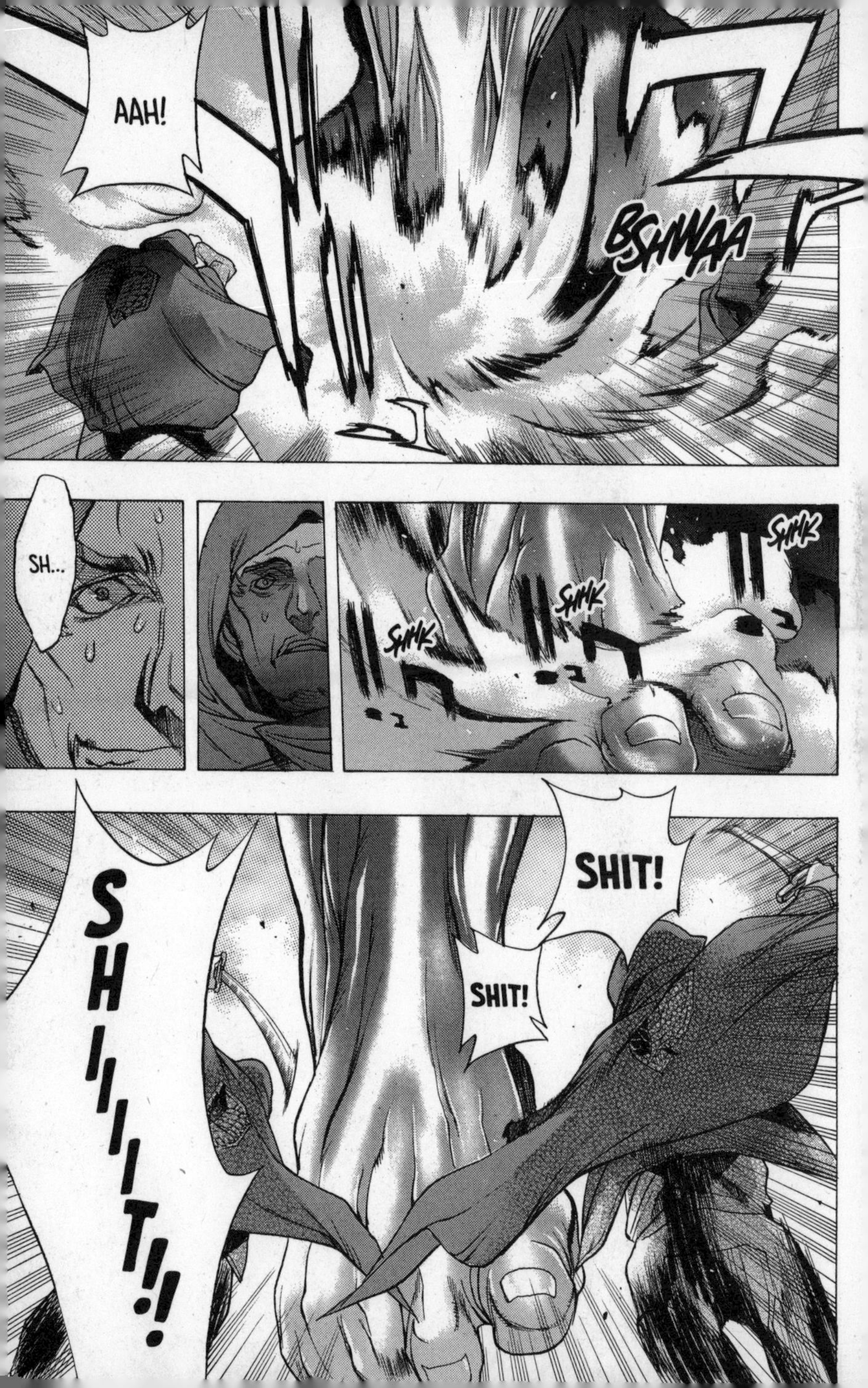
AAH!
BSHWAA
SH...
SHHK
SHHK
SHHK
SHIT!
SHIT!
SHIIIIIT!!

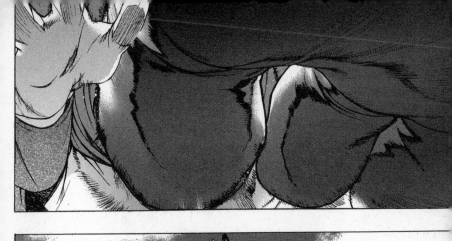

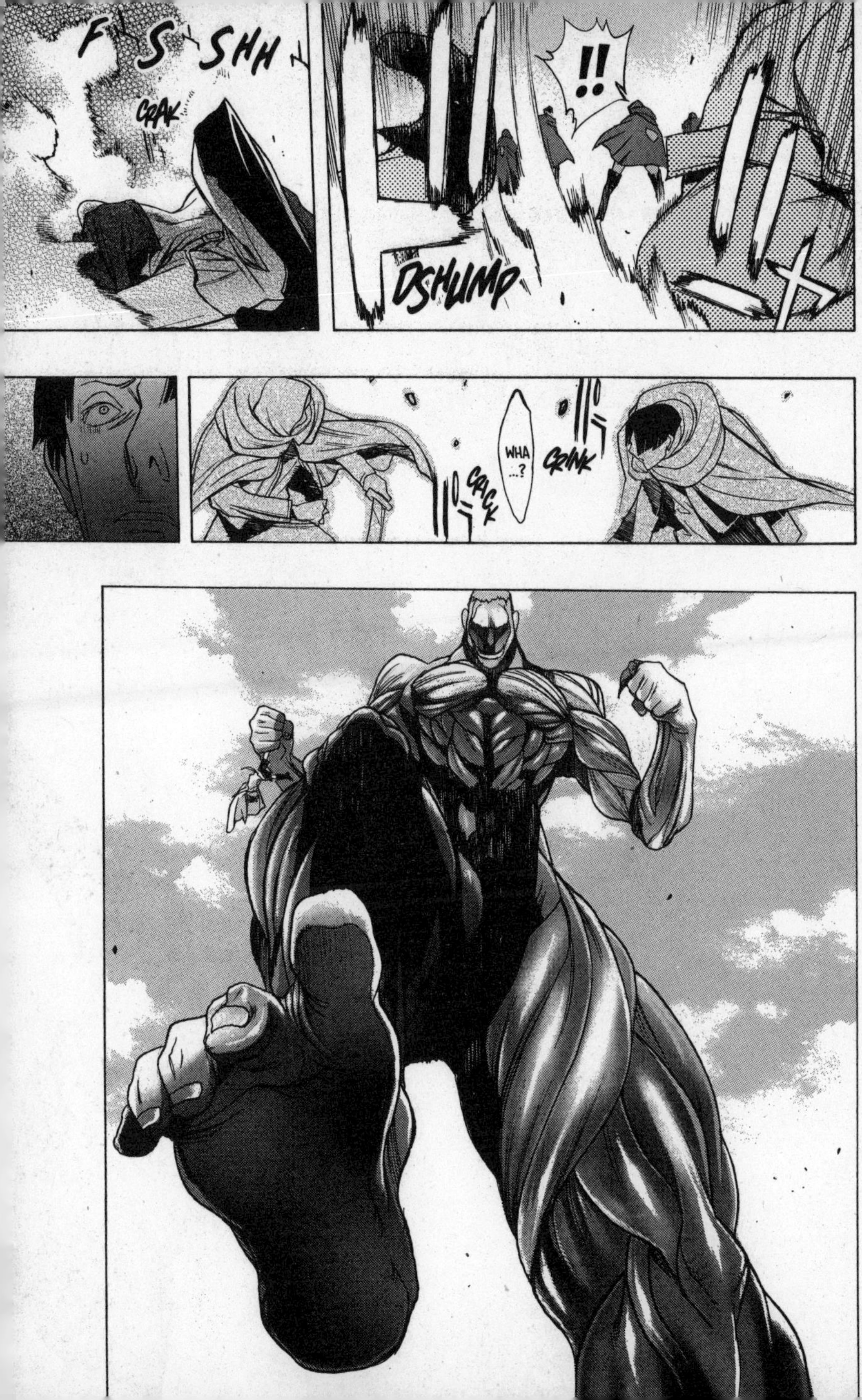

!!
DSHUMP
FSSHH
CRAK
GRINK
WHA ...?
CRACK

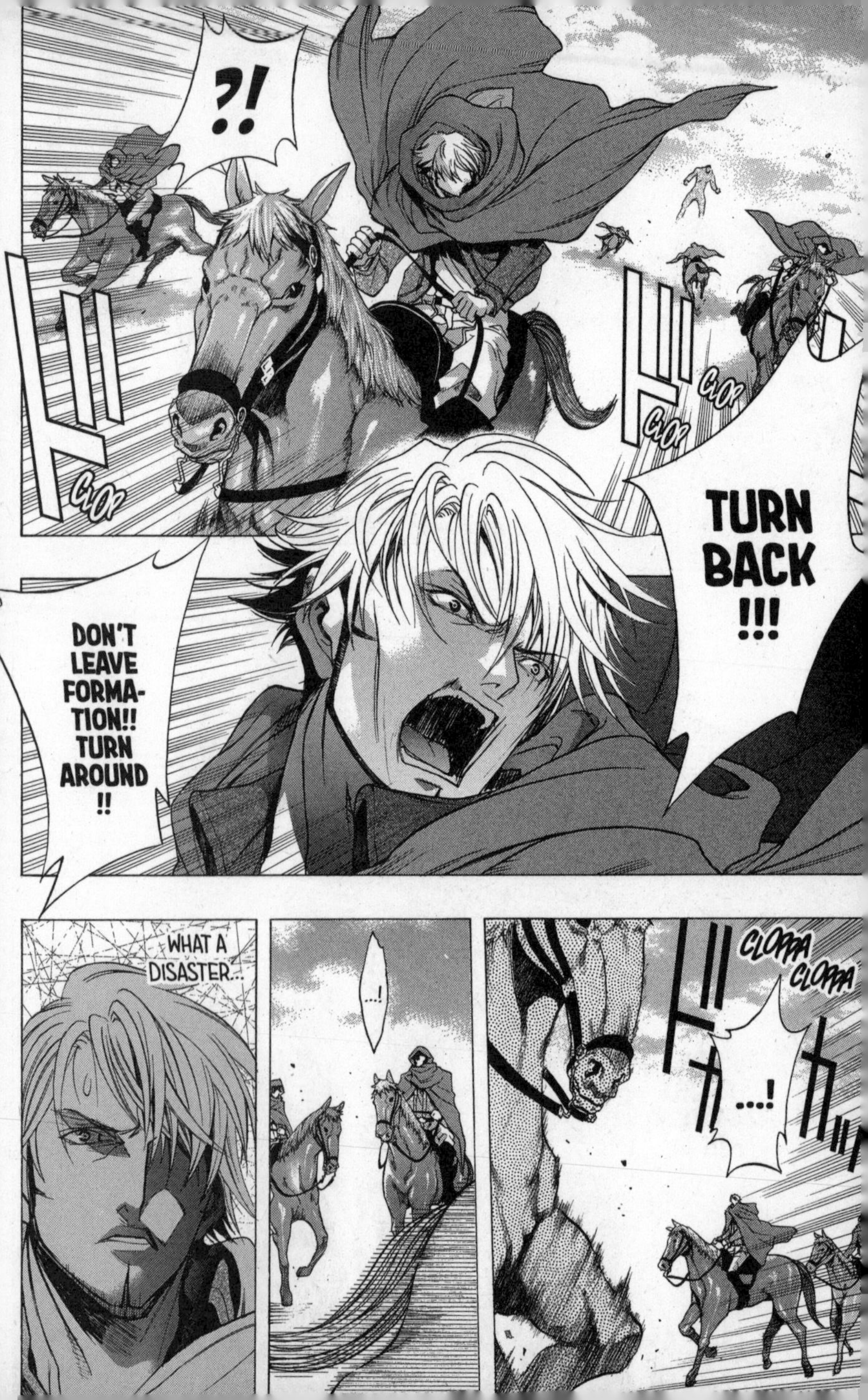
?!
CLOP
CLOP
CLOP
TURN BACK !!!
DON'T LEAVE FORMA-TION!! TURN AROUND !!
CLOPPA CLOPPA
...!
...!
WHAT A DISASTER...

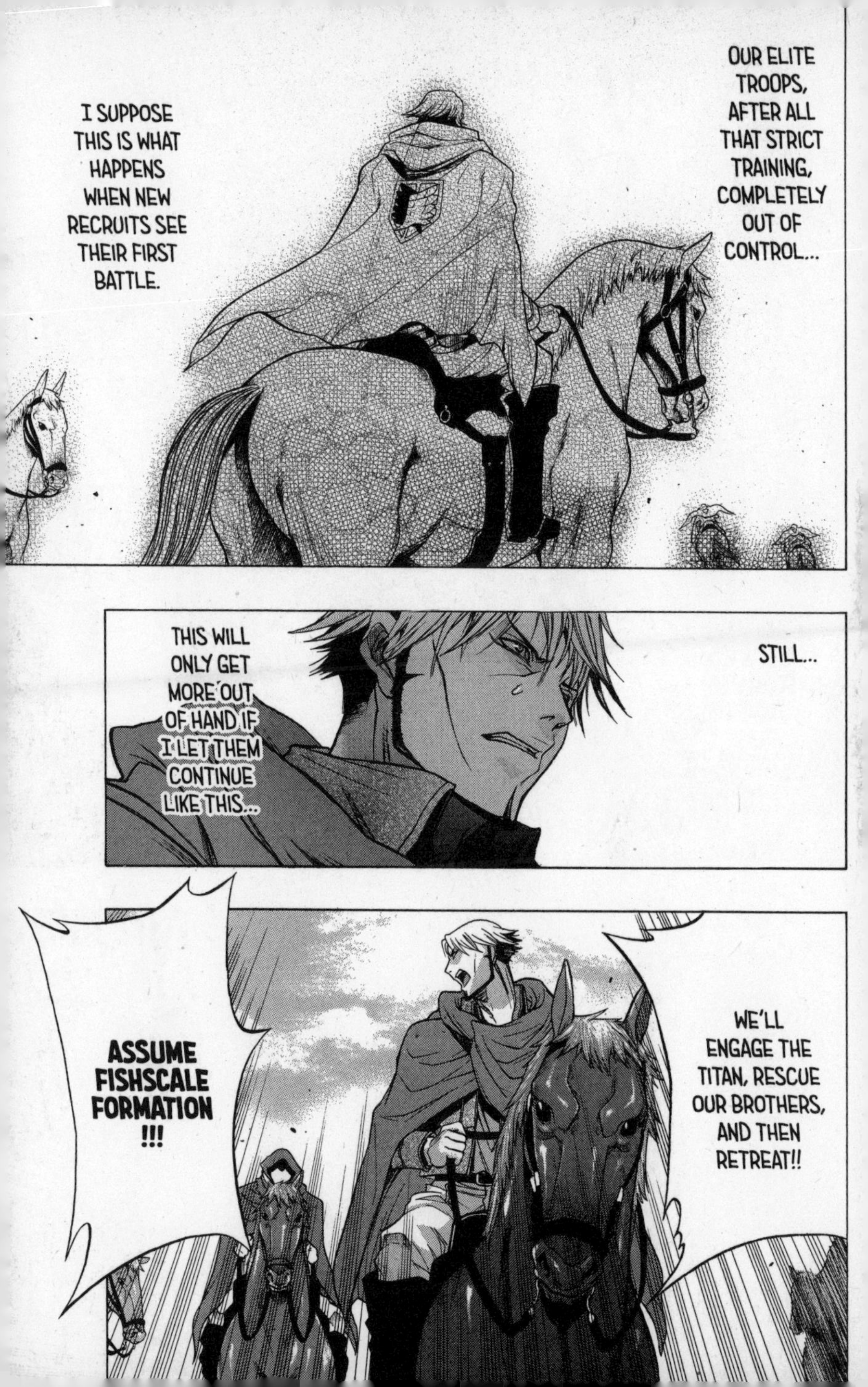
OUR ELITE TROOPS, AFTER ALL THAT STRICT TRAINING, COMPLETELY OUT OF CONTROL...
I SUPPOSE THIS IS WHAT HAPPENS WHEN NEW RECRUITS SEE THEIR FIRST BATTLE.
STILL...
THIS WILL ONLY GET MORE OUT OF HAND IF I LET THEM CONTINUE LIKE THIS...
WE'LL ENGAGE THE TITAN, RESCUE OUR BROTHERS, AND THEN RETREAT!!
ASSUME FISHSCALE FORMATION!!!

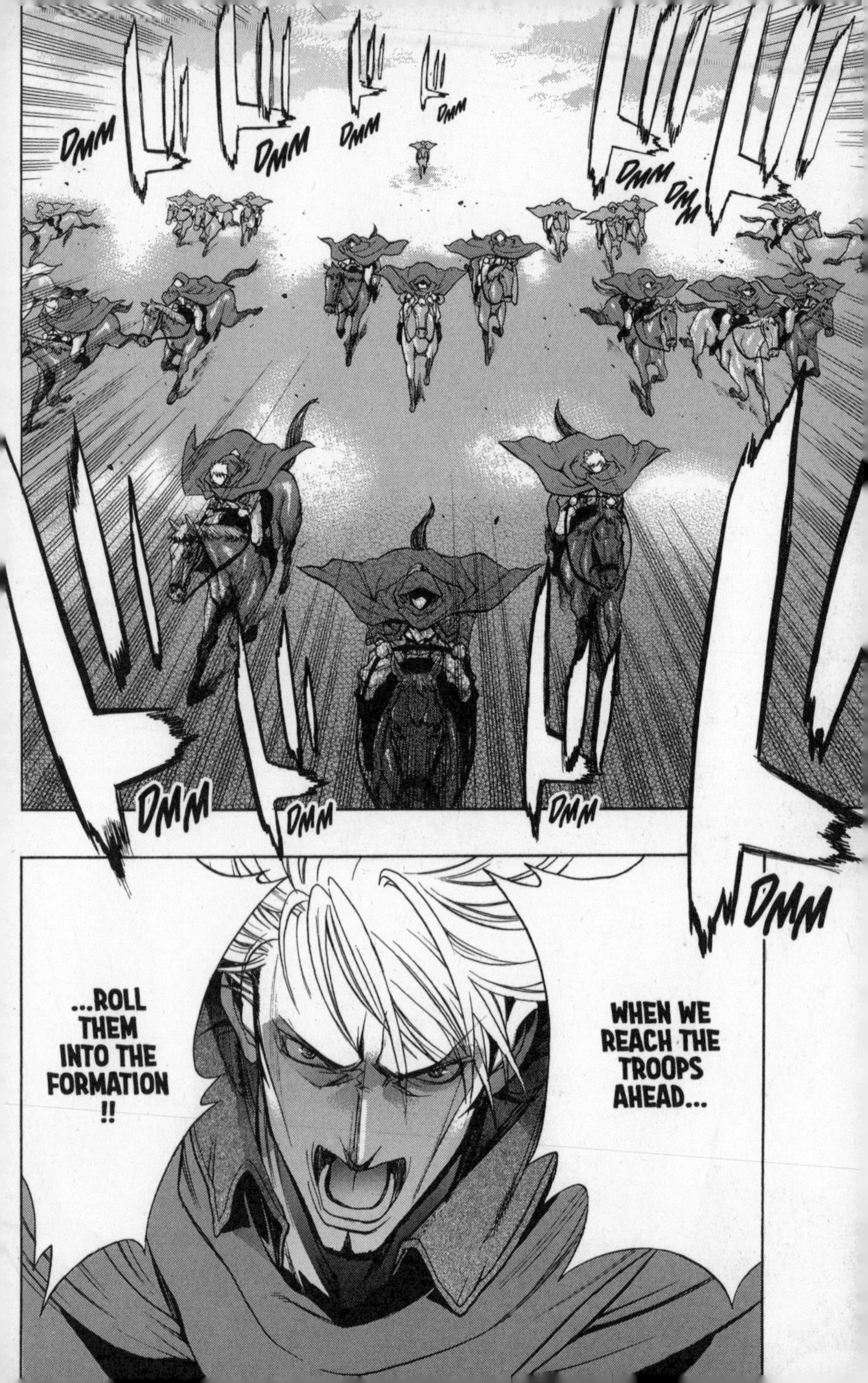
DMM
DMM
DMM
DMM
DMM
DMM
DMM
DMM
DMM
DMM
DMM
WHEN WE REACH THE TROOPS AHEAD...
...ROLL THEM INTO THE FORMATION !!

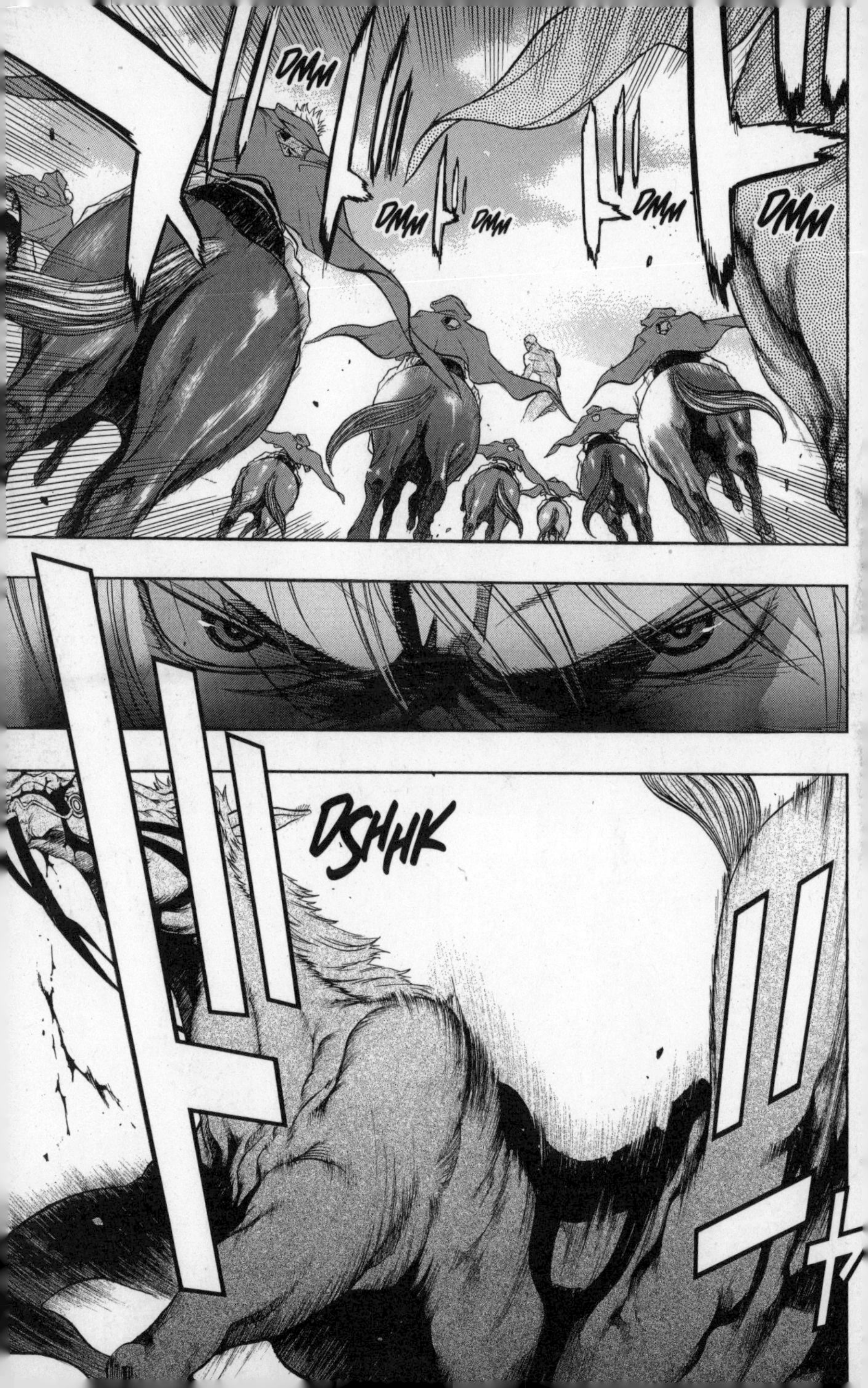
DMM
DMM
DMM
DMM
DMM
DSHHK

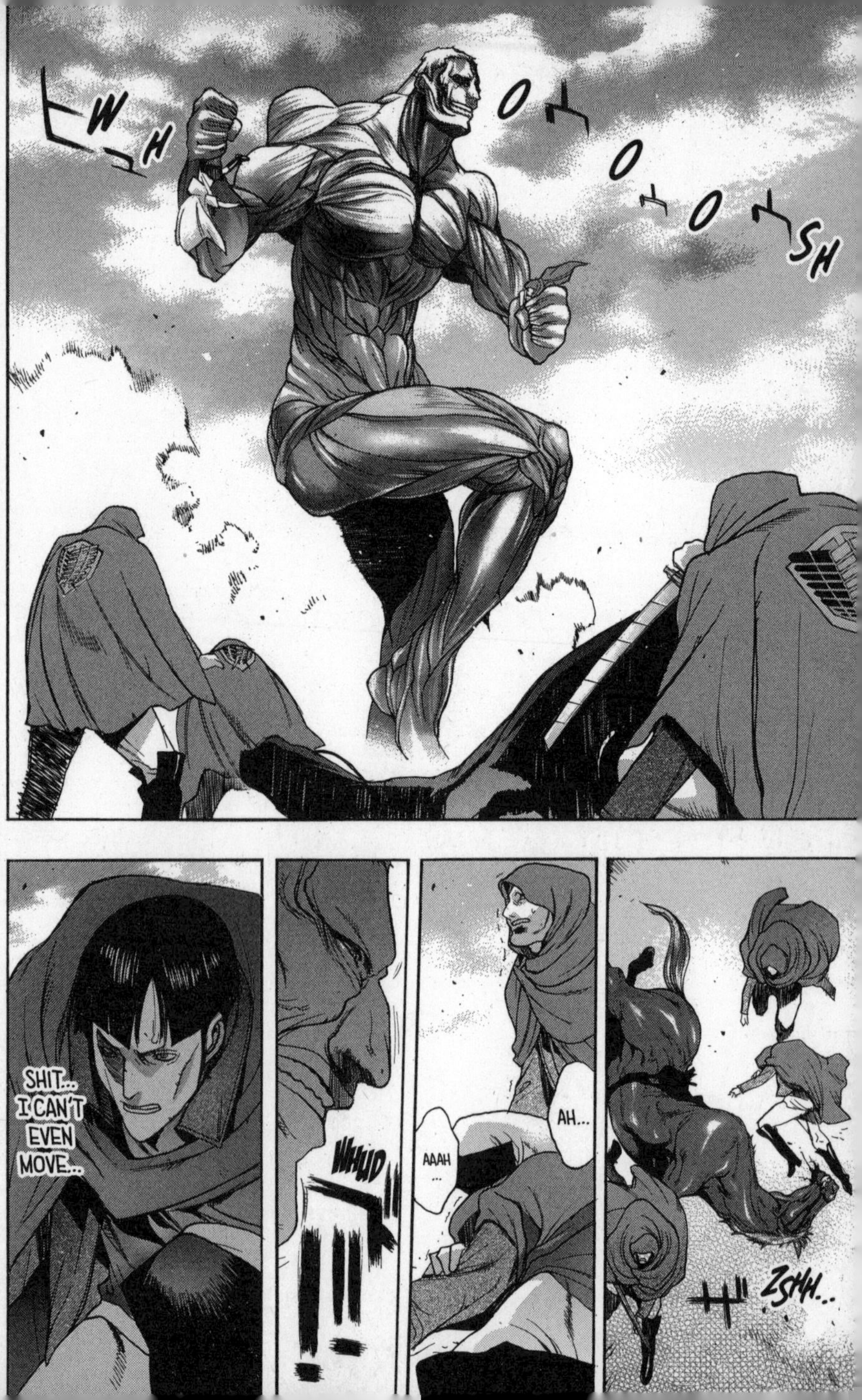
WHOOOOOSH
SHIT... I CAN'T EVEN MOVE...
WHUD
AAAH ...
AH...
ZSHH...

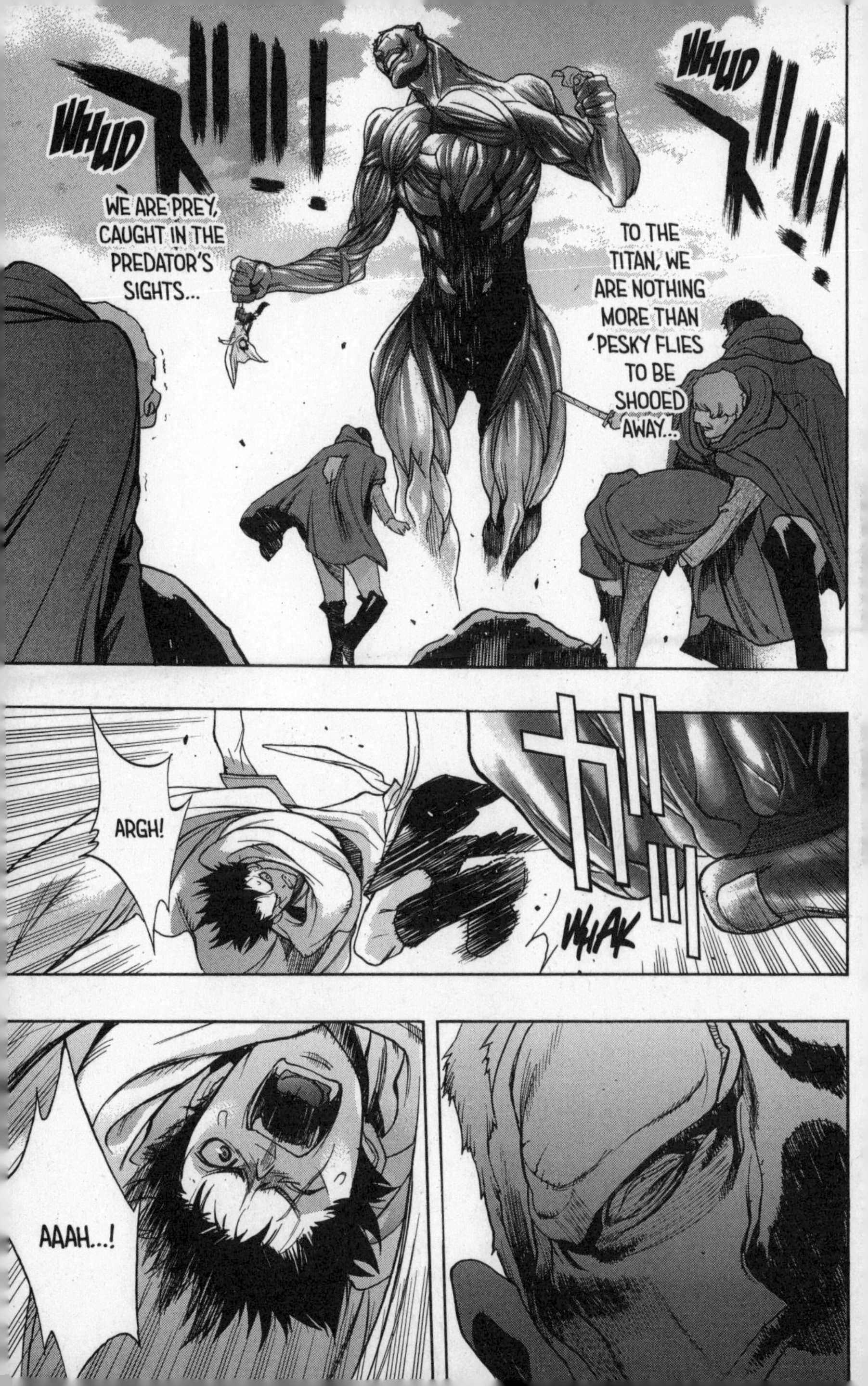
WHUD
WHUD
WE ARE PREY, CAUGHT IN THE PREDATOR'S SIGHTS...
TO THE TITAN, WE ARE NOTHING MORE THAN PESKY FLIES TO BE SHOOED AWAY...
WHAK
ARGH!
AAAH...!

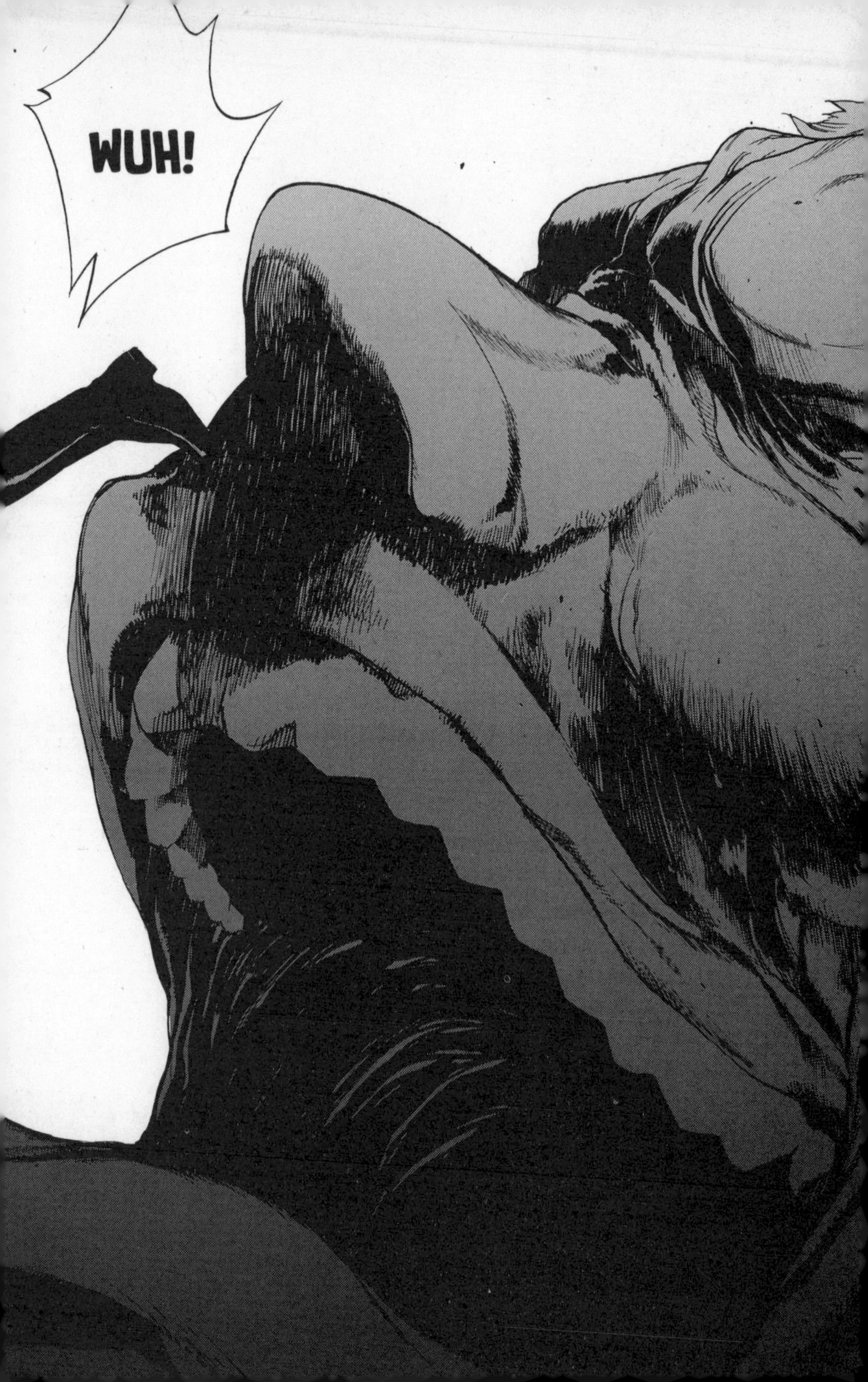
WUH!

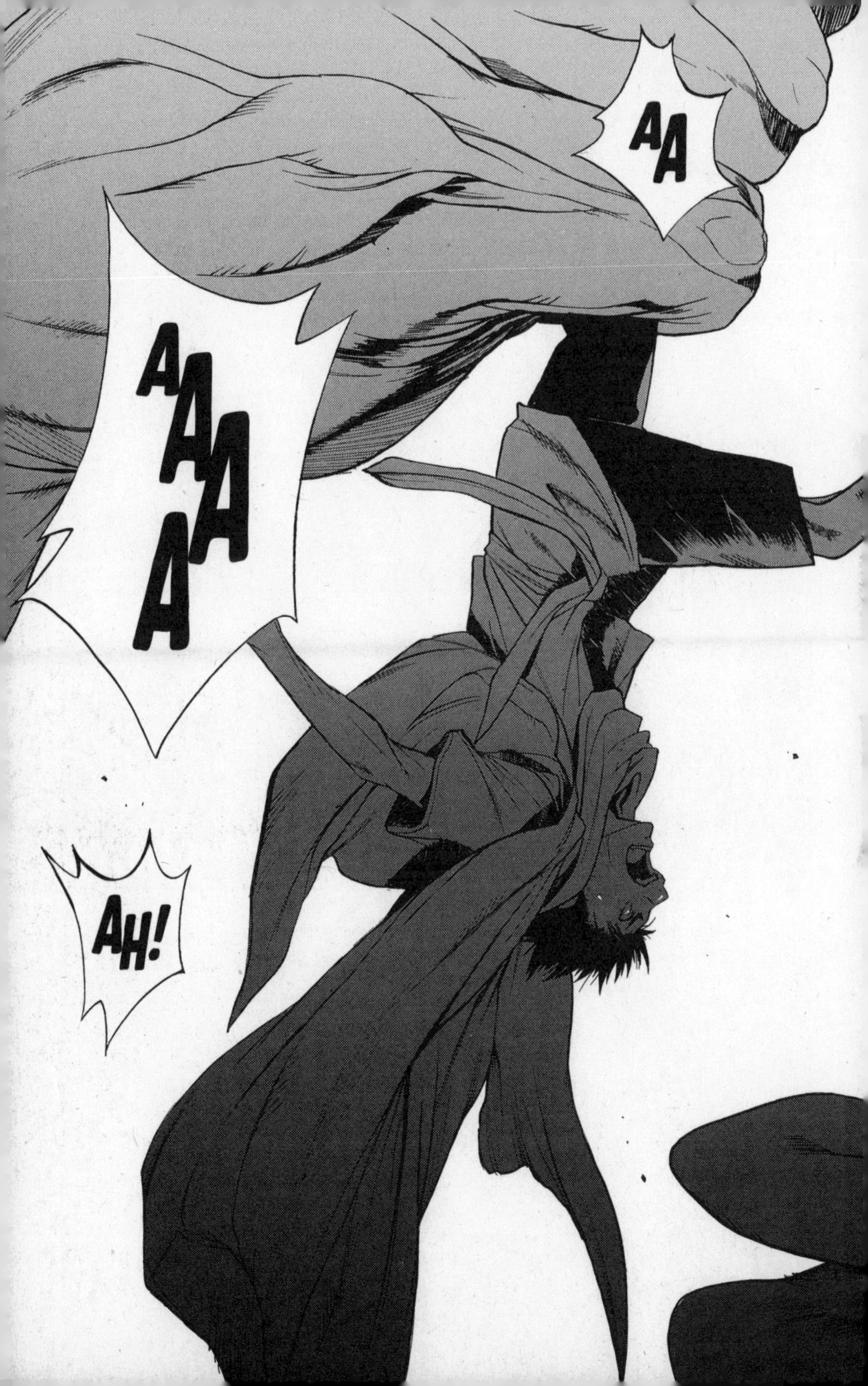
AA
AAAAA
AH!

IS THIS WHERE MY LIFE...

...ENDS...?

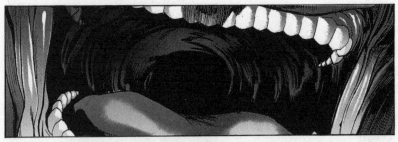

SHARLE...

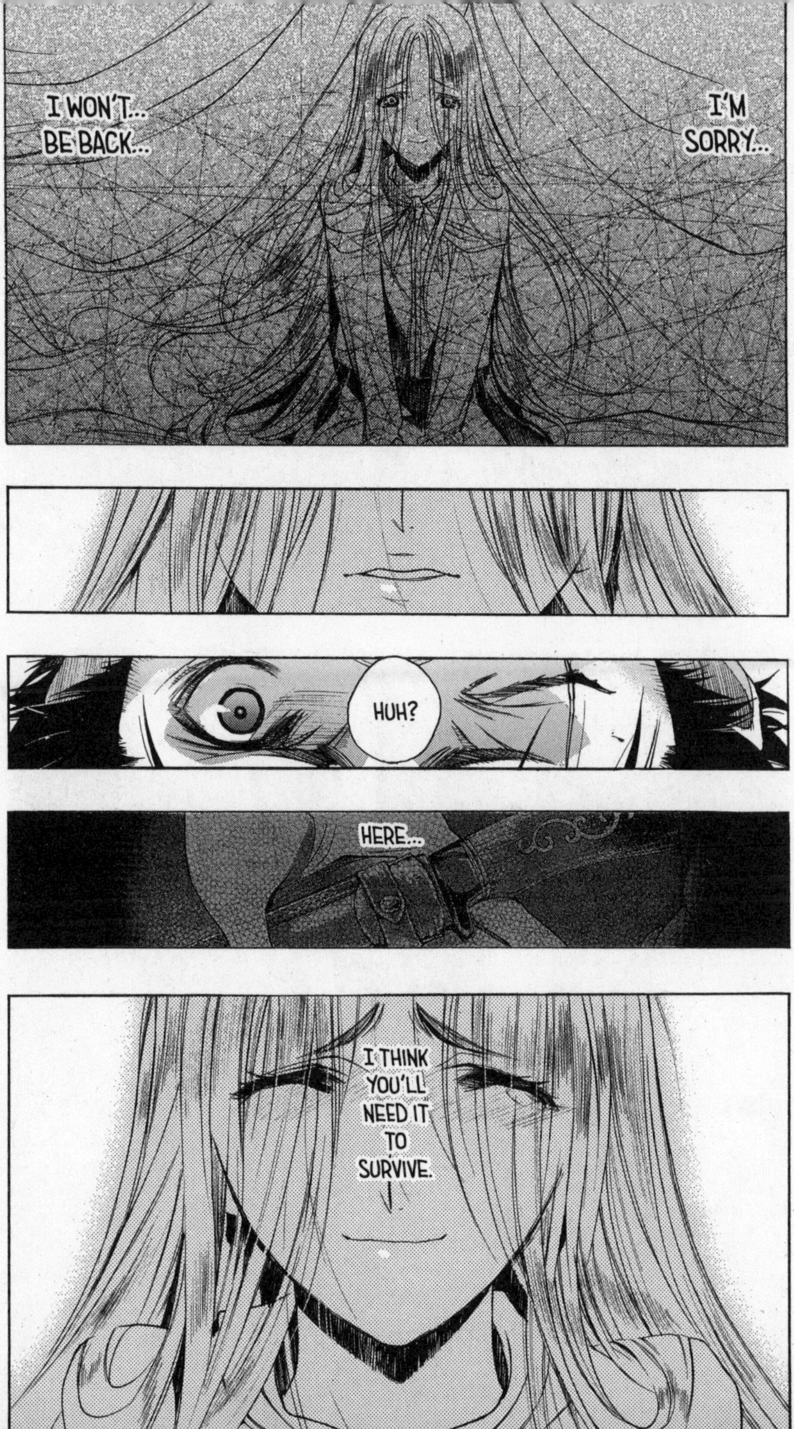
I'M SORRY...
I WON'T... BE BACK...
HUH?
HERE...
I THINK YOU'LL NEED IT TO SURVIVE.

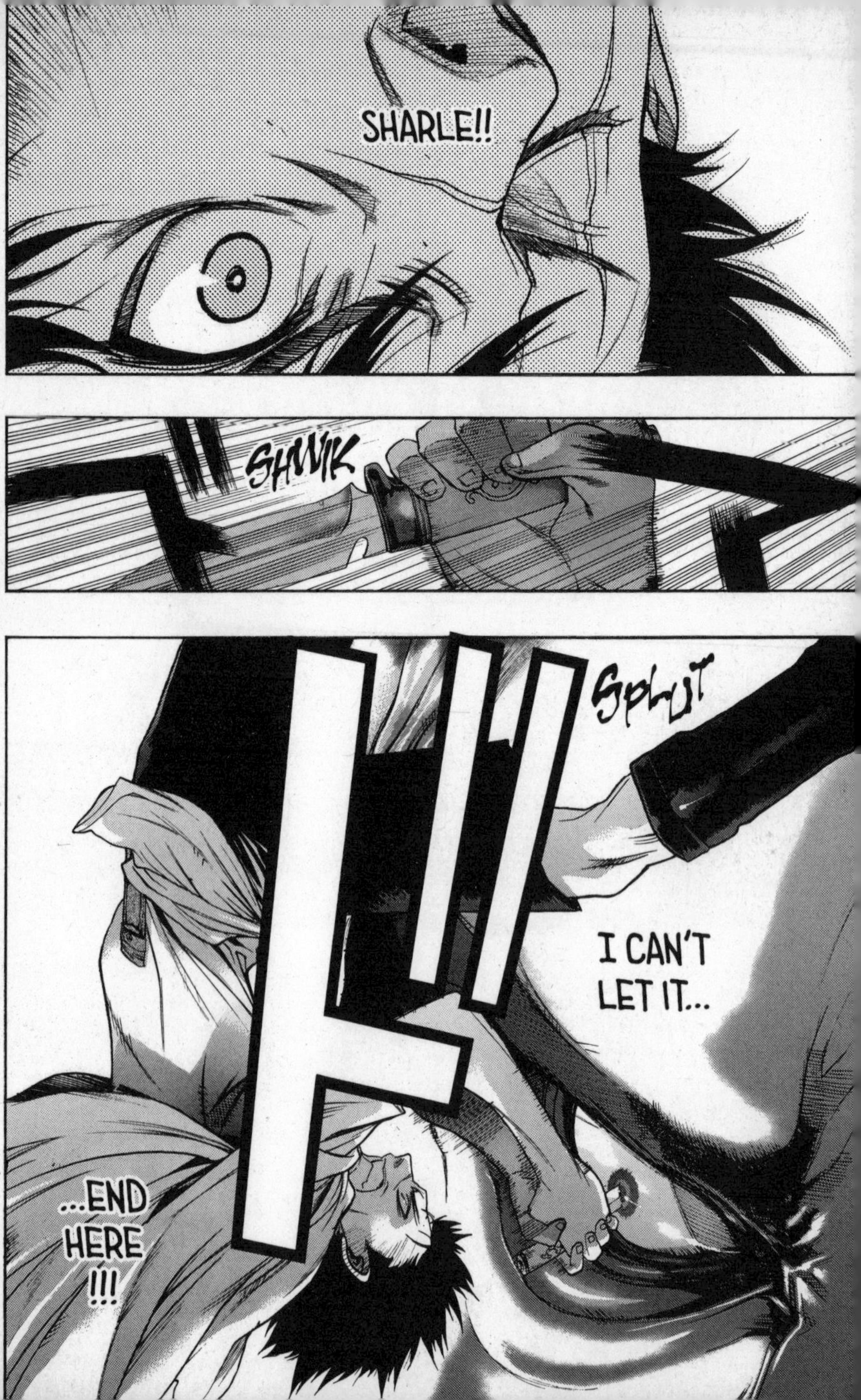
SHARLE!!
SHNIK
SPLUT
I CAN'T LET IT...
...END HERE !!!

ATTACK ON TITAN
BEFORE THE FALL

TO BE CONTINUED

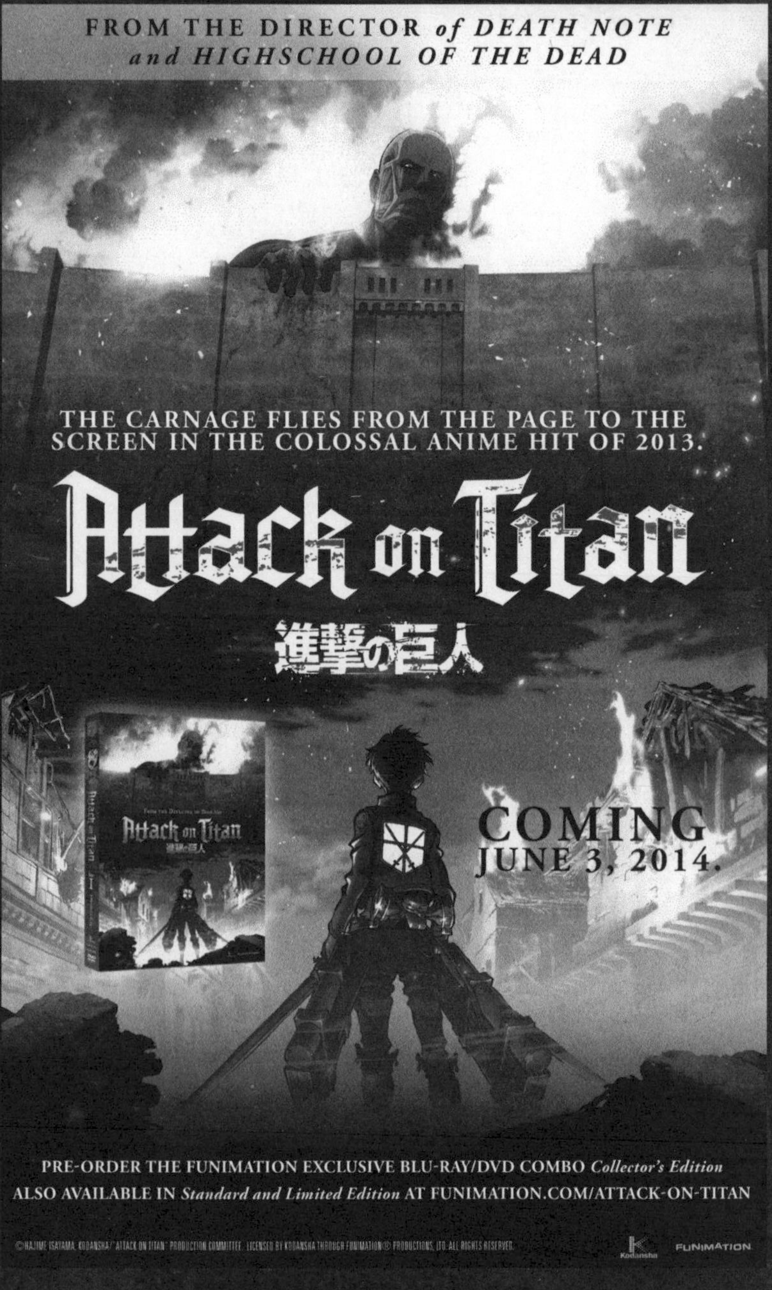
FROM THE DIRECTOR *of* DEATH NOTE
and HIGHSCHOOL OF THE DEAD
THE CARNAGE FLIES FROM THE PAGE TO THE SCREEN IN THE COLOSSAL ANIME HIT OF 2013.
Attack on Titan
進撃の巨人
COMING
JUNE 3, 2014.
PRE-ORDER THE FUNIMATION EXCLUSIVE BLU-RAY/DVD COMBO *Collector's Edition*
ALSO AVAILABLE IN *Standard and Limited Edition* AT FUNIMATION.COM/ATTACK-ON-TITAN
©HAJIME ISAYAMA, KODANSHA/"ATTACK ON TITAN" PRODUCTION COMMITTEE. LICENSED BY KODANSHA THROUGH FUNIMATION® PRODUCTIONS, LTD. ALL RIGHTS RESERVED.
Kodansha
FUNIMATION

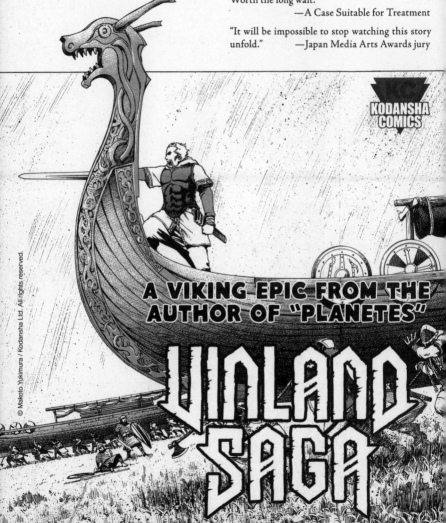

BLOODY MONDAY

Story by
Ryou Ryumon X **Art by** **Kouji Megumi**

Takagi Fujimaru may seem like a regular high school student, but behind the cheery facade lies a genius hacker by the name of Falcon.

When his father is framed for a murder, Falcon uses his brilliant hacking skills to try and protect his sister and clear his father's name.

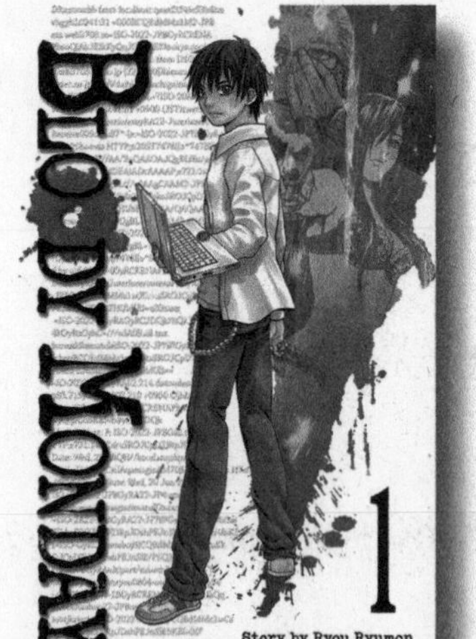
BLOODY MONDAY
1
Story by Ryou Ryumon
Art by Kouji Megumi

Special extras in each volume! Read them all!

RATING OT AGES 13+

VISIT WWW.KODANSHACOMICS.COM TO:

- View release date calendars for upcoming volumes
- Find out the latest about new Kodansha Comics series

KC KODANSHA COMICS

NO.6

A PERFECT LIFE
IN A PERFECT CITY

For Shion, an elite student in the technologically sophisticated
city No. 6, life is carefully choreographed. One fateful day, he
takes a misstep, sheltering a fugitive his age from a typhoon.
Helping this boy throws Shion's life down a path to discovering
the appalling secrets behind the "perfection" of No. 6.

KC
KODANSHA
COMICS

Praise for the anime:

"The show provides a pleasant window on the highs and lows of young love with two young people who are first timers at the real thing."

-The Fandom Post

"Always it is smarter, more poetic, more touching, just plain better than you think it is going to be."

-Anime News Network

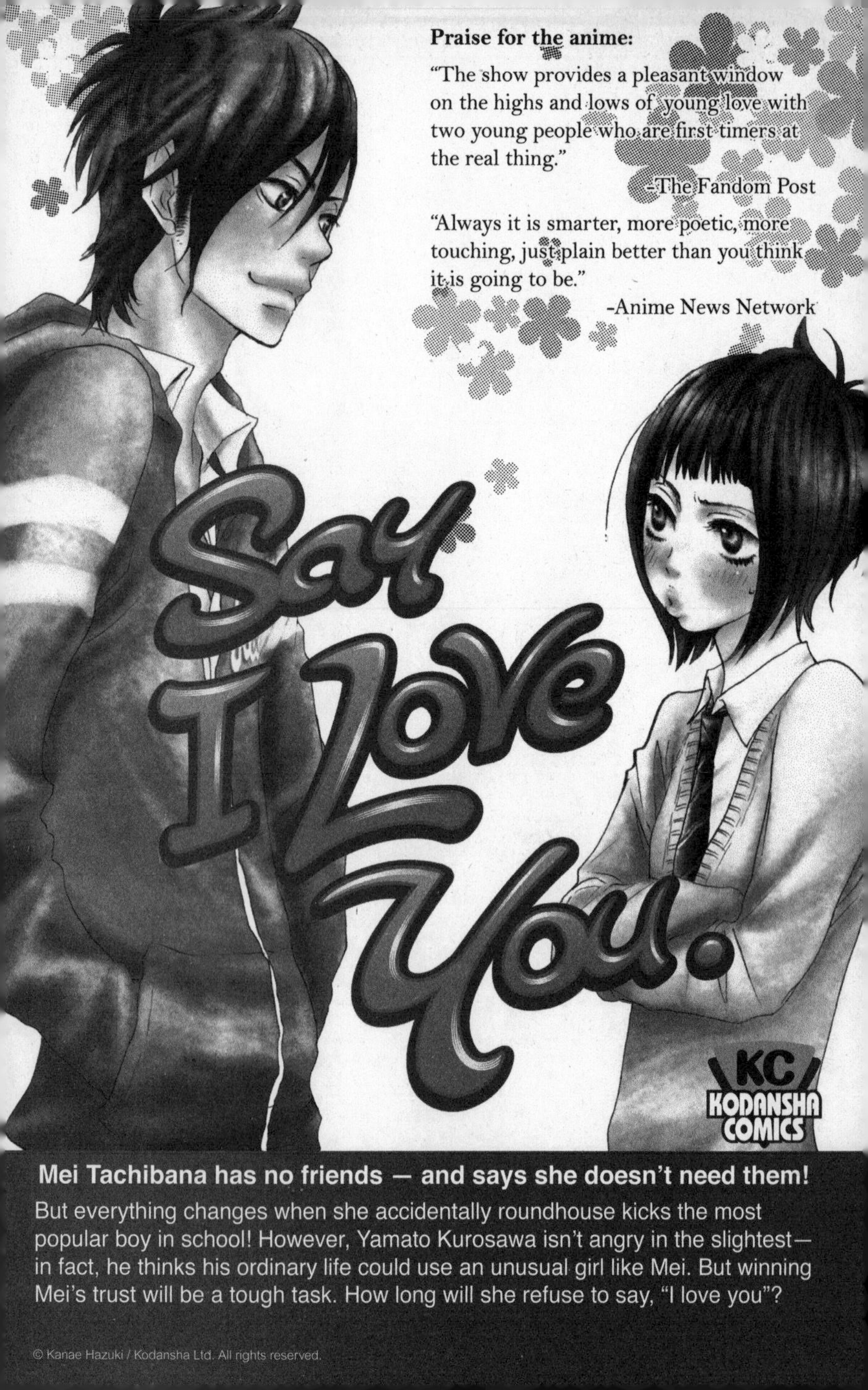
Say I Love You.
KC
KODANSHA COMICS

Mei Tachibana has no friends – and says she doesn't need them!

But everything changes when she accidentally roundhouse kicks the most popular boy in school! However, Yamato Kurosawa isn't angry in the slightest—in fact, he thinks his ordinary life could use an unusual girl like Mei. But winning Mei's trust will be a tough task. How long will she refuse to say, "I love you"?